SALVATION WITH A SMILE

JOEL OSTEEN,
LAKEWOOD CHURCH,
AND AMERICAN CHRISTIANITY

Phillip Luke Sinitiere

NEW YORK UNIVERSITY PRESS
New York and London

NEW YORK UNIVERSITY PRESS
New York and London
www.nyupress.org

© 2015 by New York University
All rights reserved

References to Internet websites (URLs) were accurate at the time of writing. Neither the author nor New York University Press is responsible for URLs that may have expired or changed since the manuscript was prepared.

ISBN: 978-0-8147-2388-3

For Library of Congress Cataloging-in-Publication data,
please contact the Library of Congress.

New York University Press books are printed on acid-free paper, and their binding materials are chosen for strength and durability. We strive to use environmentally responsible suppliers and materials to the greatest extent possible in publishing our books.

Manufactured in the United States of America

10 9 8 7 6 5 4 3 2 1

Also available as an ebook

To Jenni, Matt, Alex, Maddie, Nate, and Eli,

my oasis of love

Also, for my professor, mentor, and friend,

Terry D. Bilhartz (1950–2014)

CONTENTS

LIST OF FIGURES AND TABLES

Figures

Tables

ACKNOWLEDGMENTS

Studying Lakewood Church over the past decade, I heard Joel Osteen talk regularly about the concept of "favor." If I understand it correctly, to have favor means that one has been exceptionally lucky and has much for which to be thankful. At every stage of researching and writing this book, I have had favor—and with a smile, I gladly acknowledge the individuals and institutions that made it all possible. With a spirit of gratitude, I offer a Texas-sized thank you for the gifts of resources, labor, friendship, love, and time.

Without archivists and librarians, there would be no history. They are vital to keeping the past alive. I offer a word of thanks to archivists and librarians at the University of Houston; Sam Houston State University; College of Biblical Studies; Rice University; Houston Metropolitan Research Center; African American Library at the Gregory School; San Jacinto Baptist Association; General Baptist Convention of Texas; University of California, Santa Barbara; Regent University; Flower Pentecostal Heritage Center; University of North Carolina at Chapel Hill; Northern Baptist Theological Seminary; and Oral Roberts University. I especially want to thank Mark Roberts, director of the Holy Spirit Research Center at Oral Roberts University, for warmly welcoming me to Tulsa for research and for his enthusiastic support of this project. Most important, I thank Mark for his friendship.

Both Sam Houston State University and the College of Biblical Studies generously funded research trips during the course of this project, for which I am most grateful. I also thank *Houston History*, Palgrave Macmillan, and New York University Press for permission to include revised portions of previously published material.

I gladly recognize numerous individuals associated with Lakewood Church, past and present. Without them, this book would not exist. To those who chose to remain anonymous, I understand your reasons and respect your integrity. To those to whom I assigned a pseudonym, I appreciate your willingness to share your memories and experiences. To both the anonymous and the pseudonymous, I offer profound thanks for your time and, in some cases, the rare Lakewood materials you shared with me in the form of print and media sources. Also deserving of thanks are Saleim Kahleh and Teri Burrell.

A steady stream of friends, colleagues, journalists, and scholars either listened to me discuss the project, asked insightful questions about it, commented on portions of the manuscript, or otherwise supported my research and writing efforts in numerous ways. Please accept my gratitude, even those whom I inadvertently forgot: Julia Duin, Vinson Synan, James Beverly, Steve Bauer, Andrew Chesnut, Dan Lietha, Mara Einstein, Bob Sivigny, Ed Harrell, Matt Hedstrom, John G. Turner, Chuck Carpenter, Tommy Kidd, Scott Billingsly, Joe Parle, Bill Klages, Jarvis Taylor, Derek Hicks, Seth Dowland, France Brown, E. R. Haire, Jr., Marvin McNeese, Bernadette Pruitt, Jeff Littlejohn, Tom Cox, Jason Bivins, Ken Hendrickson, Nancy Baker, Artis Lovelady III, Ed Blum, Alex Hernandez, Paul Shockley, Susan Hill, Bart Marnitz, Tony Tripi, Gerardo Marti, Debbie Watkins, James Kirby Martin, Nic Ellen, Steve Sullivan, Darren Grem, Bill Blocker, Lance Waldie, Steve Shanklin, Jen Graber, Israel Loken, Rich Cozart, Guy Jackson, Harold Fisher, Justin Doran, Randall Stephens, Andy Woods, Virginia Garrard-Burnett, Terry Bilhartz, Sergio Estrada, David Daniels, Joel Goza, Elena Kravchenko, Miles Mullin, A. G. Miller, Edgar Serrano, Katharine Batlan, Rob Cooper, Joseph Williams, John Armstrong, Robert Crosby, Blaine Hamilton, Jessica Wilson, Mike McClymond, Mike Ayers, Todd Brenneman, Kristen Bullock, Derek Trevathan, Eddie Carson, Ty Cashion, Quentin Schultze, Doyen Blair, and Lee Bouldin.

I had the good fortune to present parts of this project to various audiences. My thanks for patient listening and thoughtful feedback: College of Biblical Studies, Society for Pentecostal Studies, American Academy of Religion Southwest Region (Southwest Commission on Religious Studies), and the University of Texas at Austin Religious Studies Colloquium. I especially thank Chad Seales for inviting me to Austin, for great food, and even better conversation.

As this book took shape, I had the pleasure to meet two students who completed research projects on Lakewood Church. Jillian Owens wrote an award-winning senior honors thesis on Lakewood's small groups in the University of Texas Religious Studies Department, and Matt Henderson's master's thesis for the University of Houston's Sociology Department examined Lakewood's racial and ethnic diversity. Thank you for inviting me to comment on your scholarship. I learned so much from the great research in each of these projects.

The original seeds for this project took root during the research for my first book, *Holy Mavericks*. In that regard, this project would not have been possible without Shayne Lee. Shayne is a good friend, and through the journey that became this book, he unfailingly encouraged my work, answered my questions, and responded to my meandering thoughts over the phone, in a text, through an email, or over a meal. Similarly, David Sehat's friendship, wise counsel, probing questions, and delightful conversation has enriched my life for many years. David's encouraging words, particularly over our "coffee talks," sustained me throughout this project. Likewise, the regular conversations with Arlene Sánchez-Walsh, Charity Carney, and Kate Bowler provided much laughter, much encouragement, and much insight as we navigated the conceptual, historical, archival, and cultural dimensions of religious history, megachurches, and the prosperity gospel. Arlene, Charity, Kate, and I shared with each other works in progress, and ideas and perspectives in process. I am most grateful for their friendship and their constructive feedback.

Two summer seminars at Calvin College (Seminars @ Calvin) provided space to reflect, research, and write—and enjoy a much cooler respite from Houston's sweltering summers. I commend the efforts of Seminars director Joel Carpenter, along with his staff. I thank both seminar leaders and seminar participants for listening and responding to my work and to my ideas: Michael Emerson, Korie Edwards, Kathleen Garces-Foley, Mark Mulder, Jerry Park, Kim Hill, Tanya Brice, Paul Gordiejew, Bruce Fields, Ryon Cobb, Erica Wong, Rebecca Kim, Luke Harlow, Rusty Hawkins, Julie Park, Karen Johnson, Gerardo Marti, Penny Edgell, Bill McKinney, Paul Olson, Jim Wellman, Lisa DeBoer, Janine Giordano Drake, Kendra Barber, Walt Bower, Lloyd Chia, Peter Schuurman, Christine Sheikh, Kevin Taylor, and Lincoln Mullen. Lincoln is a digital genius who suggested new ways to conduct online research that unearthed some of Lakewood's earliest Internet materials.

For making this book better, although not in any way responsible for its deficiencies, I especially thank New York University Press's anonymous readers, and those who read the manuscript at a late stage: Steven P. Miller, Arlene Sánchez-Walsh, Charity Carney, John Wilsey, Felipe Hinojosa, David Sehat, Kate Bowler, Tim Gloege, Roy Ledgerwood, and Betsy Cooper.

My editor Jennifer Hammer deserves a wealth of praise. She helped to shape and reshape the ideas in this book, and her expert guidance pushed me to articulate arguments and make observations with clarity. I am also very thankful for her patience and forbearance. I also express sincere gratitude to Constance Grady, Dorothea Halliday, and the NYU Press team that helped to bring this book to fruition. It was a real pleasure to work with such consummate professionals and wonderful people.

Raised on Houston's north side in the suburb of Humble, I have childhood memories of seeing Lakewood commercials and broadcasts on local television. And I recall more than once seeing "Lakewood Church: Oasis of Love" bumper stickers on cars motoring by as I traveled along Houston's sprawling highways. Houston is still the city in which I find myself, and I continue to discover that the history of this growing Sunbelt metropolis is rich with religious activity and suffused with spiritual meaning. It is also home to some of my closest friends and family. I thank my parents, Donnie and Marcia, for their constant support and sustaining love. My siblings, Doug, Andy, Paul, and Nick (along with sisters-in-law Jenni, Ashley, and Allison), inspire me more than they know. My in-laws Bill, Sandy, and Mary each in their own way made the completion of this project possible. Finally, Jenni, Matt, Alex, Maddie, Nate, and Eli remind me that life is so much more important than books and scholarship. Not only is my family unfailingly patient with my numerous shortcomings, but also they consistently fuel my passion for life and enrich my soul beyond measure. They are my oasis of love.

Introduction

I am in the upscale business complex of Greenway Plaza, near downtown Houston. After parking my car, I follow the signs directing me to Lakewood Church. Emerging from the dimly lit confines of a parking garage, I join hundreds of people surging to the church's entrance. In an energetic multiethnic mix, I walk alongside individuals, some of whom are black, others white, still others Latino/a or Asian. Some are talking with one another, while others are silent. Some walk with heads down as if in prayer. I see men wearing their Sunday best, along with women adorned in stunning white and pink hats; others come in jeans, T-shirts, and shorts. I hear the sharp strike of high heels and the flop of sandals. Some carry Bibles as they purposefully walk toward the church. I see Bibles that appear worn and creased, the result of a sustained engagement. I also observe congregants clutching *Hope for Today Bible*, a resource designed with notes and commentary by Lakewood's pastors Joel and Victoria Osteen. Shortly, at Joel's invitation in the worship service to "lift up your Bibles and say it like you mean it," congregants will thrust their Bibles into the air and make Lakewood's famous "This is my Bible" confession. A mantra started by Joel's father and Lakewood's founder, John Osteen, in the 1980s, the statement highlights the church's evangelical fidelity to the Bible and firm conviction about its spiritual power. I also observe a large group of people rolling into the church, some wheeling themselves while others proceed in electric wheelchairs. The leader of this group also ushers in other disabled persons, some with visual impairments, others with Down's syndrome. Lakewood's doors open for a diverse array of people.[1]

As I enter the building with the throngs of men, women, and children who pour in for the service, a volunteer with a nametag greets me with a warm smile and "Welcome, God bless you." I take the bulletin she hands me. I start ascending the stairs into Lakewood Church. Knowing that Lakewood is America's largest megachurch, welcoming over 40,000 members and other attendees each week, I feel as if I am in an important place. It pulsates with energy. I also notice symbols of the church's history on display. I pause halfway up the steps as I encounter a life-size bronze display of Lakewood's founding couple, John and Dodie Osteen, honoring Lakewood's fiftieth anniversary. The couple meets visitors with smiles and a Bible held in the air. The base of the bronze statue is in the shape of a heart, symbolic of Lakewood's old motto, "Oasis of Love." While John never preached at the Compaq Center, a converted sports arena that became Lakewood's home in 2005, six years after his death, his likeness, along with that of Dodie, greets visitors as they enter the church he founded. At Lakewood, the past intermingles with the present, while the future is a source of perpetual anticipation.

As I continue to walk up the stairs, to my left people enter and exit the well-stocked bookstore. On the television screen that sits in the middle of a display that contains Joel and Victoria's teachings I look over to see and hear Joel encouraging a positive mindset in the midst of difficult circumstances. In the bookstore, I browse the most recent books by contemporary Christian teachers such as Joyce Meyer, John MacArthur, Joseph Prince, and John Piper, and a substantial variety of study Bibles and study aids such as theological encyclopedias and Greek dictionaries. The bookstore contains a children's section and several rows with a variety of Spanish-language resources. I also notice that it sells framed paintings of the Christian artist Thomas Kinkade as well as spiritually themed items like T-shirts, key chains, or bookmarks that can also be found at Christian chain retail stores such as Family Christian, Lifeway, and Mardel. Just outside of the bookstore, families head quickly to register kids for Lakewood's expansive children's programs. Other people mill about like tourists, many of them visiting Lakewood for the first time, clearly pausing to take it all in. Things are buzzing at Lakewood Church, but also proceed in an orderly fashion. I notice people with official Lakewood nametags, energetic volunteers with clipboards and walkie-talkies who help the massive operation to run smoothly. Not shy, one volunteer inquires if I am interested in trying out for Lakewood's choir. Responding to her facial expression and her excitement to recruit volunteers, I return the smile—and politely decline. "God bless you," the recruiter replies as I continue walking.

Figure I.1. John and Dodie Osteen bronze display, Lakewood Church. The plaque reads, "Pastors John and Dodie Osteen, Founders of Lakewood Church, Mother's Day 1959, Edd Hayes, sculptor, Gift from Craig Keeland." Source: Photo by author.

I proceed to the worship center, and with many others, I anticipate my entrance into the 16,000-seat sanctuary. There is a palpable sense of expectation, a feeling already cultivated by Joel's popular message of self-improvement and salvation on television and published in a handful of *New York Times* bestsellers. Looking up, I see the ceiling arranged with large square white sheeting to produce a cloud effect, simultaneously reflecting blues, reds, greens, and purples from multicolored spotlights. I begin to get an inkling of the church's massive size, an architectural expression of Lakewood's signature place in American Christianity. I find a seat, and settle into place on the second level on the far left side of the auditorium. Lights bathe the stage in a glittery display as members of Lakewood's choir, wearing blue robes, find their place in the two choir lofts. The band, arranged on a retractable stage, warms up in front of a massive, bronze globe, an iconic symbol of Lakewood's historic commitment to missionary endeavors. Announcements for religious education classes and church events along with advertisements for resources available in Lakewood's bookstore flash across the three large screens that hang above the stage. I notice individuals in front of the stage and they appear to have security escorts—the Osteen family and other church leaders proceed to their seats. It is nearly time for the service to begin.

The interracial duo of singers Cindy Cruse Ratcliff and Israel Houghton begin the service by leading nearly 16,000 people in musical expressions of adoration toward God and the spiritual meaning of life in Christ. People clap in rhythm with the drums, and sing along as lyrics flash across the large screens. I also notice worshiping bodies sway with the music. The emotional temper of the music produces what appear to be moments of tender introspection; I see people with arms raised and eyes closed, and some with tears streaming. Later, prayer partners meet and pray with those in need. People cry and hug, finding individual spiritual solace among the thousands present in America's largest congregation. The service proceeds with an encouraging testimony from Victoria, a period of prayer and tithing, and a twenty-five-minute message from Joel. An altar call with a simple recitation, asking Jesus to reign as Lord of one's life, starts to draw the morning service to a close. In a final moment of affirmation, Joel asks people to clap if they are better now than when they came in. Employing positive confession, a historic neopentecostal practice of making verbal affirmations of spiritual significance—and much like his father John did at Lakewood—Joel makes several declarations. Each declaration becomes more intense as Osteen's voice rises and he bounces tiptoed as if to push his positive proclamations into every square inch of the auditorium: "I declare . . . God is breathing on your life, he's breathing on your dreams, he's breathing on your finances. . . . God will multiply your talent, multiply your resources, multiply your strength. . . . If you'll be confident in what God has given you, then I believe and declare you will overcome every obstacle, defeat every enemy, and you will become everything God's created you to be . . . if you believe it, give the Lord a shout of praise!" Joel ends the service in prayer, sending intense petitions upward with his face lifted, eyes tightly closed, hands raised, and his body moving as he speaks. He asks God to make the day's message real in everyday life. "Lord, draw them by your Spirit, let them feel your love as they've never felt it before," he prays. "A new beginning . . . a fresh new start . . . the road to victory . . . comes from a personal relationship with Jesus Christ."

The visual, auditory, physical, spiritual, even sensual dynamics at Lakewood Church are at once memorable, overpowering, and connected deeply to the history of American evangelicalism. This opening vignette provides five ways to consider thematically the historical significance and cultural meaning of Joel Osteen and Lakewood Church in American Christianity.

First, Lakewood is about *people*—the church's founders, its parishioners, members, attendees, volunteers, visitors, musicians, singers, teachers, and pastors. Seeing the concentration of 16,000 people singing, clapping and moving to worship songs or sitting in rapt attention to a sermon—or busily tweeting, texting, or gazing at the surroundings—is an unforgettable experience. Once there, one "feels" Lakewood. Although it began in 1959 with about 200 people, the congregation has been thousands strong since the late 1970s, when Lakewood became a megachurch. Outside of the worship auditorium, Lakewood's people gather for Bible study and spiritual fellowship. They donate their time and efforts to the community, whether handing out sandwiches or shoes to the homeless, or writing notes of encouragement to the depressed and downhearted. Lakewood's people worship by singing, by study, and by community service.

Lakewood is about *place*—the former Compaq Center situated near downtown Houston, a former sports arena transformed into sacred space. Lakewood's current location is a $90 million facility with an annual budget of similar proportions. Classrooms offer space for collective study, silent reflection, and individual prayer. Offices provide places to plan and strategize for the different ministries Lakewood offers. The latest recording, mixing, and broadcast technology coupled with purposeful sanctuary design ensures a professional production scripted for the maximum impact. A wall of champions displays a short pictorial history of Lakewood's move to the former Compaq Center along with the names of "champion" donors. Yet Lakewood's "place" was not always located in a state-of-the-art facility along a busy freeway surrounded by multimillion-dollar corporations and thriving retail spaces. For forty years of its fifty-year history, Lakewood called home a gritty working-class neighborhood with black and brown enclaves on Houston's northeast side, miles from where political and economic power is concentrated in the city. Small space at a feed store welcomed Lakewood's founding pastor and earliest members in 1959, with incremental architectural additions during the subsequent three decades. In Lakewood's history, place has mattered greatly: its "place" in Houston and its "place" in the Sunbelt are rich with cultural significance.

Lakewood is about *personality*. John Osteen's visionary reach coupled with a fierce willpower not only removed him from the blight of childhood poverty, it resulted in the growth of Lakewood Church and situated John as a leading figure in the neopentecostal movement, a multidenominational charismatic stirring that emerged after World War II. Infused with physical and spiritual energy after he discovered the Holy Spirit's power, during the 1960s and 1970s John built and grew Lakewood Church. Members use the words "love" and "compassion" to describe John's personality. They recall his tireless preaching on Sundays and Wednesdays, the intensity of his exhortations, the tenderness of his encouraging words, and the power of his prayers. And when Lakewood's television ministry began in the early 1980s, his personality instantaneously transcended the walls of the church, now touching not only Lakewood's people but Lakewood's "public," as well. Since 1999, his son Joel Osteen has utilized personality with a recognizable presence as the "smiling preacher"—often alongside his striking and energetic wife, Victoria—counseling positive thinking and positive confession to face life's challenges. His Texas drawl and fit body coupled with a soft-spoken but firm message of encouragement have endeared him to many. But Joel's "personality" also elicits waves of criticism. Elsewhere at Lakewood, the distinct personalities of Joel's sister Lisa and his mother, Dodie, carry John's legacy as they conduct their own services. Joel's brother Paul, a surgeon with a missionary's mindset who also represents

John's legacy, not only fixes bodies but also attempts to mend hearts spiritually through his preaching and teaching. Spanish-language pastor Marcos Witt, an accomplished musician in Latin American circles, when he worked at Lakewood between 2002 and 2012, also constituted a "personality" with his preaching and singing. Likewise, John Gray, the only black pastor on Lakewood's staff, since 2012 has riveted the congregation not only with his preaching, but also with enjoyable stories and jokes, which reflects his previous career as a standup comedian. Performance and personality mix among Lakewood's professional musicians, such as the award-winning Israel Houghton and Cindy Cruse Ratcliff. In the midst of Lakewood's more public personalities, church members and attendees express "personality" as well, constructing religious identities and articulating testimonies about how they believe God sustains and blesses them.

Lakewood is also about *Pentecost*—a term that Christians, particularly Christians of the Pentecostal and charismatic persuasion use in reference to something new: the birth of the Christian movement recorded in the New Testament book of Acts. However, this book employs "Pentecost" as a metaphor to describe Lakewood's origins and conceptually encapsulate the message of second chances that emanates from its pastors to its parishioners. Expressed in different ways by different ministers and members, the message of Lakewood Church centers on the promise of starting over. Both pastors and parishioners contend that the past is the past, and with hope and faith, one can transcend the past in order to remake the future. And while explanations of God's ways do not always satisfy the questions surrounding some of life's unfortunate circumstances, Lakewood promises faith to understand that God's orchestration of history will ultimately turn to one's own advantage spiritually, materially, or both. Lakewood's Pentecost informs the church's history even as it expresses the conceptual architecture of its core message.[2]

If Lakewood is about Pentecost and the promise of starting over, then it is also about *prosperity*. Lakewood's arrival on the American religious landscape during the genesis of the neopentecostal movement and John's focus on divine healing and positive confession oriented the church toward the prosperity gospel, a message of boundless improvement. More recently, Joel's critics have drawn out opposition to his prosperity message, categorizing him as another manifestation of the

"Health and Wealth Gospel," a dimension of the prosperity gospel that spiritualizes material attainment. The earliest moments of Lakewood's history lodged notions of prosperity in the church's message, particularly related to John's impoverished origins. But Lakewood's increasing monetary accumulation throughout the last few decades of the twentieth century made prosperity a financial reality for the church. As a wealthy church in one of the Sunbelt's most economically vibrant cities, Lakewood's prosperity gospel also means its history is as much about class as it is about religion. At Lakewood, as in Houston, God's blessings can be both spiritual and material.

This book argues that Joel Osteen is America's most powerful twenty-first-century evangelical minister. His story, and that of Lakewood, does not represent the totality of evangelicalism; rather, they collectively illuminate key trends in contemporary American Christianity. First, the constellation of historical and cultural factors that produced Osteen's privileged position includes his historic and enduring connection to neopentecostalism, his affiliation with the prosperity gospel, and the rise of Lakewood as America's largest megachurch. Second, Osteen's pinnacle position in American Christianity is the result of an innovative message delivered through television and across many new media platforms. Osteen's religious teaching is positive, predictable, redundant, and consistent in a contemporary moment of profound political change. Finally, Osteen's emergence as America's leading evangelical minister in the early twenty-first century began at a time of cultural discord, when Democrats and Republicans vociferously debated the role of religion and politics as the presidency of George W. Bush gave way to the Obama era. The fact that Osteen, at the time, was neither specifically aligned with the Christian Right nor connected to the Religious Left meant that his politics of positive thinking presented a unique alternative across America's religious landscape. Osteen's functionally conservative political positions on pressing cultural questions such as abortion or marriage equality aligned with Christian Right opinion. But he scrupulously avoided overtly politicizing his teachings, an avoidance that contrasted sharply with the combative rhetoric of religious conservatives and the equally impassioned proclamations of religious progressives. Although Osteen's sermons and social opinions were not without controversy, his approach produced a broadly affable message more acceptable to a wide diversity of individuals.

The story of Joel Osteen and Lakewood Church matters today because it is essential to understanding the history of contemporary American Christianity. This is especially true in relationship to neopentecostalism's historic versatility. Osteen and Lakewood's intersection with neopentecostalism documents the movement's vibrancy and adaptability well into the twenty-first century. In addition, Osteen's populist, positive message, delivered via diverse means, testifies to the enduring power of televangelism. Moreover, his ubiquitous, successful presence in the religious media landscape shows that in the twenty-first century popular religious teachers must diversify the modalities through which they present their messages. Osteen's arrival on the national scene paralleled the rise of social media, and his background in religious programming advantageously positioned him to embrace emerging technology; as a result, he has crafted an electronic and digital presence for the prosperity gospel that far exceeds any other minister's or congregation's. In concert with Joel's prominence across social media and the emerging digital universe, the content and tone of his religious broadcasting makes televangelism tolerable, and perhaps even acceptable—despite the long shadow of recent televangelist scandals—otherwise millions of viewers would not tune in every week, nor would his other ventures, such as his *New York Times* bestselling books, net such tremendous success. Also significant is Osteen's soothing Texas drawl and well-known cheery smile, born from his and his church's place in Houston as well as the religiously significant Sunbelt, factors that speak to a transitional moment in the contested history of religion and politics in the United States. Fewer and fewer people wish to stomach the bombastic rhetoric of the Christian Right that was so consequential in the 1980s and 1990s, while large numbers of Americans hold fast to conservative social values. Osteen's power as America's leading Christian minister delivers conservative social values—with an insistence that Lakewood welcomes *all* people—without the vicious language of cultural combat that the Christian Right has perfected and used to significant effect. At the same time, his gestures toward social inclusion, along with Lakewood's consistent outreach efforts both in Houston and around the world, reflect the social consciousness of religious progressives, even though the individualist-oriented message of positive thinking and positive confession hardly addresses in any robust systemic way social justice or economic equality. Questions of leadership and institutional history—especially with the virtually seamless transition of Lakewood from John's pastorate to Joel's church—are equally consequential for grasping the importance of Osteen and Lakewood. In the annals of American religious history, it is not often that a church's second generation outshines the founder in the way Joel has done with Lakewood Church.

The aim of *Salvation with a Smile* is simple and clear: to explain Joel Osteen and Lakewood Church's cultural significance in light of American religious history. While this study addresses aspects of Christian theology—neopentecostalism, the prosperity gospel, and New Calvinism—it presents the historical development of theological ideas, not theological analysis itself. While this book is not a biography of Joel Osteen, it deals with biographical aspects of his life, as well as those of other members of the Osteen family. Similarly, this book is not an institutional analysis of Lakewood Church; it delves into selected aspects of the congregation's institutional life. Organized around eight chapters, this volume explains how Lakewood's neopentecostal origins resulted in its emergence as America's largest megachurch. It connects the historical dots between John's adoption of the prosperity gospel and his son Joel's creative and purposeful rearticulation of that message as he ushered Lakewood into the twenty-first century. And it spells out how Joel's technological knowledge coupled with a competent understanding of American culture has translated into a staggeringly popular presence in the contemporary world. At the same time, this book demonstrates that Lakewood is far more than its founder and current pastor. Incorporating the experiences of other individuals in the Osteen family, associate ministers, and church members and attendees, it elucidates the wider history of one of America's most important religious institutions. Finally, analysis of Joel's reception among American Christians—after all, constant scrutiny is one price of celebrity—further deciphers Lakewood's historical significance and cultural meaning across America's evangelical landscape.[3]

Chapters 1 and 2 offer a biographical account of John Osteen's early life in Texas, documenting his Southern Baptist background and transition into neopentecostalism. They explain how he fostered connections in neopentecostal networks to become a nationally known minister during the 1960s, and connect the strands of John's Sunbelt story to spell out the origins of Lakewood Church. Picking up Lakewood's story in the 1970s, chapter 2 draws on John's books and sermons to explore neopentecostal preacher Kenneth Hagin's influence on his embrace of Word of Faith principles. Turning to the 1980s and 1990s, this chapter tracks the rise of John's televangelism, a vital development in Lakewood's history that paved the way for the church's transition into the twenty-first century after John's death in 1999.

Chapter 3 is the first of two chapters that specifically address Joel's prosperity gospel teachings. It draws out the historical antecedents of Osteen's message to offer part of the answer to the question, how did Joel Osteen become *Joel Osteen*? This chapter sets forth the four parts of Osteen's prosperity gospel as positive thinking, positive confession, positive providence, and finally, the promotion of the Christian body as a site of improvement. It unveils the chief influences that shaped Osteen's ministerial evolution: his father, neopentecostal evangelist Joyce Meyer, and leadership teacher John Maxwell. By establishing the most important neopentecostal and evangelical determinants of Osteen's message, this chapter pinpoints how Joel creatively refashioned a prosperity gospel message that brought him to the pinnacle of American Christianity and helped to make Lakewood Church one of America's most consequential congregations of the twenty-first century.

With the foundational inspiration for Joel's prosperity gospel established, chapter 4 analyzes the content of his teachings. Based on transcripts of his earliest sermons from 1999 along with his more recent orations, his *New York Times* bestselling books, selected interviews, and the *Hope for Today Bible*, this chapter connects Osteen's message to the neopentecostal inheritance of his father, and it discloses how his teaching has drawn heavily from Meyer and Maxwell. Furthermore, it reveals that Joel's unflappable confidence led to the presentation of a message in which God orchestrates history tailored to each individual's specific needs—what I call a providence of positive outcomes. This chapter also explains how Joel translated neopenteocostalism's emphasis on divine healing into a wider message that focuses on fitness, health, and psychological well-being, what I call his prosperity gospel of the body. Chapter 4 illuminates striking historical parallels between Norman Vincent Peale's mid-twentieth-century articulation of positive thinking and Joel's astonishingly redundant teaching about self-improvement, further unfolding Osteen's contemporary importance. Finally, chapter 4 shows that while Osteen's prosperity gospel intersects with the broader history of neopentecostalism, his positive message also comes from his cultural roots in Houston.

Coupling the content of Joel's teaching with its display across multiple media platforms, chapter 5 considers his place in the broader history of American televangelism. It fashions Osteen as a new tel-e-vangelist. Bracketing "tel" and "e," this rendering of televangelism highlights the singular importance of Joel's first career as a television producer to his subsequent arrival at the heights of American religious broadcasting as new technology and new media demanded a digital dexterity that Osteen possessed. The discussion of Osteen's tel-e-vangelism recalls the heyday of televised preaching even as it attends to the specific ways Joel harnessed new forms of electronic media (websites, blogs, podcasts, live streaming, e-votionals, Facebook, Joel Osteen and Lakewood apps) while preserving face-to-face encounters.

Establishing that the church is much more than Joel, chapter 6 sheds light on what I term Lakewood's charismatic core, aspects of its collective existence both past and present, as expressed through the congregation's other main preachers. Lakewood's charismatic core is not a hidden center of the church, but distinct manifestations of the church's congregational history and collective identity through the teachings of Dodie and Joel's sister Lisa Osteen Comes, as well as Victoria; Paul Osteen, Joel's brother; and Lakewood's first Spanish-speaking pastor Marcos Witt.

Based on documentary sources, media materials, oral history, and my fieldwork as a participant-observer in Lakewood's religious education classes, chapter 7 focuses on the congregation itself, its members, and attendees. It comments on the congregational resources from which former and current Lakewood members and attendees have fashioned both an individual and a collective religious identity. They have done so by embracing the notion of Pentecost, symbolic for a second chance in life, to attain what narrative psychologist Dan McAdams calls the "redemptive self." While members and attendees connect their redemptive selves specifically to the historic evangelical sense of salvation through

Jesus Christ, this chapter explains that the redemptive self at Lakewood has also referred to the maintenance of a spiritual makeover through activities such as prayer, Bible study, and community outreach.

Chapter 8 profiles Joel Osteen's leading critics to illuminate his place as America's leading Christian pastor. A surging movement within American evangelicalism known as New Calvinism—a group of pastors and theologians committed to intellectualism and Reformed theology—has been most vocal in denouncing the smiling preacher as spiritually weak and biblically illiterate. Detractors such as California pastor John MacArthur, seminary president R. Albert Mohler, and theologian Michael Horton, along with Christian rappers and street preachers, have castigated the Houston pastor. In turn, Osteen has responded to the scoffers by engaging in what I term his piety of resistance, a spiritualized counteroffensive composed of scriptural defenses, positive confession, and positive thinking. The upshot of the conflict between Osteen and his critics shows how evangelicalism's persistent fractures result from battles over how Christians interpret the Bible, part of what historian Molly Worthen calls its "crisis of authority."

A conclusion rehearses the book's main arguments, and points to the historical importance and cultural significance of Joel Osteen and Lakewood Church. Finally, the appendixes provide the texts of two of Joel's earliest sermons from 1999. Annotation offers brief historical and contextual commentary on these remarkable sources, since they all appeared several years before the publication of Osteen's first book in 2004.

A Note on Methodology and Terminology

The discipline of history shapes this book's interpretive framework. It draws heavily on analysis of documentary evidence; it is attentive to context and concerned with change over time. Yet the subjects of this volume—a congregation, its founders, and its members—continue to exist as an active assembly of people. Hence, this book couples archival-based historical study with participant observation in order to make more sense of Lakewood's historical and cultural totality.

Methodologically, the exploration of contemporary history offers unique opportunities and presents considerable challenges. As historians Claire Bond Potter and Renee C. Romano argue in *Doing Recent His-*

tory, reconstructing the recent past depends as much on documentary evidence as it does on newer media such as blogs and web sites. Quicker access to an abundance of primary sources via the Internet, for example, foregrounds the necessity of selectivity and highlights the difficulty of writing historically about living subjects. But with such exciting developments, methodological questions abound. Where does the recent past begin and end? From what vantage points is a subject historical enough? How is analysis of a living subject properly historical? What is sufficient historical distance from a subject in close historical proximity? How much historical distance defines the right amount of hindsight? There are as many answers to these questions as there are historians, but numerous scholars of American religion have intelligently attempted to reconstruct the recent past of contemporary movements and individuals. Studies of neopentecostal faith healers, prosperity gospel televangelists, contemporary evangelical subculture, and Oprah, for example, have collectively grappled with critical scholarly analysis of sensationalized subjects, historical investigation of living persons, and methodological quandaries of access to those subjects. These very questions and concerns surrounded the research and writing of this volume.[4]

Given the sensationalized dimensions of living subjects, researchers often face two additional concerns: historicizing contemporary figures and gaining access to those whose reputations and livelihoods may seem justly suspect. Historians who write about living individuals and movements face the fact that the final chapters are not final; they must keep in mind that the study of the contemporary can fall easily into mere description. The passage of time often fosters fuller perspectives and allows for broader analysis. Nevertheless, historical work on contemporary individuals and movements can yield insightful understanding based on cogent analysis and studied observation. Lakewood's over fifty-year history offers more than enough for historical scrutiny even if the smiling preacher is still smiling. Although repeated requests over a period of several years for interviews with members of the Osteen family proved fruitless, the research for this book surmounted this hurdle with qualitative evidence such as audio and video files of sermons, television broadcasts, and sustained participant observation. Several years of regular participant observation proved particularly fruitful. Relationships and friendships built over the course of months and years yielded a trove of material that offered plentiful perspectives on Joel Osteen and Lakewood Church.

I profess a personal ambivalence about Joel Osteen and Lakewood Church. While the church is a remarkable religious institution in terms of its size and the deeply multiracial character of its congregation— although at present Lakewood's leadership remains largely Anglo—a highly individualized spiritual message of self-improvement seems ill equipped to address the persistent, systemic injustices that plague today's world. At the same time, in my research I discovered that many of Lakewood's members and attendees actively engage the local Houston community and support, for example, efforts to eradicate human trafficking. With all of this said, I have attempted to maintain a rigorous commitment to remain flexible, patient, but scrutinizing in my historical assessments and cultural analysis of the smiling preacher and his congregation, not unlike anthropologist Susan Friend Harding's quest to reside at a "psychic intersection" in her study of Jerry Falwell and his fundamentalist world. I endeavored to produce a historically situated analysis of the church's story, even as I analytically considered through participant observation the current life of an active congregation. In light of such existential and academic intersections, religious studies scholar Manuel A. Vásquez's *More than Belief* assisted me in assessing Osteen's message and understanding religious practice at Lakewood. Vásquez elegantly elucidates his materialist approach to studying religion. "[A] non-reductive materialist framework," he writes, "begins with the acknowledgement that the practitioners' appeals to the supernatural, god(s), the sacred, or the holy have powerful material consequences for how they build their identities, narratives, practices, and environments." "It behooves scholars of religion," he contends, "to take seriously the native actor's lived world and to explore the biological, social, and historical conditions that make religious experiences possible as well as the effects these experiences have on self, culture, and nature." Vásquez's work oriented me to seek to understand the material consequences of Osteen and Lakewood's spiritual worlds as well as the spiritual dimensions of Osteen and Lakewood's material realities.[5]

Researching Osteen and his congregation during the course of this project, I have discovered that most people are not neutral when it comes to Joel. In print sources, online, and in interviews I found that Osteen's very existence was routinely the subject of effusive, ebullient praise and vicious vitriol. For some of the evangelical faithful, Joel is God's man for the global age. For others, he is one of the latest flashpoints of theological disputation in contemporary times. For some scholars, Joel is another slick televangelist with a smile in an era with vivid memories of highly publicized televangelist scandals. For others, he is a window into understanding how religion operates in American society. I concluded that it is futile to take sides either with those who insist Joel Osteen is "bad" in a theological sense or with others who claim that Joel Osteen is "good" as a motivational speaker by proffering positive thinking. In telling Osteen and Lakewood's history, I believe nuanced analysis is more constructive than taking sides in cultural or theological debates. Approaching the topic in a dualistic manner may generate headlines, website hits, Facebook likes, or retweets, but it generally fails to produce clearer understanding of the complex contingencies and changes that have been part of Osteen and Lakewood's larger story. At the same time, contested opinions about Osteen speak more to his signal importance for those trying to make sense of the contemporary moment in American religion than they do about presenting finalized assessments about America's most visible evangelical preacher. After all, he is still an active pastor and his living, breathing congregation continues to grow. Put another way, the visibility of Joel Osteen across the vast landscape of American religion—for better *or* for worse—deserves sustained, critical reflection. It is also important to respectfully acknowledge that Osteen and Lakewood matter religiously and spiritually for many people. This means that Osteen and Lakewood matter culturally and politically, too, not least to his most persistent critics. In light of the range of factors noted above, questions of distance and proximity—historical, cultural, and existential—can produce scrutiny, add clarity, and invite conversation. Perhaps this is what ethnographer Robert Orsi meant by pointing to the scholar's analytical residence at a place of "disciplined attentiveness" in between heaven and earth.[6]

It is helpful at this stage to discuss certain terminological aspects of this book.

First, uses of "evangelicalism" refer to the historical religious movement. For the purpose of readability, this book often uses "evangelicalism" and "Christianity" interchangeably, despite the wide definitional range of both terms. By referring to evangelicalism as a "movement," I intend to communicate institutional aspects as well as individual actions. "Movement" also encompasses a very broad range of denominational traditions, political persuasions and religious practices. Implicit in this definitional arrangement is the acknowledgment that evangelicalism, whatever definition assigned to it, is a complex phenomenon. History shows that it is a movement of both elites and nonelites, impacted by changes at both the macro and micro levels. References to the term in this book most specifically engage post–World War II American evangelicalism, which also includes those connected to Pentecostalism, charismatic Christianity, and neopentecostalism.

Highlighting the evangelical movement's individualist dynamics, historians of American evangelicalism also identify shared characteristics that developed over time and find expression in everyday practice: a focus on an inward, identifiable spiritual change, called a "new birth," by expressing faith in Jesus Christ; an emphasis on the Bible as authoritative for issues of both faith and practice; acknowledgment of the influence of the Holy Spirit on spiritual enlightenment, sometimes expressed through speaking in tongues; and the imperative to act on faith through evangelistic activity. Historians also point to common questions and concepts about the proper execution of human reason, the most effective place of public engagement, and most acceptable kind of political activity for individuals who adopt a religious orientation rooted in spiritual worlds accessible only by faith. This cluster of experiences, thoughts, and perspectives finds a home in the hearts, minds, emotions, and actions of those individuals discussed in this book, which also renders evangelicals in possession of aesthetic sensibilities rooted in spiritual understanding. Recognizing institutional and individual particulars of evangelicalism, readers will note the historical orientation of how I define evangelicalism as an integral part of American religious culture. This book does not address evangelicalism's theology systems, or the movement's technical, doctrinal minutiae that are the province of religious scholars and theologians.[7]

Second, I use "neopentecostal" and "neocharismatic" interchangeably. Following definitional conventions of historians David Edwin Harrell and Kate Bowler, and sociologist Milmon Harrison, these terms refer specifically to the post–World War II charismatic revival in the United

States. Some participants in the movement resisted rigid denominational lines that resulted in the emergence of hundreds of independent ministers and the creation of countless associated evangelistic agencies. Within the neopentecostal movement there emerged a distinct set of teachings called the prosperity gospel, also known as the Word of Faith movement (although the prosperity gospel's historical roots preceded World War II). The prosperity gospel's nomenclature, typically deployed by the movement's critics, also includes references to the "Health and Wealth Gospel" along with "Name It and Claim It." Like Bowler and Harrison, I use Word of Faith to refer specifically to the teaching of Kenneth Hagin as well as to identify ministers Hagin influenced. Finally, I follow religious studies scholar Candy Gunther Brown in my references to "divine healing." Brown explains that this phrase reflects how neopentecostals understand the healing process or healing event. Divine healing highlights the belief that God's divine love is the ultimate trigger for healing, the expressions of faith in God to act, and the neopentecostal conviction about the necessity of "supernatural intervention" in times of spiritual, physical, or psychological need for wholeness.[8]

Following historians Allan Anderson and Russell Spittler, I use "charismatic Christianity," the "charismatic movement," "Pentecostal Christianity," and "Pentecostalism" interchangeably. According to Anderson and Spittler, these terms reflect the conviction that in either individual settings or collective assemblies of worship God is undeniably present through the Holy Spirit, expressed not just through the words and teachings of the minister, but also through events of divine healing or speaking in tongues. Individually, charismatic and Pentecostal Christians experience the Holy Spirit through rapturous moments of intense prayer, visions, healings, or speaking in tongues. Corporately, charismatic and Pentecostal Christians respond to the Holy Spirit in similar ways but also through clapping, shouting, raising hands, applause, singing, dancing, or physical touch ("laying on of hands"). Pentecostal and charismatic Christians also believe that the Holy Spirit prompts improvisational and spontaneous embodied movements or oral expressions. Similar to my definition of evangelicalism, my use of the terms above intends to explain the lived religious experiences or "pietistic habits" of neopentecostals and neocharismatics, not to define or speculate about what they mean theologically.[9]

[1]

John Osteen's Pentecost

The Origins of Lakewood Church

Daddy knew that adversity could be a stepping-stone to
something greater. . . . He began to search the Scriptures as
never before, and he discovered the God of the Bible in a
fresh way—as a loving God, a healing God, a restoring God,
and yes, as a God of miracles.

—Joel Osteen (2004)

The year was 1939. John Osteen, a seventeen-year-old theater employee
and frequent nightclub patron, found an anchor for his wandering heart
in Fort Worth, Texas. "I surrendered all to the Lord Jesus and passed from
death into life," Osteen explained. "I became a new creature in Christ
Jesus. . . . I called my friend, who had been witnessing to me through the
years, and told him about this. He was glad and invited me to go to church
with him." That friend, Sam Martin, had long encouraged John to follow
Jesus. In his 2001 autobiography, *How I Led One and One Led a Million*,
Martin recounted the moment when John confessed the need for a savior.
"We knelt together and I led him in the sinner's prayer," Martin wrote
about that historic day in 1939. "John invited Jesus to come into his heart."
Martin encouraged John to put his new faith into action. John showed the
energetic conviction of a new convert, proclaiming, "I want all of the people here today to know that I shall spend the rest of my life telling about
Jesus." At the time, Martin and Osteen attended a Southern Baptist church
together, and soon around the city the budding ministers "preached on
the streets, in the missions, in the schoolhouses, in the jails, at the poor
farms (what they used to call nursing homes back then). We preached
anywhere we had the opportunity." John's early sermons included a meditation on Proverbs, speculation about God's will, and an oration titled
"Ambassadors for Christ." Osteen found faith in Fort Worth.[1]

This account of John Osteen's conversion introduces several important dimensions of American evangelicalism and the origins of Lakewood Church. John's early life in Depression-era north Texas not only marked the beginning of his definitive place in the Lone Star State's religious history, but it also orients his story to religion in the Sunbelt South. Second, John's Pentecost alludes to a central principle in American Christianity, second chances, a message that would become his staple. Osteen, like many evangelicals, found his life's central meaning in the story of Jesus and redemption. Third, Osteen's transformation from Southern Baptist to charismatic changed the language he used to describe religious experience. It also enhanced the public presence of his preaching career, particularly when he began to engage the vast network of neopentecostal ministries birthed after World War II. Connecting the various strands of these stories helps to explain the origins of Lakewood Church.

John Osteen's "Texas Theology"

The story of John Osteen began in 1921 northeast of Dallas in the small town of Paris, Texas. His father, Willis Jackson Osteen, owned a cotton farm until the Great Depression forced the family to sell vegetables from the bed of a pickup truck. Struggling in poverty, as a young boy John's wardrobe consisted of second-hand clothes and shoddy shoes with soles made of cardboard. For breakfast, when he had any at all, he poured water over his cereal because milk was a luxury the Osteen family could not afford. Reflecting cultural sensibilities in which music provided some sense of meaning to the chaos of a shifting existence, Willis playing the fiddle, voicing simple folk tunes as John and his four siblings sang along.[2]

Economic difficulties compelled many families in the area to migrate west to destinations such as Southern California, but the Osteens remained in Texas. Since an agricultural livelihood seemed impossible, as John got older, he worked at the Isis Theatre in Fort Worth, selling movie tickets and popcorn. These circumstances, coupled with John's conversion to Christianity, meant that he became part of the South's white "plain folk," people committed to evangelical religion, individual initiative, and conservative politics. John's plain folk experience in the context of Southern Baptist faith reflected the religious communalism of evangelicals in the South, conforming to what historian Darren Dochuk calls "Texas theology," a message "that melded traditionalism into an uncentered, unbounded religious culture of entrepreneurialism, experimentation, and engagement." John's Texas theology would not only provide the means by which he would overcome a period of existential crisis in his own life, its core message planted the seeds that would sprout a smiling preacher half a century later.[3]

John's newfound initiative inspired a commitment to transcend the spiritual and social coil of his circumstances. For Osteen, Christian education was the lamp that lit his path to Siloam Springs, Arkansas, the home of John Brown University (JBU). Here, just before Osteen's arrival at JBU, the moneyed political interests of national figures such as businessperson, politician, and civil servant Jesse Jones met the fledgling but fiery evangelistic and entrepreneurial visions of preacher and educator John Brown. At JBU, along with countless other plain folk, Osteen secured credentials that cemented aspirations toward Christian ministry. Schooled in JBU's evangelistic philosophy of striving for spiritual growth by putting faith into action peppered with commitments to free-market capitalism and entrepreneurialism, during the course of World War II Osteen completed a bachelor's degree. While John was hardly an architect of the Christian Right, attending JBU represented the first of his many intersections and affiliations with both individuals and institutions connected to American evangelicalism's halls of power.[4]

Animated by JBU's "head, heart, and hand" philosophy, Osteen moved north and enrolled at Northern Baptist Theological Seminary (NBTS). His 1944 master's thesis constructed strategies of Christian learning for the local congregation. At NBTS, Osteen developed a ministry philosophy that emphasized both preaching and Christian education. Voicing a vision of church life in language that became common at Lakewood Church, Osteen argued that in congregational life:

The people who gather in the sanctuary have a deeply felt need that only the declaration of the gospel can satisfy. Some have spent a week of victory; some a week of defeat; some have been discouraged by the onslaughts of Satan; some are weary; some have family troubles—all have another week to face; all need the voice of God for direction. . . . Sincere worshipers have come to the service to hear God's voice and to receive strength and courage and power from the indwelling Christ with which to continue the good fight of faith.[5]

Osteen contended that spiritual growth emerged through the corporate gathering of Christians in a congregational context. Hence, the "unified service" enshrined a Sunday morning schedule of worship and religious instruction. This practice emphasized the preaching role of the minister while it gave church members a place to pursue additional learning outside of the communal setting. In this way, Osteen believed the church functioned most powerfully as a "soul-winning organism." Shortly after matriculation, once again following Sunbelt migration patterns of plain folk, Osteen had occasion to test his theory of congregational life in California.[6]

Osteen applied his insights about the unified service as an assistant pastor at First Baptist Church in San Diego. Then, in the late 1940s, he returned to north central Texas as a minister at First Baptist Church in Hamlin, located approximately three hours from Fort Worth. Promotional literature published by Osteen's Hamlin church offered snapshots of his work as a young pastor. Local ministers testified to his preaching prowess. Stamford pastor Miles Hays observed that Osteen was a "man of unusual evangelistic talents. He is a constant student of the Bible, and believes it without question. He loves the Lord, and has a passion for souls." Fred Fisher, a professor at Hardin-Simmons University in Abilene, described him as a "safe, warm-hearted evangelistic preacher." Osteen left Hamlin in 1948 intending to become a traveling preacher. But a year later, in order to secure steady income for a wife and young son, Justin, Osteen settled at Central Baptist Church in Baytown, a suburb on Houston's east side.[7]

Osteen's arrival in Baytown coincided with the city's official establishment in 1948, a signal of its thriving oil industry. For the previous three decades, the Humble Oil and Refining Company—later to become ExxonMobil—had established business interests in Baytown, and assisted in the building of its infrastructure. Baytown was part of the larger area known as the East Texas Oilfield, a petroleum-rich portion of the state that fueled the region's economy. The East Texas Oilfield also included the town of Beaumont, about fifty miles east of Baytown, another

Figure 1.1. John Osteen, Northern Baptist Theological Seminary, ca. 1944. Source: Northern Baptist Theological Seminary Archives. Used with permission.

growing oil boom town featured in historian Darren Dochuk's analysis of "oil-patch evangelicals," a group of Christians whose spiritual and entrepreneurial interests focused on "God and black gold." Osteen no doubt met some of these oil-patch evangelicals, some of whose money likely assisted in the material growth of Central Baptist Church.[8]

Just as the region's oil industry reached new heights during the mid-twentieth century, Osteen's tenure in Baytown marked critical junctures in his life and career. He expanded Central Baptist's Christian education program, building from strategies outlined in his master's thesis. Osteen also oversaw the construction of a new 800-seat sanctuary. Moreover, he played a leading administrative role in the San Jacinto Baptist Association (SJBA) between 1950 and 1955. In 1950, he served as the clerk for the SJBA, and he preached the Association's annual sermon in 1953. Displaying an early interest in religious programming, in 1955 Osteen worked

Figure 1.2. Central Baptist Church, Baytown, Texas, ca. 1950. Source: Central Baptist Church Archives. Used with permission.

as a pastoral advisor to Youth on the March, a pioneering attempt at televangelism directed toward teen audiences. He served on multiple missionary committees, including a program focused on evangelism in Mexico. Despite such successes, Osteen left Central Baptist in 1956, resigning when his youthful marriage ended in divorce.[9]

Mired in despair, John found hope a few years later when he married Dodie Pilgrim, a nurse. To make ends meet in the late 1950s, Osteen worked as a salesperson and preached occasionally around Houston. He became a regular at Hibbard Memorial Baptist Church, but because he felt that his divorce disqualified him from holding a permanent pastorate, he declined the congregation's initial offer to become Hibbard's full-time minister. Nevertheless, church deacons, led by a man named Hollis

Brewer, remained impressed with Osteen's powerful preaching and persisted in their request that he become Hibbard's pastor. In time, Osteen accepted the church's offer. As an adolescent, David Russell (who would eventually become Hollis Brewer's son-in-law) spent many Sundays in Hibbard's pews intrigued, almost mystified at John's oratory. "He could say more in twenty minutes than a lot of people could say in an hour," Russell recalled. "He was so knowledgeable of the Word [and] he was a gifted preacher" who would address "repentance, sin, and the necessity to live a holy life." While at Hibbard, Osteen added a new building—which, like Central Baptist's sanctuary addition, displayed the decade's suburban affluence—and under his leadership membership soared to nearly 1,000.[10]

During John's tenure at Hibbard, he and Dodie welcomed their first daughter into the world with what appeared to be insurmountable health problems. Both doctors and parents feared Lisa would never have full mobility of her limbs nor full mental and cognitive capabilities. "When our little girl was born we saw immediately she was not a normal child," Osteen wrote in 1961. "We thought her neck was broken. She couldn't hold up her head. She couldn't hold her arms up. She couldn't hold her legs up. She was just a little blob of quivering flesh." In desperation, and perhaps interpreting Lisa's ill health as God's judgment on him for his divorce several years previous, John started to study the concept of healing in the New Testament. As a result, he and Dodie began to imagine new possibilities for Lisa's future as they prayed fervently for their daughter. Eventually, Lisa began to lead an active life, something Osteen attributed to divine influence and supernatural activity. He became convinced that he could experience in the twentieth century the supernatural power he read about in the New Testament, a notion that contrasted sharply with his Southern Baptist heritage. Elated but still in the throes of an existential crisis, John remained unsettled even after his daughter's healing. "One day there came upon me a great restlessness," John recalled in his 1961 book *Supernatural Manifestations in the Life of John Osteen*. "This restlessness turned into fear. I told my wife I felt that God was greatly displeased about something and that I need to go somewhere alone and seek His face. I rented a hotel room in downtown Houston. I locked the door and stood in the presence of God." Cloistered in prayer, in 1958 John Osteen sought and received the baptism of the Holy Spirit. Dodie

Figure 1.3. Hibbard Memorial Baptist Church, Houston, ca. 1958. John Osteen, far right, poses with Hibbard's leaders in a photograph taken by Hollis Brewer. Junior Ferguson is third from left, wearing a tie. Curtis Bell, third from right, worked closely with John when Lakewood started. Source: David Russell. Used with permission.

received the baptism of the Holy Spirit the following year at a neopentecostal revival meeting in Los Angeles.[11]

John's new and ecstatic religious experiences eventually divided Hibbard. His Pentecostal spirituality became public knowledge when deacon E. E. Ferguson spied on one of John's prayer meetings at which he heard the group speak in tongues. Many at Hibbard scoffed at his new teachings. But when several deacons and church members—including one-time critic Ferguson—began to affirm Osteen by offering their own testimonies of Spirit baptism, others spoke out in support of Hibbard's pastor. Church member Jean Martin, who later served as secretary of Osteen's evangelistic agency, became a staunch advocate. Martin found John "likeable and [he] preached sound doctrinal sermons." The turning point came when she witnessed the physical healing of those in the congregation and watched other church leaders receive baptism in the Holy Spirit. "To my amazement," Martin observed, "the chairman of the board of deacons and his wife and another deacon and his wife began to have the same strange look on their faces as Brother Osteen! They looked happy! I had known and loved these people for years. What was happening? . . . After several months the Lord Jesus baptized me in the Holy Ghost and Fire while I was praying alone in my home. Oh, what joy filled my soul!" For other former Hibbard members, physical healing confirmed the Spirit's power. A young girl named Sandra Fielding reported healing from a leg injury and Osteen claimed that Mary Celestine's "leg popped like a gun as the Lord touched her and she was healed instantly!" John had numerous supporters at Hibbard, many of whom would form the core membership of his new church. However, not everyone supported charismatic displays, so to avoid further contention he resigned on May 3, 1959. One week later, Osteen founded Lakewood Baptist Church with 190 people.[12]

While Osteen ended the 1950s on a positive note with a new congregation, he had experienced a series of difficulties and setbacks, including the rupture of his marriage, that spawned nothing short of an existential crisis. His conflicted experiences mirrored the decade's ups and downs. It took what John called "supernatural manifestation" to emerge from the valley of the shadow of death.[13]

"Pentecost Is Not a Denomination but an Experience from God for Everyone"

With testimony of charismatic, spiritual transformation, John's 1958 Pentecost moment reshaped his sermons and redirected his ministry. And he was not the only Southern Baptist baptized into a new spirit during the early post–World War II period. Fellow Texas minister Howard Conaster and Florida pastor Jamie Buckingham also participated in the neopentecostal renewal. Southern Baptist seminaries and denominational leaders issued a range of theological responses to Spirit-led clergy within their ranks. Some Southern Baptists supported openness to the Spirit, while others maintained that speaking in tongues had died with the New Testament apostles. Debate among Southern Baptists about charismatic experiences would reach a fever pitch in the 1970s, but already in the 1960s, animated discussions about the issue resulted in expulsions and resignations.[14]

Distanced from most noncharismatic Southern Baptists by 1959, John attained more flexibility by founding Lakewood. The church eventually dropped "Baptist" from its name. Untethered by denominational restraints, and with documented talents for preaching and religious leadership, John fit emerging patterns in the neopentecostal movement that prized theological training, respectability, and organizational management. Factors that contributed to Osteen's formidable presence within the movement included his willingness to receive counsel from established clergy and foresight to forge links with key figures in neopentecostal preaching networks.[15]

Osteen's horizons widened when he became involved with the Full Gospel Businessmen's Fellowship International (FGBMFI). Demos Shakarian founded the FGBMFI in the 1950s to provide a place of worship, fellowship, and encouragement for working men and women of Pentecostal conviction. With a nondenominational charismatic identity—like that to which Osteen was also passionately committed—it quickly became a locus of spiritual authority in the neopentecostal movement. In addition to its spiritual role, leaders and local FGBMFI chapters easily forged business contacts and the fellowship established new alliances that aided the funding of numerous independent, charismatic teachers. Osteen's ability to express "charismatic fervor in a dignified setting before a much broader and more sophisticated audience" struck a chord. He enjoyed the lively charismatic preaching, prayer sessions with an identifiable intensity, and elegant dinners FGBMFI offered. As a result, Osteen appeared in the regular rotation at FGBMFI conventions.[16]

Osteen first met the FGBMFI founder in 1959 through Houston businessperson Andy Sorelle. Osteen preached at the national convention in Los Angeles that year and appeared on the cover of FGBMFI's *Voice* magazine. Apparently, he made a stirring impression. A report on the Los Angeles meeting described him as an "[o]utstanding Spirit-filled speaker" who's preaching, "aroused the convention." In 1962, Osteen again spoke at the national convention in Seattle, where "the power of the Holy Ghost fell and many were filled." John's message about denominationalism tethered Christian believers to traditions that rendered the Spirit's work nearly impossible. "The church has laid its head in the lap of tradition," Osteen maintained, "And tradition has said the day of miracles is over, tongues are a farce, prophesy has passed away, and the supernatural is gone." Osteen continued voicing this message throughout the 1960s at regional FGBMFI meetings in Miami (1960), Houston (1960), Tulsa (1960), Denver (1961), Lubbock (1961), Milwaukee (1963), Denver (1965), St. Louis (1966), and Dallas (1966). John coupled his presence at FGBMFI meetings with numerous publications in *Voice* magazine. Ministers associated with the FGBMFI sung his praises. A Methodist minister who became Pentecostal, Don Scott, attributed his newfound experiential faith to Osteen's influence. Scott visited Lakewood in the early 1960s, and because of Osteen's preaching, "we were filled with the Holy Ghost and called to be witnesses for the living Christ." In addition, *Voice* editor Jerry Jensen included John's testimony in the widely circulated FGBMFI publication *Baptists and the Baptism of the Holy Spirit*. This collection registered the voices of nationally known Baptists at the time, including Billy Graham and Pat Robertson, thus notching John's signal place in neopentecostal circles.[17]

Although rich fellowship and powerful sermons through the FGBMFI bolstered John's presence on the national stage, he continued to assess the meaning of his new, neopentecostal faith through counsel from Houston area ministers, including Assemblies of God pastor J. R. Goodwin. Goodwin led Osteen through a study of scriptural passages about speaking in tongues and healing. Both Goodwin and his wife proved to be formative influences on John and Dodie. As Dodie recalled, "We went to church with the Goodwins when our children were little. We loved it. They were our good friends and tremendous shepherds. They helped us know how to pastor." John remembered, "It was with the help and in the home of Brother and Sister J. R. Goodwin of Pasadena, Texas, that I first spoke a few words in another language."[18]

In 1961, Osteen left Lakewood Church to pastor Marvin Crow and set out as an itinerant minister. Osteen and Crow met through the FGBMFI. Crow spoke at numerous FGBMFI regional conventions, including meetings in Albuquerque (1963) and Fresno (1963), and authored a chapter for the FGBMFI book on Pentecostal Baptists, the same publication in which John's testimony appeared. Outside of Houston, Osteen strategically collaborated with Tulsa-based healing evangelists T. L. Osborn and Oral Roberts. He sought wisdom and guidance from Osborn and Roberts through personal conversations and close observation of their sermons, preaching styles, and publications. In 1961, Osteen and Osborn preached together in a Juárez, Mexico, revival, and Osteen later wrote about Osborn's preaching tour to Houston—which also included healing accounts from some of Osteen's former parishioners at Baytown's Central Baptist Church. In articles Osteen published in Osborn's monthly *Faith Digest* he stated that Osborn's book *Healing the Sick* "showed [me] how to believe" in divine healing. Osteen also published an article in Oral Roberts's magazine *Abundant Life* in 1961, and preached with him at several FGBMFI national conventions, including Seattle (1962) and Houston (1963). Not only did *Faith Digest* and *Abundant Life* offer additional platforms for Osteen's message, his collaborations with Osborn and Roberts further legitimated his place among neopentecostals.[19]

Additional evidence of Osteen's growing stature within the neopentecostal movement, his name also appeared in the *Pentecostal Evangel*, the magazine of the Assemblies of God. The denomination's evangelism secretary, Burton Pierce, in a 1961 article praised the evangelistic work emanating from John's Houston church. Pierce quoted the popular neopentecostal preacher. "We want our church to be a missions center," stated Osteen about Lakewood. "Our goal is to establish a hundred churches in the Republic of Mexico." That same year, Minnesota pastor Frank J. Lundquist also commented on Osteen's evangelistic capabilities. Over 130 people received the Holy Spirit at Minneapolis's Gospel Tabernacle in a July revival, reported Lundquist. "Brother Osteen is a fine preacher who seeks to have Pentecostal liberty in each meeting. The operation of the gifts of the Spirit was evident." Finally, a testimony in the *Pentecostal Evangel* from late 1961 about baptism in the Holy Spirit quoted a phrase Osteen had made popular in neopentecostal circles, "Pentecost is not a denomination, but an experience from God for everyone."[20]

By the early 1960s, John's extensive involvement in the neopentecosal movement gave him the confidence to establish his own independent ministry. The John H. Osteen Evangelistic Association (JOEA) distributed reading materials, published books, solicited donations, and organized preaching revivals. Between 1961 and 1964, he published five books on the work of the Holy Spirit and divine healing. In his early works, Osteen interweaved his own personal transformation from a rational-minded Southern Baptist to passionate charismatic. Osteen's books in the late 1960s proclaimed the decade one of spiritual renewal and possibility. Two titles reflected the multiple moods of the 1960s by adopting then current buzzwords—*This Awakening Generation* (1967) and *You Can Change Your Destiny* (1968)—but their content was unambiguously charismatic. The awakening to which Osteen referred led him to reject fidelity to denominational traditions. "God never established denominationalism," Osteen pointed out. "The Church, which is His Body, is the important thing in this hour. . . . God loves all of His children, no matter what their denominational affiliation. His promises were not for a certain denomination, but for 'as many as the Lord our God shall call.'" His language of destiny, unlike that of others who used the term in the 1960s, referred not to achieving a higher consciousness, but to a new lease on life through healing. "Have you become convinced that your destiny is to suffer pain and disease and defeat? Have you given up and resigned yourself to the position that there is nothing that can be done about your situation?" Osteen queried readers. "You can change your destiny! Thousands of people who once thought there was no hope have come into the light of God's Word and found that by daring to believe the promises of God they could revolutionize their lives."[21]

Similar to other evangelistic organizations at the time such as Campus Crusade for Christ, which published the famous *Four Spiritual Laws* booklet, the JOEA issued numerous gospel tracts during its early years. A popular tract, *Telling the King's Household*, adopted the crisis language of the decade's larger social ethos by claiming that Satan had locked God's people behind "the high walls of tradition" as they "rush with hunger to the spiritual tables only to find them barren . . . [t]he children of God are sick and tired of being sick and tired."[22]

Modeling what John learned from the likes of Oral Roberts and T. L. Osborn, and reflective of the abundant print culture of neopentecostalism, the JOEA launched a bimonthly magazine called *Praise*, which ran from 1962 to 1965. Osteen wrote articles in *Praise* about his own charismatic experiences and included hundreds of accounts from Spirit-led Methodists, Presbyterians, Nazarenes, Mennonites, Lutherans, and Episcopalians, among many others. A reflection of his own commitment to the idea that Pentecost transcended denominations, Osteen published testimonies from charismatic Catholics. During its three-year run, *Praise* reached nearly 5,900 subscribers, which included readers in such places as Rhodesia, Japan, and France. Osteen even reported that his teaching influenced the conversion of Hindus and Muslims to Christianity, although he did not provide corroborating evidence. While *Praise* did not include testimonies from African American charismatics—unlike Roberts's *Abundant Life*—Osteen documented the revival work of numerous Mexican pastors and a minister named Hong Sit of First Southern Baptist Chinese Church in Houston. Sit's article relayed accounts of healing and charismatic revival in Hong Kong, Tahiti, Japan, and Hawaii, thus adding an international dimension to *Praise*. Sit was also instrumental in Osteen's initiation to charismatic Christian experience. At a preaching campaign during the 1960s, a man on whom Osteen laid hands began to speak in tongues. "Shawndi! Shawndi! Shawndi!," the man exclaimed. Sit explained to John that "what the Spirit was probably giving this man were the words *sheang dai*, pronounced almost exactly like *shawndi*, which is perfect Cantonese for O Most High God."[23]

While *Praise* reported on Osteen's national campaigns as well as events and personalities of the wider neopentecostal movement, it also gave additional insight into John's religious vision and spiritual practice as a minister in Houston. Harold Nichols, a Hibbard member and one-time Osteen foe, stood committed to John. "While Brother Osteen preached about the Baptism of the Holy Ghost in our sanctuary, the chairman of the deacons and I sat in the back room plotting a way to get rid of him," wrote Nichols. Upon Nichols's own Pentecost moment he exclaimed, "No words can express the praise and power that fills our lives" at Lakewood. Testimonies from Mary Clayton, Curtis Bell, and S. E. Lindsey related similar commitments from former Hibbard members. The Hobbs family, former members of Central Baptist in Baytown, attributed tongues speaking and psychological healing to Osteen's influence. John even invited the Hobbs to Lakewood Church in 1962 for a service that featured neopentecostal preacher Kenneth Hagin. John's passion impressed people, as did his shepherding practices as a pastor. Despite his distance from some Southern Baptists after his Pentecost moment, evidently many of John's former parishioners remained tied to their former pastor.[24]

While John took careful notice of how neopentecostal ministers conducted evangelistic organizations, he also had a keen sense of how both neopentecostal insiders and American society at large viewed the rising generation of popular preachers. While many teachers received adoration and praise, others experienced brash criticism from those within and without the neopentecostal movement. From within the movement, neopentecostal leaders such as Gordon Lindsay and G. H. Montgomery publicly questioned ministers' motives by connecting aggressive fundraising with lavish living. Montgomery, a former assistant to Oral Roberts, lamented the lack of accountability independent evangelistic associations enjoyed. "Men who preach the meek and lowly Nazarene to a lost and dying world, and yet live in palatial homes built on money contributed by God's poor people, cannot call themselves followers of Jesus," roared Montgomery. He also targeted the stories and statistics of perpetually successful evangelistic campaigns, which included crass peddling of "miraculous commodities" such as dirt from Israel and water from the Jordan River.[25]

Neopentecostal teachers vigorously responded to criticisms. As early as 1957, Oral Roberts published an open letter to readers of *Abundant Life* that carefully articulated that he did not oppose "medical science" as a legitimate mode of intervention. But Roberts distanced himself from the term "faith healer" with the claim that:

> I am not a healer. I am not a faith healer. I cannot heal. Only God can heal. . . . I can only trust the innate honesty of the public press to publish the truth concerning my views on the subject of faith healing. It is my purpose to pray for the sick with the laying on of hands, and to use the spoken word as a point of contact with God for the healing of the sick.[26]

Roberts continued his impassioned defense of neopentecostal teachers by criticizing journalists from *Life* magazine, whom the Oral Roberts Evangelistic Association (OREA) had given generous access for an article, for publishing work "that . . . did not truly reflect the facts, objectives and purposes of our ministry." In turn, the OREA printed a full article from *The Tulsa Tribune* that offered a point-by-point defense of Roberts, his healing services, and the OREA.[27]

Other ministers responded similarly to the criticisms Roberts addressed. Juanita Coe, who continued her husband Jack Coe's ministry after his 1957 death, published sermons and editorials defending neopentecostalism. In the January 1964 issue of *Christian Challenge*, she printed a sermon by Pastor P. C. Nelson, "Objections . . . To Divine

Healing," that defended faith teaching from claims that it involved hypnotism, psychic therapy, spiritualism, and Christian Science. Later that year, an unsigned *Christian Challenge* editorial advanced similar claims. "Scriptural Healing" practices such as anointing the sick with oil "must not be ranked among those quack remedies for human ills," the editorial claimed. The editorial also rebutted criticism that the healed thereafter avoided professional medical care. "The act of turning away from doctors, braces and medicine will not bring divine healing to an individual any more than leaving off drinking of alcohol will bring salvation to a sinner."[28]

Osteen's *Praise* featured some of the "miraculous commodities" G. H. Montgomery targeted, although it appears that John offered his prayer cloth at no charge. A small advertisement titled "Do You Need Healing?" promised believers hope: "Evangelist John H. Osteen would like to pray for you personally; since this is impossible, except in his Revival Meetings, he will be glad to pray for you and send you a prayer cloth he has prayed over. You may be healed through this faith ministry as have many others." The disclaimer that followed based the distribution of prayer cloths on Acts 19:11–12, where this New Testament passage reported healing from "handkerchiefs or aprons" the Apostle Paul had touched. This advertisement appeared in *Praise* four times throughout 1963 and 1964. Nevertheless, Osteen addressed critical voices that questioned the motives and practices of neopentecostal teachers. He issued a plea to "invest your tithes and offerings in the Lord's work today. We count each gift as a trust from the Lord Jesus and seek to use it wisely for His glory." In an early 1965 issue of *Praise*, Osteen reminded JOEA donors that "this non-profit organization is approved by the Internal Revenue and can give tax-deductible receipts for all gifts." He assured readers that the JOEA "operates in the highest ethical standards and Christian principles. Business references will be gladly given to all who desire them. We seek to walk humbly before God; act honestly toward all, and above all, to please our Heavenly Father." The specificity with which Osteen referred to both criticism of charismatic experiences and how the JOEA used money documented a clear strategy of neopentecostal legitimization.[29]

During this period, Osteen devoted considerable attention to healing. Coupled with detailed reports of revivals with generous quotations and

pages reproduced from his personal diary, he documented divine healing by publishing "before" and "after" photographs of participants in his
meetings. While John did not at this point offer medical records to legit-
imize healings, unlike teacher Kathryn Kuhlman, in his 1968 book *You
Can Change Your Destiny* he included four "before" and "after" pictures
of a young boy from India whose calloused, clubbed feet represented
what he described as "[o]ne of the greatest miracles I have ever witnessed." Several pages later, black-and-white images intended to illustrate divine healing of leprosy and severe leg injuries. At the end of the
book, Osteen provided pictorial documentation from El Salvador of a
healed leg injury and a tumor. While Osteen's approach appeared similar
to that of A. A. Allen's *Miracle Magazine* and Oral Roberts's *Abundant
Life*, both of which contained "before" and "after," sequentially arranged
photos of men, women, and children rising from wheelchairs, removing
leg braces, laying crutches aside, and displaying X-ray records, Osteen
rarely placed himself in the photograph of the healed person. Instead, he
presented a carefully organized evidentiary package to document divine
healing, a practice that reflected wider neopentecostal trends, which
he retained as part of his healing ministry well into the 1980s by using
medically confirmed evidence in television broadcasts.[30]

While John achieved a national and international reputation among
neopentecostals during the 1960s, his full-time itinerant activities slowed
down considerably by the decade's closing years. At this point, Lakewood Church, with which Osteen had maintained contact, needed a
new leader, and his family demanded more sustained attention. Strained
and stretched by travels, John was not about to lose a second marriage.
Dodie recalled that he once traveled for 37 straight days in India, including Christmas Day. "I almost dreaded to see him come in," she admitted,
because he would turn around and leave again. In tears, she said it was
probably harder on John being away in India, not having anyone. But
"I'm glad now that he went," Dodie said, because "he won a lot of people
to Jesus and saw a lot of miracles."[31]

Eventually, John applied what he had learned to build and sustain
Lakewood Church. John's rugged origins in Depression-era north Texas
birthed an unfailing conviction that through Jesus there is always the
possibility for a second chance in life. Grappling with the guilt of a failed
first marriage and the difficulties of a newborn plagued with a mysteri-

ous ailment, John's desperate search for existential wholeness led to a new beginning in the neopentecostal movement. In other words, John Osteen's Pentecost gave birth to Lakewood Church. A spiritual tenacity sustained his energetic commitment to a message of healing and new life. Access to neopentecostalism's leaders schooled John in the art of evangelistic outreach and organizational development. While his entry into neopentecostalism coincided with the birth of Lakewood Church in the 1950s, its neopentecostal origins meant that the church's spiritual and social roots in Houston fostered its growth not just in the Lone Star State but also across the world.

John Osteen's Prosperity Gospel

Faith and Divine Healing at the Oasis of Love

I am healed. I am strong. I am prospering. Every need is met. Thank God, we are what God says we are.
—John Osteen (1981)

In 1972, John Osteen first referred to Lakewood Church as an "Oasis of Love in a Troubled World." For Christians accustomed to Houston's sweltering heat, the image of an oasis proved inviting. But it also depicted Lakewood as a place to find spiritual nourishment. "People are saved in every service," Osteen proclaimed. "Many are filled with the Holy Ghost and enter in through that doorway to the supernatural. People with hungry hearts come . . . from far and near to find the true power of God that will meet their needs." After traversing the globe as an independent evangelist during the 1960s, John fashioned Lakewood as a respite from the difficulties of a world in flux. Lakewood music leader David Ingles's 1976 song "Oasis of Love" captured these realities in a powerful way. A tune of its time, his song told of a disconnected vagabond, unmoored from social contact, searching aimlessly, who ultimately finds a new community of Jesus People who provide meaning and a remade identity. Ingles sang, "Because of His love/A loser can win/ Hey you in the desert of life/Come on in/And drink from the cup of a friend." In Lakewood parlance, Ingles's weary traveler experienced Pentecost. And in the "desert of life" the weary traveler found acceptance at the Oasis of Love. Ingles's song reflected not only the period's Christian counterculture but also the faith, divine healing, and prosperity gospel that defined John Osteen and Lakewood Church from the 1970s to the 1990s.[1]

Increasingly influenced by the teachings of neopentecostal teacher Kenneth Hagin, John eagerly embraced Word of Faith principles throughout the 1970s. The ways that John fashioned these teachings to his own context, not unlike the ways he created his own place among independent neopentecostal ministries during the 1960s, paved the way for his prominent place in the prosperity gospel movement during the 1970s and 1980s. But John's prosperity gospel emphasized divine healing and privileged physical health much more than financial blessing. Continuing to nurture national neopentecostal connections he had forged in the previous decades, John's books and messages starting in the 1970s more vociferously reflected concerns expressed by the culture warriors of the Christian Right. The latter three decades of John's career also witnessed continued commitment to neopentecostalism's core teachings on healing, speaking in tongues, and faith.

The (Holy) Spirit of the Seventies

As the 1960s gave way to the 1970s, shifting sensibilities within the neopentecostal movement spawned significant changes. Anxieties related to class conflict persuaded some neopentecostals to dismiss a growing number of independent evangelists who aimed to present a healing message with more respectability. These same neopentecostals, both black and white, connected the quest for refinement to a renewed, clearly articulated message of financial prosperity, a feature of Word of Faith teachings at the time. In some cases, prosperity teachings yielded quantifiable results: more money to conduct campaigns, increased resources to publish books and distribute teaching tapes, and sufficient funding to construct larger churches. But other neopentecostals focused on divine revelation or divine healing, which increasingly put the focus of independent ministries on personality. For critics, the cost of respectability was too high. It polluted the message and the focus on a minister's charisma undercut personal integrity. Yet true to the neopentecostal message itself, fracture fostered opportunity. In turn, these developments ironically energized the movement with a distinct, ecumenical, nondenominationalism, an outlook that deemphasized denominational adherence and strident sectarianism in favor of assembling a wider Christian community.[2]

During the 1970s, John's ministry most clearly reflected the neopentecostal quest for respectability along with its established, nondenominational fervor. Already a leading figure within the movement, John continued regularly teaching at FGBMFI meetings. He addressed gatherings in Oahu (1973), St. Louis (1974), Dallas (1974), Muskogee (1975), Phoenix (1975), Honolulu (1977), Portland (1977), Orlando (1977), Chicago (1978), and Phoenix (1978), and spoke at the FGBMFI World Convention in New Orleans (1979).[3]

John's February 1973 sermon in Oahu, "The Divine Flow of God's Love," emphasized healing and expressed his fidelity to nondenominational Christianity. Retooling his 1960s mantra, "Pentecost is not a denomination but an experience from God for everyone," Osteen spoke about how he felt God's love "flow" in concrete ways. "I didn't used to love Methodists," Osteen admitted. "An Episcopalian was out of the question. Deliver me from a Catholic! But when I received the Baptism [of the Holy Spirit], the love of God was shed abroad in my heart and I'd hug them all. *The first thing that love burned off was my nondenominational tag.* I was Baptist born, Baptist bred, Baptist living, and Baptist dead." John expressed his notion of "divine flow" with references to healing. A zealous preacher, Osteen's early charismatic fervor led to sadness and frustration. John recalled praying for "an old man who was dying of everything you can imagine. I prayed for him—and he died. I went to the Lord about it and He said, 'You go out there on the platform and just preach my Word—not *your* word but *my* Word—and I'll confirm it.'" This admission of a failed healing, remarkable for a neopentecostal minister to mention publicly, led to a happier ending when John experienced another "divine flow" toward a young girl "who had a crippled foot, a spastic ankle [and] a built up brace. . . . That night Jesus touched that girl. Her ankle popped and He healed her instantaneously by His power."[4]

At the 1979 FGBMFI World Convention in New Orleans, Osteen shared the stage with some of the Christian Right's leading figures, including Chuck Colson and Pat Robertson. Neopentecostal luminaries Kenneth Hagin, Jimmy Swaggart, Oral Roberts, and Jim Bakker also spoke alongside Osteen. John's address, "Hear Ye the Word of the Lord," alluded to the marginalization of Pentecostals and charismatics, and the need for members of the "King's household" to "bear the name of Jesus Christ in the darkest hour of human history and be identified with the people of the Bible, and not be ashamed of Holy Ghost power." Reflecting the Christian Right's embattled mentality, Osteen continued, "I am glad to take my stand with those, as it were, on the outside. We need to be willing to move out against the spiritual forces of evil." As an established figure in the FGBMFI, Osteen lived anywhere but the margins. Access to evangelicalism's halls of power brought him to prestigious places.[5]

Shaped by the therapeutic dimension of American culture, John's teachings in the 1970s offered a more refined, programmatic approach to Christian living. Topics he wrote and preached about with increasing regularity included spiritual warfare and positive confession.[6]

Positive confession is the belief that a formulaic verbal articulation of wishes and sentiments coupled with genuine faith based on select Bible passages guarantees that the desired reality will come to fruition. Combining the various strands of New Thought metaphysics, the Holiness movement, and beliefs about divine healing, around the turn of the twentieth century E. W. Kenyon taught a positive confession theology that later had a tremendous impact on the neopentecostal movement. As historians Dale Simmons, Scott Billingsley, and Kate Bowler richly document, teachers such as T. L. Osborn and Kenneth Hagin, two of John's mentors, utilized Kenyon's teachings. It was Hagin who most energetically popularized Kenyon's work after World War II. John first met Hagin during the 1960s through the FGBMFI. Both men had difficult childhoods in north Texas and associated the prophetic call on their lives to events of divine healing. "After I received the baptism [of the Holy Ghost]," Osteen claimed, "it was Kenneth Hagin's teaching that really got me going on the Word." The two ministers continued to harvest a friendship and mutual respect that lasted well into the 1990s.[7]

Hagin's 1979 booklet *You Can Have What You Say!* is a concise summary of his positive confession teachings. Linking positive confession theology to the New Testament gospel of Mark, Hagin wrote, "What you say is your faith speaking. . . . If you do not believe what you are saying, you should not say it, because if you say something long enough, those words eventually will register on your spirit and will control your life." Hagin also referred his teaching to Old Testament passages. When a dozen Israelites spies traveled into Canaan to scope out the Promised Land, Hagin observed that from this Numbers 13 account only two returned with "a report of faith," whereas the majority of the spies relayed "a report of doubt" due to the perceived physical prowess of the Canaanites. "It wasn't the giants in Canaan who kept Israel from entering in," Hagin observed. "No, the 10 spies defeated themselves. It was their wrong thinking, wrong believing, and wrong talking that defeated them. . . . If you are defeated, you are defeated with your own lips."[8]

John's sermon "How to Get Confession to Work for You" adopted Hagin's emphasis on verbalizing wishes of the heart and articulating a state of mind. Osteen echoed Hagin by utilizing Bible passages to "claim" divine blessing. In this sermon, delivered during the 1970s, Osteen used the biblical text of Romans 10 to point out that Christians can claim spiritual "rights," but those rights only come by way of using the mouth properly. He believed that, since "faith comes by hearing God's word," deep faith manifested itself in speech so that one's "confession will cause to materialize whatever [one is] confessing." He encouraged the faithful to confess God's word verbally to enact a confession made "unto salvation, unto healing, unto health, unto prosperity, unto a good home peace, unto the things you desire." He also discussed the centrality of visualization, imagining oneself in better circumstances, or in possession of healed bodies or happy spirits. He admonished Christians to have the "right visualization or image of yourself in your heart . . . a scriptural image of how God sees you. . . . See yourself in the Bible [and] believe that you are the person God says you are." He continued: "I see myself primarily filled with love, wisdom and understanding from above. . . . I see it therefore I talk that way." Typical of Lakewood services, a cassette recording of this sermon captured a Lakewood congregant break into glossolalia, after which John asked for an interpretation: "Behold thy mouth is a channel of blessing," the congregant belted out to "Amen!" and "Hallelujah!" While John's sermon argued for the general power of positive confession, he recommended that congregants focus on using it for healthy marriages and families—topics he would address more frequently during the 1980s—reflecting the "family values" that animated evangelical political activism at the time.[9]

John's sermon echoed themes in several of his books from the same period. A 1972 publication, *There Is a Miracle in Your Mouth*, documented positive confession's influence on Osteen. Emphasizing the reality of miracles, the book served as a guide to prompting divine intervention. As in "How to Get Confession to Work for You," Osteen cited

Romans 10, but added a text from Proverbs 18:21, "Death and life are in the power of the tongue." Based on these passages, he argued that "[t] hough the words in the Bible may look like all the others, there is a difference. They are God's words. God has breathed life into them. When we take these 'God-breathed' words and confess them, miracles come to pass! God used words to create this world. He created everything by the word of His power. He created by using words." This logic served as the foundation on which Osteen exhorted others to adopt positive confession. Using language that his son Joel would popularize over two decades later, John recommended that Christians confess:

> I am blessed.
> By the stripes of Jesus I am healed.
> I am strong in the Lord.
> I can do all things through Christ who strengthened me.
> I am more than a conqueror.[10]

In addition to positive confession, John's teaching during the 1970s focused on spiritual warfare, the conviction among neopentecostals that "there is a very close relationship between what goes on in human life and what goes on in the spirit realm." Like many within American evangelicalism, he addressed questions of demonic possession and demonic activity in both individuals and American society at large. "Remember, prayer is a battleground," Osteen opened his 1976 book *The Confessions of a Baptist Preacher*. "So is life. But as we learn to take the Word of God and approach the throne of grace, we will see the devil routed and victory come into our lives. We must learn to take the Word of God and drive the devil from the arena of conflict, the field of battle, and stand as more than a conqueror in Jesus' name!" His military imagery fit a decade that witnessed the end of the Vietnam War but also the continuation of the Cold War. Osteen believed that in "one of the most turbulent, violent and shocking generations that has ever lived upon the face of this earth . . . untold legions of demon forces have been unleashed upon humanity." He listed youth "rebellion" and campus riots as manifestations of cultural carnage, and even cited a rise in suicides as evidence of demonic activity along with "[a]lcoholism, dope, nervous breakdowns, divorce, mental sicknesses, packed hospitals, penal institutions and psychiatric wards." "The foundations have crumbled!" Osteen exclaimed.[11]

In his 1972 book *How to Flow in the Super Supernatural*, Osteen offered a more direct interpretation of why he believed American society was in a precipitous decline. "We have seen the rapid expansion of the kingdom of darkness influencing every strata of society," he explained. "As we read the newspaper, watch television, and listen to the radio we notice the phenomenal increase in violence, lust, homosexuality and suicide." Osteen identified Satan as the cause of such societal blights. He argued that individuals who lacked the Holy Spirit engaged in "fortune telling, ouija boards, witchcraft, black magic, false religions, séances, palmistry, numerology and the reading of tea leaves . . . crystal balls, interpreting the signs of the zodiac (astrology), necromancy (the practice of talking with the dead), and astral-projection (the act of projecting one's self out the body by the power of demonic spirits)." Satan targeted the nuclear family as well: "demonic powers have been unleashed upon our children, husbands, and wives. Homes are being wrecked. Preachers are under attack and many are falling." Osteen's list of societal problems led him to proclaim in the therapeutic language of the 1970s, "Satan has bullied God's people long enough! . . . Don't be demon-conscious, but be Jesus conscious." Although he interpreted the signs of cultural change in terms of spiritual warfare, Osteen's analysis of society's problems drew on the rhetoric of political conservatives who, longing for a golden age that never existed, worried about a culture in the midst of social change.[12]

In addition to publishing books, during the 1970s John Osteen fortified the foundation of Lakewood Church and planted the seeds for its future. Physically, the church expanded, and by the late 1970s Lakewood was a bona fide megachurch with a membership that exceeded 2,000. The church's exponential growth was a sign of things to come, although another Houston congregation—Graham Pulkingham's Church of the Redeemer—was perhaps the city's most notable charismatic church. Lakewood's racial and ethnic diversity also registered as a signal achievement, though John was a beneficiary of Houston's integration since he was not present for much of the 1960s during the city's most heated civil rights struggles. Student sit-ins, led by young activists such as Eldrewey Stearns and other African Americans, and public school boycotts led by

Mexican Americans exemplified the city's freedom struggles. Some of Houston's Baptist churches animated the movement as well. First Baptist Church refused to integrate in 1963 even after protests staged by the Houston chapter of the Congress of Racial Equality. Aligned with the National Baptist Convention and led by William A. Lawson, Wheeler Avenue Baptist Church became a central venue for civil rights protests, particularly after Lawson invited Martin Luther King to Texas Southern University in 1964. Still, Osteen can be credited with maintaining his commitment to keep Lakewood situated in a largely African American, working-class neighborhood despite requests from friends and associates during the 1970s that he move the church to one or another upscale white suburb. John had tasted the bitterness of poverty in his youth and wished to lend a spiritual and material hand to the destitute.[13]

Nevertheless, while John refused to move Lakewood Church to the posh confines of Houston's suburbs, the church's leadership remained largely white and male. Along with other participants in white flight, when his stature as a religious teacher netted material blessings John relocated his family to the wealthy northeast suburb of Forest Cove, part of an area called Kingwood. Although his messages proffered hope for the hurting, staring in the 1970s he chose to reside in a part of Houston far removed from where the hurting lived.[14]

Pentecost and Prosperity at the Oasis of Love

In 1984, John Osteen's good friend and mentor T. L. Osborn, himself a leading neopentecostal teacher, penned a poem titled "Love" in recognition of his friend. "Love's the devotion of faith in action," Osborn wrote. "Love's not an ecstasy we like to live/Love's the ability to earn and give/Love's not a creed we chant with bells/Love's a seed we plant that tells," he continued. "Love's not a song to sing from the steeple/ Love is strong—it's the good we do to people." Osborn's poem expressed his appreciation for John's ministry while it also described an "oasis of love" to which the spiritually hungry would flock for nourishment, the downtrodden for hope, the weary for strength, the sick for healing, and the needy for prosperity.[15]

As John entered his sixth decade of life during the 1980s, his teaching and his church continued to find growing audiences both locally and nationally. He continued to minister at FGBMFI meetings, including the "By My Spirit" World Convention in Anaheim (1980) and the "Signs and Wonders Now" World Convention in Detroit (1983), where he again shared the stage with neopentecostal preachers such as Kenneth Hagin and Oral Roberts, along with Christian Right leaders like Pat Robertson. While on the presidential campaign trail in 1987, Robertson even spoke at Osteen's church. Osteen also preached at the national meetings of other leading neopentecostals, including Kenneth Copeland's 1983 Victory Crusade in Alabama and Lester Sumrall's 1982 and 1985 Campmeetings. Similarly, John taught classes on the spiritual life at Kenneth Hagin's Rhema Bible Training Center. In the charismatic press, he published numerous articles on the prosperity gospel, and in two major articles *Charisma* magazine chronicled the life and ministry of John, his family, and Lakewood Church. And in large measure due to the efforts of his energetic and enterprising son Joel, John became a televangelist. National cable outlets such as Pat Robertson's Christian Broadcasting Network and Lifetime carried the *John Osteen* telecast, as did numerous local stations. Promotional materials reflected viewers' unabashed praise, and national surveys also registered the impact of Osteen's televangelism.[16]

Locally, Lakewood's growth in membership and architectural scale mirrored the prosperity associated with Houston's oil fortunes in the early 1980s. Lakewood's additional expansion in 1988—the opening of a new $5.2 million, 8,000-seat sanctuary—expressed the larger growth of the prosperity gospel since, in contrast, by the late 1980s Houston's oil fortunes had plummeted. Reflecting the language of the prosperity gospel, Osteen remarked, "We just keep on sowing seeds and living very simple lives. . . . This is a very simple ministry. In 30 years, this is the first decent building we've had." But, he commented, "We're not . . . the little Pentecostal church on the corner." Construction started in early 1987 and Lakewood opened its new facility in April 1988. Not only did dignitaries attend the facility's groundbreaking ceremony, including Texas State Representative Senfronia Thompson and Houston mayor Kathy Whitmire along with neopentecostal teacher Norvel Hayes, but additional ministers and notables participated in the new sanctuary's opening services. Texas State Representative Jack Fields showed up to the inaugural service, as did longtime Osteen friends Oral Roberts, Kenneth Hagin,

T. L. Osborn, and R. W. Schambach. Osteen also invited as guests of honor some of Houston's black clergy, including Ernest McGowen and C. L. Jackson. Billy Graham sent Osteen a videotaped message for the occasion, as did FGBMFI founder Demos Shakarian and President Ronald Reagan. William Hinson, a noted minister at Houston's First United Methodist Church, recalled that Osteen "had that wonderful ability to apply the gospel to a very diverse congregation." Another Houston megachurch pastor, Ed Young, described Osteen as a "fine leader and brother" whose church labor wrought spiritual fruit. Young, president of the Southern Baptist Convention during the early 1990s, maintained, "I know many have come to know the Lord through John's ministry."[17]

Notable Houstonians also found Osteen's messages significant in the 1980s. His teaching resonated with federal judge and Democrat Woodrow B. Seals, a member of St. Stephen's United Methodist Church. "My dear Brother Osteen," Seals began an April 1987 letter, "I turned on the television Saturday night while I was preparing my church school lesson for Sunday [and] you were walking out to that small pulpit and starting a sermon." Evidently, Seals listened intently. He found Osteen's sermon meaningful. "Like everyone in Houston, I have noticed those bumper stickers, 'Lakewood Church—Oasis of Love,' for two or three years," he continued. "I have always wondered how anyone could start a church out where you started yours. But after hearing your sermon Saturday night . . . I agreed with everything you said, and I especially appreciated what you said two or three times, 'Tell the untold and reach the unreachable.'" He contrasted Lakewood's vitality with the shifting fortunes of his own Methodist church, which Seals lamented was in numerical decline. "We [Methodists] are becoming like the Episcopalians, we are slowly dying, but the Lord is raising up people like you who will save the world."[18]

As Osteen's message affected the city, the nation, and the world during the 1980s, he continued working to foster spiritual growth in the lives of Houstonians. Lakewood Church's growth allowed John to launch the Lakewood Bible Institute (LBI). Although unique in its connection to Lakewood Church, LBI was not the first attempt in Houston to make available broad-based, affordable theological and religious education. For example, in the early 1960s, African American Christians, including well-known minister William A. Lawson, had launched the Systematic

Bible Institute to train black clergy. The following decade, a black minister and teacher named Ernest L. Mays founded the Houston Bible Institute (HBI)—later renamed the College of Biblical Studies—to educate black, white, and Latino/a pastors in theology. Mays aimed to assemble a multiracial student body at HBI and to "make quality evangelical Bible training available to all Christians in Houston, particularly for minority groups," efforts not unlike those John Osteen envisioned for LBI.[19]

Although unaccredited, LBI offered classes for laypeople in the New Testament, Old Testament, principles of Bible study, healing, spiritual growth, faith, conversion, and prayer. In addition to daily chapel services, students were required to attend all of Lakewood's missions and pastor's conferences and the tapings of Lakewood broadcasts. A youth pastor internship program offered intensive training for ministerial occupations focused on children and young people. In addition to academic work, students gathered for regular intervals of fellowship to share meals or play sports. LBI promised that students "would learn how to apply the life-changing truths of God's Word in a practical way . . . you'll enjoy Spirit-filled services while you learn in a supernatural atmosphere of worship, teaching, and world evangelism." LBI also provided special access "to observe firsthand the pastoral ministry of John Osteen and learn from his powerful message of faith and great love."[20]

Osteen served as LBI's president, and J. Dennis Key worked as the school's director. Osteen encouraged students through "The Graduates' Commission," reminding them to dedicate their ministry service to Jesus: "Let him be more precious than all of the things in life. Count it the highest honor to be His ambassador. Bear His name with the greatest of dignity and integrity." LBI had regular faculty that consisted of Lakewood ministry leaders and staff members, as well as visiting faculty that included Lisa Osteen, Bill Dearman, Sven Levin, and Justin Osteen. Around this time, Justin published an evangelistic booklet titled *A Letter to My Friend*, about end times theology and the apocalypse. Live broadcasts from LBI included speakers such as Lucy Rael, T. L. Osborn, Kenneth and Gloria Copeland, Kenneth Hagin, R. W. Schambach, and Dr. Reginald Cherry. Promotional literature for LBI reflected Lakewood's racial and ethnic diversity, and students ranged from white-collar professionals to working-class wage earners. It also featured students' superlative comments on their experiences at LBI. Glenda Graves, a white female, stated, "My main goal is to not only learn the Word intellectually, but to get the Word in my spirit." Romanian student Daniel N. Matei praised LBI's focus on global missions. René Rodriguez said he "came to L.B.I. to learn as much as I could about the Word of God" and found that the school "teaches a balanced diet. I am now living a victorious and abundant life." A white male, Randy Golden planned to take his LBI education and put it to use in the U.S. Navy. Kim Murphy, a black female, appreciated the "practical knowledge" she obtained from LBI, and found that it "has developed me into a disciple of the Lord Jesus Christ by teaching me a balance of the Word." While LBI seemed to have a significant educational impact, it did not survive the 1980s. Nevertheless, its presence served as one manifestation of John Osteen's focus on Christian education first documented in his 1944 master's thesis.[21]

John Osteen's Prosperity Gospel

The prosperity gospel gained considerable currency during the late 1970s and early 1980s. Teachers preached about *Jehovah Jireh*, the God who provides. Pastors looked to the life of Jesus, both his teachings and his death and resurrection, as justification for the acquisition of material blessings. Many also found promise of financial wealth in Old Testament teaching on covenants. Since Yahweh's covenants promised blessing for obedience, Christians in modern times could expect a monetary return for their devotion. Coupled with these teachings, prosperity pastors employed countless personal testimonies of individuals who lavished in God's abundant financial rewards. Printed testimonies in ministry publications along with televised interviews worked to further popularize the prosperity gospel. As more teachers who espoused a prosperity message secured airtime in the expanding world of televangelism, opportunities for growth seemed boundless. Accomplished preachers pleaded with television audiences to "sow" into their ministries to "reap" financial blessings. Pastors also exhibited wealth themselves with well-furnished studios, adept marketing, ministry updates that almost always documented increase, and fashionable clothing that expressed fine taste and respectability. Although a number of television ministries imploded in scandals during the late 1980s, the prosperity gospel continued to produce a burgeoning class of entrepreneurial pastors schooled in the methods and committed to the message. During this period, luminaries in the prosperity gospel movement included teachers Jim and Tammy Faye Bakker, Benny Hinn, Leroy Thompson, John Avanzini, Oral Roberts, Rex Humbard, Charles and Frances Hunter, Kenneth Hagin, and Kenneth and Gloria Copeland, among countless others. As donations from listeners or viewers grew, some prosperity teachers expressed their messages through the construction of expansive megachurches. Employing strategies of congregational expansion during the 1970s, 1980s, and beyond, megachurches became a mainstay of the prosperity gospel.[22]

Historian Kate Bowler has analyzed teachings associated with the prosperity gospel as falling into the broad categories of "hard prosperity" and "soft prosperity." Hard prosperity renders faith as a law. Growing and committed faith nets increased financial rewards, whereas a lack of faith delivers very little. Soft prosperity, on the other hand, still emphasizes faith but places more emphasis on proper thinking. A keener use of psychological categories replaces a rigid formula that equates faith with wealth. A long established presence in neopentecostal circles and a keen student of Hagin's Word of Faith message, John's teachings during the 1970s and 1980s exhibited many of the prosperity gospel's characteristics. He sometimes leaned toward a hard prosperity message by articulating a divine guarantee of God's blessing, while the majority of his teachings expressed soft prosperity through an emphasis on divine healing and positive confession. Osteen continued to utilize positive confession, for example, and connected it to the possibility of financial rewards. In a 1988 sermon titled "The Power of Words," he noted that through words God created the universe. John also used the Old Testament figure of Job to exemplify the power of positive confession. Because of difficult circumstances, Osteen said, including the loss of wealth and family, the words Job's friends spoke to him could either lift him up or pillory him further with doubt and depression. Similarly, in a sermon series titled "Confession that Brings Possession," John referenced numerous New Testament passages to encourage listeners to locate their needs in the Bible, and confess scriptures specific to those needs. "See it in God's Word and believe it in your heart," John said. He encouraged his listeners to believe that "your faith can talk," making the point that literacy in biblical prosperity teachings was a necessary formula for God's blessing. Osteen was even more explicit in *Four Principles in Receiving from God.* He likened faith to the possession of a "blank check." God would honor "burning desire" for something specific, especially if it could be found in the Bible. "What would make you happiest?" queried John. "God delights in making you happy! Write down what you want from God and be specific about it. See yourself with it. Have a burning desire for it. Start talking like it is yours now. If you will not give up, it will be yours."[23]

Despite clear references to wealth and finances, John's prosperity gospel more routinely emphasized divine healing and the body, most specifically in reference to his daughter Lisa's healing. To further legitimate his perspective, John regularly offered the testimony of his sister Mary's healing, as well. John's teaching on divine healing also employed the psychology of visualization. "In your heart of hearts," he wrote, "picture yourself completely delivered from sickness, suffering and all trouble. . . . [C]onfession will be made unto deliverance, healing, safety and wholeness in body, mind, and spirit." Yet, like with Lisa, John pointed out that using a faith formula did not guarantee instantaneous healing. He believed that faith increased with more frequent use of positive confession and that wholeness came gradually. Osteen admitted that while God was the ultimate healer, positive confession in essence worked to activate faith so that God's promises came to pass.[24]

During the 1980s, John's family circumstances tested his nerves and stretched his faith. Another family crisis solidified his commitment to divine healing: Dodie's cancer diagnosis in 1981. Doctors reported that she had only a short time to live. Just as the couple prayed for their daughter, John and Dodie's charismatic faith shaped the prayerful response to this situation. The Osteen family's faith in redemption and belief in second chances fueled the persistent conviction that troubles would always turn around for the better. Medical professionals eventually gave Dodie a clean bill of health, unable to find cancer. Relieved, the Osteens attributed these medical reports to divine intervention and connected it to passages about healing found in the Bible. John's teachings shaped the specific way that Dodie narrated her defeat of cancer through prayer and positive confession. In her autobiography, *Healed of Cancer* (1986), Dodie wrote, "The Word of God is extremely important to people who are fighting a battle with their health, for often it's the only hope they have. I know I would have died if it had not been for the

Bible." She attributed her healing to verbal confession of Bible verses. "Day by day," she remembered, "I gained hope and encouragement from the precious promises that God revealed to me through His Word. I clung to my Bible and its healing promises." While the Osteens emphasized the spiritual dimensions of Dodie's bout with cancer, the family's Houston residence proved fortuitous as increased funding for research allowed doctors to battle the disease at M. D. Anderson Cancer Center.[25]

Bolstered by the application of the positive confession strategy in the defeat of his wife's cancer, John expounded upon positive confession by placing confessions at the end of his books published in the 1980s. Moreover, his well-known "This Is My Bible" confession at the beginning of Lakewood's services originated in the 1980s. Lakewood member Saleim Kahleh, a former Muslim with family roots in the Middle East and the southeastern U.S., first attended the church in the late 1970s while a student at Houston Baptist University. As Kahleh sat listening to John's preaching on a Sunday morning in the mid-1980s, John stood up, thrust his Bible into the air, and started the "This Is My Bible" confession. John continued with "I am what it says I am. I can do what it says I can do. Today, I will be taught the Word of God. I boldly confess: My mind is alert, my heart is receptive. I will never be the same. I am about to receive the incorruptible, indestructible Word of God. I will never be the same. Never, never, never. I will never be the same in Jesus' name. Amen." According to Kahleh, as the anticipation and energy built with John's inaugural "This is My Bible" confession, Osteen paused after describing the Bible as "incorruptible." In that moment, Kahleh blurted out "indestructible!" John repeated it and thereafter Kahleh's contribution became part of Osteen's Bible confession.[26]

Two of John's books, *The ABCs of Faith* (1981) and *Spiritual Food for Victorious Living* (1985), illustrated a continued commitment to positive confession. John listed "Confession" as the word for the third letter in his alphabet of belief. "The power of life and death is in the tongue," Osteen argued. "You must confess the Word of God. . . . I am going to say about myself what God says." Linking his convictions about positive confession even more explicitly to Bible passages in *Spiritual Food for Victorious Living*, Osteen exhorted, "When we meditate upon God's Word, we have to use our mouths to speak it aloud. . . . Jesus said that we will receive what we say or, as the Greek says, what we confess (Mark

11:23). Christianity is not merely a belief but it is a confession. . . . What we are today is a result of all that we have said and confessed in the past. What we are tomorrow will be a result of all that we say and confess today." The experiences of the Osteen family crystallized John's focus on the possibility of divine healing even as they testified to the continued currency of positive confession.[27]

Attention to the body in his prosperity gospel, along with a nondenominational perspective, inclined John to consider the legitimacy of stigmata, a largely Roman Catholic tradition that witnesses the appearance of wounds on Christians in the feet, hands, and other places on the body associated with Jesus' crucifixion. On Good Friday in 1986, charismatic teacher Lucy Rael spoke in Houston at Lakewood Church. Reared as a Roman Catholic, Rael moved in prosperity circles in the 1980s and amazed crowds by exhibiting stigmata while preaching. Other neopentecostal teachers, including T. L. Osborn, supported Rael's ministry and operated as mentors to Lucy and her husband, Sito. At the Lakewood service she attended, John told parishioners, "You will see strange things today," but cautioned those watching, "We better be careful about making fun of what God does." He also asked ushers to bar anyone from disrupting the service. Osteen then spoke in tongues and interpreted it: "'Oh yes, blessed be the name of the Lord, blessed be the one who is all victorious; blessed be his holy name.' That's what I said in tongues." As Rael ministered, her hands, feet, forehead, and back displayed wounds. "I'm not here to take the place of Jesus," Rael stated. The stigmata, she said, should "not draw sympathy but inspire faith," because "Calvary is not a place of defeat, but a place of triumph." She said that Jesus' resurrection represented a "breakthrough to new life." At this point in the service, John walked on stage, offered praise to God, and called on physicians to accompany him to examine Rael's wounds. Dr. Sharon Walker, a black physician, peered at Rael's hands and said, "This is amazing." Another doctor, an African American named Richard Walker, who previously had provided written confirmation of Dodie's recovery in *Healed of Cancer*, examined Rael's wounds for a few minutes, and commented, "This is real." Rael then began to prophesy, foretelling financial blessings, spiritual clarity, and blessing on missionary activities.[28]

In 1989, a Protestant teacher from California, Albert James Dager, questioned the legitimacy of Rael's claims by pointing out that she never "renounced Roman Catholicism." Dager also stated that the stigmata sometimes occurred "in conjunction with occultic manifestations" and that visuals of her wounds on television contrasted with biblical descriptions of Jesus' wounds. Dager claimed that during some preaching campaigns the stigmata of "Lucy Goosey" did not manifest at all. From this perspective, it is possible John Osteen alerted doctors before Rael's Lakewood service, persuading them to help confirm the apparent authenticity of her stigmata. Since a recording of the Lakewood service exists, it is also possible that the church's television producer skillfully manipulated and edited the images. Regardless, due to John's commitment to nondenominational Christianity, Lakewood welcomed a wide array of individuals, including Spirit-led Roman Catholics. And a teacher who exhibited the stigmata, a sign most closely associated with Roman Catholicism, found a welcome audience in Houston, with its sizable Latino/a population, many of whom had experiential knowledge of the Catholic faith. John had also previously consulted medical professionals to validate spiritual claims with respect to Dodie's divine healing, and providing visual evidence on camera was a natural progression in legitimating such claims.

Perhaps in response to Rael's critics, the same year she visited, John published a book titled *Deception!: Recognizing True and False Ministries*. He argued that legitimate ministers based their teachings on the Bible, respected the authority of local ministers, possessed a willingness to accept correction and spiritual counsel, exhibited personal qualities such as patience and humility, and established networked connections with other like-minded clergy. John warned of "false prophets, false teachers, false prophetesses and false Christs" and counseled the faithful to stay "spiritually keen. We must be full of the Holy Spirit and in touch with God. We must know the Word of God and stand on it. The time for playing is over."[29]

Harvesting Hope: John Osteen's Twilight Years

In 1994, John Osteen and Lakewood Church launched "Seven Years of Harvest" (SYH). Using the biblical metaphors of harvesting and reaping to articulate the evangelical imperative to proselytize—like many other neopentecostals—Lakewood's SYH boldly pleaded for renewed funding for missionary efforts and energetically planned evangelistic campaigns in Houston and across the globe. Osteen believed that between 1994 and the year 2000, "we're going to see millions make their reservation to go to heaven!" He continued: "We're going to reach our cities. We're going to reach our nation. We're going to reach the nations of the world. God is going to trust us with more money than we've ever had in all of our lives. . . . God is going to have a transfer of wealth. The wealth of the wicked is laid up for the just!" Invoking additional biblical images, Osteen cast the harvest initiative as a battle between good and evil. "The devil can't have Texas," he exclaimed. "We are going to have a harvest of hope in Houston, Texas," he said. "We are believing God that the schools will be turned around. We're believing the gangs will all give up and join the gang with Jesus! We're believing the power of drugs and alcohol will be broken. Pornography shops will be closed and saloons will be shut down! Our own vineyard we will keep!"[30]

According to church reports, the harvest was indeed plentiful, and the workers many. Lakewood distributed thousands of tapes and videos around the world, John and other ministers and volunteers conducted preaching campaigns in newly liberated Eastern Europe, Lakewood television production teams created documentaries broadcast nationally and internationally, and millions of dollars were contributed to evangelistic efforts in Houston, the Americas, India, and elsewhere across the globe. With over 12,000 members now at Lakewood and a large television audience for *John Osteen*, funds flowed freely to harvest hope, mirroring the era's dotcom-fueled economic boom.[31]

John's message of harvest tracked with topics and themes that occupied the last decade of his life. John and Lakewood staff members hosted several national leadership conferences during the mid-1990s. He shared personal life experiences with conference attendees, and provided a window into the operations of one of the nation's most important megachurches. John's morality-based messages reflected national discussions of traditional family values. And echoing the discourse of men's movements such as Promise Keepers, his teaching in the 1990s expressed a distinct spiritual politics of masculinity. John also started making plans for Lakewood's future: he wished for his son Joel to succeed him as the church's minister. The two had worked closely for nearly two decades, and Joel had intimate knowledge of church operations. Moreover, filming his father's sermons and editing the messages for television provided Joel with a unique perspective on the art of preaching and equipped him with an extensive knowledge of the prosperity gospel. While John's harvest of hope was ostensibly about missionary evangelism, the campaign ultimately yielded a very immediate message of hope when Joel became Lakewood's pastor in 1999.[32]

The 1990s had begun with another test of faith for John and his family. A pipe bomb rocked the campus of Lakewood Church on a brisk morning in January 1990. John's daughter Lisa opened a package about the size of a shoebox that exploded in her office. She was rushed to the hospital with burns and cuts on her legs and abdomen; doctors effectively addressed her injuries and she survived.[33]

Already attuned to a narrative of survival, Lisa attributed her recovery to divine intervention. "The Bible says . . . God [will] protect us," she declared, and "God performed a miracle in my life." National Christian media produced a similar spiritual interpretation of Lisa's recovery—her second major one, along with her healing in the late 1950s. Osteen family friend and *Charisma* editor Stephen Strang proclaimed that God had preserved Lisa from debilitating injury and that ultimately God had protected John and his church. Strang quoted Lisa's brother Joel, who said that his sister's survival "show[ed] everybody there's a God who's alive and who will protect you."[34]

Lisa's second escape from death's door coupled with the church's intensive evangelistic impulse led to a stunning Lakewood Media Productions documentary, *Death & Beyond*. Produced in 1993 by Joel Osteen and intended to prompt viewers to consider their eternal fate, the documentary explored the meaning of near-death experiences. John marshaled several medical experts to discuss scientific opinion on the subject, including Raymond A. Moody and Maurice Rawlings. He presented the well-known story of Kenneth Hagin's divine healing testimony—an alleged near-death experience in which Hagin saw fire at the gates of hell—as the most authoritative account of a near-death experience. John oriented the film as a Christian apologetic, calling on theologian Joel B. Green to validate the historicity of Jesus' death and resurrection. Without explicitly rejecting science, John predictably concluded the documentary in evangelistic mode by arguing that God's unconditional love transcended both science and religion.[35]

John's use of medical experts outside of evangelical circles provided a counterpoint to countless other evangelicals who spiritually "anointed" evangelical experts on a variety of subjects, a process central to establishing what historian Randall Stephens and scientist Karl Giberson call evangelicalism's "parallel culture." Unlike the declarations of many evangelical cultural warriors in the 1990s, *Death & Beyond* refused to engage in an "adversarial juxtaposition" of religion and science. But this decision also reflected an aggressive marketing strategy Lakewood employed in the early 1990s. "What we find is that the TV, the advertising, the billboards," Joel Osteen told the *Houston Chronicle* in 1992, "they all work as the pieces of a puzzle." Contextually backdropped by Lisa's survival, the Trinity Broadcasting Network–distributed evangelistic documentary also anticipated John's "Seven Years of Harvest" campaign in 1994.[36]

Paralleling the Christian Right's discourse of family values, John's final years focused on the traditional Christian family. In *Active Faith* (1996), conservative Christian activist Ralph Reed linked America's precipitous decline to the implosion of the Christian family. "Families are disintegrating," the Christian Coalition leader claimed, "fathers are abandoning children [and] abortion is the most common medical procedure in the nation." For Reed, these trends contributed to unsafe, mediocre schools, systemic drug use, youth gangs, and "inner city illegitimacy." According to Reed, the "pro-family agenda" provided the proper antidote to the "social chaos" created by this constellation of political and social problems. Similarly, John's pro-family message centered on resistance to a "satanic attempt" to demolish the traditional Christian home by following the Bible's instructions to develop "God's due order" of strong male Christian character. "The devil is out to destroy your home," Osteen announced in *A Miracle for Your Marriage*. "He wants to destroy and divide every husband and wife. Families are under attack, leaving husbands, wives and little children wounded and scarred. Thousands of homes are disintegrating and falling apart." In a sermon titled "Building Secure Homes in an Insecure World," John counseled Christian men to "guard" their families by "chasing the devil off" and to "beautify" their wives with "good dresses" and "good gifts" because "[e]very husband will give an account to God for their family." Likewise, in *Love & Marriage* Osteen wrote, "You husbands, be men. Do not be

Figure 2.1. Lakewood Church billboard advertisement, Houston, ca. 1990s. Source: ©
Houston Chronicle. Used with permission.

dictators and bosses. Be lovers. Be somebody who will guide and guard
and protect your wife. Make her proud of you."[37]

Coupled with John's focus on the family, in his last years he also ex-
pressly examined the centrality of faith. Building on the work of E. W.
Kenyon, a leading predecessor in the prosperity movement, and expressing the free market confidence of the Reagan years, *Unraveling the Mystery of the Blood Covenant* (1987) offered a detailed theology of divine
guarantee. Osteen reasoned that the blood covenant activated by faith
guaranteed blessing and prosperity. He explained that Yahweh's blood
covenant with Abraham—which included a bloody animal sacrifice coupled with Abraham's own blood from the rite of circumcision—bound
God and his people together both in Abraham's time and for future generations. Such a covenant, Osteen wrote, obligated God to preserve his
people even as it demanded their strict obedience to God's laws. Breaking the covenant invited curses, which then necessitated a high priest to
offer a sacrifice to redeem the infraction. If a blood covenant bound God
to his people in the Old Testament, then for Osteen the blood of Jesus
provided the ultimate blood sacrifice for a "new covenant." Rather than
a literal incision, those of the new covenant experienced a "circumci-

sion of the heart" by which Osteen meant faith that Jesus Christ's blood erased sin and damnation. Faith in the "blood covenant" through Jesus Christ thus enacted a divine guarantee of blessing. "God respects the Blood Covenant," Osteen argued. "He could not and would not break the covenant because He is a covenant-keeping God. And He respects his covenant-keeping people." Osteen exhorted readers who expressed faith in the blood covenant to embrace the identity of a "new breed" as "covenant-men" or "covenant-women."[38]

John's final book, *Seven Qualities of a Man of Faith* (1990), which deployed the number seven so important to Christians, presented the Old Testament prophet Elijah as a "man of faith." Osteen carefully articulated what faith meant. First he likened faith to muscles in the body—muscles grow with regular use; likewise, exercising faith only increased it. Osteen then referenced the Greek word *logos*, a term that implies faith and salvation, and the Greek word *rhema*, which "is a word God speaks to you. Suddenly a scripture comes alive as if God himself spoke it to you. . . . Once God speaks a scripture to you, believe it is easy because with that *rhema* comes faith." Similarly, Osteen pointed out that because he exercised faith in Yahweh, Elijah defeated the prophets of Baal. These actions, according to Osteen, demonstrated that those with faith believed without seeing, petitioned God for things found in the Bible, remained steadfast when prayers went unanswered, and found their experiential anchor in the Bible.[39]

By the end of his days, John Osteen's message of nondenominational, charismatic evangelicalism had endeared him to many. Drawing from more than five decades of neopentecostal teachings on prosperity and positive confession—as he moved from distinctly Southern Baptist connections to an ever-expanding network of independent, neopentecostal teachers—John spent the last few years of his life imparting the lessons of a lifetime of preaching and teaching. Speaking at Carlton Pearson's AZUSA 93 Conference in Tulsa, he preached on "Don't Limit God." Osteen told the pastors present to transcend negative thinking about their ministries, to remember that one's background did not determine one's future, and to maintain steadfast faith in God's healing power. Three years later, he delivered the 1996 baccalaureate address at Oral Roberts University. Other ceremonial events in which he participated included giving the inaugural prayer in 1998 for newly elected Houston mayor Lee Brown.[40]

Increasing health problems plagued Osteen in the closing months of his life. Faltering kidneys and residual cardiac problems from open-heart surgery in the 1980s slowed his pace. Ultimately, he succumbed to a heart attack in January 1999. Thousands attended his memorial service, and friends and family paid tribute to Osteen's sixty years of preaching and teaching. After John's death, Texas State Representative Senfronia Thompson (D-Houston) proposed a resolution honoring his years of service to Houston. Passed as H.R. 57, the resolution stated that Osteen "was a great man of faith and compassion, and his strength of character enabled him to grow profoundly in his life and to improve the lives of others." In the years following John's passing, neopentecostal ministers such as Ed Dufresne and Kenneth Copeland continued to circulate his teachings by making available audio versions of his sermons. Family members also sought to keep John's ministry alive. In 2010, his son-in-law Gary Simons, pastor at High Point Church in Arlington, Texas, published a book on church growth, a strategy he attributed to the years he spent at Lakewood with his "spiritual mentor." That same year John's daughter (and Gary's wife) April Simons delivered several sermons on her father's influence titled "The Legacy Lives On." By 2014, Joel had edited four collections of his father's writings, repackaging and republishing most of John's teachings from six decades of ministry. But in life as well as in death, John had always taught that the end of something always signaled a new beginning.[41]

Joel Osteen's Prosperity Gospel, Part I

"We Believe in New Beginnings"

God is enlarging our vision. . . . I believe [Lakewood's] greatest days are ahead.
—Joel Osteen (1999)

Change was on the horizon at Lakewood Church in 1999. The year
started with health problems for John Osteen. The kidneys in his
seventy-seven-year-old body were not functioning as they should, and
heart trouble had slowed down the seemingly indefatigable preacher.
In the midst of these illnesses—and as it turned out one week before
he died—John asked his son Joel to preach. John's daughter Lisa and
son-in-law Gary Simons had been preaching regularly, but this time
John tapped his youngest son. As he had done many times before, Joel
refused. Yet, as Joel recalled in his 2004 book *Your Best Life Now*:

> Daddy's words kept flitting through my mind, and with no other provo-
> cation, I began to have an overwhelming desire to preach. I didn't really
> understand it at the time, but I knew I had to do something. Keep in
> mind, I had never even prepared a sermon, let alone considered standing
> up in front of thousands of people to speak. . . . I studied all week and
> prepared a message, and the next Sunday I spoke at Lakewood Church
> for the first time.[1]

Joel has breezily repeated the story so many times it rings familiar.
Shortly after he delivered his first sermon at Lakewood, his father passed
away and an unassuming, shy television producer who had for years
rebuffed John's invitations to preach became the minister of a megachurch. Within five years, Joel published his first book, *Your Best Life
Now*, and in 2005, with national fanfare, he moved his church into the

Compaq Center, a former basketball arena. Several more *New York Times* bestselling books followed, as did annual appearances on network talk shows such as *Larry King Live* and *Piers Morgan Tonight*. In addition, his "Night of Hope" (NOH) preaching rallies packed sports stadiums across the United States. These accomplishments resulted in soaring popularity for Osteen, making him one of America's most visible religious celebrities. The "smiling preacher," as *Washington Post* writer Lois Romano called him in 2005, became a household name with a recognizable grin. But, how did Joel Osteen become *Joel Osteen*?

Tracing out the historical contours of Osteen's prosperity gospel is one way to answer this question. Joel's prosperity gospel has four parts: positive thinking, positive confession, positive providence, and finally, the promotion of the Christian body as a site of improvement. Before getting to the detailed contents of Osteen's prosperity gospel, the subject of chapter 4, it is imperative that we first grasp the chief influences on his overall message. While Joel's teaching is his own, his sermons and publications pay tribute to those who shaped his ministerial evolution: his father, neopentecostal evangelist Joyce Meyer, and leadership teacher John Maxwell. Connecting the historical dots between John's prosperity gospel, Meyer's positive thinking, and Maxwell's motivational program, this chapter establishes the important neopentecostal and evangelical antecedents to Joel's message. Moreover, it aims to pinpoint the ways that Joel creatively refashioned a prosperity gospel message that has established Lakewood as one of America's most consequential congregations of the twenty-first century. In addition, grasping the larger religious landscape of Houston, as chapter 4 explains, presents the fuller picture of Osteen's prosperity teachings, thereby adding crucial context to its historical and cultural significance.

Joel Osteen's Lakewood Genesis

On Sunday, January 24, 1999, Dodie Osteen and her family announced that Lakewood's founder and beloved minister had died. Sad yet remarkably composed at that Sunday service, she recounted John's declining health in his final hours but commented on his resolute faith—despite inevitable death, he had proclaimed, "[God's] mercy endures forever!" She remembered her husband of over four decades as "a man loved by the whole world" and a minister who "had the ability to preach simple sermons yet profound." Dodie also related the story that as John lay dying in the hospital, the family stepped outside to pray and "committed him to the Lord." Family members thereafter washed his feet as a symbolic ritual for one who spent his life in the service of God's people. Other family members spoke during the service, including John's daughter Lisa Osteen Comes, son Paul Osteen, and son-in-law Gary Simons. Most notable, however, was Joel's reflection. His appearance as the service's second speaker following his mother suggested the likelihood that he would succeed his father while it also revealed, if in embryonic form, shades of his core message of faith, positive thinking, and unflagging optimism. With tears welling up in his eyes, Joel said, "My dad, he was a great friend. . . . Daddy built this church on such a solid foundation." Committed to extending his father's legacy, Joel maintained that the "Osteen family" would "carry out his vision, and the desires that God has for this church" by working to "minister and show God's love and compassion." He concluded his comments with a resolute proclamation that exhibited the aspirational shape of his future teachings. Joel's closing prediction portended Lakewood's growth and expansion: the Oasis of Love soon became the new Lakewood Church. Three days later, on January 27, Lakewood Church held a memorial service for its founding pastor. Musical by Gary Simons, Oliver Jones, and Vestal Goodman punctuated tributes by Houston mayor Lee Brown, and Houston First Baptist Church pastor John Bisagno, along with neopentecostal teachers Richard Roberts, T. L. Osborn, R. W. Schambach, Kenneth Hagin, and Kenneth Copeland. A fitting homage to a neopentecostal giant, John's memorial service also reflected a changing of the guard for Lakewood Church.[2]

The Oasis of Love became the new Lakewood Church on October 3, 1999. "We Believe in New Beginnings" now served as the church's official tagline. On that fall day, dubbed "Vision Sunday," Joel systematically unveiled his plans for the church. He seized the moment to acknowledge his father's influence, but also to begin to chart his own course. "I think it's so interesting that my daddy, Pastor John Osteen, died just 11 months before the new millennium," Joel stated at the beginning of his first sermon as Lakewood's "official" pastor. "He could have gone to heaven a year from now or three years. But I believe God ordained it before the foundation of the world that you and I would be standing here at this very time about to launch this church into a new century. We are people of destiny." Building on what his father preached, Joel unpacked an aggressive plan to fund evangelistic efforts in Houston, the United States, and around the world. "And I have to warn you, I have big dreams," he declared. Impacted by John's interest in Christian education, Joel also spoke about new spiritual growth classes for Lakewood's members devoted to creating "strong families and strong leaders for the kingdom of God." In addition, Joel promised classes on marriage and English-language classes for Spanish speakers, along with job training seminars and the creation of health clinics. He also announced a stunning list of guest preachers he had lined up to speak at Lakewood. Reflecting a generational shift then taking place within neopentecostal Christianity, the list reads like a who's who of both veteran and emerging neopentecostal teachers: Joyce Meyer, Rodney Howard-Browne, Jesse Duplantis, Jerry Savelle, Nicky Cruz, Kenneth Copeland, and R. W. Schambach. "Daddy has passed the baton to me and to you. Now this is our day," Joel concluded his inaugural sermon. "I believe that we're entering into a whole new dimension today and that our greatest days are just ahead. This is a time of New Beginnings!" Like his father, in Joel's inaugural oration he preached about determination, hope, and destiny. His opening sermon bridged Lakewood's past and present even as it announced that change was around the corner.[3]

Joel's declaration of Lakewood's destiny, wrapped in both appreciation for his late father as well as providential musings used to bolster his position, rolled out ambitious plans. Osteen purposed to support local religious and social initiatives as well as build on the international reach Lakewood had developed over the decades. Joel's confident announcements, while perhaps a vigorous cover for internal self-doubt, nevertheless sprung from a burning desire to honor, respect, and uphold the legacy he felt John had delivered to him.

Embracing the Inheritance: Like Father, Like Son

The primary and most important influence on Joel Osteen undoubtedly came from his father. John's Texas theology, which included a boundless optimism, tethered to a functionally conservative political persuasion, shaped his message deeply. From his father, Joel adopted positive confession, although he repurposed his declarations for a wider audience. John's nondenominationalism also left its mark on his son; Joel continued to open wide Lakewood's literal and virtual doors to the world. John's Southern Baptist seminary training cemented a hermeneutical analysis of the Christian scriptures that prized literal interpretation and a valorization of Bible characters as moral exemplars. Although Joel's preaching style and pulpit performance differed markedly from the energetic orations of his father, he embraced the inheritance of John's positive confession, nondenominationalism, and biblical literalism, which assisted him in building a foundation for future ministry endeavors.

While it is true that Joel never obtained a formal seminary education, he apprenticed to his father by watching, listening to, and editing John's sermons (and those of other neopentecostal teachers who preached at Lakewood) in preparation for television broadcasts. This process began in 1982 when Joel started Lakewood's television ministry, and it constituted his religious education and theological training. For nearly twenty years, Joel listened to his each of his father's sermons at least half a dozen times as he edited the footage to fit the thirty-minute *John Osteen* broadcast he produced. "[A]fter my dad would speak on a Sunday morning, we would get everything he said typed out," Joel stated in 1999. "And then I'd have to time it out. So by the time it was finished, by the time the program aired I'd probably gone over the sermon 5 or 6 times. So I knew exactly—I knew daddy's train of thought. I could finish any story. I could finish any sermon." Osteen once estimated that he had listened to approximately 1,500 of his father's sermons. As Joel viewed his father's sermons multiple times for the best cinematic angles and television-friendly presentations, he also absorbed much of their content.[4]

One of John's imprints on his son included Joel's use of positive confession. Staring with his 1999 sermons, Joel continued to employ John's Bible confession at the beginning of every service. He rhetorically linked Lakewood's past and present by invoking his father's well-known phrases. Within John's confession was a reference to Bible teaching that represented "the ever living seed of the word of God," a prosperity gospel concept John adopted from Oral Roberts's "seed faith." Like his father and Roberts, Joel too used the language of investing in faith with the hopes of receiving God's blessing in return. With the Bible confession, Osteen encouraged listeners to assent to God's supernatural intervention, generate positive thoughts, and speak or "confess" biblical passages to elicit hopeful faith for dire circumstances. At the core of Osteen's Bible confession was an evangelical emphasis on the Bible that informed a personal spiritual transformation. Joel's energetic recitation with a smile on his face added to his listeners' anticipation that they would receive useful skills and practical encouragement to grow in a life of faith. In his *Hope for Today Bible* (*HFTB*) published in 2009—one of the few study Bibles published by a prosperity preacher—Joel included the Bible confession with scriptural verse references for each phrase of the confession. He recommended that readers recite the confession to themselves before Bible study. "Each time we open God's Word," he wrote, "we anticipate what he will say to us. As we read, we find daily bread, living water, and life-changing truth. We meet God in the pages of Scripture . . . we prepare to hear God's Word by saying these phrases together." As it turned out, Joel's use of the Bible confession heralded his routine use of the Christian scriptures in his teaching and books.[5]

Building from the Bible confession, Joel also adopted John's formal practice of positive confession. In contrast to his father's positive confessions, which focused on the recitation of Bible passages, Joel's positive confessions emphasized the enhancement of personal qualities in order to establish a more positive frame of mind and to generate feelings of encouragement. Joel's positive confessions referenced God and the attainment of Christian virtues such as trust and faith, but his language also promoted feelings of happiness and well-being. In a note on Proverbs 18:21 ("The tongue can bring life or death") in the *HFTB*, a verse John cited regularly in defense of positive confession, Joel wrote, "Your words have creative power, and when you speak those words of faith and victory, you are bringing them to life." Joel's sermons and books argued that words have the power to heal or to hurt, to confirm or to condemn, and to uplift or undermine.[6]

Joel also embraced his father's focus on the body, but as with his adaptation of positive confession, adjusted it to his own understanding. In books and sermons, John regularly related accounts of divine healing, particularly those of his daughter Lisa, and his wife, Dodie. Joel rarely invoked accounts of divine healing outside of retelling the story of his mother's victory over cancer or his sister's defeat of cerebral palsy. However, very much like other neopentecostals, he more subtly inter-faced neopentecostal notions of embodiment—particularly since he had not directly experienced dramatic divine healing stories like his father had—by dispensing encouragement and advice about God's plan for fitness, physical health, and emotional stability. Joel's prosperity gos-pel of the body, as chapter 4 explains in detail, expressed in the con-text of a therapeutically informed, image-oriented cultural landscape, ironically tethered his message to historical forms of neopentecostal understanding.[7]

Joel also inherited from his father a literalist hermeneutic of scripture study, a hallmark of conservative evangelicalism and fundamentalism in the United States. While Osteen employed a literal hermeneutic, he simultaneously deployed a figurative reading of Bible passages in which he took the stories of well-known characters and presented their lives as symbols of struggle, success, faith, and achievement. Osteen's HFTB of-fers a stunningly rich site in which to observe the adoption of his father's biblical literalism.[8]

The Old Testament account of the Jewish prophet Jonah is a case in point. According to the Old Testament, Yahweh commanded the prophet to deliver a message of grace and mercy to Israel's enemies in Nineveh. However, Jonah ignored these instructions and sailed in the opposite direction. After admitting that he was the ultimate cause of a storm that put the ship in jeopardy, the vessel's crew dumped him over-board into tumultuous seas. Thereafter the text reads that a "great fish" swallowed Jonah, and that he survived for three days in its entrails until the fish spewed the prophet out. Only then did Jonah deliver God's mes-sage to Nineveh. Osteen commented that as Jonah sat "trapped in the belly of a great fish . . . I can imagine it was cold and dark. Jonah was covered in things he didn't even know how to describe!" While Osteen employed the story of Jonah to teach that God always provided second chances, he nevertheless explained it as if Jonah literally survived three days inside of a fish before winding up spewed out on a beach.[9]

Similarly, Osteen used a literal hermeneutic to interpret the Old Testament story of Shadrach, Meshach, and Abednego. A narrative of Israel's Babylonian captivity during the eighth century BCE, the Old Testament book of Daniel relates the story of three Jews who refused to honor a Babylonian deity, thus defying the command of King Nebuchadnezzar. The king then condemned the men to death by fire only to discover that Shadrach, Meshach, and Abednego—and a fourth figure whom Nebuchadnezzar identified as a god—survived the fiery furnace unscathed. Osteen explained that the Babylonian king heated the furnace up to ensure a painful demise for the obstinate Israelite dissidents, but the three "weren't panicking. . . . They weren't full of anxiety. They didn't get upset or become afraid. No, they were in complete peace. . . . God brought them through the fire without even having them smell of smoke." When pressure increases and negativity is on the rise, Osteen explained that during the "fires" of life those with hope trusted that "God has something great in store for you just on the horizon." Suggesting that Shadrach, Meshach, and Abednego literally survived the fires of Nebuchadnezzar's wrath, for Osteen deliverance and hope were the ultimate morals of the story.[10]

Osteen's commentary on Jesus' life and teachings also illustrates his literalism. In Luke 1:46–47, the Bible records an angelic visit to a teenage girl in Nazareth. Joel took Jesus' virgin birth at face value. He did not try to explain how a woman might become pregnant outside of coitus, but rather emphasized the concepts of assurance and affirmation. Osteen stated, "When God gives us a promise, it may not make sense to our mind. It may be out of the ordinary. . . . Simply trust in God; for with God all things are possible!" Furthermore, Osteen commended Mary's faith, and promised that if his readers pursued her example, blessings would soon follow. Commenting on Jesus' resurrection, another cardinal evangelical doctrine, Osteen proclaimed, "Jesus is risen! That's what we celebrate today and every day. The cross is bare, and the tomb is empty—forever." For Osteen, Jesus' resurrection also symbolized starting over. "As Christians, we believe in new beginnings," Osteen commented about Matthew 28:6 ("He isn't here! He is risen from the dead, just as he said would happen. Come, see where his body was lying."). "Jesus gave us unconditional love and unlimited possibilities. . . . That same power that resurrected Jesus from the grave can resurrect your dreams; it can resurrect your marriage, your health, your future."[11]

Joel's use of positive confession echoed the teachings of his father, as did his definitive literal analysis of biblical passages and focus on the exemplary faith of characters in the scripture. While Joel embraced particular parts of John's neopentecostal inheritance, certain aspects of his teaching moved beyond his father's shadow, influenced most explicitly by Joyce Meyer and John Maxwell.

Positive Thinking with Joyce Meyer

Joyce Meyer's impact surfaced in Joel's teaching about the mind. From her teachings, he constructed an approach to spiritual growth organized around emotional health and positive thinking. When Joel introduced Meyer to his Lakewood congregation during her February 2013 appearance at the church, he recalled her deep encouragement in the weeks following John's death. In his introductory comments, Joel noted his debt to Meyer's 1995 book *Battlefield of the Mind* and admitted to ordering between 200 and 300 of Meyer's taped messages as he began his preaching career. Osteen stated that Meyer was "a gift to the body of Christ" and played a major role in his development as a minister and teacher.[12]

Meyer's teaching career began in the mid-1970s, but she did not grab national attention until the early 1990s. Rooted in Midwestern Lutheranism, she became a charismatic and ventured out into independent ministry in 1980. Headquartered in St. Louis, throughout the 1980s she steadily gained a regional, then national following through radio. Meyer eventually extended her impact through the publication of books and other teaching materials. She also engaged in significant missionary endeavors outside of North America. Her organization Hand of Hope coupled preaching with the creation of food distribution networks, orphanages, medical missions, and the construction of water wells. A preaching slot in 1993 at Carlton Pearson's AZUSA revival— the same year neopentecostal minister T. D. Jakes debuted—helped to propel Meyer into the prosperity gospel's national spotlight. Historian Scott Billingsly attributed Meyer's importance to the ways she used her own history of mistreatment and abuse to create a message focused on emotional wholeness, what he terms her "commonsense approach to everyday problems." As Meyer's stature rose in the prosperity gospel community during the mid-1990s, her practical message resonated in Houston with Lakewood television producer Joel Osteen.[13]

Positive thinking rooted Meyer's commonsense approach to the Christian life that Joel appropriated. Meyer invoked Norman Vincent Peale's power of positive thinking, and expressed a similar message in two books, *Battlefield of the Mind: Winning the Battle in Your Mind* (1995) and *Power Thoughts: 12 Strategies to Win the Battle of the Mind* (2010). She stated, "The mind is the leader or forerunner of all actions [since] [o]ur actions are a direct result of our thoughts. If we have a negative mind, we will have a negative life." Meyer summarized her teaching this way: "Positive minds produce positive lives. Negative minds produce negative lives. Positive thoughts are always full of faith and hope. Negative thoughts are always full of fear and doubt." According to Meyer, God is by nature positive, therefore, careful reading and Bible study produced positive thinking. Employing therapeutic language, Meyer advised the faithful to become "righteousness-conscious" and remain "God-loves-me minded" in order to resist reliving negative experiences and defeatist thinking, what she called "power-draining" thoughts. Like many prosperity gospel teachers, Meyer coupled positive confession with positive thinking. She suggested using "word weapons" to counter negative thinking. "I recommend that you not only purposely think right thoughts," Meyer said, "but that you go the extra mile and speak them aloud as your confession" since, she claimed, spiritual congruence existed between "having a positive mind and mouth."[14]

Meyer's prosperity teaching also saw positive thinking as leading to a healthy body and stable emotions. "Our thoughts are silent words that only we and the Lord hear," Meyer argued in *Battlefield of the Mind*, "but those words affect our inner man, our health, our joy, and our attitude." Similarly, she observed in *Power Thoughts* that "disciplining [the] mind" avoided emotional instability, where "[o]ne day, you may be calm, peaceful, sure of yourself, and confident in God. Another day, you may be anxious, worried, insecure, and full of doubt." Meyer's spiritual teaching correlated positive thinking and a healthy body, as exemplified by her own youthful appearance. She cited a verse from Proverbs 4 that connected meditation on God's words to good health. Meyer contended that "[m]editating (pondering, thinking about) the Word of God in our mind will actually affect our physical body. . . . People tell me that I actually look at least fifteen years younger today than I did when I first began to diligently study the Word and make it the central focus of my entire life." Meyer thus articulated a prosperity gospel that was about far more than money. Abundant "talents" (a biblical term for money) should dispense blessings, she argued, but a "holistic approach to prosperity" concerned both "the body and the soul. When our bodies prosper, we are strong and physically healthy." "Our moods, countenance, conversation, and even our body can begin to droop in a downward position" when we obsess on negative thoughts, Meyer said, citing a host of scientific findings that correlated mental and physical health. "If we want to live healthy lives," she emphasized, "we have to have healthy minds—and that starts with thinking positively instead of negatively."[15]

Meyer's self-styled holistic prosperity gospel sought to strike a balance between a message of material accumulation and teaching that promoted fitness and faith. As scholar Kate Bowler explains, Meyer's dual focus cohered with neopentecostalism's history of prosperity teachings that defined abundance, in part, as the maintenance of healthy choices and a healthy lifestyle. It also aimed to bring nuance to the prosperity gospel as a message that did not merely fixate on money. Meyer's teaching on a holistic prosperity gospel informed Osteen's prosperity gospel of the body. As the next chapter more fully shows, Joel hitched together John Osteen's emphasis on divine healing and Meyer's broader presentation of prosperity.[16]

Osteen has alluded to Meyer's imprint on his messages, and she has also conducted a number of preaching campaigns and conferences at Lakewood. While Joel's personal history of material comfort and emotional stability contrasted sharply with Meyer's difficult past, he has nevertheless drawn inspiration from her teachings on positive thinking and stable psychology. In 2012, Joel returned the favor to one of his mentors by preaching at Meyer's Love Life Women's Conference, a meeting in honor of her thirty years of ministry.[17]

Motivated for Spiritual Success with John Maxwell

Joel's message of positive thinking also pivoted on a belief in the inevitability of spiritual success. Promoting an aspirational attitude in which those with deep faith foresee their hopes being actualized in reality, Joel based much of his dream and discovery discourse on the teachings of motivational speaker and leadership expert John Maxwell. Osteen formulated a framework that encouraged his followers to articulate dreams and develop success-oriented imaginations.

In the earliest days of Joel's pastorate, as he learned how to preach and worked to develop core aspects of his message, he admitted to experiencing several "periods of self-doubt." As he attempted to gain confidence in his abilities, he revealed, "I still didn't feel at home [at Lakewood]. I was very unsure of myself on Sunday mornings." In the midst of this episode, Joel received a letter from John Maxwell. "I had never met him before. I had only admired his writing and teachings," Joel wrote in his book *Every Day a Friday.* "I opened that letter as quickly as I could, and then I was touched by what he'd written." According to Osteen, Maxwell commented, "I watched you on television on Sunday and you were outstanding. . . . I've got to tell you, you've got what it takes. . . . You keep it simple. You've got a good personality." This important letter birthed a mentorship and close friendship. "I arranged to meet with John a few weeks after I received his note," Joel recalled. In October 2000, only a year after Joel became Lakewood's pastor, the church hosted one of Maxwell's leadership conferences, and he has visited ever since.[18]

In April 2012, Osteen invited Maxwell to guest preach at Lakewood when he and the church staff conducted an NOH event in Washington, D.C. In a taped message to Lakewood before Maxwell's Sunday morning sermon, Joel alluded to Maxwell's impact. He described Maxwell as "one of my favorite people in the whole world . . . a great friend of our ministry, he's been a friend behind the scenes, he's encouraged me when I first started [preaching] . . . he's one of the heroes of faith . . . he's written so many books that I use all the time, I still study from them." While Joel did not identify which of Maxwell's books most influenced him, Maxwell's studies that addressed motivational attitudes and achieving personal success most clearly aligned with Joel's messages.[19]

Maxwell started his career as a minister in Indiana in the late 1960s, pastored Faith Memorial Church in Ohio during the 1970s, and throughout the 1980s and 1990s worked at Skyline Wesleyan Church in southern California. In the mid-1990s, he expanded his preaching career into motivational speaking and leadership consulting. With expert communication skills, he developed a motivational message that bridged the American evangelical world and nonreligious settings. Joel adopted Maxwell's approach and developed his own vocabulary of spiritual success to create a message at once religious and motivational. Put another way, John Maxwell helped Joel to realize his own dreams.

Maxwell addressed these topics most specifically in *Be All You Can Be! A Challenge to Stretch Your God-Given Potential* (1987) and *The Success Journey: The Process of Living Your Dreams* (1997). California minister Robert Schuller, a former minister at the famous Crystal Cathedral in Orange County, influenced Maxwell's teaching about cultivating inner potential and achieving personal success. A vocal advocate for what he termed "possibility thinking," Schuller penned the foreword to *The Success Journey*. In this foreword, which echoed a pamphlet he had published, *The Miracle of Thinking Big*, Schuller wrote, "I happen to believe in success, because I do not follow a loser. My Lord is a winner, and he doesn't believe in failure." In Schuller's teaching, as in Maxwell's message, success, possibility, and abundance connected to "thinking big." The Schuller–Maxwell connection is significant. Insofar as Maxwell impacted Joel's teaching, Schuller's motivational message of personal possibility and spiritual achievement was an indirect influence on Joel's articulation of positive thinking and his emphasis on spiritual success.[20]

In *The Success Journey*, Maxwell argued that "success" is unique to each individual, and specific to the particular circumstances of an individual's potential. Maxwell's formula for success is the realization of an individual's life dreams. "It's the thing we were born to do," he explained. "It draws on our talents and gifts. It appeals to our highest ideals. It sparks our feelings of destiny." In *Be All You Can Be!* he stated, "They have a dream that is bigger than themselves. . . . [T]he happiest people in the world are those who are living out their dreams." For Maxwell, a dream took "an active part in shaping the purpose and meaning of our lives . . . when pursued [it] is the most likely predictor of our future." For Maxwell, as for Osteen, a dream expressed and achieved was the distinguishing feature of a successful person. [21]

Maxwell's process of achievement involved envisioning success. "Paint a broad picture," he suggested, so that supporters can "catch your vision." The achievement process also required the dreamer to write down the vision in order to articulate a "philosophy of travel for the success journey." To "seize the dream" manifested potential. For Maxwell, one's success statement developed over time as one embraced the objectives of being a "continual learner" and determined to transcend fear. "Feed your faith," Maxwell suggested in *Failing Forward* (2000), "not your fear. . . . Both fear and faith will be with you every minute of every day. But the emotion that you continually act upon—the one you feed—dominates your life."[22]

Shaped by Robert Schuller's "possibility thinking," Maxwell eventually prophesied his own dreams and articulated the parameters of his own achievement. Drawn from the Bible and his own experiences as a business leader and entrepreneur, Maxwell's teachings influenced and informed not only business leaders but also religious celebrities. Joel Osteen translated Maxwell's teachings on spiritual success and personal fulfillment into a formula for achieving his own dreams.

Into the Pulpit with Joel Osteen

In his 2007 book *Become a Better You*, Joel recalled the numerous times his father commented that he looked forward to the day when 20,000 people would worship at Lakewood. While his father had a big dream about the church's future, Joel admitted, "God used his children to complete it. . . . Daddy sowed the seeds; he paved the way, and my family members—as well as millions of other people—have enjoyed the blessings as a result." Despite Joel's confident recollections of the past, Lakewood's large membership and cultural impact were neither guaranteed nor inevitable. Rather, Joel achieved them through the specific calculus of John Osteen's inheritance, Meyer's teaching, and Maxwell's leadership strategy. But before the big time, the bright lights, and the bountiful blessings of bestselling books and large buildings toward which Joel has pointed as his successes, he stepped into Lakewood's pulpit with knocking knees, sweaty palms, and a parched mouth. Wearing his father's old shoes and suit and tie, and firmly clutching his Bible, Joel's early sermons from 1999 and 2000 drew from what he knew and from the teachings with which he was most acquainted. If Lakewood really believed in new beginnings, then it was with Osteen's rookie sermons that new days dawned.[23]

Transcripts from nearly two dozen of Joel's earliest sermons, analyzed in this book for the first time (two of which appear in the appendixes), shed light on the opening months of his preaching career that gave shape to the substance of his teaching. Prior to becoming Lakewood's official minister in October 1999, Joel preached most of the sermons that year. Some of the sermons were topical in nature, others occasioned by Christian holidays such as Easter. Still others Joel organized into specific serialized subjects. The sermons depict a rookie preacher, familiar with the congregation, but in an unfamiliar position in front of the audience. Osteen's addresses display a familiarity with the Bible, expressed in neopentecostal categories and evangelical language. In his preaching, Osteen discussed the need to formulate dreams in order to imagine a future devoid of self-doubt and pregnant with possibility. He addressed the battlefield of the mind in order to champion positive thinking and promote living a life of victory by transcending negative circumstances, all topics closely tied to the teachings of his father, Meyer, and Maxwell.

Joel titled his inaugural sermon series at Lakewood Church "Holding onto Your Dreams." Delivered between February and May of 1999, Osteen's orations included anecdotes about his deceased father, and several accounts of his sister Lisa's healing and his mother Dodie's defeat of cancer. Numerous illustrations alluded to his "dream" to start Lakewood's television ministry along with stories from his marriage to Victoria and the travails of raising young children.

Referencing a Bible passage from Habakkuk 2 ("Write the vision and engrave it so clearly that anyone who even goes by fast will see it quickly and easily."), Joel preached, "The first thing we need to do if we're going to hold on to our dreams is to write the vision down clearly. In other words, what are you believing God for?" Osteen suggested composing visions for better marriages, reducing debt, and more dedicated Christian service. He then applied visionary language to Lakewood, articulating a "dream" for more funding of missionary work and evangelistic campaigns. In another sermon, he called for Christians to "step out in faith" and "get out of our little comfort zones and know that God wants to bless us. And reach for [y]our dreams" with a "shameless persistence" of religious devotion. "Holding on to your dreams and desires," Osteen explained, is "getting into that place of fulfillment in your life through Jesus Christ" and "develop[ing] this unshakable confidence in God." He said that struggles or difficulties might defer dreams, but should not deter them. Humans placed limitations on "the flow of God's blessings" through "doubt and unbelief," he claimed, because "[t]he enemy, Satan himself can put thoughts into your mind." Osteen preached that building faith instead of embracing fear achieved spiritual success. "Our faith is being tested in the fiery trials we face," he said. "In your hour of distress, don't give up. Don't turn away from God. Run to God . . . your victory is just right around the corner. Hold on to your dreams. God will see them come to pass." Joel's series of messages on dreams of spiritual success that drew on language and concepts from John Maxwell defined the first few months of his preaching career through mid-1999. In the midst of concerns about the coming millennium and questions about a potential Y2K disaster, not to mention the difficulties of pastoring a large congregation inherited from his father, Osteen chose to face the future through imagining positively his success journey.[24]

Joel's second sermon series more directly utilized the teachings of Joyce Meyer. Echoing the title of her *Battlefield of the Mind*, Joel delivered sermons on "Winning the Battle of the Mind" between May and August of 1999. Osteen considered the mind as one of the most important domains of the Christian life. He described it as a "soulish area" in which reside the "will and emotions." The mind is a "gateway," he said. "[E]verything starts with a thought." Ultimately, he explained, the mind was a spiritual battleground, the "bull's eye of Satan's target" where "tremendous warfare is going on." Osteen continued, "You must understand that the only entrance that the enemy has into your personality, into your emotions, into your thoughts is through your mind." He declared, "I'm amazed at people in 1999 who don't believe in the devil and demon forces. Can you believe that? You don't have to look around this world very far to realize that there is an evil influence in the world." To illustrate this point, Osteen cited the Columbine massacre, which took place in April 1999, a month before he began his battlefield series. "You can't tell me the devil wasn't having a heyday in their minds," he said about the shooters. "That is the devil and demon forces at work. We must realize who our enemy is. It is the devil and demon forces. We know we're in a warfare." He warned, "Don't be ignorant of the enemy's mind-oriented strategy," because Satan wished to "blind [the] mind to the Gospel of Jesus" and persuade the faithful that "God's out to get them" by "remind[ing] people of their past failures and their past mistakes." Osteen recommended that the solution to this dilemma was to "bring every thought into the captivity of Christ" by prayer, confession using Jesus' name, worship, and meditation on the Bible.[25]

While Osteen's direct references to "Satan" echoed standard neopentecostal teaching and evangelical language, these references later gave way to more generalized descriptions of "the Enemy" or negative influences. Nevertheless, early on in his ministry Osteen drew from his neopentecostal understanding of the world to link life problems and national calamities very specifically to demonic influences.

In the face of spiritual warfare, Osteen's expression of neopentecostal faith paralleled Joyce Meyer's with his recommended focus on cultivating spiritual virtues to generate a positive outlook on life. He stated, "wrong thinking patterns will hold us back from being all God wants us to be . . . your attitude's affected, your emotions are affected [and] your personality is affected." "Satan knows that by [a]ffecting the way we think," Osteen declared, "he can manipulate and control our personality, our emotions. He can even keep us in bondage." Examples of such "bondage" included "suicidal thoughts" and "poverty thoughts" along with watching too much television, spending too much time on the computer, and fixating upon highly sexualized advertisements. In addition, Osteen promoted intensive recitation of Bible verses to shape one's mental outlook, a practice he embraced as positive confession. He said the faithful must "stand guard faithfully over [their] mind." Osteen warned that with a "polluted thought-life . . . it will be extremely difficult for you to hear the voice of God when He speaks to you." He promised that "God has given each and every one of us this tremendous ability to imagine," therefore "[y]ou cannot think poverty and expect to get out of debt. You can't think depression and expect to have joy."[26]

Joel's new position at Lakewood Church in 1999 provided him an opportunity to acknowledge his father's leading role in the congregation's history even as it gave him an open forum to present foundational religious ideas and spiritual concepts that he continued to revise, retexture, and refine. These orations were a crucial step in Osteen's development as a minister because he drew very specifically from the teachings he felt he knew best. It is notable that Osteen's opening sermon series on spiritual success mimicked the specific aspirational language of John Maxwell while his sermon series on positive thinking employed Joyce Meyer's description of the mind as a "battlefield" on which spiritual struggles take place. In addition, his deployment of distinctly neopentecostal frames of spiritual expression throughout his inaugural sermons directly reflected his father's imprint.

The months and years during which Joel cemented the central themes of his teaching witnessed a sustained focus on positive thinking, the routine use of positive confession, and a language of spiritual success, all core elements of his neopentecostal heritage. In time, he developed his own distinct teachings. He refashioned his father's nondenominationalism through transforming specifically neopentecostal language into more ecumenical discourse. Osteen's message of living a blessed life explained not only the path to material acquisitions, but also affirmed psychological wholeness through the cultivation of personal happiness by a healthy lifestyle, balanced nutrition, and regular exercise—a message strikingly representative of Joel's own life, as he grew up far outside of the shadows of poverty that so defined John's ministry and message. While Joel's job as Lakewood's pastor starting in 1999 literally embodied the church's belief in new beginnings, it also established an important prosperity platform from which he would continue to reach for new heights. As he repeated numerous times during his inaugural season as Lakewood's pastor, improvement was inevitable.

[4]

Joel Osteen's Prosperity Gospel, Part II

The Mind, Mouth, and Body Becoming Better

Osteen and I are strangers, but his praise still felt tender and good, like having my hair stroked. I wondered how many people in the arena never hear words like that except here. I'd show up every week too.

—Emily DePrang (2014)

By 2001, Joel Osteen had started to solidify the core themes of his overall message: positive confession and positive thinking. At the same time, he had identified the trajectory of his teaching and preaching repertoire: encouragement and improvement, optimism and expectancy, all articulated in aspirational language tied broadly to Christian concepts of redemption and restoration. Since 1999, Joel had regularly acknowledged the ways that his father's teaching had informed his own. Moreover, as the previous chapter documented, to establish his ministerial footing in the opening months of his role as Lakewood's new pastor, Joel used the teachings of John Maxwell and Joyce Meyer for inspiration.

Looking back on the early years of his ministry, Osteen stated, "When my father went to be with the Lord, I had to accept the fact that the purpose for my life was different from my father's. His calling was to help bring down the denominational walls between churches, and he went around the world telling people about the fullness of the Spirit." Osteen recalled that as he contemplated the direction his ministry would take, he felt his way into the future: "[W]hen I searched my heart, deep down I knew my calling was to plant a seed of hope, to encourage people, to let them know about the goodness of God." Taking his own advice to push away negative thoughts and critical voices of doubt, he found biblical sanction for his purpose in the Old Testament: "David fulfilled God's purpose for his generation." At the moment he read that, Joel said that a divine message resonated "right down in my heart." The communication Osteen received discouraged him to live in imitation of his father. Instead, he concluded, "I don't have to be like my father. I don't have to fit into a certain mold; it's okay to run my race. I am free to be me."[1]

Liberated from the confines of John's mold, yet firmly planted in the rich soil of Lakewood's history, Osteen bloomed in new directions. The months and years during which he began to express the twin tenets of positive thinking and positive confession, Joel retooled John's nondenominational orientation by effectively neutralizing distinctly neopentecostal language into more affable spiritual discourse broadly ecumenical in nature. He repackaged neopentecostalism's teaching of divine guarantee into an emphasis on a providence of positive outcomes. Osteen's message of providential promises, a version of what religious studies scholar Helje Kringlebotn Sødal identifies as his "rhetoric of hope," prized notions of expectation, confidence, and possibility. His teaching on living a blessed life explained not only how to achieve spiritual advancement and material accumulations, but also psychological health, nutrition and fitness, and the cultivation of personal fulfillment through his prosperity gospel of the body. Thus well into the first decade of the twenty-first century, Osteen had effectively adjusted his prosperity gospel to promote betterment through the mouth, the mind, and the body.

A Can-Do Mentality: Joel Osteen's Positive Thinking

The core elements of Joel's teaching connect him to a long historical line of individuals scholar Donald Meyer calls "positive thinkers." Meyer states that "popular psychologies promise power," and Osteen's brand of positive thinking pivoted on various elements of power: God's power accessed through Bible study to create a more positive mental outlook and an individual's power to imagine a better future for him or herself.[2]

Many of Joel's earliest sermons engaged positive thinking in relation to Joyce Meyer's concept of the battlefield of the mind, but his own articulation of positive thinking began to crystallize around 2001, two years into his preaching career. In a sermon from that year titled "Be Positive," he elaborated on the disposition of happiness in the midst of difficulties. He reminded listeners that Jesus cautioned that his followers would encounter adversity. To transcend "negative situations," Joel suggested that individuals dwell on a positive "attitude of faith," and resist adopting a negative mindset "on the inside." The development of a positive mindset produced a balanced emotional state in which Christians "choose joy as [the] dominant emotion." Similarly, in a 2002 address, "Developing a Warrior Mentality," Osteen advocated that his listeners adopt mental tenacity to produce "victors and not victims" and to become "more than conquerors." Describing the relationship between a warrior mindset and spiritual warfare, he declared that the "enemy of debt, the enemy of marriage trouble, the enemy of sickness [or] the enemy of depression" are "no match for Jesus." Just as biblical characters David and Paul encountered troubles, and thus served as spiritual exemplars for Christians, Osteen attested that a "warrior mentality" avoided discouragement and negative thinking.[3]

A sermon series from 2003 titled "Thinking the Right Thoughts" expressed Osteen's positive thinking even more explicitly. He exhorted his listeners to "cast down" negativity by "thinking God's thoughts." He elaborated on this theme: "God's thoughts will fill you with faith and hope and victory. God's thoughts will build you up and encourage you. They'll give you the strength you need to just keep on keeping on. God's thoughts will give you that can-do mentality." A booklet he published that same year, 30 Thoughts for Victorious Living, similarly recommended, "Begin today to think the way God thinks. . . . Start expecting the unexpected and look at life through your eyes of faith." Osteen wrote that such thinking produced a "restoration mentality" of being "strong-willed and determined." Those with determination, for Osteen, considered "obstacles [as] opportunities for advancement." Likewise, in another 2003 sermon, "Get Up on the Inside," he stated, "[P]eople that are going to fulfill their destiny are people who have a made up mind" because they can "get up on the inside." An interior focus meant a positive frame of mind reflected in a spirit of determination. To live in a positive frame of mind, Osteen counseled listeners in a 2005 address to "precondition" their minds to succeed and "reprogram" their minds for success. His focus on positive thinking delivered a powerful cognitive message that emphasized the possibility of change and the likelihood of positive outcomes to unpleasant circumstances. He did not say to deny difficulties or ignore bad health, but to respond to problems with a "positive attitude of faith." In a 2008 message, "Freedom from Wrong

Mindsets," Osteen claimed that negative thinking was a "stronghold" that put limitations on achievement and advancement. He pronounced the importance of "can-do thoughts, possibility thoughts [and] well-able thoughts." He likened negative thinking to a computer virus, and argued that new mental "software" resulted in proper thinking to foster "more faith, better health, divine connections, and supernatural opportunities." Placing limits on the horizon of possibility made life difficult, said Osteen, because "wrong mindsets will keep you from your destiny."[4]

Just like his sermons, Osteen's books enthusiastically embraced the power of positive thinking. In his first book, *Your Best Life Now*, published in 2004, Osteen located this philosophy both in the Bible and in the science of psychology. Since the New Testament book of Romans recommends personal transformation though mental renewal, he reasoned that "when you align your thoughts with God's thoughts and you start dwelling on the promises of His Word, when you constantly dwell on thoughts of His victory, favor, faith, power, and strength, nothing can hold you back. . . . If you transform your mind, God will transform your life." Positive thinking offered a divine guarantee of blessing, and positive thinking related to science. "Psychologists are convinced that our lives move in the direction of our most dominant thoughts," he claimed. To "become a better you," the title of Osteen's second book, released in 2007, Osteen cautioned against associating with negative minded people. "Get around people who will inspire you to rise higher," he encouraged. "Be careful with whom you associate, especially when you feel emotionally vulnerable, because negative people can steal the dream right out of your heart. . . . Dwell only on positive, empowering thoughts toward yourself."[5]

Osteen related the quest for happiness to the power of positive thinking. In his 2011 publication *Every Day a Friday*, he counseled readers to find a "voice of victory." Drawing on his background in television production, Osteen promoted positive thinking by utilizing the imagery of television channels. "Pay attention to what you're thinking. Some people have been tuned into the Worry Channel so long they could be lifetime members. . . . Pay attention to your thoughts. Make sure you're tuned into the right channel," he recommended. It may be necessary to "[c]hange the channel. You've got to guard your mind . . . [y]ou control what you think about," he cautioned. Known for his stalwart commitment to health and fitness, Osteen also used clinical imagery to voice his message of positive thinking. "When you dwell on what you can't do and the hurts you've felt and the challenges you face," explained Osteen, "you are focusing on the toxic thoughts that can do as much damage as toxins in your body. . . . If your mind is polluted, your whole life will be damaged." The solution he proposed centered on developing new thought patterns. "You make a decision you will not dwell on those [negative] thoughts anymore. You starve those toxins. . . . If you ignore toxic thoughts and keep your mind filled with thoughts of hope, thoughts of faith, then those toxic thoughts will grow weaker, and before long they won't have any effect on you."[6]

Whether from the pulpit or in print, during the first decade of the twenty-first century Osteen argued that a changed mindset invariably resulted in a changed life, always for the better. Drawing from biblical texts and popular psychology, Osteen promised happiness and contentment for a mind perpetually focused on what could and should be best in one's life. In addition to one's individual initiative, Osteen drew a connection between personal fulfillment and associating with "positive" people. Building on the "positive" experiences of his own life—being born the son of a respected preacher, the comfortably bourgeois circumstances of his childhood and adult life, and the successful creation of Lakewood's television ministry—Joel's energetic advocacy of positive thinking in his sermons and books personalized the triumphant application of his religious principles, a historical practice of celebrity ministers.[7]

Words Are Like Seeds: Joel Osteen's Positive Confession

Like positive thinking, positive confession emerged as a hallmark of Osteen's message. Joel's use of positive confession exhibited the most direct influence of his father's teaching. He did not always connect confessions to specific verses from the Bible like his father, but most often employed the practice of making positive declarations about good health, abundant finances, healthy relationships, or meaningful occupations.

While Joel's earliest sermons dealt more specifically with positive thinking and motivational encouragement, by 2001 he had clearly articulated elements of positive confession. In a 2001 sermon series titled "The Power of Words," he focused on the transformative importance of religious utterances. Not only did what one say shape human relationships, Osteen contended that words revealed the contours of one's past while they simultaneously shaped one's future. Osteen remarked, "You are who you are today in large part because of the words that you've been speaking. . . . You've got to begin to see yourselves as the overcomers God made you to be." Referencing stories and quotes from his father, Osteen recalled a catchy rhyme John repeated on many occasions: "Great it is to dream the dream, when you stand in youth by the starry stream; but a greater thing is to fight life through, and say at the end the dream is true." According to Osteen, words possessed transcendent power: "You've got to give life to your faith by speaking it out.[8]

A very telling 2004 sermon series, "Life-Changing Words," presented additional facets of Joel's message of positive confession. He spoke of "faith-filled words" that promoted encouragement and personal spiritual growth. "You can change your world by changing your words," preached Joel. "[Q]uit prophesying defeat, quit prophesying lack, quit prophesying mediocrity." Speaking "faith-filled words" also referred to giving encouragement in the midst of difficulty, or simply providing a compliment to someone. He said that verbalizing encouragement after being prompted by positive thoughts demonstrated that God moved in the heart to "sow a seed" of blessing. For Osteen, positive confession aided people in reaching goals and achieving dreams.[9]

Osteen's 2007 bestseller *Become a Better You* echoed these early sermons. Joel stated, "Words are like seeds. They have creative power. It says in Isaiah that 'We will eat the fruit of our words.' That's amazing when you stop to consider that truth: Our words tend to produce what we are saying." "Think about it," he continued. "Your words go out of your mouth and they come right back into your own ears." For Osteen, this placed a premium on "positive, biblically accurate statements about yourself," such as "I am anointed; I am approved; I am equipped; I've been chosen, set apart, destined to live in victory." He wrote in his 2009 book *It's Your Time*, "Our words truly do have creative power. . . . Change your words. Change your life. . . . Your words prophesy what you become." Drawing an application from this message, Osteen counseled daily confession. "Positively or negatively, creative power resides in your words, because you believe your words more than you believe anybody else's. . . . That's why it is so important that we get in the habit of declaring good things over our lives every day." His practice of positive confession, much like his father's, aimed to encourage hearers to find meaning in the midst of trouble by "confessing" alternative spiritual and material scenarios.[10]

In 2012, Joel published two additional books that demonstrated his fidelity to positive confession. An edited collection of his father's writings, *Your Words Hold a Miracle: The Power of Speaking God's Word*, testified to this focus. Osteen suggested that Christians should replace complaining with confessions of abundance and prosperity. In so doing, Joel adopted his father's famous phrase "miracle in your mouth." Commenting on his father's writings, Joel wrote, "Our words have tremendous power and are similar to seeds. By speaking them aloud, they are planted in our subconscious minds, take root, grow, and produce fruit of the same kind. Whether we speak positive or negative words, we will reap exactly what we sow. . . . Use your words to *change* your negative situations and fill them with life." Referencing the New Testament book of Romans, chapter 10, a passage popular in the realms of positive confession, Osteen stated, "When you believe God's Word and begin to speak it, mixing it with faith, you are actually confirming that truth and making it valid in your own life." In addition, Joel began his fifth book, *I Declare: 31 Promises to Speak over Your Life*, by writing, "I have written this book of thirty-one declarations so you can bless your future one day at a time, one month at a time. . . . [Y]ou've got to send your words out in the direction you want your life to go. . . . You give life to your faith by what you say . . . don't talk about the way you are. Talk about the way you want to be."[11]

Deeply shaped by the neopentecostal tradition of positive confession, Osteen adapted the popular practice to his own ministry. As Joel refined his style and the core components of his message, he found that reformatting positive declarations into principles applicable to wide audiences achieved the successes he spoke of for his own future.

If God Wills It: Joel Osteen's Providence of Positive Outcomes

Osteen's focus on positive confession and positive thinking—most akin to the prosperity gospel's conception of victory—connected to an outlook that deemed God's activity in the everyday lives of ordinary Christians as fundamentally beneficial. Osteen's positive, upbeat message promoted the conviction that God worked behind the scenes in positive ways despite trying or seemingly hopeless circumstances. He contended that God rearranged the broken pieces of a shattered life into something new, pristine, and ultimately positive. While he stopped short of saying that God caused calamities, he urged Christians to believe that God maintained control of events and transformed all trials and tribulations to one's personal benefit. Osteen taught that in a hopeful frame of mind rested the conviction that something positive materialized. His decidedly affirmative, unflappable confidence that God turned troubles into triumphs expressed his providence of positive outcomes, the notion that God has predestined good fortune and beneficial circumstances.[12]

In *Your Best Life Now*, Osteen provided one of his clearest statements about the providence of positive outcomes. He encouraged readers to "trust God's timing" and to "relax knowing that God is in control" of life's circumstances. He cautioned against treating the possibility of God's blessing "like an ATM machine, where you punch in the right codes and receive what you requested." Instead, he counseled followers to express faith and concentrate on how the Christian waited on "God's timing" since "God sees the big picture." As David in the Old Testament settled for the status of shepherd for much of his life, Osteen wrote that in "due season" the shepherd eventually became a king. He also linked a more general trust in the providence of positive outcomes to specific prayer requests. "God already has the answer to your prayers before you have the need," he explained. "He has already been arranging things in your favor. . . . Let God do it His way." Osteen fleshed out his philosophy of positive providence with this statement:

Understand, God is at work in your life whether you can see anything happening externally or not. In fact, one could almost make a case that God often works the most when we see it and feel it the least. You may not see any progress. Your situation may look the same as it did three months or even three years ago, but you must trust that deep inside your life, God is at work. Beyond that, behind the scenes, He's putting all the pieces together. He's getting everything lined up, and one day, at the appointed time, you will see the culmination of everything that God has been doing. Suddenly, your situation will change for the better.[13]

Osteen contended that God worked for one's good and ultimately brought about something positive. For Osteen, embracing God's cosmic mystery involved absolute and unwavering trust in God's provision and protection.

If "living your best life now" involved recognizing positive providence, then for Osteen the same principle applied to "becoming a better you." To "become" suggested an orientation toward the future, which connected specifically to the sense of expectancy Joel developed for his message. "Waiting should not be a passive thing," he wrote in *Become a Better You*. Tethering the prosperity language of "seed faith" to expectancy—in a manner similar to that formerly articulated by Oral Roberts—Osteen wrote, "[Y]ou have to let the seed really take root. But you can't stop there. You must move on from believing to expecting." Joel wrote that he adopted this disposition as Lakewood negotiated to acquire the Compaq Center, which illustrated the necessity of "planning for blessing" associated with positive providence. Faced with several setbacks in his attempts to acquire property for a new church location before Lakewood obtained its new building, Osteen treated his own disappointment as a fortuitous juncture leading to the inevitable enactment of divine blessing.[14]

Similarly, Osteen also urged individuals to push uncertainty out of the thought process. He suggested exercising faith that life's rough patches actually revealed opportunities in disguise. Osteen's book *It's Your Time*, published in 2009 during a debilitating recession, sought to teach positive providence coupled with expectancy. "Sometimes, God pushes us out of our comfort zone and into a growing zone," he observed. "[Y]ou need to understand that what is unfamiliar and uncomfortable may also be exciting and beneficial." Instead of contemplation on the unknowable, Osteen emphasized faith in a divine plan. "Do not dwell on unanswered questions. Believe God is in complete control. He will show up and show out in unusual ways. He will transform your scars into stars. He will make your mess into your message." Using the language of providence, Osteen wrote that God "already released favor, supernatural opportunities, [and] divine connections. The breaks you need have already been preordained to come across your path."[15]

A final key to Osteen's providence of positive outcomes is what he called the "anointing of ease." A very familiar neopentecostal term, Osteen defined "anointing" as "a supernatural grace, a favor that lightens the load and takes the pressure off. Scripture describes this as God going before you and making crooked places straight, rough places smooth." Osteen illustrated the "anointing of ease" with a discussion of successful businesses, successful careers, and people who achieved financial stability by overcoming personal difficulties. Once someone "step[s] into [an] anointing of ease," Joel resolutely proclaimed, "[y]ou need not worry. Your life will not be a constant struggle. Yes, there will be hard times and challenges, but don't you dare dwell on them. God has lined up the right breaks, the right opportunities [and] the right people in your future. Those hard times will end and give way to the best of times." Osteen admitted that problems may persist, but it is far more likely that favor inhabited the future since "God likes to outdo Himself. He doesn't just meet your needs. He doesn't just make our lives easier. He does more for us than we can think to ask of Him."[16]

Osteen's providence of positive outcomes resonates with historic themes in prosperity gospel teaching and it rescripts his father's Texas theology, which offered a sense of hopeful expectancy. However, it also relates to a much longer conception of predestination, what historian Peter J. Thuesen calls America's most "contentious doctrine." Thuesen describes the idea of providence as the sense that "the divine superintendence of all events [moves] toward preordained ends." Spanning centuries of intense debate and fractured reflection, the contention about predestination revolved around personal notions of salvation connected to eternal destinations while it also informed contemplation about natural disasters or environmental calamities. If Christians of an earlier era assigned an element of mystery to the doctrine of predestination, Thuesen argues that many modern Christians—as illustrated by Rick Warren's 1995 book *Purpose-Driven Life* and the purpose-driven ethos at Warren's Saddleback Church—jettisoned the mystery in favor of a more pragmatic and populist message of God's divine guarantee, a perspective more stylistically amenable to megachurches. "In the rise of the megachurch," Thuesen concludes, "these old acids simply evaporated, leaving behind a residue of providential language." If a residual providential language existed at Warren's megachurch, then it has also shaped the messages at megachurches elsewhere in the country, including Lakewood Church.[17]

America's Fittest Pastor: Joel Osteen's Prosperity Gospel of the Body

In early 2012, a photograph of a shirtless Joel Osteen vacationing in Hawaii hit the Internet. Several news outlets picked up the story, including the celebrity gossip website TMZ. "Good God, He's RIPPED!!!" screamed the headline. The TMZ story and photo were the standard fare of tabloid reporting, yet they also said something about the Christian body. "Besides being one of the most famous preachers in the world," the TMZ piece read, "Osteen is also a health nut . . . who dishes out diet advice on his web page. Judging by his sculpted physique, dude knows what he's talking about." The *Christian Post*, in an article titled "Megachurch Pastor Joel Osteen's 'Healthy' Physique Stuns Public," reported that as the photo went viral, ABC devoted airtime to the image, the British press gave it attention, and Osteen's hometown newspaper the *Houston Chronicle* printed a story about the preacher's abs.[18]

Then, in March 2014, Houston-based fitness guru Samir Becic, who teaches fitness at Lakewood, released a list of the "Top 10 Fittest Christian Leaders" to the *Christian Post*. Osteen topped the list, apparent evidence of God's divine favor of faith, fitness, and the Christian body. Becic praised Osteen's self-discipline and commitment to fitness, and applauded his decision to eat healthy, exercise, and "take care of [the] temple," a New Testament reference to the human body in which Christians believe God dwells spiritually. Becic directly related physical health and spiritual well-being, and commented that healthy Christian bodies might serve as an evangelistic tool of religious outreach. "They can be great ambassadors for the Christian community," stated Becic about the fit pastors, especially for individuals who "might be struggling with their physical health." Becic's observation proposed profound connections between ideals of faith, fitness, and the Christian body.[19]

What prompted so much media attention to a forty-nine-year-old white Christian male's "sculpted physique"? Why should a celebrity minister's "healthy physique" stun the public? What is significant about Osteen's reputation as America's fittest pastor? While a never-ending public fascination with celebrity might explain these questions, the larger story behind the headlines ties into historical concerns about fitness, health, and the ideal Christian body in American religious culture, as the work of religious studies scholars R. Marie Griffith and Lynne Gerber documents. Griffith explains how the cultural significance of "body politics" in American Christianity with respect to weight loss and dieting, "offer[s] a model for tracking the ways that ordinary middle-class white bodies have been tutored in the obligatory hungers and subtle yet stringent regulations of consumer capitalism." Gerber interrogates the cultural politics of evangelical weight loss ministry by exploring its reflexive relationship with American society. Despite evangelical desires to influence culture in a spiritually meaningful way through weight-loss ministry, Gerber argues that American cultural ideals of body image prove most determinative in the execution of ministry activities, the result of which invariably casts moralizing judgments on what is a "proper" fit body. Read alongside the work of Griffith and Gerber, Osteen's prosperity gospel of the body points to the larger cultural significance of the fit Christian body, the moral meaning of which sits at the historical intersection of contemporary American Christianity and the prosperity gospel.[20]

Since his entrance into the wider landscape of American religious culture, Osteen has continuously attempted to demonstrate that the prosperity gospel is a message not just of faith and finances, but also of faith and fitness. For example, when asked to define the prosperity gospel in a 2012 *Christian Post* interview, Osteen maintained, "The way I define [the prosperity gospel] is that I believe God wants you to prosper in your health, in your family, in your relationships, in your business, and in your career. . . . [I]f that is the prosperity gospel, then I do believe that." Echoing Joyce Meyer's holistic notion of prosperity, Osteen's prosperity gospel of the body augments the prosperity gospel's material emphasis by presenting the Christian body as a gift from God, and as a site of improvement.[21]

An analysis of Joel's prosperity gospel of the body must attend to not only how the message trumpets the consumer benefits obtainable through capital, but also how the message explains embodied aspects of material attainment in the form of good health, emotional wholeness, and psychological well-being. Moreover, the contemporary historical context that indelibly shaped Osteen's prosperity gospel of the body means that his message of faith and fitness emphasized the possibility of second chances and achievement in the midst of difficulty. As Griffith and Gerber indicate, such ideas reinforce notions of health that prize as normal or standard the able-bodied, physically fit, emotionally balanced, and psychologically healthy Christian body.[22]

Joel's teachings include close attention to the Christian body, but not in the same way that the neopentecostal inheritance of his father emphasized divine healing. Understanding this connection is crucial to making sense of Osteen's prosperity gospel of the body. For the duration of his sixty-year ministry, John explained his conversion from Southern Baptist to Pentecostal in three distinct ways. He credited divine intervention when he overcame depression and regained emotional health during the 1950s and 1960s. John explained his daughter's recovery from cerebral palsy in 1958, and his wife's defeat of cancer in 1981 as the result of divine healing. John also regularly referenced many other accounts of divine healing he gathered for public testimonials used in his books and sermons.

Joel grew up hearing the story of his father's battles with disappointment and his sister's recovery, and lived through his mother's defeat of cancer, so the concept of divine healing was an integral part of his neopentecostal upbringing. However, neither in his books nor in his sermons does Joel cite any experience of divine healing of his own. His accounts of divine healing uniformly depended on the experiences of others, such as the stories of his sister's and his mother's health struggles. Joel's invocation of divine healing by proxy created for him the opportunity to retranslate this central tenet of neopentecostalism into a message of faith and fitness. Thus, the absence of Osteen's personal testimony of divine healing results in a repurposing of the neopentecostal focus on the Christian body to one of health, fitness, and self-improvement.[23]

Also critical to understanding Osteen's prosperity gospel of the body is his privileged background. When Osteen has presented autobiographical details in books and sermons, he has related stories of an active and athletic youth coupled with rigorous exercise as an adult and active participation in sports such as basketball, weightlifting, and jogging—all of which translated into an adulthood of health and physical fitness. Coupled with an able-bodied lifestyle of physical exertion, when Joel was young the Osteens moved to Kingwood, a middle-class suburb of northeast Houston, reflecting a distinctly bourgeois boyhood. Although largely unspoken in his sermons and books, there is a distinct class component to the relationship between Joel's privileged upbringing, able-bodied health, and focus on fitness and faith. As a result, Osteen's prosperity gospel of the body has reinscribed divine healing as a bourgeois neopentecostal embodiment of attainment, opportunity, potential, and possibility both spiritual and material. This means that Osteen's prosperity gospel of the body is replete with a certain kind of "body politics," to employ Griffith's phrase, and in possession of particular moral meanings attached to fit Christian bodies.[24]

Although Joel Osteen has always lived in close proximity to healed Christian bodies, in his teachings he has vicariously approached neopentecostalism's focus on divine healing. By repositioning neopentecostalism's emphasis on divine healing into material concerns about fitness and faith, in his publications, sermons, and writings Osteen's prosperity gospel of the body presents the Christian body as a gift from God, and as a site of improvement.

Associating health with prosperity, in his *HFTB* Osteen commented on the New Testament passage of 3 John 2 that states, "Dear friend, I hope all is well with you and that you are as healthy in body as you are in spirit." Based on this verse, Osteen accentuated the connection between physical health and spiritual health. "We have to take care of our physical bodies so that we can do what God has put in our hearts to do," he observed. "The apostle John is telling us that physical health is just as essential as spiritual health, so begin making whatever changes you need in order to live in health in your physical body." Invoking the Bible's temple imagery for the human body, Osteen stated:

> But so many people today make life harder for themselves than it needs to be. They're in a hurry, don't get adequate sleep, and don't eat healthily. They grab a candy bar on the go instead of an apple. They have a couple of donuts in the office and eat dinner at 10:00 p.m. and then stay up until one or two in the morning checking email. They go to sleep with the

BlackBerry and wake up to their iPod. Friend, that's not the best way to take care of the temple of the Most High God.[25]

As a neopentecostal, Osteen has assumed divine activity in the world. However, regarding Christian bodies, Osteen has presented the idea of preventing temple pollution as a spiritual ideal, a way to maintain the Christian body as God's gift.

In an appearance on *The Dr. Oz Show* in 2011, Osteen also invoked biblical references to the body as God's "temple" by asserting that God expects the faithful to commit themselves to the pursuit of health because there is a correlation between physical health and spiritual health. Titled "Medical Miracles," the show provided Osteen with the opportunity to cite his mother's account of defeating cancer. A Lakewood member, Anna, also appeared on the show. She attributed her defeat of cancer to divine healing, and said she had found encouragement in Dodie's story. To explore the potential connection between religious faith and health, Dr. Oz reviewed Anna's medical records and spoke with her cancer doctors. Osteen stated that spiritual intangibles, "unseen" factors of people praying for one another, or "God's breath" working to heal Christian bodies offered possible explanations for Anna's recovery. Joel emphasized his prosperity gospel of the body through a tacit support of divine healing by proxy. In addition, in exchange for God's gift of the Christian body, Joel reasoned that God's people should care for the "temple" by cultivating a healthy Christian body through faith and fitness.[26]

If Joel's prosperity gospel presented the Christian body as God's gift, it also emphasized the Christian body as a site of improvement, a literal embodiment of second chances. Osteen stated some of his clearest expressions of starting over in *It's Your Time*. In a section of the book titled "It's Time for Restoration," he commented on cancer diagnoses and ill health. Osteen referenced a story about a man named Kyle, who, he explained, adopted a mentality of victory and eventually defeated cancer. In addition, Osteen indicated that in hospitals, patients sometimes watched his television broadcasts. "I tell them never to view their illness as a permanent condition," he wrote, and recommended positive confession to restore health to the Christian body: "This cancer is not welcome in my body. It goes against the blessings that God has put on the inside. It is a trespasser. It is on private property. And as a child of the Most High God I have the authority to say, 'Cancer, you've got to go back. You will not defeat me. You will not steal my joy. You will not take one day of my divine destiny.'" With his emphasis on recovery stories, Osteen presented the body as a site of improvement and championed a spiritual prescription of second chances for healthy Christian bodies.[27]

Osteen's teaching series "Healthy Living" was the most sustained articulation of his prosperity gospel of the body. Preached in 2006, these sermons advocated strategies for maintaining physical health, finding balanced nutrition, and achieving optimal body weight. In the opening sermon, Osteen connected physical health and spiritual vitality, using temple language, and invoking the New Testament passage of 1 Corinthians 6:20 that states, "honor God with your body." As the Christian body is the "temple of the most high God," Osteen stated that "the most spiritual thing you can do" is to exercise and increase heart rate to release endorphins; after all, he observed, God made natural chemicals in the body and physical exertion therefore participates in a divine plan for the ideal Christian body. While Joel recommended deeper faith and regular prayer to achieve a healthy Christian body, he also cautioned that without proper exercise prayer and faith might prove fruitless. Since John Osteen died from a heart attack, in his sermon Joel said that while he spiritually invoked God's wrath against heart disease, he attempted to alleviate cardiac problems through regular exercise. Referencing his own Christian body as a site of improvement, Joel explained that his health-conscious fitness regimen had provided a second chance his father never had.[28]

Osteen preached in a second sermon that bad nutrition "abuse[d]" the Christian body. Instead of consuming unhealthy foods while praying for a divine miracle of bodily health, Osteen said, "discipline yourself to make healthy choices" by reading labels and heeding advice offered in scientific studies. Similarly, while he praised God for what he deemed a purposeful, divine dimension to the body's remarkable immune system, he strongly cautioned against the consumption of processed foods, sugary snacks, and fried meals. Instead, he proposed adopting a kosher diet as found in the Old Testament. Anticipating the popularity of the Daniel Diet—in 2013, fellow megachurch pastor Rick Warren and two physicians published *The Daniel Plan: 40 Days to a Healthier Life*—Osteen praised the Old Testament prophet Daniel, who resisted Babylonian imperial rule through his dietary decisions and in turn garnered a divine blessing. Invoking the moral example of an Old Testament figure to promote the Christian body as a site of improvement, Osteen's prosperity gospel of the body promised divine blessing in exchange for adhering to biblically sanctioned nutritional habits.[29]

Osteen's third sermon in his "Healthy Living" series, "Living at Your Ideal Weight," diagnosed obesity and fatness not as the consequences of morally deficient overeating, but as unfortunate by-products of faulty nutritional choices due to lack of information. "Take what God has given you, and make the very most of it," he preached. Osteen linked overconsumption to mindless snacking habits and to interior trauma; he suggested that for many food filled an emotional void. To optimize weight, Osteen maintained that it was wise to watch portions and track caloric intake. Yet implicit in Osteen's message was the imperative to decrease body size, thus casting fatness as abnormal and undesirable. Most of Osteen's examples, both in this sermon and in his books, allude to overweight women, although this distinct gender bias is not uniform throughout his messages. In the end, Osteen recommended the habituation of healthiness by avoiding the temptation of overconsumption; curtailing consumption and harnessing desires for food translated into "healthy living." For Osteen, a healthy mindset equated to a healthy Christian body, because "God will help you live at your ideal weight."[30]

While TMZ's 2012 story on Joel Osteen's chiseled abs exclaimed "Good God, He's RIPPED!!!" and other news outlets fixed a journalistic gaze on the physique of America's fittest preacher, there is more than meets the eye to Osteen's healthy Christian body. Osteen's association with the neopentecostal movement, and the close proximity to healed Christian bodies in which he has long lived, acquainted him with neopentecostalism's emphasis on divine healing, even though according to his books and sermons he has never been the recipient of it. An enterprising minister conscious of the most salient cultural trends of self-help and self-improvement, when Osteen became Lakewood Church's full-time minister in 1999 and affiliated his core teachings with the prosperity gospel, he adamantly insisted that the prosperity gospel was not just about financial progress, but also about attaining good health. Osteen's repurposing of the prosperity gospel's material message to one of finances *and* fitness, hope *and* health, paved the way for the eventual articulation of his prosperity gospel of the body. Osteen's prosperity gospel of the body as a gift from God and as a site of improvement resonates in a therapeutic culture where in the hearts, minds, and most importantly, bodies, of millions of individuals his message of self-improvement and second chances has found welcome homes.

Joel Osteen's Prosperity Gospel in History and in Houston

Having established the main contours of Osteen's prosperity message and its relationship to his father's teachings, the messages of Joyce Meyer, and the writings of John Maxwell across this chapter and the preceding one, a more concise rendering of Joel's historical development places his ministry more clearly in the broader cultural landscape of American Christianity. It begins with the Cold War context of Norman Vincent Peale's positive thinking. Peale's message, like Osteen's today, offered predictability in unstable times. Moreover, on a local level, the themes of Houston's religious culture pulsate through Osteen's message, which ultimately helped to define his cultural stature. Finally, the shifting political fortunes of evangelical Christianity during the early 2000s also proved highly determinative of Osteen's future; he entered the national scene at a time when his positive thinking proved politically persuasive.

What makes Joel's message culturally meaningful and historically significant? Nationally, his message is a contemporary manifestation of positive thinking that has its roots in the New Thought of the nineteenth century. The immediate historical foundation of Osteen's cheery articulation of Christian hope, however, comes from Peale, that mid-twentieth-century guru of positive thinking. Preaching, teaching, and writing at a time of increasing anxiety due to heightened fears about communism and existential crises connected to the material fruits of capitalism's abundance, Peale's power of positive thinking provided a predictable message in the unpredictable days of the early Cold War. Peale's "uncomplicated spirituality," as historian Carol V. R. George observes, fostered self-improvement aimed at happiness and fulfillment in life experienced at a frenetic pace, as it capitalized on the valorization of individual achievement and accomplishment. "Pealeism," as George calls it, emanated from Peale's books, from his pulpit in New York City's

Marble Collegiate Church, from his articles in *Guideposts* magazine, from his teaching available through the Foundation for Christian Living, and from Positive Communication, Inc., his film company.[31]

Without minimizing the differences between Peale and Osteen—their denominational histories, for example, as well as Peale's very intentional foray into conservative politics—important parallels between the ministers connect Joel's message and its meaning to key moments in American religious history. Today, Osteen's message of spiritual meaning rooted in positive thinking and positive confession provides predictability in an anxious age of global terror, late capitalism's ferocious economic uncertainty, and dizzying technological change, promising connection in a starkly individualistic historical moment. Despite its ability to spiritualize material inequalities and the structural deficiencies of capitalism, much like Peale's teachings, Osteen's counsel to find your best life now, become a better you, and declare yourself happy, confident, and content offer possibility and hope to many in extraordinarily unstable times. Ultimately, Osteen's teachings have found their cultural and historical currency through an inalterable predictability and astonishing redundancy. It once seemed that his penchant for thematizing nearly every sermon and every book with a quip about positive thinking or a scripture passage to enhance positive confession would reach its terminus sooner rather than later. However, an enormous reserve of anecdotes has animated Osteen's messages with what cultural critic Barbara Ehrenreich calls "bright-sided" thinking. It is precisely the predictability and redundancy of Joel's bright-sided teaching that leads to its popularity.[32]

While the contemporary popularity of Osteen's message finds its closest historical reflection in Norman Vincent Peale, equally important to Joel's currency are his Houston origins. The acquisitive orientation of Osteen's teachings percolated from his Houston heritage. Journalist Joel Kotkin, for example, cited economics, population growth, and shifting wage scales to describe Houston as an "opportunity city." Similarly, in 2010 essayist Kerry Hannon ranked Houston the number one city in which to restart a career. Getting a second chance at life is not only foundational to Joel's message, it is part of Houston's cultural DNA. Although not without its financial difficulties, Houston is a powerful, sprawling metropolitan area reflective of the Sunbelt's global horizons. Articulating this ethos, Bill White, Houston's mayor in the early 2000s, once described the largest Gulf Coast metropolis as a "can-do city." The city's first LGBT mayor, Annise Parker—at whose 2012 inauguration Osteen prayed—claimed that for Houston "the future is already here." Echoing a positive thinking mentality and using the language of opportunity, Parker described Houston as a place where one can bring to fruition unlimited potential: "It is the blessing and curse of Houston to never be satisfied with where it is, to always be reinventing itself. Ours is a city of opportunity and optimism—never stopping at why we can't do something, but always seeking how we can get it done. We are a city that knows how to turn potential problems into possibilities. We dream great dreams, but then make them happen." While Joel linked his message of hope to God's heavenly desires, it is also a positive message profoundly rooted in Houston's culture.[33]

Osteen's positive message also proved powerful in the midst of Houston's vibrant religious landscape. Joel's congregation was neither the only megachurch in town nor Houston's only site of religious significance. The nation's fourth largest city has a religious makeup and a religious history that are seemingly as diverse as its inhabitants.

According to the Houston Area Survey (HAS), longitudinal analyses of religiosity in the city indicate that since the early 1980s over half of Houstonians have found religion very meaningful in their everyday lives. The majority of religious Houstonians are Protestant—although increasing numbers identify as Roman Catholics—and Baptists and nondenominational churches such as Lakewood represent the highest percentages of Protestant identification. Average weekly church attendance has stayed stable over the last decade at approximately once per every seven days. Regarding religion and technology—Houston has had industry leaders in both religious television and radio—the HAS found at particular points that religious programming on television proved more popular than religious-oriented radio programs. In terms of specific religious orientations, over the last three decades—the years during which Osteen has worked in professional ministry in Houston—the HAS revealed a more or less equal percentage of fundamentalist, conservative Christians and liberal, more progressive Christians. The number of nones in Houston, the HAS found, has steadily risen, which reflects national trends. While the HAS's statistics and data offers fascinating and important measures of Houston's broader religiosity, additional evidence also fleshes out contextual factors that shed light on the local roots of Osteen's broader cultural and historical impact.[34]

Since Osteen became Lakewood's pastor, a number of new cowboy churches affiliated with the General Baptist Convention of Texas have emerged to provide havens of religious community in largely rural areas. Botanicas service Houstonians who practice religions such as Santería. Local traditions practiced by some of Houston's Mexican immigrants have shaped the religious lives of devotees to Santa Muerte, a Mexican folk saint. A local church affiliated with the Iglesia La Luz del Mundo (Light of the World Church) denomination based in Mexico has offered another religious option for the growing numbers of Latinos/as who call Houston home. Some mainline Christians in Houston have engaged in mystical labyrinth-walking rituals, while others of evangelical conviction have chosen to practice a Christian version of yoga called PraiseMoves. Religious radio also became popular across the city's airwaves. For over three decades, 89.3 KSBJ, headquartered in Humble, has offered a broad evangelical flavor with contemporary Christian music artists, while the Roman Catholic Radio María Houston for Spanish speakers launched in 2003. KROI Praise 92.1 has dubbed itself the "Inspiration Station" and made inroads into Houston's African American religious communities. The sprawling metropolitan landscape has welcomed a number of vibrant immigrant religious communities from Latin America, Africa, and Asia who represent not only a wide variety of Christian traditions, but also practitioners of Hinduism, Buddhism, and Islam, including some Latino Muslims. In addition, in the early 2000s Houston became the home of a Roman Catholic cardinal—His Eminence Daniel DiNardo— along with motorcycle evangelistic ministries, NASCAR outreaches, an interfaith movement led by women, and a surging population of nones who have organized gatherings of freethinkers, agnostics, atheists, and humanists. The Catholic Charismatic Center has embraced Catholics of Pentecostal persuasion and offered Mass in multiples languages. Millionaire attorney Mark Lanier established the Lanier Theological Library, with 100,000 volumes for biblical study and academic reflection. And Father Cedric Pisegna, a Passionist priest with a ministry called Live with Passion!, has published books and appeared on local Houston religious television to present a message of hope and healing. As an ad-

Figure 4.1. Lakewood Church, ca. 2009. Source: © Houston Chronicle/Eric Kayne. Used with permission.

vocate of the "New Evangelization," Father Cedric's teachings across social media and television have commonly encouraged the quest for joy, inspiration, happiness. Moreover, his presentations, with titles such as "Challenges Make Champions," "The Power of Positivity," and "You Are God's Champion," not only reflect the Roman Catholic Church's outreach techniques in the New Evangelization, they also echo the promise of possibility that has been part of Houston's cultural identity.[35]

While the HAS findings and numerous accounts of Houston's religious communities offer demographic perspectives on the city's recent religious past, the preponderance of megachurches also define Houston's religious context. According to data compiled by the Hartford Institute for Religion Research, out of approximately 206 megachurches in Texas, the greater metropolitan area of Houston is home to fifty-one. The top tier of Houston's megachurches—here defined as churches with 10,000 members or more—includes Lakewood, Second Baptist, Woodlands Church, and New Light Christian Center. On the one hand, Houston's megachurch population reflects national trends: the majority of mega-

Table 4.1. Houston's Top-Tier Megachurches, 2015 (10,000+ members)

Church/Pastor	Membership
Lakewood Church/Joel Osteen	43,500
Second Baptist/H. Edwin Young	20,656
Woodlands Church/Kerry Shook	18,385
New Light Christian Center/I. V. Hilliard	13,500

Source: I developed this table from the Database of Megachurches in the U.S., Hartford Institute for Religion Research, http://hirr.hartsem.edu/megachurch/database.html. The figures included in this table reflect data available as of April 2015.

churches have roots in the Southern Baptist Convention, while a sub-stantial number identify as nondenominational. On the other hand, in contrast to the national figures, Houston has a large number of mega-churches with a United Methodist Church affiliation. The Southern Baptist roots of Lakewood and its nondenominational label tie the church's specific history to national trends. Since Joel became pastor, the church has grown to be the largest church in Houston *and* in the United States.[36]

While Lakewood sits atop certain measures related to megachurches in Houston, in Texas, and throughout the nation, it also achieves significance in the delineation of megachurches specifically related to the prosperity gospel. Historian Kate Bowler has compiled a list of 115 prosperity megachurches throughout the United States—and of the five largest, three are in Texas (two in Houston, one in Dallas). Figured another way, of the largest fifteen prosperity megachurches across the United States, six are located in Texas, and half of those churches reside in Houston. Within Texas itself, the Dallas–Fort Worth metroplex hosts nine prosperity megachurches, the most of any city in the state. Houston claims six prosperity megachurches, followed by San Antonio with three, and Austin, Amarillo, and El Paso, with one each. Of Texas's prosperity megachurches, the three oldest are St. John Church, in the Dallas area, founded in 1921, along with Houston's Lakewood and Fountain of Praise, both founded in 1959. The genesis of all other prosperity megachurches in Texas dates to 1975. While table 4.1 presents the largest megachurches in Houston of various denominational backgrounds and affiliations, table 4.2, which adapts data from Bowler's book *Blessed*, lists megachurches in Houston connected specifically to the prosperity gospel. Differences in membership totals between the tables are attributable to their different documentation dates and methods of data collection. These tables provide indicators not only of Lakewood's size compared to other congregations, but of how to consider where it fits in the contexts of Houston and Texas.[37]

While maintaining his Houston roots in the midst of extensive religious diversity and in a local congregational community of other leading megachurches, in the early 2000s Joel started to chisel out his own place in history. It was not only Lakewood members and other Houstonians who took notice of Joel's new beginnings. Because of John's historical record of accomplishment within neopentecostal circles, the Osteen name garnered some recognition. Popular Christian magazine *Charisma*, for example, which had published a large profile of John and Dodie in 1988, added additional chapters to its Lakewood archive with feature stories on Joel in 2000 and 2004. Profusely praising Lakewood's newly minted minister, *Charisma*'s articles chronicled Osteen's maturation as a pastor, the development of a national and international ministry, and the strategic hiring of musician Cindy Cruse Ratcliff, Latin Grammy–winning singer and minister Marcos Witt, and African American singer Israel Houghton. These hires proved a major draw for Lakewood congregants. Along with the dissemination of Osteen's teaching across the television airwaves and through audio cassettes, video tapes, and later CDs and DVDs, the *Charisma* articles assisted in establishing a place of prominence for Joel in the neopentecostal world. And it was not long before Joel hit the national stage, which allowed him to transcend regional limitations, thus exemplifying aspects of American religion's "southernization."[38]

Table 4.2. Prosperity Megachurches in Houston, ca. 2011

Church/Pastor	Membership
Lakewood Church/Joel Osteen	38,000
New Light Christian Center/I. V. Hilliard	29,000
Fountain of Praise/Remus Wright	16,000
Windsor Village United Methodist Church/Kirbyjon Caldwell	14,000
Higher Dimension Church/Terrance Johnson	12,000
Abundant Life Christian Center, La Marque/David and Vicki Shearin	3,000

Figure 4.2. Lakewood Church auditorium, balcony view. Source: Bill Klages, New Klages Inc. Used with permission.

Outside of drawing attention in the national religious press, changes afoot in American society in the first decade of the twenty-first century also shed light on how Joel Osteen became *Joel Osteen*. First, shifts among the Christian Right in the early 2000s registered the desire for a different kind of public evangelical voice in American culture. Partisans of the Christian Right cheered in 2000 as they seemed to score a meaningful political victory when George W. Bush became president. Similarly, many evangelicals supported Bush in his 2004 reelection, despite his slim margin of victory. However, concerns that there were too many conservative appointments to the Supreme Court, coupled with the personal implosions of Texas politician Tom DeLay in 2005 and Colorado megachurch pastor and National Association of Evangelicals president Ted Haggard in 2006—key figures connected to the Christian Right— led to more than one forecast that the Christian Right was losing influence. Moreover, after the Democrats regained control of both houses of Congress in 2006, a 2007 *Time* magazine article confidently announced that the Democrats finally "got religion." The case for this perspective seemed to gather strength with books by Christian activist Jim Wallis, journalist Amy Sullivan, theologian David Gushee, and columnist E. J. Dionne that sought to exposit this critical moment in American political culture. Wallis stated in an interview, "I think the time is just about over where the religious right will be seen as the only voice, and we are right before the tipping point." Survey data from the election of Barack Obama in 2008 documented that the Christian Right was not, in fact, on life support but working through a generational identity crisis. Reports indicated that the culture warrior posture embodied by figures such as Jerry Falwell was giving way to a younger evangelical politics oriented more toward social justice. As historian Daniel K. Williams argues, deeper recognition of "cultural pluralism" and the eschewing of a "polarizing brand of politics" began to distinguish younger evangelicals from their aging counterparts.[39]

Similarly, in consideration of Osteen's message that attributes to God the providential inevitability of good fortune, positivity, and happiness,

Figure 4.3. Lakewood Church auditorium, panoramic stage view. Source: Bill Klages, New Klages Inc. Used with permission.

political geographer Jason Hackworth has pointed out that the contemporary populist orientation of the prosperity gospel's providentialism may not be so positive after all. Hackworth explains that the "religious neoliberalism" of the prosperity gospel traffics in providential language to offer "divine absolution for accumulating capital" and "sanctifies private property as an expression of piety." It shifts the material circumstances of the contemporary world—both for the 1 percent and for the 99 percent—into spiritual realms that assign divinity to the wealthy and nonwealthy alike. Hackworth observes that religious sanctioning of individualism, especially during the decade that Joel ascended to public view, often worked to baptize the dismantling of the welfare state. According to Hackworth, this reveals two logics at work: if individuals are the ultimate architects of their material acquisition, then they are also the primary cause of their economic debilitation and demise. In a complementary analysis of the prosperity gospel, religious studies scholar Kathryn Lofton comments on Marxist theory and the study of American religion. Purveyors of the prosperity gospel, she argues, work as "designers of their own hegemony [because] participants imagine they are the ultimate agents of their religious life and their economic life." Osteen's message has embodied certain aspects of the neoliberal political logic Hackworth identifies, and the smiling preacher's prosperity gospel has exhibited the kind of acquisitive orientation Lofton describes. The class markers that Hackworth and Lofton discuss also draw attention to religious studies scholar Sean McCloud's conception of "socially habituated subjectivities" in relation to embodiment and the prosperity gospel. His conception of religious identity and class based on language, praxis, and community connects to the corporeal of the prosperity message because it "entail[s] not just what people think and do but *how* people go about thinking and doing."[40]

Joel Osteen's ascension to prominence in America's religious landscape occurred during tremendous changes in American society and world culture. A noted local pastor in Houston starting in 1999, and a recognizable figure in neopentecostal circles after the biographical features *Charisma* published in 2000 and 2004, the publication of his first book *Your Best Life Now* in 2004 coupled with his appearance on *Larry King Live* in 2005 made Osteen a household name. A 2004 *New York Times* feature on Lakewood's impending move to the Compaq Center also put him on the national radar. Lois Romano's 2005 *Washington Post* feature not only christened Osteen "the smiling preacher" but offered observations that spoke to the historical moment. Romano noted the power of Osteen's "general appeal" to a wide audience with an "energetic, New Age gospel of hope and self-help" that was "notably devoid of politics and hot-button policy issues." Osteen affirmed this point later that year on *Larry King Live* by saying that he did not address politics in the pulpit although he "ha[d] thoughts" on political issues such as marriage equality and abortion. "I don't think that a same-sex marriage is the way God intended it to be. I don't think abortion is the best," Osteen told King. "I think there [is] a better way to live your life. But I'm not going to condemn those people. I tell them all the time our church is open for everybody." Joel's national ascendance during 2004 and 2005 along with his string of bestselling books and talk show appearances during the next eight years established a stark contrast between Osteen's public apolitical stance as the smiling preacher and the embattled culture warrior clergy, who, at times adopting what religious studies scholar Jason Bivins calls a "religion of fear," continued to vie for the Christian Right's love and affection. Joel's meteoric rise as "the new face of Christianity" in America during the first decade of the twenty-first century suggested that positive thinking and self-improvement were more attractive than the historically combative cultural politics of the Christian Right. Furthermore, as a minister who rose to public prominence in the early fear-filled years of America's War on Terror, Osteen's upbeat and encouraging message offered a consistently safe spiritual tonic in a world where political and material realities looked anything but promising. Not unlike how Norman Vincent Peale dispensed positive thinking's power in the 1950s to those in search of solace amid the threat of nuclear war, Osteen's message on positivity and personal affirmation provided an anchor of predictability in a world unhinged by the threat of global terrorism and economic collapse.[41]

The complex intersection of religion and politics in the United States during the first decade of the twenty-first century proved fortuitous for Joel Osteen. Although his father had courted luminaries of the Christian Right during the late 1980s, Joel had never officially thrown his lot in one ideological direction or the other, let alone identified with a political party. Nevertheless, his overall message was a theologically conservative evangelical one, and to the extent that he commented directly on cultural issues, Osteen's politics seemed functionally conservative. When pressed on marriage equality, for example, he maintained a fidelity to heterosexual marriage, while he also adamantly stated that Lakewood welcomed everybody. The fact that Osteen was generally nonpartisan—or openly opinionated with a smile on selected political issues—his politics of positive thinking proved attractive at a time of intense partisan bickering on the social and cultural front during the first decade of the 2000s.

Joel Osteen's prosperity gospel—inspired by the likes of his father, Joyce Meyer, and John Maxwell—eventually took a shape of its own. Emphasizing positive thinking, positive confession, a providence of positive outcomes, and a prosperity gospel of the body, the ascendance of Joel Osteen in the first decade of the twenty-first century was as much about those who influenced his prosperity gospel as it was about the swirl of historical and cultural circumstances in which he found himself in the early 2000s. Since then, Osteen's teachings have influenced numerous constituencies across the globe. But it was also his innovative use of religious media in the early 2000s that worked to spread his message of positive Christianity further and wider than he ever imagined—an abundance his prosperity gospel promised.

[5]

Joel Osteen's Tel-e-vangelism

The Message and Its Media

I'm not a national TV preacher. I don't even know if I can
preach. Who is going to want to listen to me?
—Joel Osteen (2004)

Throughout several of his *New York Times* bestselling books, Joel
Osteen has unveiled selected snapshots of his own engagement with
religious television. In *Your Best Life Now*, he admitted that before discovering his ability to preach he felt less than hopeful about Lakewood's
broadcasting future when he first became the church's minister. Despite
his integral involvement in the creation of Lakewood's media ministry,
Joel questioned whether he could garner the viewership that his father
maintained, so he canceled the church's national television program. He
knew what it took to make it on national television, and he doubted he
could compete. However, Osteen soon changed his mind, and arranged
a new national television slot for Lakewood. That decision changed
history.[1]

In *Become a Better You*, Osteen wrote that despite a burning desire to
work in television birthed when he was an adolescent, he failed in his
attempt to gain employment at Oral Roberts University's campus television station while a student there in the early 1980s. Overcoming this
setback, he subsequently moved to Houston to start Lakewood's television program, which he took as proof that "God had hardwired television production into me." In *Every Day a Friday*, Joel counseled readers
to use their smiles to communicate encouragement. "Let your joy be
seen and pass it on. Be friendly. Smile on purpose and without condition," he stated. "When things are difficult, smile by faith. Don't wait
until you feel better. Smile, and the feelings to support that smile will
catch up. . . . If you develop a habit of smiling, God will reward you with

His favor." For Osteen, a smile also communicated powerfully through television. "People write me all the time and say they can't remember the sermon's message," he admitted, "but they were touched by the joy in my face. They felt love coming through on the screen." In Osteen's world of positive thinking and a providence of positive outcomes, the blunting of his aspirations to gain valuable broadcasting skills as a college student ultimately worked to birth Lakewood's successful television ministry.[2]

During the early years of Joel's role as Lakewood's producer in the 1980s, the field of televangelism experienced a number of high-profile scandals, most of which took place in ministries associated with neo-pentecostalism. As a result, he learned quickly what did and did not make for attractive religious programming. When he became Lakewood's head minister and continued his involvement with religious media, he was effective because he knew well viewers' skepticism, suspicion, and cynicism about television preachers. Moreover, as a television and media producer, he understood, and as it turned out, anticipated the directions religious broadcasting eventually took.

Drawing on his experience with televangelism, Joel, in concert with an expert team of ministry colleagues and media consultants, developed innovative strategies for the placement of his message across multiple media platforms in the early 2000s. In an auspicious conjunction of circumstances, his national ascendancy as a popular religious figure coincided with the rise of new media. As someone already oriented toward religious broadcasting—in possession of more extensive media production experience before becoming a preacher than any other current televangelist—Osteen effectively harnessed his ministry to emerging digital technologies. This process spotlights how he became a new tel-e-vangelist. By bracketing "tel" and "e," my rendering of "televangelism" emphasizes the tremendous changes in media culture during the early 2000s. It highlights how Joel has adopted the traditional methods of televangelism on screen while it also alludes to how he has purposefully embraced new media to diversify the modalities on which he presents his message. His first career as a television producer for his father is vital to understanding the process by which he became a tel-e-vangelist. As a pastor and a media producer, Osteen developed the skills necessary to launch the most recognizable ministry in the early twenty-first century. Similarly, based on his wide media experience, Osteen quickly recognized the potential new media held at the dawn of the twenty-first century to distribute his teachings further and wider than ever before. As a tel-e-vangelist, Osteen has also rescripted American religious programming. His television broadcast is not only excellently produced, but it is also intentionally predictable and free of the spectacle generally associated with televangelism: activities such as speaking in tongues, pleading for money, dramatic healing, or slaying people in the Spirit. Instead, a half-hour message of positive thinking, hopeful expectation, and positive confession—in other words, a message of salvation with a smile—have come to define Osteen's broadcast.

Osteen's tel-e-vangelism is of historical consequence and cultural importance. A full accounting of his relationship to American televangelism links him to the foundational figure of Oral Roberts. In addition, the launch of Joel Osteen Ministries early in Joel's tenure as Lakewood's pastor, under which he eventually published the digital magazine *Hope for Today* (*HFT*) and birthed his monthly NOH stadium events, some of which he recorded, televised, and simulcast, mirrored the start of his father's evangelistic association, cross-country and international preaching crusades, and ministry magazines *Praise* and *Manna*. At a particularly ripe moment of both political change and cultural opportunity in the early 2000s, ministry colleagues Duncan Dodds and Jon Swearingen, as well as media consultant Phil Cooke, helped Osteen to inaugurate his innovative tel-e-vangelism. The careful calculus of Osteen's media synergized traditional religious broadcasting with the use of new media tools such as email, blogs, apps, YouTube, Facebook, Instagram, Twitter, iTunes, and starting in 2014, SiriusXM Radio. Religion scholars Pradip N. Thomas and Philip Lee term the twenty-first century's conjointment of traditional religious programming, the use of new media, and market concerns a "digital convergence." In a description that illuminates how Osteen has artfully approached the dissemination of his message, Thomas and Lee explain that "televangelism is no longer limited to television but is increasingly a new media phenomenon—amplified and shaped on social media sites and accessed by mobile technologies in ever more complex circuits of production, distribution, and consumption."[3]

Framing Faith: Joel Osteen and Televangelism's History

As part of the modern communications revolution, televangelism's roots date back to the 1920s and the advent of religious media with figures such as Father Charles Coughlin, a Roman Catholic, and the Protestant preacher Aimee Semple McPherson. During the same era, black ministers also frequented the realm of religious media. Recorded sermons, what religion scholar and Christian ethicist Jonathan Walton calls "religious race records," popularized African American religious practice through the work of ministers such as Missouri's J. C. Burnett, along with J. M. Gates, from Atlanta, and Mother Rosa Horn of Harlem. As the screen became as popular as the speaker, also integral to televangelism's history was the formation in the 1940s of the National Religious Broadcasters, which eventually added political muscle to the movement. Federal Communications Commission and congressional rulings during the 1950s and 1960s were highly consequential as well, providing evangelists with unprecedented visibility by making it easier to get on the air. Early on, Roman Catholics such as Bishop Fulton J. Sheen took to the television airwaves with popular shows. Mainline Christians and evangelicals of multiple denominational backgrounds seized opportunities to build on an established radio presence and branched out to televangelism.[4]

By the 1950s and 1960s, preachers such as Oral Roberts and Rex Humbard began to learn the ins and outs of television ministry, attempting to skillfully take the Christian gospel message to new audiences. During the same period, Pat Robertson launched the Christian Broadcasting Network, and shortly thereafter Paul Crouch established the Trinity Broadcasting Network. Billy Graham's crusades were also a mainstay on television. Meanwhile, from California, Robert Schuller hit the airwaves by the 1970s, and across the country, individuals such as Kathryn Kuhlman and Frederick Eikerenkoetter II, also called Reverend Ike, continued operations. Moving into the 1980s, Jim and Tammy Faye Bakker started the *Praise the Lord* telecast, and ministers such as Creflo Dollar began to expand their cultural influence through religious broadcasting. Men and women, black and white, nondenominational and neopentecostal, televangelism was in no way one-dimensional. These ministers and their ministries coupled religious broadcasting with books, in-person appearances, and other marketing-based strategies to gain name recognition. In the increasingly crowded market of religious programming, not all of the televangelists employed the same methodologies. Neither did they present their religious messages in the same way. More and more, higher ratings and larger audiences became central to the success of the televangelist enterprise, and those audiences constituted a significant political block as President Ronald Reagan came to office in the 1980s and as evangelicals became particularly animated about the culture wars.[5]

Significantly, the 1980s were also a decade of controversy for televangelism, as the Bakkers and Jimmy Swaggart were embroiled in financial and sexual scandals. Around the same time, Pat Robertson's presidential campaign in 1988 led to the lumping of televangelist scandals with the convergence of religion and right-wing politics. As a result, televangelism as an enterprise and televangelists themselves underwent a crisis of credibility. People for the American Way (PFAW), for example, distributed a pamphlet in the late 1980s for the "Media Fairness Project"; featuring images of religious conservatives Robertson, Jerry Falwell, and James Robison, the pamphlet targeted the "moral majoritarians: urging their nationwide audiences to view anyone who disagrees with them as a sinner and anyone who won't conform to their narrow orthodoxy as un-American." In an interview, PFAW founder Norman Lear criticized televangelists as "manipulators to the extreme who use those good people, for their purposes, for their own power-grabbing, political purposes." Solidified as never before by the late 1980s, the commingling of televangelism with conservative politics coupled with public religious controversy meant that televangelism's legacy remained suspect well into the twenty-first century.[6]

Colorado pastor and National Association of Evangelicals president Ted Haggard's drastic fall from grace in 2007 in conjunction with suspected drug use and sexual encounters with a male escort further tarnished televangelism's reputation. That same year, Senator Charles Grassley (R-Iowa), under the auspices of the Senate's Finance Committee, called for a congressional investigation into the financial holdings and spending habits of several well-known prosperity televangelists that included Creflo Dollar, Eddie Long, Joyce Meyer, Paula White, Kenneth Copeland, and Benny Hinn. He attributed the committee's interest in the matter to concerns expressed in media reports. Grassley's investigation ended in early 2011 with no televangelist formally charged. Nevertheless, the investigation clearly questioned the credibility of the targeted televangelists, as articulated in letters Grassley exchanged with the Evangelical Council for Financial Accountability (ECFA). He insisted that the ECFA continue "setting standards for accountability and transparency for churches and religious organizations." Grassley's public, inquisitorial critique further presented prosperity preachers and televangelists as money-obsessed, luxuriously living religious frauds.[7]

The televangelist scandals of the 1980s, along with subsequent spectacles and controversies, seemed to spell the end of televangelist enterprises. Yet, as ethnographer of religion Susan Friend Harding writes, the "spectacularizing forces" of the scandals actually made televangelism an enduring cultural presence in American society. She points out that in "the 1980s electronic churches were anomalous, mercurial, protean creatures, at once religious, economic, and political. Far from being premodern relics, atavisms of an earlier age, the televangelists were a late capitalist crossbreed of symbolic production, consumption, and social reproduction." Although rooted in specific cultural and historical circumstances, Harding notes that televangelists artfully portended future change as "harbingers of an emerging political and economic order in which the stakes were collective identities, cultural ideas, and symbols as well as profits, markets, political power, and lost souls." It is true that televangelists are suspect, routinely dismissed, and scathingly critiqued, but they have not disappeared; nor has their programming. It remains on television screens and, largely due to the pioneering efforts of Joel Osteen and many others, highly active across social media and digital platforms.[8]

Osteen's approach to tel-e-vangelism seemed to intuit future developments in religious broadcasting. A 2014 Pew Research Center on Religion and Public Life survey concluded that while generational differences existed between Millennials and Gen Xers in terms of media consumption, electronic religious media has remained attractive to Americans whether delivered through television or in digital formats. New media has not superseded old media. Rather, formats of new media and old media augment one another. This suggests that contemporary televangelists must be both conversant with traditional practice and able to adapt quickly with each new season of technological advancement. Joel's pioneering tel-e-vangelism practices have remained on the cutting edge.[9]

Osteen has learned the tools of the televangelist trade through innovative practice, local religious television programming in Houston, and attending meetings of the National Association of Broadcasters. However, he did not become a tel-e-vangelist of his own accord. Industry knowledge coupled with the advice of ministry colleagues and the expertise of media consultants rooted Joel's tel-e-vangelism in solid ground, ultimately yielding his ascendancy to televangelism's pinnacle.[10]

Joel Osteen: America's New Tel-e-vangelist

During the period that Oral Roberts was a leading neopentecostal televangelist, Osteen learned a great deal from the Tulsa prosperity preacher that would help him achieve his own unparalleled status as a television producer and religious broadcaster. Joel received tremendous benefit from his father's relationship with Roberts. A steady stream of Oral Roberts University–affiliated broadcasting, communications, and programming specialists assisted him with the creation and maintenance of Lakewood's television media. Joel depended on the Tulsa–Houston connection to develop Lakewood's television ministry, and he continued to draw on it as he expanded the church's reach. The simultaneous pastoral- and production-focused strategies of Lakewood's leadership team in the early 2000s combined to shape Joel's imagination well beyond the confines of Houston and the Sunbelt. At the same time, the circumstances of Joel's first decade as Lakewood's television producer—including the widely publicized televangelist scandals of the late 1980s—left an indelible impression on his production-oriented focus. He proved an able student of American religious history and an expert observer of the technological tastes of media consumers, which eventually propelled him into a place of prominence.

Understanding Osteen as a tel-e-vanglist begins with Joel's earliest days as Lakewood's television producer. As his older siblings had done, after graduating from Humble High School in 1981, Joel started college at Oral Roberts University (ORU) in Tulsa. Since he had developed an early interest in cameras and television, he studied broadcasting in Tulsa.

Perhaps homesick, but also embracing an entrepreneurial impulse and imagining the possibility of a future in media production, Joel left ORU and returned to Houston. He was not sure his family would support his leaving college. After all, his siblings had graduated from ORU, and his brother had even completed medical school in Tulsa. Joel recalled that his father supported his move into television programming, although Dodie initially balked at her son's decision to forego college. In time, the family fully embraced his vision to become a television producer. In *Become a Better You*, Joel explained how he sought to bring his occupational desires to fruition:

> From the time I was ten or eleven years old, I was fascinated with television production. I loved the cameras, editing, and the production of television shows and movies. Every part of the process excited me. As a young man, I spent most of my weekends at Lakewood Church. . . . At the time, the church owned some small industrial cameras, and I'd spend all day Saturday playing with the television equipment. I didn't really know how to run it, but I was fascinated by it. I'd turn the camera on and off, unplug it, plug it back in, coil the cables, and get the equipment ready for Sunday. I was passionate about it because it was what came naturally to me. When I got old enough—maybe thirteen or fourteen years of age—I began helping to run the camera during the services; I became pretty good at it, too. In fact, I soon became one of the best cameramen that we had. It wasn't hard for me; quite the contrary, I loved it; to me working behind the camera seemed almost like a hobby. . . . I went to college and studied broadcasting for a year, returned home, and started a full-fledged television ministry at Lakewood Church.[11]

Osteen considered his interest in television production as his appointment with divine destiny. But he also worked assiduously to acquire the tools of the trade to produce his father's television show and firmly establish Lakewood's media ministry.[12]

While Joel did not leave ORU with a degree in hand, he evidently left an impression on those involved with Oral Roberts's television ministry. In 1983, a former Oral Roberts television associate named John Connolly joined Lakewood's staff. An experienced television producer, Connolly mentored Joel through countless hours of hands-on training. "He was knowledgeable, talented, and had a great personality," Joel remembered from Lakewood's early television ministry. "I watched very carefully how he put the programs together and how he chose certain camera shots. I was learning so much from him."[13]

Connolly taught Osteen the mechanics of television production, and alerted him to the performance dimensions of modern televangelism. Recollecting a 1983 suggestion to mute the volume when editing his father's sermons in order to focus on John's performance, Joel wrote that with this exercise he began to discover that "the key to learning how to communicate in television is to turn down the sound and observe the speaker's facial expressions and body language, and then to note the feelings they stir in you." Joel took the suggestion to heart. He canvassed broadcasts and attuned himself further to the intricacies of televangelist performance by "tr[ying] this with several ministers. Some appeared very passionate, but without the sound they came off as angry and intimidating. You didn't want to watch them very long. The ministers who smiled and had a pleasant, unthreatening demeanor were more likely to draw you in even without sound. . . . I do know that people who watch television are more likely to tune into a smiling face than any other." Connolly's coaching and Joel's intense study of televangelism made him readily aware of how viewers perceived television preachers. This awareness no doubt became more acute during the late 1980s when Joel began to understand just what was at stake with a national (and international) television audience.[14]

Surviving VHS tapes of John Osteen's broadcasts document some of Joel's media broadcasting practices and illustrate a variety of approaches he adopted to present Lakewood to the larger television public. One video, a message on positive confession produced in 1988, began and ended with a series of testimonials from an ethnically diverse group of male and female Lakewood members. John and Dodie opened the broadcast with comments on the miraculous nature of religious programming and the verified results of positive confession in the form of Dodie's defeat of cancer. In a broadcast on Christian internal spiritual peace produced in 1989, Dodie stood in Lakewood's pulpit, welcomed the television audience, and then shared the story of a Christian woman who lived in rural Pennsylvania without cable television, but whose friend taped the *John Osteen* show and provided copies. This proved,

Dodie suggested, the miracle of television ministry. After she called John to the stage, Lakewood's pastor began, "Hold up your Bible and make the devil mad and Jesus glad," and then chanted his well-known Bible confession. At the beginning of his message on positive confession, John looked into the camera and stated that he was not a televangelist, but rather a "tele-pastor" whose work was tied to Houston even though it was broadcast across the globe. A shrewd move to distance himself from the televangelist scandals of the era, John's comments distinguished his show from other religious programs. At the broadcast's conclusion, he delivered an evangelistic appeal on the connection between faith in Jesus and spiritual contentment.[15]

John Osteen broadcasts ran in thirty-minute slots, and typically included a segment in which John and Dodie personalized the message with a preview or a summary of its contents, and prayer for viewers. Dodie added a further personal touch by reading viewers' letters to report on healings and spiritual success stories. Rather than performing the healing touch or physically displaying the spiritual victories on screen—the type of programming about which most viewers were skeptical—John and Dodie let viewers speak for themselves. This practice distinguished their broadcast from other television ministries, even as it reflected Joel's programming decisions as Lakewood's media production director. A testimony to Joel's work as a broadcaster, and a preview of his subsequent media activity, a viewer survey conducted in 1990 about religious television listed the *John Osteen* show among the leading televangelist programs.[16]

Equally illustrative of Joel's approach to broadcasting, a mid-1990s "Welcome to Lakewood" video he produced featured an introductory message by John in which he encouraged new members to seek the gift of speaking in tongues, and practice regular church attendance, missionary efforts, healthy living, and consistent tithing. A second segment of the video introduced viewers to the congregation. Joel assembled a rich collection of images to support a description of Lakewood first as a congregation of "people who have come together to share their difficulties, their successes. And most of all their love; love for each other and love for Jesus Christ." The video touted Lakewood's multicultural character and non-denominational identity. Shots of congregational worship, Bible distribution, prison ministry, children's ministry, the Tribe of Judah motorcycle fellowship, deaf ministry, evangelistic outreach, the church's bookstore, Joel with headphones working busily in the television control room, and John greeting Lakewood members—including a young boy with Down's syndrome—aimed to present the church as a place of buzzing activity, religious outreach, and inclusion and acceptance. The video ended with biographical clips of John and Dodie's life, followed by the 1993 evangelistic documentary *Death & Beyond*, a show that Joel had produced.[17]

Additional evidence of Joel's work as a tel-e-vangelist comes from his own broadcasts, which he has continued to produce in his nearly two-decade preaching career. In conjunction with media consultants, Osteen has constructed taglines to express the core of his message. Early in his preaching career, Lakewood's tagline was "We Believe in New Beginnings." In cooperation with media consultant Phil Cooke, discussed more extensively below, Joel's "new beginnings" mantra encapsulated his emphasis on second chances, while it also literally narrated a comparison between Osteen's ministry and that of his father's. Osteen put the tagline into a song, which played at Lakewood's services and introduced each cassette tape message he distributed. "At Lakewood Church we're here for you. We believe in new beginnings, we believe in you!" the song exclaimed.[18]

Once Joel had settled on positive thinking and positive confession rooted in the notions of possibility and hope, he launched a new tagline: "Discover the Champion in You." This phrase communicated not just a fresh start, but also a message of triumph and victory. A "Discover the Champion in You" music video presented a message that captured Joel's central teaching themes. The song included the following lyrics, sung by Lakewood musician Cindy Cruse Ratcliff: "Till we see the new horizons, believing the best is yet to come. Yeah! You're an overcomer, more than a conqueror, called to be a champion in life. All things are possible, and every river's crossable. At Lakewood, discover the champion in you." Coupled with images of individuals, words appeared onscreen to drive the message home: "new horizon," "the best," "overcomer," "conqueror," "champion," "life," "possible," and "Lakewood."[19]

In the video, Osteen presented images of ordinary Houstonians—including members of the extended Osteen family—all of whom smiled or appeared exceptionally happy. A racially and ethnically diverse assembly of people accurately reflected Houston's demographics, while it also communicated to viewers outside of Houston that ordinary people not only deserved a second chance, but had achieved success via adoption of Joel's message of victory. The images showed that people came to Lakewood from everywhere in Houston. The introductory scenes ended with Joel and Victoria, arm in arm against a backdrop of Houston's skyline, offering a welcoming smile to viewers. The Osteen family had discovered their inner champion, and encouraged others to achieve the same state of mind.[20]

The sermon portions of Osteen's videos included wide-angle screen shots of Lakewood's interior, as well as row shots of Lakewood members listening intently. Television broadcasts typically excised the musical performances. As a production of Joel Osteen Ministries, the thirty-minute broadcast focused on Joel. Early on, in what would become a mainstay of his broadcasts, Osteen included a welcome message thanking viewers for tuning in and inviting them to visit Lakewood in Houston. At the broadcast's conclusion, not unlike that of the *John Osteen* telecast, Joel made a formal statement on the Christian gospel of Jesus' life, death, and resurrection, followed by an affirmation of faith and belief and the born-again experience. This part of the broadcast not only underscored Osteen's evangelical credentials, but also tied it to central themes of his overall message, second chances and starting over—the Pentecost of Lakewood's institutional DNA. The visuals that Joel chose for his broadcast communicated that his success resulted from applying the advice his own message offered. As Osteen wrote in his 2014 book *You Can, You Will*, he took considerable care in the production of his broadcast. "We're in a very competitive marketplace," Joel admitted. "If you're not growing, improving, and learning new skills, then you're falling behind." To enhance the value of his broadcast, Osteen revealed that every Sunday afternoon he and the production team edited his sermons for television. "I've done over 625 messages in fifteen years," he calculated. "I'm constantly evaluating and analyzing not only my speaking performance, but also the production, the lighting, and the camera angles." Coupled with his editing experience from the *John Osteen* show, Joel's media training and expertise is unparalleled among prosperity gospel preachers.[21]

While one part of Osteen's rationale for rescripting American televangelism literally focused on considerations about how a smile, other facial expressions, and even bodily postures in front of the camera affected perceptions and ratings, he consciously sought to produce noncontroversial shows such as *John Osteen*, and later his own broadcasts, to which viewers would turn their attention. For all of the reasons stated above, Joel knew that as a result of the storied scandals of the 1980s, television viewers, whether Christian or not, harbored profound skepticism about television preachers. Too many had used the camera and the stage to solicit money, Joel reasoned, or preached one thing in the pulpit, such as sexual purity, but engaged in adulterous liaisons outside of the camera's view. Moreover, preachers who gallivanted across a stage, screamed frightfully about sin, or demonstratively slayed people in the Spirit, for many seemed more about entertainment than respectful worship. Most controversially, South African pastor Rodney Howard-Browne's identification as the "Holy Ghost bartender" and the manifestations of laughing, jerking, ticking, roaring, or even barking in the Spirit associated with the Toronto and Brownsville revivals of the 1990s passed as at best gimmicky, at worst bizarrely strange. As a full-time television producer of religious programming while such events transpired, and as a keen student of American religious culture—not to mention the criticism of televangelists that dated back to the movement's earliest days—Osteen knew of viewers' reservations about and profound suspicion of televangelists. Queried by Larry King on his show about the topic of television preachers requesting money, Osteen stated, "When we started way back with my father back in 1983, we made the decision not to [ask for money]. . . . Not that that's wrong, but I didn't want to do anything that would turn people off, because I know people are skeptical [of televangelists] anyway."[22]

Osteen's comments to Larry King suggested that he clearly grasped the power of televangelism, as well as its potential and its pitfalls. As a result, upon launching his own television ministry, he devoted considerable energy to cultivating a distinct message and a unique persona across the airwaves. In this way, Joel embodied Lakewood's themes of both personality and prosperity, putting his own stamp on them. Perhaps the label "smiling preacher" speaks to Osteen's achievement in this regard. While his smile secured his spot as one of America's most famous ministers, the ministry and media experts who advised Joel over the years also played an integral part in his tel-e-vangelism.

Christian media consultant, innovator, and critic Phil Cooke has advised Osteen over the years of his work in television production. With a friendship and partnership that dates back to the late 1980s, during the early 2000s Cooke and Osteen's synergy translated into Joel's successful presence across many media platforms. Drawing on Cooke's years of experience, the successful equation that Cooke and Osteen have seemingly perfected has been one part branding and marketing, and one part cultivating and maintaining a deep and perpetual media literacy. An effective and inspirational leader, Cooke has pointed out, is vital to the maintenance of the brand. "I speak the language of Christianity, and I also speak the language of media," Cooke wrote in his book *Branding Faith*. "I don't believe there's simply a connection between branding and religion; I believe that religious experience is what the core of branding is all about."[23]

For Cooke, the need for religious leaders to proceed thoughtfully and strategically about visibility in today's global age is vital at a time when people are both highly skeptical of televangelists as well as possessed of more choices across the cable programming and digital media landscapes. In his book *The Last TV Evangelist*, Cooke asserted that "the new media world is about connection, community, and conversation. It's about being networked . . . *change isn't coming—it's here*." The immediacy of connection in today's world also suggests, Cooke contended, that perception is critical. The case that Cooke used to illustrate the power of perception was an early moment in Joel's ministry in which he attempted to develop an innovative branding approach "that would capture Joel's unique gifts and brand story." Cooke explained that he and Osteeen settled on "We Believe in New Beginnings." By helping Joel to identify core themes of his teaching, Cooke masterfully succeeded in equipping the smiling preacher to effectively deliver his message as a tel-e-evangelist, whether it was through quality cameras and recording equipment, the proper positioning of lighting, or hiring expert practitioners of digital religious media.[24]

The influence of Cooke's approach to marketing and ministry was apparent on Osteen's broadcasts. Media studies scholar Mara Einstein singles out the successful script format of Osteen's religious programming—both on television and online. A joke or funny comment followed by the Bible confession always started the sermon. Einstein points out that church camera operators used a combination of wide-angle camera shots to display Lakewood's large scale, and screens of individual members or attendees worked to personalize the viewer's experience. A message bathed in positive advice and encouraging comments shaped the sermon's content, and advertisements punctuated the telecast: upcoming NOH events, special offers on books and messages, and reminders about the ministry's online presence. Osteen's website secured a viable digital presence, writes Einstein, with easily navigable links and accessible information about free ministry resources and products to purchase. Moreover, in the late 1990s Joel purchased a Houston television station, KTBU (called "The Tube"), for $2 million, where he then worked as general manager. KTBU provided Osteen with more broadcasting capabilities for Lakewood's religious programming. Eventually, Joel's pastoral duties demanded significant time, and ownership of a local television channel was less necessary for broadcasting once Lakewood acquired its own in-house production capabilities. Osteen sold The Tube for $30.5 million in 2006, and thereafter, according to Osteen's brother-in-law Don Iloff, paid off some of Lakewood's debt. In the end, the consistent formulas for marketing that Cooke supported, coupled with a philosophy of adaptability that kept Osteen nimble and flexible in a changing media marketplace, made Joel, to use Einstein's phrase, an ever-present "brand of faith."[25]

Another minister and marketing expert, Duncan Dodds, also proved central to Osteen's emergence as a tel-e-vangelist. Dodds, who served as Lakewood's executive director from the late 1990s until the early 2000s, possessed a unique skill set as an ordained Southern Baptist minister and a marketing specialist. Dodds's many accomplishments as the church's executive director included helping to create the specific "Joel" brand to popularize Osteen outside of Houston and the articulation of a biblical rationale for Lakewood's branding and missionary outlooks.

At Lakewood, Dodds's inauguration of Joel Osteen Ministries and the moniker "Joel" proceeded from a critical marketing perspective that sought to associate ideas with products. At a church leader's conference in 2006 that offered an inside look at Lakewood operations, Dodds queried the participants in a breakout session on marketing to identify products associated with particular words. When asked to identify luxury cars, members of the group blurted out "Lexus!" and "BMW!"

When Dodds mentioned coffee, many in the session intuitively stated "Starbucks!" Dodds then said boldly and provocatively that when people thought of religion in America he wanted "Joel" to come to their minds and roll off their lips. In effect, Dodds strategically started Joel Osteen Ministries to leverage Osteen's influence as far and as wide as possible. True to form, Lakewood ministry events outside of Houston have emphasized Joel Osteen Ministries. The pulpit from which Joel preaches when he travels does not have the Lakewood logo with an "L" on it, but an oval design with an "O" or a "J" in the middle.[26]

Combining his fields of expertise, Dodds articulated the need for a focused branding strategy with biblical concepts related to the evangelical imperative for missionary work. He insisted that brands had to be "tangible" and "appeal to the senses." A smile is certainly tangible, and as Joel himself has stated, it communicates visually in powerful ways. From an institutional view, Dodds suggested that a vertical alignment of a church's message succeeds when the "[p]astor says it, [the c]hurch reflects it, [and the] members say it." In turn, effective media engagement assisted in communicating the message, while an "experience" at Lakewood or a Joel Osteen Ministries event, or through television, in essence "deliver[ed]" the brand's promise. Moreover, a message's "continuity" across a variety of mediums or "platforms" rooted its brand in a particular market. In accordance with this methodology, Dodds supported a marketing blitz for Osteen's books. In 2007, for example, upon the release of *Become a Better You*, for five straight days, book excerpts appeared in the *Houston Chronicle* and Joel appeared on numerous morning and evening talk shows, including *Larry King Live*. This practice continued for Joel's subsequent publications, for which Dodds helped to transform immediate saturation into broader media exposure and higher sales.[27]

While as a marketer, Dodds excelled at innovation, as an ordained pastor he has linked his motivation and outlook to the Bible. The New Testament book of Acts describes the evangelistic imperative of "making disciples" in terms of the spread of the Christian message outward from Jerusalem: "ye shall be witnesses unto me both in Jerusalem, and in all Judaea, and in Samaria, and unto the uttermost part of the earth" (Acts 1:8). In Dodds's formulation of marketing Joel's message, "Jerusalem" stood for the local market, "Judea" was the market of regional churches in Texas that have competed with Lakewood, "Samaria" translated into the national media market, and the "uttermost" related to Joel's message in the global context. During Dodds's tenure at Lakewood, Joel began a series of daily "e-votionals" that arrived at subscribers' inboxes with a short, positive thought and a prayer for blessing. In addition, Lakewood's extensive web site has hosted daily and weekly events, and Joel and other Lakewood staff have blogged about church events, offered encouragement, and disseminated spiritual wisdom for all those who are interested. Dodds also assisted in the inauguration of the NOH preaching and ministry events that since 2004 have been held across the nation and around the globe.[28]

A YouTube channel and Facebook page, along with iTunes, Instagram, and SiriusXM, have delivered Joel's message into additional markets. With the exception of Instagram, which updates with new images, the content on each of these platforms is rarely original. It is mostly derivative material from Osteen's sermons and publications, repackaged for the appropriate format. SiriusXM has aired the content of previously presented sermons, live sermons, and even NOH events. Osteen messages run twenty-four hours a day. An unscripted call-in feature on Osteen's channel called *Joel Osteen Live*, which broadcasts from a radio studio inside Lakewood Church, has added unique content to this platform. About his radio venture, Osteen has expressed a rationale similar to that he has given for his television broadcasts: "We're reaching a whole new group of people. . . . We've done church services, on-the-road events, books, but we've never done radio. . . . Our outreach is to people who don't necessarily go to church. . . . SiriusXM has such a broad reach. It was very interesting, and here we are today." It seems that Osteen's media work has come full circle now that he is on satellite radio, a fitting new direction for a tel-e-vangelist committed both to an evangelical message and to media innovation. In a sense, Osteen has "redeem[ed] the dial," as historian Tona Hangen describes the history of religious radio.[29]

While marketing and ministry consultants assisted in the creation of Joel Osteen Ministries and launched specific strategies to leverage and expand Lakewood's reach, additional mediacentric practices in which Joel engaged further exemplified his novel and timely execution of tel-e-vangelism. He took great care, for instance, to design a television friendly stage and seating arrangement before Lakewood moved into the Compaq Center.

In *Your Best Life Now*, Joel alluded to design and architectural strategies for religious programming. "A few years before my dad went to be with the Lord, we decided that we were going to remodel the platform area at Lakewood Church," he explained. "At the time, I was working behind the scenes in the television production department [and] I wanted the new set to look the best that it possibly could. We worked several months with the architects and the designers, and after they got it all drawn up, I had a mock-up made of everything. I wanted to see it through the camera before we built anything permanently." Soon the design team situated a massive revolving globe on stage, illustrative of John's affection for missionary work. A specially designed podium for John appeared next, which the design crew "sized . . . just for him, fine-tuning every detail. When we got it all built, we spent several weeks working on the lighting." About ten years later, Osteen applied the same fastidiousness at the Compaq Center when it was time to create a new stage.[30]

Lakewood's acquisition of the former sports arena not only provided a new visibility for the church along one of the city's and the nation's busiest thoroughfares, it also offered Osteen a unique opportunity as a tel-e-vangelist to design a viewer-friendly space that would welcome thousands of worshipers and images of which would be beamed into millions of homes. Intimately involved in the creative process, Joel worked closely with one of the church's production specialists, Jon Swearingen. An ORU graduate, Swearingen learned broadcasting with the Oral Roberts television team. He came to Lakewood in 1991, worked under Joel for nearly a decade before John passed away, and was promoted to an executive production position when Joel assumed pastoral duties. Over the years, Swearingen found production inspiration from Grand Old Opry shows, music videos, and evangelical Hillsong worship from Australia. Influences on his directing included Roger Flessing and Greg Flessing, brothers who worked on Billy Graham's television endeavors. Moreover, Swearingen counted Phil Cooke as a friend and mentor.[31]

Given his training with one of the more important neopentecostal televangelists in Tulsa, Swearingen's role at Lakewood has resulted in additional chart-topping religious programming. His meticulous preparation for Lakewood's broadcast created compelling television by what he described as "letting the viewer feel like they're in the room." According to Swearingen, "the subject of [the] sermon is the pastor," and therefore camera angles and camera shots have focused on members who are engaged in the service, listening intently. He also orchestrated congregational shots to document "the vastness of the room" and create images that conveyed Osteen's popularity. On a 2006 tour of the worship center at Lakewood's ministry conference, Swearingen led guests from the back of the sanctuary to the stage. He pointed up to his left and right at the stationary cameras. He discussed the lighting, tripod cameras, and the control desk toward the back of the worship space. He mentioned how the sanctuary seating was intentionally sloped to focus both viewer and worshiper on the stage, and therefore on Joel. While on stage, he pointed to the choir seating and its design with the moving platform for Lakewood's band. About the production of Joel's weekly broadcast, Swearingen explained how the production team zeroed in on sound, stage movement, and shots of the crowd and audience, and the need to provide an experience and present a story to viewers. He mentioned that he typically attended Lakewood for the Saturday evening service, the first of three weekend gatherings at Lakewood, so that on Sunday, with a service participant's knowledge, he could more effectively direct the production before editing it with Joel in preparation for the television broadcast. Swearingen also adopted the same methodology for Joel Osteen Ministries' NOH events. For example, he visited Nationals Park in Washington, D.C., no less than eight times in order to assess camera angles and other factors that would be crucial to his production. While Swearingen provided an insider's perspective on Lakewood's design and its intentional enhancement of television production value, his comments offered an illuminating backdrop to contemporary developments in church architecture and religious broadcasting.[32]

The process of careful calculations by which Osteen, Swearingen, and the design teams refashioned the Compaq Center's interior into Lakewood's worship space reflected historic evangelical architectural practice even as it prized innovation for a twenty-first-century audience. According to historian Charity Carney, the populist nature of Osteen's message, which offered a spiritual teaching for everyone, coupled with an accessible architectural style paralleled historic patterns of evangelists such as Charles Grandison Finney, who preached at Broadway Chapel during the Second Great Awakening revivals of the 1800s. The modern mega-church, as religious studies scholar Jeanne Halgren Kilde points out, presents an important site in which to understand the complex intersec-tion of religious and cultural trends. Considerations of a megachurch's location and how a congregation communicates its message to the world connect intimately, she writes. For Kilde, understanding the lighting, design, projection screens, and the overall focus on production both ac-centuate individual religious meaning and provide for a "shared experi-ence" between participants and viewers. Thus, the "transversal areas" of a megachurch's interior, especially the interior as seen on camera, say as much about the message as the articulated sermon itself. Carney's his-torical observation and Kilde's spatial analysis help to explain Joel's pin-nacle position as a tel-e-vangelist. His extensive background in religious programming and television production, which is not shared by the ma-jority of contemporary prosperity gospel televangelists, equipped him to not only deliver a religious message, but also a predictable, inviting, and innovative experience onscreen. Joel's coupling of religious television with new media at a heightened historical moment of digital innovation in the early 2000s powerfully defined his tel-e-vangelism and has made him one of the most powerful pastors in American Christianity.[33]

An elaborate ceremony led by Joel's brother Paul Osteen when Lakewood moved into the Compaq Center in 2005 illustrates how a television-friendly auditorium combined with specific design choices to present the smiling preacher's place in the congregation's history. Paul deployed Old Testament biblical symbolism punctuated by family testimonies that recognized Joel's debt to Lakewood's past while simul-taneously archiving his place in the church's larger story. Paul reminded attendees that just as the children of Israel once made a historical pas-sage into the Promised Land as Yahweh provided dry ground on which to pass through the Jordan River, Lakewood had remade the former Compaq Center into a site for God's work in the present age. Before the Israelites completed the journey, Paul pointed out, the Israelite leader Joshua gathered rocks from the Jordan River's dry bed, which he assembled into a physical reminder of provision, protection, and blessing so that subsequent generations could find inspiration from the recollection of miraculous moments. Assembling various "stones" of Lakewood's past across the church's wide stage, the grandchildren of John and Dodie Osteen presented various artifacts of the church's past. Paul emphasized the spiritual significance of the selected material objects. A pair of John's dress shoes symbolized a bold pastor who not only stepped out in faith but also a compassionate minister who lived and walked through life with great faith. A chair from Lakewood's original location was intended to remind the faithful about the congregation's "humble beginnings," sparse in resources but rich in faith and hope. Another chair from the church's previous campus symbolized the "sawdust trail" that many repentant individuals walked at Lakewood to discover newfound faith. An Oasis of Love bumper sticker recalled the church's open arms and open doors to all. A display of John's tattered, marked-up Bible demonstrated deep fidelity to Christianity's sacred text. Contrasting the ministries of John and Joel while he suggested a certain spiritual continuity, Paul stated that "God found another man who was willing to leave his comfort zone and find his God-given destiny. . . . [Joel] leads with skillful hands and he leads with integrity of heart." An oversized golden key with "December 1, 2003" and the Lakewood logo covering the Compaq Center logo served as a final material reminder that the church stood in the good graces of Houston politicians who approved a multimillion-dollar lease of the former sports arena. While church leaders used the 2005 opening day ceremony to interpret the church's new future as the supernatural orchestrations of divine favor, the church's bountiful financial resources also funded accomplished lobbyist Dave Walden in his efforts to persuade city officials to approve Lakewood's move into the business district of Greenway Plaza.[34]

If architectural, visual, and performance aspects of Lakewood's physical location helped to forward Joel's message through creative religious broadcasting, then an important digital resource also helped him to realize his innovative vision as a tel-e-vangelist. Expanding upon John's use of print magazines as a ministry resource, several years into his preaching career Joel launched *HFT* magazine through Joel Osteen Ministries. More akin to *Manna* than *Praise* for its spiritually focused articles, advertisements, and television listings as opposed to testimonies about speaking in tongues or divine healing, *HFT*'s innovative digital format provided for a crisp delivery of content and its online availability no doubt led to wider distribution. By 2013, Joel exhibited a fresh media approach; he ditched the digital PDF delivery of *HFT* and instead made the magazine available on Apple's iPod and iPhone, in Android, and through Amazon's Kindle Fire.

The standard format for each *HFT* issue included articles by Joel, Victoria, Dodie, and Paul. Occasional contributions from Lakewood's first Spanish-speaking pastor, Marcos Witt, and music leaders Da'dra Greathouse and Cindy Cruse Ratcliff provided readers with a diversity of voices and distinct spiritual advice. Running advertisements on the magazine's footer announced new NOH events, Joel's latest book, the television broadcast schedule, and a link to donate money to Joel Osteen Ministries. Ads sprinkled the magazine for Dodie's book *Choosing Life* and Lisa's book *You Are Made for More!* along with the *Hope for Today Bible*. For a more personalized touch, each issue included a video testimony from a Lakewood member or ministry leader, or printed statements from readers about overcoming a difficulty or achieving spiritual growth. An occasional video announced a new pastor or ministry leader at Lakewood, providing biographical details and interesting facts about their preparation for service to the church. In addition, links to "Stay Connected, Be Blessed" promised the spiritual value of digital technology in the form of podcasts and "Today's Word," the daily e-votional. A special contributor category, "Champion of Hope," called readers to make an even bigger spiritual impact with a larger donation, in exchange for specialized ministry resources.

To illustrate the range of *HFT* contents, in 2012 Lakewood music leader Da'dra Greathouse, member of the gospel duo Anointed, shared painful memories of childhood bullying to explain how the biblical principle of "overcoming lies with the truth" led ultimately to a loving marriage and award-winning musical career. "I didn't know it back then," she explained, "but these were all seeds of lies that the enemy planted to hinder my growth and progress in life. Why? Because he knows that if I rejected those lies and believed the truth about who God says I am, then I would flourish and accomplish many things that would oppose his operation in the lives of many people." In nearly every issue Paul Osteen, a physician, included an anecdotal account from his medical missionary work in Africa. In stories from Kenya and Cameroon, he discussed seemingly insurmountable medical conditions, overcome through both surgical skill and the spiritual work of prayer.[35]

It is now common for televangelists to employ multiple strategies of marketing, product placement, and visibility to leverage the widest possible influence across the media and digital landscape. However, Joel Osteen was the first tel-e-vangelist who most effectively harnessed his message of second chances to the broad range of new media choices. Social media's ubiquity across today's vast and growing digital landscape overshadows the very short history of its rapid emergence. iTunes only arrived in 2001, Facebook became public in 2004, and the following year YouTube hit the digital scene. Twitter launched in 2006, and Instagram became available in 2010. Osteen understood that finding a spot on each of these media platforms as they came into existence was necessary to stay competitive. At the same time, he and his ministry colleagues articulated a spiritual rationale for Lakewood and Joel Osteen Ministries' media choices. While Joel has explained that through prayer he considers the strategy of ministry operations and business decisions, he has also read the media world with the eyes of an expert and has executed choices on the digital frontier that have outshined those of his competition. While Joel had television production experience and a keen approach to religious programming, Phil Cooke, Duncan Dodds, and Jon Swearingen lent their expertise to the smiling preacher and participated collectively in the construction of a message for a diversity of platforms. As a tel-e-vangelist, Osteen's method of messaging has depended heavily on technology, but it has also involved a more traditional method of expression: that of the traveling evangelist.

The New Camp Meeting: Joel Osteen's Night of Hope

The creation of Osteen's NOH events is also part of his work as a tel-e-vangelist. Since 2004, once per month he has visited arenas and sports stadiums in the U.S. and abroad to host NOH meetings. In essence, the camp meeting of the twenty-first century—a historical reference to the inventive outreach procedures of traveling evangelists during the nineteenth century's Second Great Awakening—part of the logic behind NOH was to circulate Joel Osteen Ministries outside of Houston. But the NOH events also reserved space for a short presentation of Lakewood's history along with a concertlike musical accompaniment. As the events developed during their first decade, Osteen's approach adapted to the localities in which NOH meetings took place. In addition, several times per year Lakewood members traveled to NOH events and conducted charitable work in local communities, what the church called a "Servolution." Selected stadium events dubbed "Historic Night of Hope" (HNH) in locations such as Chicago, New York City, and Washington, D. C., highlighted Lakewood's Servolution through a television partnership with Trinity Broadcasting Network. Mirroring the historic practices of Oral Roberts's traveling ministry, Osteen began to host HNH events with local pastors in the cities where HNH travelled. At HNH events, pastors sat on stage, and then offered prayers during the festivities. Additionally, employing Osteen's tel-e-vangelism methodology, in conjunction with live broadcasts, simulcast HNH events by Joel Osteen Ministries hosted real-time online chats. Thus, a close relationship between Osteen's message and its media has come to define his original, timely approach to tel-e-vangelism.[36]

One of the first NOH events, at the time called an "Evening with Joel Osteen," and the first recorded and DVD-distributed meeting took place at Madison Square Garden in late October 2004. Remarkably, New York City government officials recognized Osteen's presence at the NOH. Frederick Lewis, special assistant to the Manhattan borough president, named Thursday, October 21, and Friday, October 22, 2004, "Joel Osteen Day" in New York City. The event, held on Friday night, began with praise music by Lakewood musicians Israel Houghton and Cindy Cruse Ratcliff. Dodie shared her story of defeating cancer and Joel's brother Paul offered a short meditation on the story of the prodigal son, followed by an altar call—just like the historic camp meeting and complete with a dramatized reunion of a loving father and a wayward son. Osteen's message of hope emphasized the importance of positive thinking and positive confession. "If you will see it and you will say it," Joel stated, "then I know God will begin to work supernaturally in your life."[37]

The 2004 NOH event was full of symbolism and intersected with key points in American religious history. For example, Joel's sermon in New York City that year, not unlike that of another well-known New York minister from a previous era, Norman Vincent Peale, focused ultimately on the power of positive thinking. As we have seen, Osteen's articulation of positive thinking rests partly on Peale's legacy of presenting a message of encouragement and hope. Whether or not Osteen intentionally chose positive thinking as that night's topic is uncertain; more than likely, he simply reprised a theme of his book *Your Best Life Now*, released just before the NOH event. However, the New York City nexus of Osteen and Peale's positive thinking is striking. It is also notable that Osteen chose Madison Square Garden to record live an early NOH meeting. Almost five decades previous, in 1957, Billy Graham led a four-month-long crusade in New York City, one of his most important and enduring evangelistic campaigns. Live recordings of Graham's sermons went out across the airwaves and beamed into viewers' homes. As historian Grant Wacker notes in his biography of Graham, the 1957 Madison Square Garden campaign proved to be a turning point in Graham's use of media and technology to leverage influence and present his message. Similarly, Osteen's Madison Square Garden NOH, and the fact that it coincided with the publication of his first book, proved determinative for his national notoriety. Furthermore, Lakewood producer Jon Swearingen's admitted acquaintance with Billy Graham's media practices revealed a singularly calculating, and successful, association of Osteen's future with Graham's legacy.[38]

The successful execution of the first recorded NOH event mirrored future innovations and practices that have assured the attraction of NOH events to viewers and attendees alike. Two of Osteen's NOH events in Texas illustrate these practices and innovations.

A 2006 event in the central Texas city of Killeen confirmed the power of Osteen's appeal. As it was located close to one of America's most important Army bases, Fort Hood, Osteen knew military personnel and their families would show up to the Bell County Expo Center. Inside the arena, the smell of pretzels and popcorn mixed with eager anticipation, the buzz of people, and tables set up with Osteen books, tapes, and CDs for sale. Short videos with images of urban and suburban spaces along with landscape shots of a Southwestern theme, all centered on texts of Bible verses, grabbed attendees' attention while they waited for the main program. In addition, advertisements encouraging attendees to financially and prayerfully collaborate with Joel Osteen Ministries flashed across the screen. Finally, a recorded testimonial by someone who attributed release from prison and recovery from addiction to Osteen and his church added to the crowd's anticipation.[39]

Similar to the large majority of NOH events, at the central Texas meeting Cindy Cruse Ratcliff and her musical attachment led attendees in thirty minutes of praise songs, punctuated by Dodie's testimony and Victoria's short sermon from Jeremiah 29:11. Victoria stated that Lakewood prayed regularly for military spouses, and Joel's sister Lisa delivered a special message to the military personnel in attendance. With the crowd on its feet to show respect and with a U.S. flag displayed prominently on the large screen behind the main stage, Lakewood's music team followed the military message with a resounding "God Bless America." Joel's message came next. He crafted a sermon from Psalm 91:11. With military and national defense references discernible, Osteen preached that sometimes God had sent angels as secret agents to deliver messages and protect the faithful. Above all, he encouraged hearers to stay faithful and believe in God's ultimate protection.[40]

A 2011 NOH event in Texas rehearsed a very similar script in terms of music and format—although in Corpus Christi, Osteen emphasized growing faith in second chances. "God is the God of another chance," he preached. He identified 2011 as a "resurrection year" and spoke in support of a new initiative in which he and Lakewood had become involved: Save the Children. The charity participated in humanitarian projects across the globe, and Osteen not only encouraged attendees to donate to Save the Children, but also promised a blessing in return for giving. Personalizing the message, both he and Victoria described their "adoption" of children from the charity, and how they contributed prayerfully and financially to each child's future. The Osteens emphasized the importance of "investing in another human being" and bringing food, clothing, and education to impoverished areas across the globe. Artfully associating the Christian concept of resurrection with personal, individual change, Osteen characterized support for Save the Children as making possible the resurrection of endangered youth from bleak circumstances.[41]

Building on the popularity of NOH events, Osteen's HNH programs brought the new camp meeting into a stadium setting. HNH meetings included a brief history of Lakewood Church, a short presentation about how Joel and Victoria met, and a recitation of how Dodie conquered cancer. Joel's messages reflected his focus on thinking positive thoughts and making positive, verbal confessions. For the events, he and the Lakewood team first visited Yankee Stadium, followed by an event on the West Coast at Dodger Stadium. In August 2011, Osteen held a HNH meeting at Cellular Field, where the Chicago White Sox play, and organized a similar event in Jerusalem that same year. At the Los Angeles event, for example, he emphasized the importance of positive thinking and encouraged the faithful to "train your mind to think about what is right," since "[y]our life is going to follow your thoughts." For the Chicago meeting, Joel Osteen Ministries designed a separate website about the event with a countdown screen, links to purchase tickets, and a live chat option once the event started. This heralded a new interactive feature for the HNH events. Moreover, each of the HNH events, unlike the typical NOH meetings, aired live on the Trinity Broadcasting Network.[42]

The Jerusalem event introduced an additional feature, a new message taken from the New Testament book of Hebrews that presented a roster of exemplary individuals to whom Joel referred as the "hall of faith." Osteen innovatively concluded the hall of faith with his father John as a member of the illustrious group. In his discussion of this hall of faith, Osteen stated that "all the saints of old are pulling for us" and "cheering us on." If these faith heroes offered contemporary testimonies, Joel preached, King David, who as the Bible records slayed Goliath, encouraged the defeat of life's "giants" and emphasized a life of faith to overcome and conquer difficulties. The Old Testament figure of Joseph, said Osteen, had his future planned out until he was sold into slavery. Osteen averred that Joseph's life taught that in dreams deferred, God ultimately set right life's future course. "God is a God of another chance," Joel exclaimed. He also pointed to Rahab, a Jericho prostitute whose positive life transformation reflected "a testimony of God's mercy" as a "trophy of God's grace." Job, who the Old Testament indicates lost everything, eventually received double what disappeared; therefore, Osteen stated, Christians should pray and believe for "twice as more." Turning to the New Testament, he told the story of the evangelists Paul and Silas, who exhibited joy despite persecution and incarceration; about Lazarus, Osteen emphasized the account of his miraculous return to life— exemplifying a "resurrection year" of second chances. Finally, while he choked up and battled tears, Joel told the story of his father's rise from poverty to plenty, from destitution to a life in God filled with faith and renewed purpose. "I can hear my father still cheering us on," he said.[43]

Coupled with his new hall of faith theme, in Jerusalem Joel also focused on positive confession. "[Y]ou [have] got to act like you're blessed to be blessed," he exhorted, because God will cease his blessings "if you have a poor mouth." Joel counseled deeper faith to keep a positive outlook in the midst of life's vicissitudes. "If you don't speak to your storm it will speak to you," he said. He reminded his audience that by literally speaking to one's difficult circumstances, "God's word coming out of your mouth is alive and full of power." He concluded with a dramatic recorded message set in front of the location where Christians believe Jesus was buried and from where they contend he was resurrected. Echoing the traditional end of his regular television broadcast, Joel stated:

> I'm not here to condemn anybody, but here to help you find a new beginning. It's so easy. Your sins have already been forgiven, the price has already been paid, Jesus has died, he's risen again, and now you have the opportunity to receive him. If you believe on the Lord Jesus it talks about how you will be saved. Another scripture says that if you call on the name of the Lord you shall be saved. So I want you to know today that God is standing before you with his arms held open wide. He's not mad at you. As I said, your sins have already been forgiven. All you've got to do is accept the free gift of Christ's salvation. Will you do it today? . . . We don't come to Christ because we're perfect. None of us would've had a chance. You come to him just as you are . . . the scripture says today is the day of salvation.[44]

As Osteen declared on his television broadcast, "Know today the moment you prayed, the scripture says God forgave all your sins. That means that you are starting afresh and anew, with a fresh, clean slate." He continued, "Get up every day knowing that God is smiling down on you. Talk to him. Prayer is simply talking to God like you'd talk to your best friend . . . then I'd encourage you to read your Bible. You may not understand everything but just read and it will get on the inside. I know when you do that you're going to see amazing things. God's going to take you places that you've never dreamed of." With cameras rolling, at Jesus' tomb Joel simultaneously summarized his sermon and focused on faith. As a master of tel-e-vangelism, he created a stunning visual back-drop in Jerusalem that Christian viewers of the HNH event no doubt found deeply meaningful, exhibiting another innovation that befit his approach to religious programming.

Osteen's NOH and HNH events reflected a creative aspect of his tel-e-vangelism born directly from his experience as a television producer and religious broadcaster. From the speakers and pastors, to the music, to the celebratory and spiritual themes of the messages, NOH and HNH gatherings have emerged as signature elements of Osteen's strategy for achieving and maintaining broad-based popularity. While the carefully planned meetings have generated attention for the smiling preacher out-side of Houston, Osteen's hometown has featured prominently in spe-cific parts of the programming. As the camp meeting of the twenty-first century, the thoughtful orchestration of the NOH and HNH engage-ments speaks to the broader context of contemporary evangelical perfor-mance, what theater scholar Jill Stevenson calls "sensational devotion." Stevenson's formulation of sensational devotion emphasizes the affective aspects of a particular religious brand. However, sensational devotion is not merely about market share, it is about the totality of how a particular institution creates a setting and establishes a context for individuals to have a religious experience. Stevenson explains how in a megachurch the worship space, praise music, sermon, preacher, media, audio/visual elements, and cultural context collectively provoke sensational devotion. The totality of the religious event—the sights, sounds, visual setting, and words spoken or sung—generates attachment and prompts affiliation. In this sense, Stevenson's notion of sensational devotion helps to explain how the NOH and HNH have been important, integral parts of Joel's tel-e-vangelism, and why Osteen and his team have planned these meetings with exquisite precision. Specialized Joel Osteen Ministries events have aimed to offer sensational, indeed unique, experiences, while they have simultaneously endeavored to inspire religious devotion and connection to God.[45]

If Joel has contended that he possesses natural hardwiring for televi-sion production, then the circuitry of his pastoral program has trans-mitted clear signals as America's tel-e-vangelist has taken to Lakewood's stage and preached from many other venues. Working as a television producer during both the heyday and precipitous decline of American televangelism proved ultimately fortuitous for Osteen's ministerial career. He simultaneously learned what did and did not make for effective religious programming. Having forged strategic relationships with media consultants and ministry experts, the combination of Joel's experience and ingenuity with the historical context at the dawn of the digital age paved the way for his effective tel-e-vangelism. Opting to take risks with the new possibilities that social media had to offer, Osteen embraced fully his belief that he was made for TV. At the same time, he decided to stay tied to traditional televangelism while employing historic methods of stadium revivals, arena events, and a radio program. In other words, Joel Osteen the tel-e-vangelist has carefully designed both his message and its media.

Lakewood's Charismatic Core

Healing Hurts, Extending Hope

I was the first miracle at Lakewood Church.
—Lisa Osteen Comes (2009)

In 2009, Lakewood Church celebrated its half-century mark. The commemorative service, punctuated by prayers, praise music, and preaching, simultaneously tracked the church's history and speculated about the next fifty years of the congregation's life. During the festivities, longtime members offered appreciative reflections on what the church meant to them, including former drug addict–turned–motorcycle minister Ben Priest, who attributed to Lakewood both his survival and his salvation.[1]

Dodie Osteen, Joel's mother; Lisa Osteen Comes, his sister; and Joel headlined the event as the evening's main speakers. Joel's sermon, "It's Your Year of Jubilee," underscored the inevitability of divine blessing through "thinking jubilee thoughts." He preached confidently that God's favor and blessing "[is] going to happen faster than you think . . . the word I hear down in my spirit is 'acceleration.'" Lisa followed King David's injunction to "remember" God's goodness by looking back on Lakewood's neopentecostal origins. About her recovery from muscular difficulties at birth, she stated, "God used this miracle to really catapult my parents into the supernatural dimension of God and bring about the founding of Lakewood Church." Lisa emphatically promoted miraculous renderings of biblical references and remarked, "My Daddy looked at the gospels . . . and he realized that Jesus is a healing God [and that] we serve a God of the supernatural." She grippingly described Lakewood as a congregation "that is founded on the Lord Jesus Christ, he is our rock. A church that is led by the Holy Spirit and a church that has always believed in the supernatural power of God with signs and wonders and miracles following." Similarly, Dodie, who as the church's living legacy received a boisterous standing ovation that brought her to tears, invoked Lakewood's former tagline of the "Oasis of Love" to remark on its ultimate foundation. She recalled tenderly her late husband's spirituality, skilled church leadership, and servant's heart. Dodie ended her address with a comment on Joel's inaugural Historic Night of Hope event at Yankee Stadium. As she sat in her seat getting ready to speak to the sold-out crowd about her defeat of cancer, she smelled popcorn in the stadium. Immediately, her mind rushed back to John's early years as a movie theater employee. At that moment, she tearfully yet joyfully juxtaposed the generations of Lakewood's leadership between father and son. "I thought back, here was a young man, seventeen years old, popcorn salesman in Fort Worth, Texas. And here's his son preaching at Yankee Stadium. What goes around comes around. Hallelujah!"[2]

At this fiftieth anniversary event, each of Dodie, Lisa, and Joel's sermons considered the meaning of Lakewood through their own life experiences. Both Dodie and Lisa rooted their comments in the past tense, recalling the spiritual power of John Osteen's life and ministry, while Joel's address only gestured toward the church's past in favor of emphasizing its imminent growth. While Joel's sermon declared that positive thinking and positive confession would usher in Lakewood's resplendent future, Dodie and Lisa's messages on miracles and healing praised the church's historic charismatic orientation. Joel's discourse on destiny looked excitedly forward; glancing backward, Dodie and Lisa in essence saluted the church's neopentecostal roots. The contrast could not have been more striking. Yet all three messages presented aspects of Lakewood's collective existence both past and present, its charismatic core.

Discussion of Lakewood's charismatic core builds on the previous chapter to affirm that while Joel has emerged most recently as the face of Lakewood Church, he is not the sum total of the institution. A focus on the charismatic core unveils not a hidden center of the church—internal access to discussions, deliberations, and decisions of the congregation's leaders is impossible—but distinct manifestations of Lakewood's congregational history and collective identity through the teachings of Dodie and Lisa, as well as Victoria, Joel's wife, Paul Osteen, Joel's brother, and Lakewood's first Spanish-speaking pastor Marcos Witt. Biographical profiles coupled with how each of the pastors has communicated Lakewood's charismatic core demonstrate ultimately that Lakewood is much more than its current pastor Joel Osteen.

Healing, Hope and the Holy Spirit: Dodie Osteen

Dodie Osteen grew up in the Houston suburb of Baytown. Located on the city's east side, for a century Baytown has been home to racially and ethnically diverse populations as well as some of the city's leading petrochemical companies. In Dodie's recollection, her parents, Roy and Georgia Pilgrim, exemplified Christian humility and practiced hospitality. Dodie's father adhered to the Protestant work ethic while he often took the graveyard shift at Exxon's facility in Baytown. His experience of poverty during the Great Depression, like that of John Osteen, coupled with the loss of his parents early in life led to a rugged, unstable, working-class adolescence. As a result, Roy's commitment to frugal living and intense family loyalty offered a stable home life. He regularly spent time with Dodie's five children, worked as a taxi to the kids' sporting and school events, and took them on special excursions to hunt or fish. Dodie's mother, Georgia, created a home that exhibited warmth, and often a full table of food. Whether it was her legendary pecan pies or pumpkin desserts, food, family, and faith anchored the Pilgrim household in which Dodie grew up. Reared in a Christian environment, her childhood experiences anticipated a faith-filled life although her relative material comfort did not prepare her for the hardship of health and testing of faith she eventually encountered. As she later told the story, she would need a heavy dose of the Holy Spirit to survive her struggles.[3]

Before Dodie married John, her occupation as a nurse mirrored the spiritual helping hand at Lakewood for which she became known. John and Dodie met during the 1950s at a hospital in Baytown, where John visited with and prayed for ailing members from Central Baptist Church. Early in their marriage, which would last for nearly half a century, John and Dodie started a family. In time, a large family brought joyful delight to the couple, but a full calendar of activities and John's intense schedule as a traveling evangelist induced stressful difficulties. Nothing was more taxing, however, than Dodie's bout with cancer in the early 1980s.

In the fall of 1981, after a series of tests, and after the Osteens had returned to Houston from a visit to Tulsa where some of their children attended college, including their oldest son, Paul, who was at the time enrolled at City of Faith, Oral Roberts University's medical school, doctors diagnosed Dodie with metastatic liver cancer. Devastated, John and Dodie reeled in disbelief and bewilderment. John questioned how he would survive without Dodie; Dodie wondered how her kids would fare without her prayers and encouraging words. Fortunately for the Osteens, Houston's well-resourced medical community gave them access to cutting-edge treatment, a fact that no doubt assisted in her recovery. As people of faith, John and Dodie also turned to their spiritual resources: a network of charismatic Christians at Lakewood and from around the world who believed deeply in the possibility of divine healing; the power of prayer, which they believed God heard and to which they insisted God promised to respond according to the Bible; and positive confession. After Dodie's diagnosis, leading neopentecostals phoned her to offer encouragement and to stand prayerfully with her: Oral Roberts, T. L. Osborn, Kenneth Copeland, and Kenneth Hagin. Dodie recalled that Hagin promised her that "every vestige of this [cancer] will be gone soon." T. L. Osborn's wife, Daisy, one of Dodie's good friends, paid a visit to Houston to spend time with her ailing spiritual sister. Dodie also reported that she received spiritual encouragement to continue her cancer fight through charismatic experiences she described as "visitations" from God. A closeness she felt to God buoyed her spirits and bolstered her faith. Despite having to "cast down imaginations" that led to doubts and fear, Dodie stated, "I had that confidence in God's word that I was healed" according to Hebrews 10:23, and she abided by the Bible's injunction to "hold fast" to her religious confession of faith.[4]

However, it was Dodie's husband, John, who stood as her strongest rock in the struggle against cancer. Ascribing to him a spiritual authority as her husband, Dodie remarked, "John, you're the head of the house so, you need to take authority over this cancer." Her description reflected gender questions many neopentecostals and evangelicals debated at the time. In neopentecostalism, notions of authority did not always mean hierarchies of politicized power relations. Instead, they sometimes referred to one's documented exhibition of spiritual power in the form of divine healing, speaking in tongues, or other manifestations of the Holy Spirit. For Dodie's sickness, John's authority resided in the realm of positive confession. John for many years had adopted positive confession in

Lakewood's services, and by 1981, he had authored several articles and books on the topic. "John and I believed and confessed God's Word," Dodie wrote in her 1986 autobiography, *Healed of Cancer*. He "anointed me with oil as we both got on the floor in our bedroom, face down before God, and he took authority over any disease and over any cancerous cells in my body." In addition to John's prayerful intercession, Dodie adopted the practice of positive confession, selecting about forty Bible passages that she would pray through daily. "The Word of God saved my life," Dodie emphasized. "Every day I would read many scriptures. . . . To this day, I never leave my home without reading healing scriptures. I know them by heart, but I still look them up and read them. It does something for me." So important were Dodie's "healing scriptures" that she eventually placed them on Lakewood's website and made them widely available at the church for easy access.[5]

After months of struggle and difficulty, Dodie eventually received a clean bill of health. She boldly claimed that through divine orchestration, her prayers, her confession of sin, and her practice of positive confession had healed her. To confirm what she counted as miraculous, Dodie approached Osteen family friend Dr. Reginald Cherry, who practiced in Houston and appeared regularly on the Trinity Broadcasting Network, to run tests on her liver. Multiple tests confirmed that she was cancer free. Cherry's printed testimony in *Healed of Cancer* offered confirmation that Dodie "was healed, not in the traditional medical sense, but supernaturally, in answer to prayer. I thank God for the healing Dodie Osteen has experienced." Cherry also connected Dodie's positive outlook to the long-term outcome of her health. "We're discovering some tremendous things in medicine today," Cherry commented. "We're learning now that a person's positive attitude in fighting and refusing to accept illness can literally change white blood cell counts in the body. It can actually activate a defense the body naturally has against disease and against cancer in particular." Following Cherry's confirmation in *Healed of Cancer*, a physician named Dr. Richard W. Walker, Jr., a specialist in obstetrics and gynecology, and Dr. D. L. Moore also confirmed Dodie's clean bill of health. It seems that her inclusion of medical testimony aimed to elicit faith among and build hope for her readers. At the same time, whether or not Dodie's practice of documentation either confirms or denies the validity of divine healing, her assembly of health reports by medical professionals conformed to the historic neopentecostal practice of what historian Candy Gunther Brown terms "testing prayer." Brown's studies present the broader history of neopentecostal evangelists who under the spotlight of scrutiny attempted active legitimation of divine healing by marshaling printed, medical documentation, important in today's era of "evidence-based medicine."[6]

About the experiences she chronicled in *Healed of Cancer*, Dodie observed, "I have learned that the word of God works." Not content to merely state what she feels is obvious—her divine healing—since 1981 she has devoted her life to extending hope and encouragement to others experiencing health difficulties. Since John's death in 1999, Dodie's work has continued to build Lakewood's charismatic legacy. For example, her 2001 book *Choosing Life One Day at a Time: A Daily Devotional for Men and Women* offered explicit support for divine healing and hope for miraculous intervention. She referenced the New Testament gospel of Mark concerning Jesus' performance of extraordinary feats to demonstrate spiritual power in contending that Lakewood "has become a place where miracles are commonplace. We love miracles. Every time I step up to the platform, our congregation sees a miracle because I was supposed to die around the end of 1981." Not only has Dodie written about charismatic healing experiences vis-à-vis evidence she found in the Bible, her attempt to usher in similar divine activities led her to conduct monthly healing services at a chapel in the Texas Medical Center in Houston. In a similar fashion, starting in 2010, in addition to Dodie's regular healing service inside of Lakewood, she began to hold drive-through healing services at the church for those whose illnesses prevented regular church attendance. The depth of Dodie's faith meant that this idea was neither a gimmick nor a laughing matter. "[God] just said in my heart, why don't you have a drive-by healing service?" she told reporter Deborah Wrigley of Houston's ABC affiliate, KTRK. "And it's the first one I've ever had. I didn't know what would happen, but if one person comes that doesn't matter. I'm doing what God told me to do." Her boldness also manifested itself during Joel's monthly NOH events, where Dodie's testimonial, in essence the story she documented in *Healed of Cancer*, represented Lakewood's neopentecostal origins. Thus Dodie's activities, both inside and outside of Lakewood in the form of healing services, presentations about her experience with cancer, and devotional publications, demonstrate that she has expressed the church's charismatic core and has therefore preserved a vital link to the church's neopentecostal past.[7]

Bountiful and Beautiful through Bruising: Lisa Osteen Comes

The second of Dodie and John Osteen's five children, Lisa Osteen Comes, has served as one of Lakewood's pastors. Her life, by her own admission, has been marked both by troubles and triumphs—a compelling biography that positioned her to eventually exemplify Lakewood's charismatic core. Born with muscular problems, as an infant her medical condition gradually improved, a development her parents—and later Lisa herself—attributed to divine intervention. A highly organized individual, Lisa did well in her classes at Humble High School and subsequently graduated from ORU. At ORU, she worked as a student chaplain, a role that anticipated a life of pastoral care and Christian service. Later, she worked at Lakewood, assisting her father in teaching duties and filling executive roles as an integral part of the church's leadership team. While at the time Lisa's claim that she was Lakewood's first miracle carried weight around the church, several other events in her life led to further assertions of miraculous intervention and a teaching ministry rooted in the notion that difficulties led to divine deliverance.

At twenty-four years old, Lisa found herself a divorcée, an identity she neither sought nor desired. She married her college sweetheart, a man named George Allan Jackson, also a pastor's kid who had designs on leading a church himself. Serving in the church together proved all that Lisa's heart desired; she was happy. Eighteen months into her marriage, George and Lisa began to grow apart. She eventually returned to spend time in Houston, hoping that the distance would make her and George's hearts grow fonder. Instead, Lisa was served with divorce papers. She fell into a downward spiral of debilitating depression, spiritual struggle, and emotional death. She recalled:

> I . . . returned to my childhood home broken, disillusioned, and full of rejection and shame. Not only had I failed in my marriage, but I felt as if I had failed God and my parents. Somehow, and I didn't even have a clue as to how, I'd failed [my husband]. I wanted to just stay on the floor in my

room and not go anywhere or see anyone, I was so ashamed and grieving. These were the darkest days of my life.[8]

Lisa's days of trouble, however, as had been the case for other members of the Osteen family, turned into a testimony of triumph. She received warmth and encouragement from her parents and siblings. Close friends, associates, and family surrounded her at Lakewood. Wise counsel from her father, John, as well as an encouraging conversation with neopentecostal minister T. L. Osborn pushed Lisa out of her existential "pit," as she described her situation. As she recalled, her father's optimism proved particularly timely. "He knew that just because I'd known tragedy, I wasn't a tragic figure," she wrote, "that just because I had a marriage that failed I wasn't a failure, that even though I'd suffered loss I wasn't a loser. . . . I was made for victory."[9]

She took her father's words and other friendly sentiments to heart, and decided to turn her "scars into stars." First, she married a man named Kevin Comes. Originally from Iowa, an engineering and construction job brought Comes to Houston. He eventually made his way to Lakewood Church, where he and Lisa met. In 1988, Lisa inaugurated a writing ministry, publishing a small book, *6 Lies the Devil Uses to Destroy Marriages*. In her book, Lisa drew on her own experiences and linked marriage dissolution to demonic influence that spawned selfishness, secrets, and sin that resulted in bitterness, lack of forgiveness, and emotional and psychological devastation. She ended her book with a marriage prayer: "I know, Father, that You have a specific plan and purpose for me and my mate together. And I thank You for perfecting that which concerns me (see Psalm 138:8). Amen." Not only did Lisa's book reflect life lessons born from the crucible of marital strife she had experienced, but it also echoed broader evangelical concerns in the 1980s with family values.[10]

While Lisa once again found a bountiful life through remarriage and a renewed commitment to Christian outreach, despite the emotional and psychological bruises from her divorce, trouble once again returned in January 1990. A pipe bomb exploded in Lisa's office at Lakewood Church. When she opened a shoebox-sized package, shrapnel and nails pelted her office and sliced into her midsection. Amazingly, she survived. The Houston media suggested that John's decision to welcome

1988 presidential candidate Pat Robertson to Lakewood's pulpit might have made the church a target of political retaliation. The Houston Police Department and U. S. Postal Service quickly launched an investigation, in which the FBI and ATF also participated. Investigators queried West Virginian Jeffrey Mack Boggs, a suspect in other pipe-bomb cases, as well as Lisa's ex-husband, but to no avail. A popular television show hosted by Robert Stack, *Unsolved Mysteries*, later profiled Lisa's case in an attempt to bring to justice those responsible.[11]

Meanwhile, the Osteen family supported Lisa through her hospital stay. Her brother Joel handled the media attention the bomb blast generated. She also received encouraging messages from high-profile figures, including then President George H. W. Bush. Within two months of the blast, she returned to Lakewood. Having overcome muscular difficulties as an infant, survived a divorce, and lived through a bomb explosion, Lisa's first Lakewood presentation after her hospital stay drew from the well-known Psalm 23, "The Lord is my shepherd." Plodding through some of her life's most difficult valleys produced a vitality and spirit of survival; it also led to Lisa's second book. Appropriately titled *Overcoming Opposition: How to Succeed in Doing the Will of God*, her 1990 book used the Old Testament figure Nehemiah as a moral exemplar. Lisa wrote, "When God calls you to a task, He anoints you to do it. He equips you and empowers you. He gives you the strength, courage, and boldness you need to see it done." Representative of perseverance, patience, and great faith, Lisa found in Nehemiah's life a biblical rationale to conquer fears and overcome difficulties, with which she was intimately familiar.[12]

From tragedy to triumph, the script of Lisa Osteen Comes's life has been one of persistence and patience, one of fortitude and ultimately faith. She has expressed Lakewood's neopentecostal legacy in two distinct ways. She articulated her multiple survivals as divine healing and divine providence. Secondly, her sermons, typically delivered during Lakewood's midweek church gathering, have deployed unmistakably neopentecostal discourse. For example, Lisa has long preferred to describe the Christian life in terms of divine destiny. As we have seen, John often used this concept to encourage Christian faithfulness, and his oldest daughter has followed suit. In two sermons delivered in 2009, Lisa's messages focused on destiny and what she described as God's divine call and preparation for a life of service. God's urging to pursue particular tasks or opportunities, Lisa stated, depended on "anointing" and pure intentions. In neopentecostal parlance, anointing has historically meant a distinct sense of the Holy Spirit. In a 2012 sermon, "The Joy of Speaking in Tongues," Osteen Comes unfurled a justification for glossolalia; she argued for its apostolic origins, and its specific connection to individual Christians for enhanced prayer, wisdom, and spiritual power. On Lakewood's stage, while the cameras rolled and recorded, Lisa illustrated speaking in tongues by voicing what she called her "personal prayer language." This particular expression of neopentecostal spirituality, which had not taken place on any of Lakewood's live telecasts since at least 2005, exemplified how Osteen Comes supported Lakewood's charismatic core.[13]

Leadership and Latino/a Pentecostalism: Marcos Witt

In 2002, Joel Osteen invited Marcos Witt to lead Lakewood's Spanish service. An accomplished performer and talented speaker, Witt was an established presence in Latin America who promised to add musical depth and pastoral leadership to the church's Spanish-speaking ministry. Witt's books, including his 1997 work *Señor, ¿en Qué Puedo Servirte?*, further legitimated his role as one of Lakewood's premier leaders. While at Lakewood, Witt published another important book, *How to Overcome Fear and Live Your Life to the Fullest* (2007). With a distinct brand of humor, stories, and spiritual counsel from the Bible, Witt authored a practical approach to the Christian life. He suggested replacing psychological fears and fears of demons and occult practices with a fear of God expressed in "reverent admiration" of God's power, a "devotional respect" in learning God's word, and a "relational trust" that prized a feeling of closeness to divine plans for everyday life.[14]

Lakewood's move into the former Compaq Center only three years after Witt's arrival signaled additional growth and a larger platform for his presence at the church. This expansion continued through 2012, when his tenure at Lakewood ended. Hired in 2002, Witt promised Osteen at least a decade of service, and ten years later Witt and his ministry partner and spouse, Miriam, felt that they had fulfilled their role at Lakewood Church. The Witts' concluding service at Lakewood included appreciative statements from Joel and Victoria, as well as prayers offered by the new Spanish-speaking pastors, Danilo and Gloriana Montero. Danilo thanked Marcos and Miriam for their work at Lakewood, and invoked the notion of harvest in praise of their efforts. About his new role at Lakewood, Montero stated, "Un gran honor y una gran responsabilidad! Honramos a Marcos y Miriam." Through tears Joel expressed deep affection for the Witts, and praised their commitment and service to the church. Similarly, Victoria applauded Marcos and Miriam's realization of "changed lives" in Lakewood's Spanish-speaking congregation.[15]

With significant name recognition among Spanish speakers, Witt often does not get enough credit for solidifying Lakewood's presence in Houston—particularly since the city has long been a hub for Latin American immigration. Also, his participation in initiatives related to Latino/a leadership and immigration reform brought Lakewood an important role in national political issues. Religious studies scholar Gastón Espinosa's research on Latino Pentecostals documents Witt's affiliation with the Reverend Samuel Rodriguez and the National Hispanic Leadership Conference. Witt, Rodriguez and other leaders such as Noel Castellanos met in 2006 with then presidential candidate John McCain on immigration reform. An examination of Witt's local and national activities is one way to discern how he has communicated Lakewood's charismatic core.[16]

To understand Witt's tenure at Lakewood, it is imperative to consider that his hire had a deep connection to the congregation's history. In 1964, in the early days of John Osteen's international evangelistic endeavors, Witt's parents, Jerry and Nola, spoke at Lakewood about their plans to travel to Mexico and establish a training and leadership school for pastors and teachers. John decided to help pave the way for further missionary work. "Pastor John Osteen was stirred and moved," Witt recalled, and provided his parents with a $600 offering. The Witts gratefully accepted the financial assistance, and eventually purchased a sixteen-acre plot in Mexico on which they built a Bible school that trained thousands of ministers. Jerry also regularly flew over Mexico, and dropped from the plane Spanish translations of the New Testament gospel of John. Unfortunately, Jerry died in a plane crash shortly after visiting Lakewood, but as Marcos stated in 2009, "The seed that Lakewood sowed in that ministry lives to this day."[17]

The historical connection Witt made between his parents' visit to Lakewood and his eventual leadership role as the church's Spanish-speaking pastor exhibits one of the ways that he has emblematized Lakewood's charismatic core. Born in San Antonio but reared in Durango, Mexico—Joel once referred to the Spanish-speaking pastor as a "multicultural man"—Witt was especially well positioned to forge spiritual and material connections between Lakewood and Latin America via his bilingualism as well as the cross-cultural competencies he acquired from living and traveling there.[18]

Another way that Witt exemplified Lakewood's charismatic core expressed itself through his pastoral work. A congregation of around 6,000 members, the large, cacophonous assembly brought multiple cultural traditions from across Latin America. Aside from mixing with the cultural customs of locations such as Argentina, Cost Rica, Chile, Brazil, and Mexico, Pentecostalism shaped numerous Latin American immigrant identities, even those affiliated with Roman Catholicism. As historian Andrew Chesnut explains, over the last half of the twentieth century, and well into the twenty-first, Pentecostal and neopentecostal traditions and religious expressions enveloped Latin America's religious landscape. This not only transformed religious life across Latin America, it also factored into the religious backgrounds Latin American immigrants retained as they relocated to places such as Houston. These historical trends produced the broad and diverse charismatic character of Lakewood's Latino/a congregation.[19]

An additional manifestation of Witt's connection to Lakewood's charismatic core occurred when his mentor, evangelist Alberto Mottesi, visited Houston in 2012. On Lakewood's center stage, Mottesi offered a prophecy for Witt's future. Wielding a sword that symbolized wisdom in the tradition of the ancient Israelite King Solomon, Mottesi claimed that a more expansive influence was in store for Witt. He praised Witt's ministry, its cross-cultural influence, and the Spanish-speaking pastor's commitment to God's work in the form of preaching, teaching, and leadership. Mottesi's dramatic ceremony in essence commissioned Witt for a new chapter in his life and ministry. His prophetic display was rich with neopentecostal significance and highly meaningful to those in the audience of Pentecostal background.[20]

Moreover, two Pew Research Center on Religion and Public Life studies of Latin American religion have documented the overwhelming influence of Pentecostal spirituality among Latino/a Roman Catholics in the U. S., especially former Roman Catholics who have joined evangelical churches, such as Lakewood. In addition, several measures of distinct Pentecostal spiritual expressions, such as divine healing, speaking in tongues, and casting out demons, found that over half of Latino/a charismatics (whom the Pew studies have termed "renewalists") identify personally with such practices. Since such practices also formed part of neopentecostalism's history, and since that tradition shaped the course of Lakewood's past, as minister of its Spanish-speaking congregation these data suggest that Witt retained a significant and substantial part of Lakewood's charismatic core in his pastoral work.[21]

Happiness, Hope, and the Home: Victoria Osteen

In the fall of 2013, Victoria Osteen appeared on the morning talk show *Great Day Houston*, which aired on CBS affiliate KHOU. Host Deborah Duncan, who had attended Lakewood, asked questions about family and faith. They also discussed Lakewood's attempt to deliver hope around the world in the form of material and spiritual support to churches, pastors, and individuals. Duncan asked about Lakewood's annual fashion show, which Victoria created to provide a gender-specific forum promoting fun, community, and encouragement. However, when Duncan asked Victoria about ministering alongside of her husband, Joel, she offered a unique glimpse into the characteristics of leadership at Lakewood. She correctly pointed to John as a "forerunner" of gender equality in the pulpit, since Dodie ministered with him, and then referenced some of Lakewood's other female ministers, including Lisa Osteen Comes. Victoria praised Joel for creating a prominent place in the pulpit for her early on in their ministry together. Victoria stated the Joel "saw the validity in having a woman, a feminine heart [in the pulpit] to be able to speak to the feminine heart . . . it's great to be able to get up there and know that I represent women." She continued, "We're a team . . . there's male, there's female, and to minister to the whole body is so important."[22]

Victoria's comments in the *Great Day Houston* interview acknowledged John's support of religious gender equality at Lakewood and praised the ministry of Lisa Osteen Comes. And in relation to both John and Lisa—and Joel—Victoria has achieved a distinct and distinguished place among Lakewood's leadership, and in her role, she has paid tribute to the congregation's historic support for female ministers. She has emphasized her specific message, and her specific place in Lakewood's operations, and by so doing, she has adopted a form of representational politics. In the role of "speak[ing] to the feminine heart," Victoria has occupied an important place in the church leadership. The ways in which she has presented her role at Lakewood are akin to the spiritualized notions of social and cultural power among evangelical women that religious studies scholar R. Marie Griffith's work explores. Griffith uses intimate prayer groups to connect material, political realities of female empowerment to specific expressions of religious practice as evidence of the "power of submission" to spouses and to God. Based on the power of submission, Victoria has created her own teaching platform at Lakewood that she has used to authorize a message by, for, and about women.[23]

Victoria has expressed Lakewood's charismatic core through her teachings on hope and happiness. The notion of joy, manifested in physical expressions such as jumping or clapping, explained as a state of mind, or presented through a rhetoric of victory, is a central sentiment in neocharismatic Christianity. While happiness and joy were themes Victoria developed in her teaching, they came in quite handy in response to two very public controversies in which she was involved.

Reared in Houston, Victoria Osteen grew up in a financially comfortable middle-class family. In the 1960s, her father worked as a NASA mathematician on space programs and her mother managed the family's fine jewelry business, Iloff Jewelers. As a young woman, Victoria studied psychology at the University of Houston and worked at Iloff Jewelers, where she met Joel. With family roots in the Deep South, Victoria's maternal grandparents and great-grandparents were wealthy landowners and business managers in Georgia. Unlike Joel's father and grandfather, Victoria's family survived the Great Depression financially intact; their local grocery store in Columbus profited handsomely during tough economic times. Victoria recalled the inspirational qualities of her grandmother as a distinguished Southern woman of deep faith and sincere Christian conviction. "Meemaw," as Victoria affectionately recalled her grandmother, was a student of the Bible who always found a way to offer encouragement and direction through scripture verses. Christian commitments evidently continued to the next generation, because Victoria described her own upbringing as one in which devoted prayer and regular scripture reading were central to family life. As an adult, Victoria looked to her grandmother's deep faith and family values to shape her own message of hope, inspiration, and encouragement.[24]

When Joel became Lakewood's pastor, he quickly welcomed Victoria as his co-minister. In a February 1999 sermon, Joel envisioned shared labor as an extension of his family life. "I know for my household, I have the vision very clear that Victoria and I and our household, we're going to serve God one hundred percent," Joel stated. "We're going to be an example to this city and to this world of what it means to live a godly, spirit-filled life." Victoria explained from the story of Jesus, two fish, and five loaves of bread that even though it appeared she had little talent, God increased her ability as one of Lakewood's ministers. "Instead of thinking about all the reasons that I couldn't do it, I started thinking about all the reason that I *could* do it," she recalled. "I encouraged myself and allowed the Word of God to empower me. . . . I knew that God wanted me to step into my position and begin to encourage people. So I took a step of faith and He was right there with me." Victoria used the sense of purpose she gained from her initial years as Lakewood's pastor to settle on the core components of her message.[25]

Like her husband, Victoria has no formal theological training, but for nearly three decades her exposure to neopentecostalism, including years of listening to Joel's sermons, has shaped the focus of her teaching to include positive thinking and positive confession, although Victoria's emphasis on them was not as pronounced as her husband's. As a wife and mother, Victoria also settled on teaching that promoted the development of faith and finding fulfillment in the traditional heterosexual family. Although she never shied away from teaching illustrations that presented her privileged class status, she made attempts to connect with working-class women, impoverished single mothers, and homeless females. Her teaching also made persistent use of market language that reflected her bourgeois life experience. Victoria's message of faith, family, and hope found expression in positive thinking and positive confession—common articulations of the prosperity gospel—while it also supported traditional gender roles for evangelical women. A purposeful focus on education resulted in a line of illustrated children's books. The primary vehicle for Victoria's teachings was her 2008 book *Love Your Life: Living Happy, Healthy & Whole*. Like her husband's books, not only did Victoria's present a breezy combination of advice about self-respect, self-fulfillment, and service, it also attained *New York Times* bestseller status.

Positive thinking is a dominant theme in *Love Your Life*. One of Victoria's starting premises claimed that spiritual concerns originate in the mind. She piled up illustrations of interior fears and failures from Bible stories, from her doubts as one of Lakewood's emerging leaders, from the struggles of 2007 Miss USA title winner Rachel Smith, from the difficulties of Paula Deen's early career, and from the life of baseball great Babe Ruth. In turn, she insisted that reformulated thinking was a key to spiritual success. She called on the Old Testament account of David and Goliath, and attributed David's victory to confidence in God. "Don't make the mistake of replaying the negative images on the You-Tube of your mind," she suggested, "replay your victories. Replay your accomplishments. Replay the good things God has done in your life." She counseled to take careful notice of thought patterns, to monitor "internal dialogue" to ensure a focus on positivity. "As a first step toward a positive perspective, it's good to take inventory of your thought life. . . . Identify any self-defeating can't-do-it thoughts and decide not to dwell on them." Victoria suggested that a divine relationship with God based on abiding faith ultimately guaranteed beneficial results.[26]

Victoria's book also promoted her version of positive confession less as personalized declarations of individual improvement and more as purposeful pronouncements directed at friends and family, what she called "being a people builder." She demonstrated her fidelity to positive confession and relationship building through encouragement. Victoria stated, "a blessing is not a blessing until it is spoken." She reminded readers that close companionship and healthy relationships thrived on verbal blessings of a complimentary nature or a simple "I love you." Victoria marshaled numerous anecdotes from family life, involving interactions with Joel, her mother, her son, and her daughter, and framed these ordinary accounts around her philosophy of people building: "You have the power to speak words of faith and victory into your family, and you must recognize the weight your words carry and the influence you have on those closest to you." Her positive confession promised personal benefits and divine favor from praising others.[27]

While Victoria's message often illustrated teaching points drawn from many of her own personal experiences, in concordance with postwar conservative evangelical family values yet also tied to neopentecostal feminine faith, she used episodes from familial interaction to project practices of traditional evangelical womanhood. Victoria's formulation of a stable domestic scene built around God, the Bible, and each individual's personal fulfillment as divine destiny is another way that her work relates to R. Marie Griffith's study of "God's daughters," evangelical women with devotional lives rooted in commitment to traditional gender roles who work toward social empowerment through spiritual growth.[28]

In *Love Your Life*, Victoria presented her then decade-long marriage to Joel as idyllic. While not problem free, Victoria narrated her union as one of perpetual relational and spiritual growth. Communication improved, Victoria said, when she realized that "insensitive" and "unkind" verbal outbursts pierced the heart of her sensitive spouse. After prayer and reflection, Victoria stated that she longed to love her husband in a God-honoring way, in a fashion of mutual accord. "The more I treat Joel like a king, the more he treats me like his queen," she explained. "The more I focus on the good in him, the more he focuses on the good in me. We have grown together." This perspective gave Victoria a realization that prompted her to develop a deeper self-giving love that supported her husband. Over time, admitted Victoria, she "studied" Joel's habits and mannerisms as a way to better understand his interior motivations, and in turn, love him in mutual submission to God. "We have to be willing to give the people in our lives what *they* need, which may not necessarily be what *we* need," she stated. To assure potential critics that blind patriarchy did not define her marriage, Victoria maintained that by attending to Joel's needs she was not "changing who I am; I'm changing the way I communicate so I can have a better relationship with my husband. I want Joel to hear me, so I adapt to the way he listens best. It is good for me and good for him." She presented a marriage that demanded effort, and one that was delightful and happy based on mutual service and respect and dependent upon God, the Bible, and prayer.[29]

In historical terms, Victoria's presentation of relative marital stability—in light of her position as one of Lakewood's ministers—reflected post–World War II evangelical concerns around domestic order and harmony. It also echoed themes of Christian Right gender norms expressed by individuals such as Marabel Morgan, whose 1973 book *The Total Woman*, mostly known for its evocative advice about making marriages "sizzle," presented "The Total Woman" as "not just a good housekeeper; she is a warm, loving homemaker. She is not merely a submissive sex partner; she is a sizzling lover. She is not just a nanny to her children; she is a woman who inspires them to reach out and up." Morgan's teaching also addressed cultural power, a topic toward which Victoria's writings alluded. "A Total Woman is a person in her own right. She has a sense of personal security and self-respect. She is not afraid to be herself. Others may challenge her standards, but she knows who she is and where she is going." At the same time, Victoria's autonomous place as a Christian woman and female minister spoke to more recent gender debates within evangelicalism, a space of potential "fresh social dialogue" historian Margaret Lamberts Bendroth considers in her research on gender and fundamentalism.[30]

Victoria has committed to literacy through the publication of numerous children's books. As a writing ministry to enhance familial relationships, spiritual instruction formed the overall rationale for her children's publications. "Now more than ever, I realize we only have a small window of time to pour unconditional love and wisdom in [our children], and I don't want to miss a single opportunity to lay a foundation of faith and hope in their hearts," wrote Victoria. "I pray that these little books will bring your family together for a fun time of sharing, laughter, and love." In 2009, she released a trilogy called "My Happy Heart Books." Titled *Hooray for Today!*, *Hooray for Wonderful Me!*, and *Hooray for My Family!*, the trilogy offered a version of Lakewood's positive thinking message for kids. For example, in *Hooray for Wonderful Me!*, at a swimming lesson a young girl said, "God gave me oomph to never quit. I always try my best. I have a can-do attitude. Just watch—I'll pass the test." While she played with friends, the same girl stated, "God gave me lots of love to give. I show love every day. I take turns going first in line and choosing what we play." The books depicted an overwhelmingly stable domestic setting with happy heterosexual families and joyful children. And although they featured only Anglo families, the books presented children at playtime with kids of diverse backgrounds. Two larger-print books, *Unexpected Treasures* (2009) and *Gifts from the Heart* (2010), delivered messages of positive encouragement along with instructional references for parents and guardians. *Unexpected Treasures* chronicled the maritime voyages of children whose sense of adventure focused on the quest to locate an elusive treasure. In the story, the young treasure seekers met frustration, but Captain Jon and his friend Sue stepped in to offer encouragement, echoing the teachings at Lakewood Church. "Success will come, if you just stick with it!" the captain said. Sue chimed in, "Success takes work. But it's not far away. Just keep believing! Don't give up! You'll reach your goal someday!" *Gifts from the Heart* detailed a medieval theme of a knight and princess who live an adventurous life in the kingdom. At the book's conclusion, Victoria included a didactic section called "Kingdom Thoughts" that read very much like positive confessions for young kids. "You may not wear a golden crown, but you are royalty deep down," wrote Victoria. "Just give your best in all you do. Your gift will make a way for you." A "Royal Q&A" offered further instruction with five follow-up questions about giving the gift of love and compassion.[31]

While Victoria's emphasis on "hearts" in her children's books offered affirmations of positivity any conscientious parent seeks to instill, her language reflected wider expressions of spiritual emotion in contemporary Christianity. Historian Todd Brenneman's study of religion and sentimentality addresses the place of children and children's literature within evangelicalism. He finds nineteenth-century origins for the current evangelical focus in children's literature on cultivating emotional relationships with God, the presentation of a stable domestic home life, and instruction in proper religious behavior. Nostalgia over pleasant emotional memories is also a key feature that Brenneman's study documents. In addition, his work also shows how "[s]entimentality and branding combine to instantiate the authority of the author or other producer of popular culture." A context of associational connections is thus created between the consumption of products and emotions and the work of procuring spiritual and religious values for children. Like the evangelical video series *VeggieTales* and youth products created by Texas minister Max Lucado—topics Brenneman addresses in his book— the fixation of Victoria Osteen's children's literature on the heart, nostalgia, and religious emotions of positive encouragement has deep roots in American Christianity. Her approach to teaching joy in children's books thus modeled one dimension of Lakewood's charismatic core in a unique way.[32]

Victoria's teaching on joy, hope, and happiness has anchored her life as a woman, wife, mother, daughter, pastor, and celebrity. Her message is thematically oriented toward notions of personal, spiritual, and psychological victory. As historian Kate Bowler argues, the practice of overcoming difficulty—the achievement of victory—is a sentiment central to neopentecostalism's history. Similarly, historian Paul Alexander explains that within the larger charismatic world, "positive expectation of good" is a fundamental tenet of neopentecostalism. In these specific ways, Victoria's teachings have articulated Lakewood's charismatic core. However, her deployment of joy, hope, and victory proved useful on more than one occasion when her celebrity status brought unwanted attention. She explained that difficulties in her own life led to renewed expressions of joy, and victory over her critics.[33]

The first public controversy in which Victoria was involved occurred in December 2005. Reports surfaced that in preparation for a vacation flight to Colorado, a dispute erupted between Victoria and a flight attendant named Sharon Brown. The Osteen family eventually deplaned, and Victoria paid a $3,000 FAA fine. Although details about what led to the conflict differed—apparently Victoria requested that Brown clean up the tray table or armrest of the first-class seat in which she planned to sit, while Brown insisted that Victoria shoved her—Brown filed suit against the celebrity minister for 10 percent of Victoria's net worth, an apology, and counseling fees, claiming that she had experienced physical and spiritual trauma as a result of the quarrel. The case went to trial in August 2008. A Houston jury found that Victoria did not assault Brown. In post-trial comments, Brown's attorney depicted Victoria as someone who felt that she could live life by a different set of rules, while Osteen's lawyer suggested that the trial was simply an attempt to bilk money from a celebrity. Even the jury foreman described the trial as "a complete waste of time" because, while he and the jurors agreed that a run-in took place, they did not deem it an assault.[34]

Reports of the Osteen–Brown rumble, along with trial coverage, framed the story as another high-profile scandal involving a religious celebrity. Bloggers and pundits immediately assumed the worst about Victoria and her actions. Similarly, cultural critic Barbara Ehrenreich labeled Osteen's actions as "pastors go[ing] postal," a class-based critique of a millionaire minister's picky traveling preferences over which Victoria became "mightily pissed." While there is much about celebrity behavior that deserves scrutiny, a point Ehrenreich makes about Osteen in comparison to California pastor Robert Schuller's 2007 airplane argument, it is equally true that the case of Victoria's 2005 conflict presents a site in which to observe her expression of Lakewood's charismatic core. For example, immediately after her dispute with Brown went public, Victoria issued a public statement. She downplayed the conflict by describing it as a "minor misunderstanding" and "a most unfortunate event and I truly regret that it happened." She proceeded to spiritualize the fracas, stating, "I value the position that God has placed me in and I can assure you that I will always walk in love and integrity. While I am not perfect, I will always seek to be a peacemaker and seek the high road." She then adopted the neopentecostal notion of joy to explain the situation. "As many of you have told me, I know that God has me in the palm of His hand," she stated. "I know that God causes all things to work together for our good—and I truly believe that when faced with adversities we all emerge better and stronger than when we were before." In 2006, Victoria echoed these sentiments in an appearance on *Larry King Live*. Uncomfortable with King's query about the flight fight, Victoria reminded the talk show host that she felt uneasy speaking publicly about the matter. She then deployed the language of Lakewood's charismatic core. The incident, Victoria said, led ultimately to her discovery of a greater purpose for her life, reason for her to express joy and gratitude. "I have taken the high road," Victoria boasted. "I realized it's made me stronger. And that's what I choose to do now. It's made me see things in me that I've never seen before. It's made me have more compassion on people. And so that's why I've chosen not to even combat, you know, something that was blown out of proportion." Although Victoria's critics found her evasions unacceptable, her comments nevertheless expressed ideas associated with Lakewood's charismatic core.[35]

Another controversy erupted in the summer of 2014 when someone posted a sermon clip on YouTube in which Victoria, during a Lakewood service, stated, "I just want to encourage every one of us to realize when we obey God, we're not doing it for God. . . . We're doing it for ourselves, because God takes pleasure when we're happy. . . . Just do good for your own self. Do good because God wants you to be happy. When you come to church, when you worship Him, you're not doing it for God really. You're doing it for yourself, because that's what makes God happy." The thirty-second clip went viral. Critics posted and reposted, tweeted and retweeted Victoria's statement, and many Christians roared with disapproval. Southern Baptist leader R. Albert Mohler described Osteen's message as one that "aims for so little," a larger issue he attributed to the deficiencies of the prosperity gospel. Charismatic writer Michael Brown wrote an open letter to Joel and Victoria that chided the couple for not teaching "the whole counsel of God." Brown provocatively suggested, "It would be better for you to see your TV ratings fall and your crowds dwindle than to displease the Lord. (Perhaps if you preached the whole counsel of God your audience would end up even bigger.) . . . The reality is that our lives are supposed to revolve around God; He doesn't revolve around us." Writer Matt K. Lewis suggested a more humane response to Victoria's comments and pointed readers to his conviction that "[w]hile blessing may follow obedience, our highest priority should be love for God."[36]

Based on an already unfavorable assessment of Joel, most of Victoria's critics found in her words even more proof of theological bankruptcy. Astonishingly, none of the critics seemed to ask who posted the clip, when Victoria made the statement, or even point out that a thirty-second clip might not reflect the totality of that day's message. In addition, nearly all of those who blasted Victoria for the abysmal theology of her statement launched similar-sounding attacks on the prosperity gospel, a point that speaks both to the echo chamber of interweb criticism as well as larger cultural judgments of the prosperity message.

In response to her detractors, Victoria issued a statement of clarification to the online news source *The Blaze*. She admitted that she "could have been more articulate in my remarks," but emphatically stated, "I stand by my point that when we worship God and are obedient to Him we will be better for it." Victoria further clarified that she "did not mean to imply that we don't worship God." At the point of incredulity, she abrasively dismissed the pundits' comments as "ridiculous, and only the critics and cynics are interpreting my remarks that way." Victoria pointed to church members who "have experienced firsthand the joy and victory of a Lakewood Church worship service, and the honor, reverence and gratitude we show God" as evidence that her message of happiness found its roots in divine blessing rather than merely human enjoyment. While Victoria's 2014 reply to scoffers mirrored her 2005 public comments, they were far more direct and confrontational. At the same time, like her 2005 statement, Victoria's 2014 retort exhibited Lakewood's charismatic core by referencing happiness, victory, and joy in connection to experiencing God in the midst of trouble. In the final analysis, even if viewers of Victoria's comment about God on the You-Tube clip did not have the full context of her statement, her references in the video to elation, gladness, and delight in worship fit right in with the general contours of her spiritual message on enjoyment, hope, and happiness.[37]

Medicine, Missions, and Miracles: Paul Osteen

Paul Osteen is the oldest of John and Dodie's children. He joined Lakewood's staff shortly after his brother assumed the position of head pastor. A medical doctor with extensive experience in numerous surgical procedures, previously Paul had his own medical practice in Arkansas. At Lakewood he focused on equipping others for leadership and participating in ministries of caring and encouragement. In a 2004 sermon, for example, Paul used the New Testament passage of Matthew 28 about Jesus' teaching on burdens and rest to admonish Lakewood members to slow down their lives, take time to pray, and "find balance" in everyday life. Eventually, Paul zeroed his attention on medical missionary work. His sermons on the subject included a message on the New Testament story of the Good Samaritan from Luke 10, and he counseled listeners to pay attention to the needs of those around them, and to help in the midst of difficulties and struggles. This philosophy influenced the rationale he adopted to undertake global missionary work. As a neopentecostal

Christian, Paul believed heartily in the power of miracles and supernatural work and his travel reports from missionary trips regularly explained fortuitous material circumstances as divinely planned. Yet, as a surgeon, Paul also possessed knowledge that medicine played a decisive role in health outcomes. Merging his interests of medicine and missions, Paul, along with his wife Jennifer, a registered nurse, set out to traverse the globe in search of miracles and healing. Starting in 2008, Paul and his family began to chronicle their travels via web updates about their global medical excursions to Africa and the Caribbean.[38]

Paul's reports generally reflected positive outcomes emblematic of short-term Christian missionary travels (STM). It is also the case that the expansive budget of Lakewood Church played a vital role in the self-reported "successes" of Paul's medical missions. While Paul attributed the triumphant medical outcomes of his missionary travels to divine intervention, and drew out spiritual lessons from the evangelistic activities in which he engaged, anthropologists point to how overwhelmingly positive STM reports overlook and simplify the historical and operational legacies of Western imperialism in places such as Africa and Asia. Moreover, scholars also show how funding from the mammoth budgets of American megachurches necessarily influence the "social organization of missions," again complicating contemporary cross-cultural encounters in light of Western colonialism's history. Thus, while Paul's STM writings leave the impression of deeply rewarding and prosperous missionary work, his travelogues document substantial transnational connections between Lakewood Church and global ministries—what sociologist Robert Wuthnow terms "boundless faith"—and offer a clear window into understanding how his work has exemplified Lakewood's charismatic core. To date, Paul's medical missionary travels have focused on Cameroon, in western equatorial Africa, and Kenya, on the eastern side of the continent. Following the 2010 earthquake, he also traveled to Haiti with Samaritan's Purse, the missionary organization led by Billy Graham's son, Franklin.[39]

In Kenya, Paul's work took place at Tenwek Hospital, a facility located in the western part of the country. On the left side of the hospital sign, it reads "We Treat," on the right side, "Jesus Saves." While this message seems appropriate for a hospital started in the 1930s by missionaries, it also reflects Paul's missionary philosophy. During his

2010 visit to Kenya, Paul told the story of a woman named Stella, whose leg tumor had caused her tremendous physical discomfort for over a decade and led to a long season of depression. After successful surgery, during which Osteen amputated part of her leg, Paul traveled to Stella's home village for a visit. He reported that joy had returned to her life, and remarked how donors in Houston forged a transnational connection across the world through money and support. In another account about surgery at Tenwek, Osteen related the account of a thirty-year-old woman named Jackie. Medical complications from an abortion led to a severe abdominal infection, and an HIV-positive diagnosis made life excruciatingly difficult for her. The highlight of Paul's story was not just that he had successfully performed surgery on Jackie, but that she had also found Jesus and joined a local congregation. He commented on the importance of transnational contacts between Lakewood Church and medical programs in east Africa: "It's incredible that God uses some concrete and steel [at Lakewood] and a whole lot of His children to work together to offer hope and healing to men, women and children in our neighborhoods, our cities, our nation, and all around the world."[40]

Similarly, Paul told the story of a successful operation at Cameroon's Ngaoundere Protestant Hospital on a young boy named Solomon, whose severe burns made it impossible for him to walk. Equally miraculous, in Osteen's opinion, was how Solomon and his family had survived an attack on their way to the hospital, conflict related to broad-based political unrest in central Africa. Paul's wife accompanied him on the journey to Cameroon, and provided post-op care for Solomon as his health improved and his strength returned. As before, Paul derived a spiritual lesson from the international missionary work in which he participated.[41]

In a 2012 sermon at Lakewood, Paul reported on a recent trip to Zambia. He reminded church members that "medicine is a tool for evangelism." He recounted precarious medical situations and seemingly terminal diagnoses, while he also pointed out that prayer coupled with expert medical care assisted his patients in making complete recoveries. Remarkably, he also told of a patient named Michael whom he described as demon possessed. As Paul treated Michael in an attempt to relieve his pain and assess his psychological well-being, the seasoned doctor also employed a spiritual approach to treatment. He told Michel about Jesus. In one session during which he described Michael as supremely "agitated," Paul reassured his patient that "Jesus loves you." Shortly thereafter, according to Paul's recollection, the patient "screamed at the top of his lungs" and responded in a "guttural snarl" that spooked the doctor. Paul and Michael's eyes met, and in the grip of fear, Paul described Michael's "evil, hate-filled demonic stare." Michael eventually calmed down; the change was gradual, but ultimately effectual, as Paul described his patient as living in "complete deliverance," the result of doing "spiritual battle." While much of Paul's travelogue reporting exhibited Lakewood's charismatic core by charting the development of missionary efforts, the 2012 report from Zambia alluded to the spiritual battles of demon possession, existential predicaments about which Paul's father John Osteen vividly reported during the 1960s.[42]

Illustrative of well-sourced STM funding streams made available by wealthy megachurches, in early 2014 Paul reported to donors that Lakewood had provided new ultrasound machines to hospitals in India, Burundi, and Malawi. "Each and every ultrasound will go to help people in some of the most impoverished areas of the world," he noted in his report. He further stated that the medical equipment "help[ed] people with little or no access to quality medical care, [while] reaching out to these people with the kindness and compassion of Jesus." Osteen praised donors for their efforts, but directed his most superlative praise "to God for all he IS doing and all He is GOING to do this year. It is such an honor to be part of advancing His Kingdom." Osteen's report of Lakewood's distribution of medical equipment and the congregation's help in facilitating the construction of medical facilities conforms to larger patterns of U S. megachurches' financial impact on global missionary networks. In addition, Lakewood's delivery of medical equipment and funds depended upon extensive charity and humanitarian networks that connected American churches with global partners.[43]

Lakewood's charismatic core shows that Joel Osteen is not the totality of the church. While he has attained the congregation's most notable presence, other ministers have delivered Lakewood's collective identity through an emphasis on divine healing, a presentation of happiness and joy, global missionary efforts, leadership, and Latino/a Pentecostalism. It is Lakewood's charismatic core who, along with Joel, have presented hope and healing as vital dimensions of the church's past and integral aspects of its current course.

The Redemptive Self

Finding and Forging Faith at Lakewood Church

What's inside Lakewood Church?
—Connie Selvaggi (2010)

In January 2012, *Salon* writer Alexis Grant provocatively claimed, "I fell in love with a megachurch." In the article, she described a tragic betrayal by someone she loved. To her surprise, Grant found love in the last place she expected to encounter it. She attended Lakewood, where "emotion pulsed through the crowd. People sang loudly, with both hands out-stretched, palms toward their God as if to receive whatever he offered. I put my hand out too. . . . As they waved their arms in the air, I hoped their strength would rub off on me." By contrast, she recalled attend-ing Mass as a young girl, where she experienced a stilted repetition that rarely moved her. "Catholics were stoic," Grant explained. "We repeated the same words every Mass, pausing when we were supposed to pause, sparing our prayers the wrath of inflection, showing neither happiness nor sadness. We showed nothing. . . . I was used to leaving church feeling guilty for my sins from the previous week, for letting my mind wander to sex while Latin words rolled off an old priest's tongue." Grant wrote that Lakewood "felt more motivational than religious" as she listened to Osteen's sermons and heard encouraging phrases and promises that life would get better. "[S]urrounded by people so full of faith and hope, I sensed an escape route for my ache. If I could just let the heaviness out of my chest, believers around me would absorb it, eat it up and digest even the tough parts." In an intensely moving emotional and corporeal expe-rience, like others in the crowd, Grant lifted her arms and let the tears flow. "It was freeing," she described, "crying in that crowd, anonymous yet part of something bigger than myself. I was among strangers, yet I felt less broken and alone than when I'd walked in."[1]

Grant's vivid description of her Lakewood visit depicts the existential experience and narrates the emotional context of communal worship services at America's largest megachurch. Drawn to the church by one person—Joel—Grant's snapshot of her time there presented a sense of Lakewood's congregational totality. Moreover, her experience captured profoundly what has endeared the congregation to so many: the hope for a new beginning. The central dynamic that has fueled religious identity at Lakewood has been redemption. Tethered to the notion of Pentecost, symbolic of starting over, redemption at Lakewood has referred both to the historic evangelical teaching of forgiveness through Jesus Christ and to the possibility of commencing individual religious change, of obtaining a spiritual makeover. The aspirational ethos of Lakewood's boundless encouragement, unflappable optimism, and belief in new beginnings has provided an impetus for attendees and members to continue their spiritual quest.

Lakewood's evangelical convictions resonate with therapeutic currents deeply embedded in contemporary American culture. This aspect of the congregation's identity tracks closely with what narrative psychologist Dan McAdams terms the "redemptive self." He writes that generativity, a focus on creating a positive legacy for the future, defines the redemptive self. Moreover, the redemptive self seeks to transcend suffering in the interest of achieving a progressively improving situation. McAdams explains that when individuals invest religious meaning in notions of the redemptive self, they assign a divine shape to their life experiences. Applied to those who have found a redemptive self at Lakewood, life experiences, or "testimonies" in neopentecostal parlance, have posited that positive results invariably emerge from negative circumstances, that the triumph of good routinely occurs in the face of evil, or that the presence of grace in the midst of sin signals ultimate hope.[2]

During the last half century, Lakewood has grown in membership size, it has moved locations and expanded its physical space, and it has transcended the confines of Houston, and the United States, through its media outreach. It has solidified its status as an independent church, despite its Southern Baptist origins. Lakewood has also diversified racially and ethnically—although as of 2014 there was only one black pastor on staff, John Gray, whom Joel hired in 2012. As a result, its "ethos of inclusivity," to use sociologist Matthew Henderson's phrase, has resulted in Lakewood becoming one of the nation's most diverse congregations in the nation's most diverse metropolitan area. These changes over time have also translated into increases in its material and economic worth. Over the course of its history, members of Lakewood Church have developed a sense of social and material connection, a collective identity around spiritual values, ideas, and language. Moreover, structural transitions in leadership have signaled institutional evolution; not just because Joel became pastor after his father, but also as the church hired new ministers and musicians.[3]

These institutional developments at Lakewood Church have connected it to the larger story of congregations in American history. Congregations are voluntary entities that fundamentally order religious life in the United States. And congregations are much more than the physical, architectural space in which they assemble. They are comprised of people. They have founders and leaders. Congregations fashion collective identities by bundling particular customs, norms, and expectations, and they develop common categories of language and discourse to narrate spiritual perspectives and explain material realities. Congregations grow and contract in size based on generational dynamics, internal conflict, demographic shifts, and economic changes. And congregations exist in geographic places, social settings, cultural locations, and historical time.[4]

As we have observed, from its genesis as a congregation, and throughout the church's five decades of existence, Lakewood's leadership has proffered a message of redemption and recovery. John Osteen's nondenominational outlook opened wide the church's doors to anybody who showed up, and teachings about transcending difficulties and finding spiritual meaning promised a more hopeful future through faith in Jesus Christ, knowledge of the Bible, and social engagement with the local community. What John Osteen once termed the "Oasis of Love in a troubled world," Joel effectively translated into a popular list of memorable spiritual aphorisms such as "we believe in new beginnings" and "discover the champion in you." As powerful mantras of encouragement and self-affirmation in America's recovery culture of second chances, these aphorisms have been connected by Joel and other religious teachers at Lakewood to a distinct collection of congregational resources in the form of religious instruction on prayer, Bible study, Christian fellowship, positive confession, positive thinking, and community outreach. At Lakewood, these spiritual adages have not been merely ideas to live by or formulas to repeat. They have been life. They provide a window into understanding how people at Lakewood have explained divine activity on the individual level.

As we turn to the voices and stories of selected Lakewood members and attendees, we observe the congregation's shared spiritual outlook and collective identity. In turn, we are in a position to understand the place of the redemptive self at Lakewood. The consistent presence of a message of second chances is, on the one hand, an idea central to the Christian gospel message, particularly in its neopentecostal expression. On the other hand, the idea of starting over speaks to new purposes in life—the intention to love and accept others, the ability to assist both friends and strangers financially, the avenue to share with somebody words and ideas that lead to existential change and spiritual understanding. Lakewood members affiliated with the congregation throughout the last fifty years have explained that they came to the church in search of a repurposed life, and invariably felt that they had attained it. Some narrated personal transformation as finding spiritual respite in an oasis of love, while others worked to discover personal routes to fortune and success. While individuals at Lakewood offered details of their own individualized spiritual journeys, they typically did not report that they experienced spiritual highs and lows in isolation. They did not travel their roads of faith in a solitary environment. Congregationally, therefore, Lakewood's larger curriculum of religious education has provided both a context and a framework for participants to learn in communal settings. The focus on the redemptive self at Lakewood, according to members and attendees, has fostered individual transformation and sought to institute meaningful social change in the world, akin to what sociologist Robert Wuthnow calls "the practice of spirituality."[5]

The articulation of a redemptive self at Lakewood is not unlike the emphasis on "champions" at another prosperity megachurch, Oasis Christian Center in Los Angeles. It makes sense that the teaching of redemption has thrived in the American cultural center of redemption narratives, Hollywood. The three-decade-old Hollywood-based congregation is much younger than Lakewood and is located in a different environment. However, the ways that Oasis members and their pastors,

Philip and Holly Wagner, have constructed individual and collective identities in the context of a multiracial, neopentecostal assembly of people provides a useful parallel in our efforts to understand the importance of congregational history and social change. In addition, a further connection between Lakewood and Oasis dates to the early 1980s, when pastor Philip consulted with John Osteen on church leadership and prosperity theology. He published his conversation with Osteen—along with those of Lester Sumrall, Charles Capps, Norvel Hayes, T. L. Osborn, and Kenneth Copeland, which revealed Wagner's strong connection to neopentecostalism—as part of a book titled *Insights from Men of Faith*.[6]

Sociologist Gerardo Marti explains that the "moral community" of Oasis has equipped members to cultivate personal holiness as they have wrestled with the necessity of individual ambition in the entertainment industry. In other words, the "Hollywood faith" of Oasis is connected deeply to its cultural context. As a result, the messages of Philip and Holly Wagner delivered in the church's Destiny Theater, like Lakewood's teachings, have offered self-affirming spiritual instruction that has promised ultimate deliverance from difficulties and triumph over troubles. Marti contends that not only do the Wagners' teachings reflect actual situations in which laborers in Hollywood's entertainment industry have found themselves, but also the concepts of deliverance and triumph tied to the prosperity gospel. From these teachings, Oasis attendees have embraced individualized orientations and a collective identity of what Marti terms "champions of life." At Oasis, and in similar ways at Lakewood, the cultivation of an individual relationship with God in the gathered setting of a moral community has resulted in the production of "empowered achievers" whose sense of redemption has fueled a new purpose in life used to affect the congregation and effect social change in the world.[7]

Religious Education and Bible Study at Lakewood

A common quandary in contemporary megachurch life is finding a way to connect meaningfully to individuals in a large and often impersonal setting. Forging relationships in a congregation that hosts tens of thousands of people is difficult. Not everyone who has attended a megachurch like Lakewood has stayed, of course; there is no doubt many have left and never returned. But for attendees or members who have chosen to stay, the congregational resources have been extensive. Over the years, to facilitate community Lakewood has supported K–12 youth activities, small adult social groups, and Bible study classes. It has produced a series of DVD programs to encourage connection as well as sponsored numerous outreach initiatives.

During John Osteen's tenure, outside of formal Sunday and Wednesday gatherings, Bible study meetings facilitated scripture memorization, basic knowledge of the Christian faith, and community outreach. Brady Mitchell, an African American, first attended Lakewood in 1976. He commented that as white flight led to Anglo suburban growth and the demographics of the area around Lakewood changed, black Houstonians and Spanish-speaking Christians started to attend the church in larger numbers. In addition, as the neopentecostal movement expanded during the 1970s, Mitchell recalled that black charismatics who left Baptist and Methodist churches found a new home at Lakewood. In fact, he remembered seeing black preachers such as Earl Allen and Kirbyjon Caldwell—who later led Houston's Windsor Village United Methodist Church—at Lakewood, as well as singer and teacher Carlton Pearson, who at the time worked with Oral Roberts. In terms of Lakewood's religious teaching, Mitchell adopted John's approach to positive confession and employed it in his own life. He received John's messages to "always look for Jesus in the Bible," and connected this advice to extensive advances in his spiritual knowledge and personal growth. "I'll never forget that," he said. In addition, Lakewood inspired his interest in outreach and social change; Mitchell once traveled to Guatemala with congregation members on a missionary and humanitarian mission to build homes.[8]

In the early 1980s, a white bivocational pastor and welder named Preston Wilson arranged for groups of newly arrived Vietnamese immigrants to attend Lakewood. In the spirit of community outreach, Wilson lined up transportation for them to and from church, assisted in English-language classes, and sought out potential employers for hourly wage jobs. In addition, based directly on John's encouragement and guidance, for a year Wilson taught a Sunday school class for immigrants. John's support of missionary work—Osteen "hungered to reach the world," he stated—inspired him to participate in Lakewood's annual missions conference. At the meetings, Wilson learned that Lakewood had provided the funding to establish early in the post-Communist era the first congregation on a Russian army base; locals referred to it as "little Lakewood." He also assisted with youth camps through the church, including outreach events for middle school and high school students at one of Houston's theme parks, AstroWorld. One of those young people, a black teenager named Jarvis Middleton, participated in Lakewood's youth programs. He began attending the church with his mother during a transitional time due to a family tragedy, and found Lakewood a welcoming place that both represented and respected all cultures. Middleton described communal worship experiences filled with music, speaking in tongues, and buoyant praise in a multicultural mix that, he reasoned, "heaven must feel like." During Middleton's time at Lakewood in the late 1980s and early 1990s, John's daughter April and son-in-law Gary Simons oversaw the youth ministry. On Friday evenings, teenagers met for worship, games, spiritual instruction, and prayer meetings. A focus on the Bible anchored the Simons' teaching, and expectations of scripture memorization aimed to promote spiritual growth. During this time, Middleton served as one of Lakewood's youth leaders and in collaboration with youth pastors had mentoring opportunities. Mentor relationships allowed selected youth leaders to work as prayer partners during Lakewood's Sunday morning services and plan churchwide youth conferences. Eventually, Middleton attended seminary and became a minister and spiritual teacher. In retrospect, he connected some of his experiences at Lakewood with Bible instruction, leadership training, and spiritual practice to his current outlook as a pastor.[9]

The recollections of Brady Mitchell, Preston Wilson, and Jarvis Middleton from the 1970s, 1980s, and 1990s reveal the historic presence of congregational resources such as Bible teaching, outreach programs, mentorship opportunities, and communal worship. Their accounts identify what shaped their individual experiences of personal renewal and what informed a communal identity rooted in the notion of second chances and redemption at a church called the Oasis of Love.

While Lakewood had established classes and learning environments for members and attendees of all ages during the years and decades of John's ministry, initiatives and plans have continued to expand during Joel's tenure. For instance, under the auspices of the KidsLife program, elementary school–aged children receive spiritual instruction according to grade level. Similarly, Lakewood offers classroom teaching about the Bible and spiritual life for middle school– or intermediate school–aged students as well as those in high school.[10]

One influential example of Lakewood's religious education is the Champions Club, a cutting-edge program developed for special needs children that began in 2008 and has served as a model for similar developments throughout the United States and the world. The creation of Lakewood minister Craig Johnson—himself the father of an autistic son—the Champions Club aims to address the needs and concerns of young people along the autism spectrum. Designed to tackle autism disorders that affect communication and socialization, for example, the Champions Club provides instruction focused on spiritual learning, sensory engagement, and physical therapy, all aimed at attending to autism in a "holistic" manner. Thus tackling both physical and spiritual concerns, Johnson ultimately hoped to create a welcoming space at Lakewood for families with special needs children. Part of Johnson's inspiration for the Champions Club—along with Joel Osteen's material, institutional, and spiritual support for the project—came when his young son Connor, who had spoken very few words over a period of several years, recited Joel's Bible confession after watching DVDs of his sermons. As a result, the Champions Club curriculum included "This Is My Bible" as part of its instructional package. Both Osteen and Johnson attributed Connor's earliest spoken phrases to divine intervention, describing his words as miraculous, incontrovertible evidence of a new beginning that signaled even more positive change in the future. While Osteen and Johnson looked to the spiritual side of Conner's life for confirmation of God's work, they in fact assembled the financial and professional resources to provide the best chance for children along the autism spectrum to make developmental progress and live meaningful lives.[11]

Small social groups and adult education classes provide settings in which Lakewood members and attendees meet, greet, learn, and fellowship. Small groups called LifeGroups convene in many homes around the greater metropolitan Houston area. As religious studies scholar Jillian Owens documents, small groups at Lakewood organize for encouragement, prayer, community, and Bible study. They provide a forum for participants to connect socially while reinforcing the church's teachings on daily Christian living. Lakewood has also hosted a blog for LifeGroup leaders to post encouraging testimonies, thoughts, and updates about the importance of close-knit fellowship. In June 2012, for example, a post by Joel and Victoria about LifeGroups stated, "Life is a group experience. You were not created to exist on your own. You were created to live and thrive through relationships; first, your relationship with God the Father, then your relationships with others." That same month, Lakewood member Tuan Hoang connected the welcoming "atmosphere" of a LifeGroup to growth in the Christian faith. "The objective of Lakewood LifeGroups is to create an atmosphere where people have an encounter with the presence of the Lord by engaging with others," Hoang wrote. "We welcome and acknowledge the Lord's presence best when we create an atmosphere of love and acceptance for others. . . . If you desire wisdom, guidance, and direction for our life acknowledge His presence by joining others in the *right atmosphere*. In His presence we get the answers to the questions that trouble us."[12]

One of the ways that LifeGroups expressed their faith in action took place in early 2013 through a project called the Hope for Freedom Walk-a-thon. Lakewood collaborated with a nonprofit group, Force 4 Compassion, to cultivate awareness, raise funds, and network with like-minded individuals to end human trafficking in Houston. Participants in the march included Congresswoman Shelia Jackson Lee and Houston mayor Annise Parker. In an interview on Houston's Fox affiliate, KRIV, Lakewood's Jackelyn Viera Iloff, Joel's sister-in-law, stated that the church wished to leverage its high profile to spotlight human trafficking, which has long been a problem in Houston. Lakewood's attempt to bring attention to the issue with the intention of making social change exemplifies what anthropologist Omri Elisha characterizes as "moral ambition," which he writes is "organized benevolence and social outreach" in the form of collective social engagement. When evangelicals engage socially in American society, Elisha argues, "they simultaneously work to inspire others to adopt the appropriate moral dispositions necessary to enhance volunteer mobilization. In other words, their aspirations pertain not only to what they desire for themselves but also what they have come to expect of others, including those who share their religious outlook as well as the larger secular and nonevangelical public." He also notes that "moments of creative agency . . . are at once fueled and constrained by the ideological demands of the institutional contexts in which they emerge. They are also complicated by multiple and at times conflicting historical, cultural, and theological influences that coexist within those contexts." Lakewood members' creative agency resulted in work with individuals in Houston's political and activist communities to get rid of human trafficking, cutting across ideological, religious, and cultural lines. Despite the church's proffering of a very individualized spiritual message—one that often seems powerless to address systemic, structural problems—the irony is that some of Lakewood's communal activities, inspired by religious ideals, focus on fostering social and political change outside of the church's walls.[13]

While LifeGroups met across the city of Houston, adult education classes gathered Saturdays and Sundays onsite at the church. For example, the New Beginnings class taught the basics of the Christian life. Class lessons defined the concept of faith, commended daily Bible study, and recommended a religious identity oriented toward future growth and development. Literature produced for this entry-level class included a fifty-page booklet titled *God's Promises for a New Beginning*, authored by Joel and Victoria. Published in 2008 and replete with nature imagery to symbolize new growth, the booklet explained the meaning of the term "Christian," suggested ways to build on life's difficult circumstances, recommended developing new friendships of positive influences, encouraged the cultivation of godly moral habits, and proposed the pursuit of contentment. Stocked with over 130 Bible verses, *God's Promises for a New Beginning* referenced its teachings about Christian identity to the Bible. "The Christian life isn't about rules and regulations," wrote Joel and Victoria, "it's about a relationship with God, through Jesus Christ, that will transform every area of your life!" *Foundations: Building Your Life with Christ*, a companion sixty-page study guide authored by Steve Austin in 2012, offered extensive training in Christian devotion. Presented with images of wooden two-by-fours, hammers, and wrenches, and employing architectural discourse in booklet sections titled "Master Plan" and "Construction Zone," the *Foundations* guide offered a six-lesson, step-by-step approach, inviting attendees to define faith from Bible study, understand the necessity of the Holy Spirit and spiritual warfare, the role of prayer in decision making, the application of spiritual gifts, and the importance of exhibiting morals inspired by the teachings of Jesus Christ. While New Beginnings teachers facilitated weekly discussions in class, workbooks such as *God's Promises for New Beginnings* and *Foundations* also served as personalized spiritual instructional manuals that encouraged Bible memorization, daily prayer, and close-knit fellowship with like-minded Christians.[14]

While LifeGroups offered teachings on a wide variety of topics and subjects and worked out in the Houston community to make social change, Lakewood produced small-group instruction through the creation of a DVD series titled *Growing Strong: Six Keys to Grow in Christ.* Narrated by Lakewood minister Lisa Osteen Comes and former Lakewood Spanish pastor Marcos Witt, the videos offered instruction on love, patience, determination, faith, obedience, and listening to the Holy Spirit. Lisa, for example, illustrated the Christian understanding of salvation by pouring water into an empty glass. She stated that the glass represented "you, as a sinner, . . . empty" without God's love. The water represented Jesus, who "pours himself into you" and "fills you up with his incredible, unconditional love." A full glass of water represented the Christian "full of the Holy Spirit" and "full of the love of God right now." Marcos Witt emphasized complementary principles, but focused on the topic of determination. For Witt, living a life of determination translated into obedience and promoted patience, illustrated by the Old Testament account of Job. "Patience comes through tribulation," he said, because "a good attitude" reflected a "spiritual maturity" and competent biblical understanding of the Christian life.[15]

"The Compass" educational track at Lakewood offers attendees more choices based on a variety of factors including marital states, age, and gender. A middle-aged white woman named Susie led a mixed-gender and ethnically diverse class titled Developing Faith for the Mercies of God and His Comfort. Having attended Lakewood since John led the church, Susie attributed her deep faith and excitement about the Christian life to divine healing from cancer and biblical promises for spiritual growth that she felt materialized in her everyday life. Observing that the Bible contained over 300 specific references to faith, Susie stated, "You successfully live the Christian life the same way you started it, by faith."[16]

A substantial part of Susie's message zeroed in on the concept of mercy—defined as compassion—a necessary ingredient to the Christian salvation process. In addition to an objective, intellectual understanding of mercy, she advocated memorizing Bible passages on the topic, which she said numbered over 260. In this context, Susie recalled a common exhortation John Osteen gave to "get the word [of God] in you before you need it." Based on the idea of internalizing the Bible, she exhorted students to "Go to the Word" and "Get rid of 'I know God can, I'm not sure He will,'" and instead find encouragement in Christian "testimonies to build your faith." Her teaching to engage scripture and draw meaningful conclusions aligned with anthropologist James Bielo's notion of "biblical relevance," a practice that evangelical Christians adopt to "establish how they relate to what is being portrayed" in the Bible based on social or cultural situations. At Lakewood, Susie's teaching on mercy, therefore, insisted that members personalize the biblical text—"get the word [of God] in you"—in relation to particular life circumstances.[17]

Susie's classes routinely ended in sessions of intense and meaningful prayer, as class members voiced requests for divine healing, employment, and growth in their fledging faith. The prayers expressed during these meetings cohered with what anthropologist T. M. Luhrmann calls "a more intimate, personal, and supernaturally present divine." Similarly, the passion of such petitions and praises embodied what Luhrmann refers to as an "emotional performance" of enunciating prayers as heartfelt language directed toward God.[18]

The structural aspects of Lakewood Church presented above provide formalized frames of spiritual guidance and social interaction under the auspices of classroom meetings, small-group fellowship, and organized Bible study curriculum both in print and in media format. Such formal mechanisms provide certain organizational insights into the congregation's larger impact. In addition, the personalized stories and narratives of individual Lakewood members and attendees offered below add further perspective on congregational life. While these stories are necessarily selective, given the size of the congregation, they are representative of Lakewood's collective identity. Moreover, the qualitative evidence emphasizes how attendees have both accessed and experienced congregational resources for establishing a moral community devoted to spiritual growth. These accounts convey stories that encompass the tenures of both John and Joel. They illustrate a wide array of spiritual and social journeys for finding a redemptive self in light of communal experiences at Lakewood.

Connie's Story: Inclusion and Embrace

Connie had hit rock bottom. In the months following September 11, 2001, her husband lost his job and the family's finances became precarious. However, Bill initially concealed the family's financial woes from his Columbian wife, until one day Connie confronted her increasingly stressed husband at his office. The startling revelation sent her into an existential tailspin over several years' time. On the verge of committing suicide in her home, Connie glanced over toward her ottoman and noticed a book she had purchased some months earlier: *Your Best Life Now*. She called Lakewood and demanded to talk to Joel Osteen. Instead, she had a conversation with Pastor Leo Taylor, who employed positive confession and pleaded with Connie to forego suicide and travel immediately to the church. "In the name of Jesus, through His blood, do not do that. . . . I declare in Jesus' name that you have to come to my office," he said. Still in a stupor of anger, hopelessness, and despair, Connie made her way to Lakewood. Despite some very tense moments, with counseling and comfort from her distraught husband, she decided not to end her life. Shortly thereafter, she and Bill started attending Lakewood and eventually received healing and hope. Over the years, Connie has found new meaning in life from Joel's teaching. She stated that he "presents a God full of love and compassion, a God who doesn't just exist to punish sinners. His message is one of hope for everyone who is tired of walking in life without seeing relief of their emotional conflicts or the real problems in their lives." Ultimately, she found love and acceptance that Lakewood members have insisted are central not only to the congregation, but also to their own religious identities. Through inclusion and embrace, Connie found her redemptive self at Lakewood.[19]

Stanley's Story: Meaning and Manhood

Stanley grew up in Oklahoma, and after college worked in New York and San Antonio before moving to Houston in 1981 after a job transfer. Having attended Baptist congregations, as an adult he strayed from his religious upbringing by indulging in drug use, partying, and drinking. As a self-described "young, angry, frustrated black man" who survived the racial indignities of living in the South, when he attended Lakewood for the first time in 1985 his initial encounter with John Osteen revolutionized his life. "He accepted me for who I was," Stanley said of John, "he looked at me with eyes of love." The love he experienced at Lakewood led him to a keener focus on the Bible, service in the church as an usher, and a wider understanding of the prosperity message through the teachings of preachers such as Kenneth Copeland and Kenneth Hagin. Stanley purchased a copy of John's 1985 booklet *Spiritual Food for Victorious Living* and adopted the practice of positive confession. In addition, speaking in tongues and the healings Stanley said he witnessed at Lakewood added legitimacy to the new teachings he had learned. "I wanted to learn how to flow in this kind of power one day. I wanted to know how this kind of power is available to the church today," he said. Stanley took what he learned from John—he was a "Word man," said Stanley of John's fidelity to the Bible—and dove into deeper scriptural study, learning more and more about the Holy Spirit and about the Christian doctrine of grace.[20]

Stanley also worked in the church's outreach programs, which eventually led him from volunteering as an usher to managing church operations. However, he insisted that the most important part of his attendance at Lakewood was the spiritual growth he has experienced in the church's men's ministry. Just as John had affirmed Stanley's identity as a black man, as a charismatic Christian, he sought to extend spiritual encouragement to a new generation. The men's ministry in which Stanley participated focused exclusively on concepts of Christian manhood. The class he facilitated addressed manhood in terms of temptation and spiritual warfare. It recommended the guided practice of Bible reading, prayer, and Christian service. Class handouts, adopted from instructional materials produced by California minister Chip Ingram's Living on the Edge ministry, linked the idea of spiritual warfare to the New Testament passage of Ephesians 6:12, which states, "For we wrestle not against flesh and blood, but against principalities, against powers, against the rulers of the darkness of this world, against spiritual wickedness in high places." Based on this verse and related concepts, Lakewood's men's ministry supported the idea that the Bible acted as spiritual "armor" against temptation and sin. In his capacity as a ministry participant, Stanley emphasized the integral role of the Holy Spirit in a life of obedience.[21]

If teachings on the concept of manhood at Lakewood invoked figurative armor based on Bible knowledge, they also adapted material from Arkansas pastor Robert Lewis's *The Quest for Authentic Manhood* to instruct participants in servant-leadership. Messages at Lakewood on authentic manhood, articulated through individualized "manhood plans," described men as "head" of their households, and instructed them to express "courage" and take "responsibility" for their lives and families. The text used military metaphors and conflict imagery, and adopted a masculinized reading of the Bible, reflecting what religious studies scholar Ryan Harper calls "post–Promise Keeper" Christian manhood. Stanley encouraged the men at Lakewood to find meaning in life through dependence on the Holy Spirit. He also counseled the men to maintain the strength of their spiritual armor, and to execute servant-leadership as a legitimate expression of Christian manhood.[22]

Richard's Story: Healing and Hope

It was 2010, and Richard had just received bad news: he had cancer. The disease had a deadly grip on his bladder and prostate. Shock and devastation set in, and tears welled up, but Richard knew exactly where to go. A long-time member of Lakewood who sat through John Osteen's teaching for a year before Lakewood's founder passed away, he said he had witnessed the Holy Spirit's work within the congregation, most specifically through the work of Dodie Osteen. Encouraged by his knowledge of the New Testament verses of James 5:14–15—"Is anyone among you sick? Let them call the elders of the church to pray over them and anoint them with oil in the name of the Lord. And the prayer offered in faith will make the sick person well"—Richard believed in the power of divine healing. Since Dodie had survived cancer, Richard sought out the Lakewood charismatic leader to offer a "prayer of faith" on his behalf. As he faced chemotherapy and surgery, Richard also had a chance to pray with Paul Osteen. Given that Paul was a physician, with a deeper knowledge than most about cancer's threat, Richard found his prayer for strength and healing moving and deeply meaningful. Richard drew tremendous hope from these prayers, and attributed his eventual defeat of cancer to the spiritual approach he took to battling the disease.[23]

If Richard found healing at Lakewood, he also discovered endless wells of hope in the messages he heard, the church members with whom he fellowshipped, and the music ministry. He said he absolutely loved the music on Sunday mornings at Lakewood, whether from Cindy Cruse Ratcliff or the moving harmonies of the church choir. "I feel the Spirit of God," he excitedly communicated, and every week prayed that he would "get out of the way" in worship so that God received all the glory. He also adamantly maintained, "Joel knows the Word a lot better than people give him credit for." Richard commented that Joel's maturation as a preacher across the span of a decade confirmed that delivering a consistent message of encouragement constituted Joel's specific "anointing."[24]

Communal experiences also animated Richard's attachment to Lakewood. An active participant in Lakewood's men's program, he insisted that he found great benefit from teachings on Christian manhood. With other men in the church, including Stanley Morrison, he met regularly for prayer and encouragement. Not only did he facilitate discussion and lead prayer in Lakewood's men's group, but also he worked as an usher at NOH events. He traveled to the Alamodome in San Antonio and even to Yankee Stadium on his own dime, which Richard said was a small sacrifice for the large spiritual benefits he received from not only attending, but also assisting in the events for Joel Osteen Ministries.[25]

In the midst of life's difficulties, Richard insisted that Lakewood offered a refreshing spiritual respite. Encouraged by the church's consistent message of victory and achievement, he found spiritual strength as his faith deepened through prayer, worship, and communal fellowship. And despite seasons of sadness and struggle, at Lakewood Richard ultimately found a second chance through hope and healing.

Raymond and Angela's Story: Faith and Family

Raymond and Angela first met Joel Osteen in 2000 when they attended Lakewood during a visit to Houston. They had watched him on television several times, drawn in by his smile and visible warmth. Raymond and Angela found themselves quite attracted to Joel's message. They both spoke favorably of what they called his "authenticity." Angela raved about the worship at Lakewood. "We loved the music," she said, "it was phenomenal." As a pastor's kid, Angela had a distinct perspective on church operations and programs. After attending Lakewood for the first time, she left moved and impressed. Raymond too was elated after he attended his initial service at the church. An inquisitive Christian, over the years he made it a regular practice to learn about the churches he attended. Not only was Raymond interested in what ministers preached from the pulpit, as someone in the sales industry he was also keen to understand how churches presented themselves outwardly. He and Angela had occasion to meet Joel and Victoria after the service, and they found the ministers' accessibility meaningful and commendable. Raymond saw Lakewood's diversity exciting, and described the congregation as a "friendly church."[26]

After their visit to Houston, the Gordons continued to watch Joel Osteen on his national broadcast. They even contributed financially to Lakewood during the fundraising campaign in anticipation of the church moving into the Compaq Center. As fate would have it, the Gordons attended two NOH events in 2004. On vacation in New York City, their trip coincided with an early NOH meeting at Madison Square Garden. It was an exhilarating event to attend, they said, and added to their very favorable opinion of Osteen. Then, the Gordons purchased tickets for the Raleigh, North Carolina, NOH event, a short distance from their home at the time. As financial contributors to Lakewood, the Gordons received an invite to meet the Osteens as part of the NOH festivities. It was another signature moment for the couple in their exposure to the teachings of Osteen and Lakewood Church, and their relationship to the ministry would develop dramatically in the coming years.[27]

In 2011, Raymond's job brought the Gordons to Houston. The following year, they started to attend Lakewood full time. Raymond started to learn about an entirely new side of Osteen's ministry now that he and Angela saw the church up close and personal. Fellowship and friendships increased. With two children, life was full and busy and as the kids got older, the family looked for ways to participate in church activities. With extensive background knowledge about the adoption process and requirements for fostering children, when the Gordons discovered that Lakewood's outreach efforts supported such initiatives, they said they found their purpose at the church. Very soon, the entire family became involved in fostering and adoption training at Lakewood. They became familiar with Texas state policies, and began the process to become a foster family. Interviews and home visits followed extensive education at the church. Spiritually equipped and legally certified, the Gordons eagerly welcomed their first foster child. The Gordons loved and cared for the child as their own, and their two biological children enjoyed having another sibling in the house.[28]

Shortly after the Gordons began fostering, their family circumstances changed dramatically. They discovered that their oldest son had visual difficulties, and soon doctors diagnosed him with Marfan syndrome. A genetic condition with potential complications involving the heart, eyes, spine, and lungs, those with Marfan tend to be exceptionally tall with extremely long limbs. An early diagnosis led to successful eye surgery. Baylor basketball player Isaiah Austin brought renewed attention to Marfan in 2014—his diagnosis, which occurred on the eve of the NBA draft for which he had declared himself eligible, led to his retirement from basketball—and the Gordons' son has become involved with Austin's foundation and its efforts at education, empowerment, and research related to the syndrome.[29]

Amid this confluence of circumstances—the new adventure of fostering children and their son's Marfan syndrome diagnosis—the Gordons experienced hope and encouragement at Lakewood. Through the classes that prepared them for the fostering process, the Gordons said that they experienced a new and deeper understanding of the Christian message. Angela stated that she felt she could "be Jesus" to the foster child and the child's family, by which she meant she could consistently offer unconditional love and a second chance. Moreover, she said that the short fostering period provided an opportunity to present "hope and encouragement to others" in a time of stress and difficulty. During the early days of their son's Marfan diagnosis, Raymond revealed that the presence and prayers of Lakewood's youth leaders and pastors Craig Johnson and Paul Osteen buoyed their spirits, not to mention provided encouragement for their son. At the same time, their son's involvement with the Isaiah Austin Foundation produced an additional surge of optimism. Ultimately, Raymond stated that the totality of what his family learned at Lakewood helped to make a difference in how they survived the difficulties of life. "Joel's messages always remind us no matter what is going on in our lives God is still in control," he said. "He reminds us that what [our son] is going through is all part of [God's] plan." The

Gordons' articulation of the redemptive self emphasized the role of providing a second chance for someone else. While their experiences undoubtedly affected them personally and individually, their orientation of service to others projected the redemptive self outward to society in religious expressions of family and faith.[30]

Teri's Story: Rescue and Redemption

Teri grew up in a stable environment on Houston's north side, but her life took a difficult turn when her parents divorced. Unwilling to face the emotional turmoil and conflicts of a new stepfamily, she sought an escape. After she struggled to assemble a clientele as a personal trainer, Teri commenced a career as an escort and strip-club dancer. For three years, she said, she easily made "fast money" as a stripper. Nice clothes and expensive things became an obsession. To work long hours and deal with the emotional and psychological trauma of the precarious situations in which she found herself, Teri admitted that she became addicted to cocaine and drank heavily. Nightlife took its toll and she experienced a drowning hopelessness. One evening, right before Teri decided to forgo stripping, police raided the club at which she worked and she found herself in jail. As she progressed through trials and litigation, a compassionate attorney offered her a job as a receptionist. "God removed the scales off my eyes," she said, and the "open door" of a stable and much safer occupation provided a glimmer of hope.[31]

A short time later, Teri got pregnant and had a child, and at the suggestion of her son's grandmother she attended Lakewood for the first time in October 2006. "That's where it all started," she recalled. As she began to regularly attend Wednesday and Sunday night services, Teri's spirits lifted. "I was so discouraged from my past," she commented, and Joel's sermons on second chances resonated deeply. She longed to start over and wished to pursue what she said was a more respectable occupation. Then, in early 2007, Teri received baptism at Lakewood, which she said, marked a turning point in her spiritual journey. Inspired by an increased knowledge of the Bible—she credited Lakewood with providing her a clear sense of "God's grace"—and possessed of a broad understanding of Christian service, Teri sensed it was time to reach out to sex workers with the kind of message she felt had rescued her. In the midst of listening to one of Joel's sermons at Lakewood, Teri stated, "God spoke on my heart that I needed to go back to the clubs."[32]

This thought eventually led to her founding Unconditional Love Ministries (ULM). "This ministry is about showing God's love to these women who may not know of this kind of love," she wrote of the ULM mission. "We are giving them hope when they feel there is no hope. Their hope is in Jesus. If this means to walk the streets alongside of them or to go to the clubs, then so be it." Under Teri's direction, ULM has actively promoted outreach to sex workers in Houston in an attempt to teach hope and provide the tools and skills necessary for a stable existence. Volunteers hand out gift packages with a message of encouragement. ULM representatives often pray with dancers. The ministry has been the subject of local news features, garnering praise for making a positive contribution to society.[33]

Teri explained that attending Lakewood for several years buoyed her spirits and helped her discover a redemptive self. Yet as a "new season" in her life dawned, she found a Houston congregation called The 429. At The 429, Teri nervously told her story, not knowing if the church would reject her because of her past. She found both acceptance and support at The 429. In the midst of sharing about her past life, she tenderly recalled an encouraging statement from one of the church leaders: "You have moved from a stage in the dark, to a stage in the light." Terri's second chance, the result of lucky breaks and those willing to lend a helping hand, led to rescue and redemption.[34]

The attention paid to the quest for the redemptive self at Lakewood speaks to the vast collection of congregational resources that the church has offered to fashion individual and collective identities. Teachings based on the Bible and recommended practices of spiritual meditation and Christian service in the form of outreach, whether expressed in the teachings of John and Joel as well as other Lakewood pastors or dispensed through Christian education classes, offer rich insight into what has attracted attendees to affiliate with the congregation and how members have maintained a spiritual perspective while in the context of a moral community. Over the course of Lakewood's history, opportunities to find and forge faith have existed at the structural level of congregational life and in the individual lives of members, resulting in innumerable discoveries of the redemptive self.

[8]

Joel Osteen's Piety of Resistance

New Calvinism and Evangelicalism's Crisis of Authority

> *Osteenification* is nothing short of the wholesale transforma-
> tion of American Christianity. . . . From Genesis to Revela-
> tion, Osteen simply uses Scripture to communicate whatever
> he wants. Not even Mormons or Jehovah's Witnesses treat
> the Scripture with such disregard. They at least attempt to
> grapple with the *biblical languages*. Osteen does not so much
> as seriously consider the *English* text. Indeed, that is what
> the Osteenification of Christianity is. It is conforming Scrip-
> ture to cultural norms as opposed to allowing the plain read-
> ing of the text to transform. . . . Osteen's . . . Scriptorture . . .
> abuses Scripture.
>
> —Hank Hanegraaff (2014)

The summer of 2005 was characteristically warm in Houston. Humid
mornings gave way to sweltering afternoons, which in turn made evenings in the nation's fourth-largest city suffocatingly hot. But solar
energy was not the only cause of Houston's heat. Joel Osteen was surging. He had published his first *New York Times* bestseller the year
before—*Your Best Life Now*—and in July 2005 moved his congregation
into the Compaq Center, a Houston landmark. Sensitive to the historical moment and conscious of his place in Houston's religious culture,
Osteen narrated the auspicious occasion: "For nearly thirty years they've
crowned champions in the sports field in this building, but I believe for
the next thirty years we can crown people champions in life. We're going
to let them know that they are victors and not victims, we're going to let
them know they can do all things through Christ." A media frenzy surrounded Lakewood's opening-day services, parking was at a premium,
and seating turned quickly into standing-room only.[1]

Another notable event in Joel Osteen's unforgettable summer of 2005 generated heat as well: his first appearance on *Larry King Live*. On the show, King asked about the history of Lakewood Church, how Osteen became a minister, and about the rapid success of his first book. King then queried Osteen as to the eternal fate of those who did not consider themselves Christians; he challenged him about the exclusive claims of the Christian message. Osteen affirmed his belief in heaven, but maintained that God is the ultimate judge of one's personal beliefs. He emphasized that his message centered on encouragement. King persisted. He asked Osteen, "What if you're Jewish or Muslim, [and] you don't accept Christ at all?" Osteen replied, "You know, I'm very careful about saying who would and wouldn't go to heaven. I don't know[.]" King again: "If you believe you have to believe in Christ? They're wrong, aren't they?" Osteen: "Well, I don't know if I believe they're wrong. I believe [. . .] here's what the Bible teaches and from the Christian faith this is what I believe. . . . I just think that only God will judge a person's heart. I spent a lot of time in India with my father. I don't know all about their religion. But I know they love God. And I don't know. I've seen their sincerity. So I don't know. I know for me, and what the Bible teaches, I want to have a relationship with Jesus."[2]

In the days that followed Osteen's appearance on *Larry King Live*, evangelicals bellowed with disapproval. Many interpreted his exchanges with King as a spiritual shuffle; they believed Osteen had in effect denied Christ on national television. He received numerous questions and complaints about his statements. After reading the transcript of *Larry King Live*, Osteen posted a letter on his website in which he apologized for his unclear statements. He articulated his convictions about the evangelical doctrine of salvation. "I believe with all my heart that it is only through Christ that we have hope in eternal life. I regret and sincerely apologize that I was unclear on the very thing in which I have dedicated my life," Osteen wrote. "I believe that Jesus Christ alone is the only way to salvation." Chastised, he stayed true to his core philosophy. "I will use this as a learning experience and believe that God will ultimately use it for my good and His glory," he promised. The following December, Osteen again appeared on *Larry King Live*. King noted the controversy surrounding his comments about salvation, and gave the humbled minister a second chance. "I believe that Jesus is the only way to heaven," Osteen stated.[3]

Despite Osteen's clarification about his fidelity to evangelical doctrinal orthodoxy, his first appearance on *Larry King Live* gave rise to a chorus of religious critics. Osteen's detractors first surfaced in 2005, and redoubled their efforts following the publication of *Become a Better You* in 2007. They have posted criticism on the Internet, mounted pulpits to denounce him, registered their disgust in print, and preached against him in person both outside of Lakewood Church and outside of arenas and stadiums during his well-attended NOH events. Some critics have denigrated him as theologically vapid and desperately shallow, while others have labeled him as merely motivational and a self-help specialist barely, if at all, Christian.

A significant number of Osteen's most persistent critics are affiliated with the New Calvinists, a surging movement within American Christianity focused on intellectualism and Reformed theology. As the New Calvinists have gained influence, the evangelical public stage on which they compete, as scholars Daniel K. Williams and Steven P. Miller argue, has undergone momentous alterations. Political realignments, generational shifts, and changing demographics, these historians write, have rendered the combative rhetoric of evangelicalism's historic culture warriors less palatable. But the New Calvinist's specific orientation to a particular style of confrontational cultural engagement has persisted. The soaring popularity of Osteen during the last decade, bringing him to the pinnacle of American Christianity, has not stopped self-proclaimed guardians of American evangelicalism from pronouncing doctrinal judgments on the smiling preacher. United in their denunciations of Osteen but different in their specific points of contention, critics such as California pastor John MacArthur, seminary president R. Albert Mohler, and theologian Michael Horton, along with enterprising Christian rappers and bold street preachers, have castigated the Houston minister. In turn, Osteen has responded to the scoffers through the articulation of a piety of resistance, a counteroffensive composed of scriptural defenses, positive confession, and positive thinking.

The backdrop for understanding the contest between Osteen and his religious critics is, on the one hand, a territorial battle over evangelicalism's past. On the other hand, his deriders have reasoned that they are also in a contest for the movement's future. These conflicts, at once theological, philosophical, and cultural, are at the center of historian Molly Worthen's study of evangelicalism's twentieth-century intellectual life. A movement with diverse constituencies and denominational traditions that have long vied for cultural legitimacy and political power, evangelicalism's fidelity to the Bible has rendered it deeply fractured organizationally—what Worthen calls its "crisis of authority"—and splintered over scriptural interpretations and ways to engage the world around it. "We must recognize that American evangelicalism owes more to its fractures and clashes, its anxieties and doubts," she writes, "than to any political pronouncement or point of doctrine." The clash between the broader propositional philosophical framework in which Osteen's New Calvinist skeptics judge the world—an epistemological orientation that prizes predictability and order—and Osteen's equally predictable and consistent message of positivity and second chances brings a rich historical irony to the debate. It also speaks inversely yet powerfully to Osteen's role as America's most important Christian leader. The intramural conflict between conservative Protestants that the Osteen–New Calvinist contest has represented is not merely insider theological drama; it is a cultural laboratory in which to observe contemporary evangelicalism's crisis of authority.[4]

Joel Osteen's New Calvinist Critics

In recent years, growing interest in Reformed theology has become the preoccupation of a significant number of New Calvinist evangelicals. They dip into the writings of the Puritans, and carefully pore over the publications of the eighteenth-century theologian Jonathan Edwards. Contemporary writers and pastors such as John MacArthur, Michael Horton, John Piper, Tim Keller, Mark Dever, and R. Albert Mohler, who represent a variety of denominational traditions, associate with New Calvinism. The movement has featured a loosely structured leadership that is largely male and predominately white, although groups known as the Reformed Blacks of America and the Reformed African American Network have developed as well. White New Calvinist leaders such as John Piper have started to address matters of race and ethnicity, though Piper has emphasized correct belief and richer relationships over structural adjustments for things like economic democracy and political equality. New Calvinist teaching is promulgated through theology conferences, evangelistic outreach societies, and Bible study groups. In 2009, *Time* journalist David Van Biema identified New Calvinism as one of the "10 Ideas Changing the World Right Now." The New Calvinists fixate on "an utterly sovereign and micromanaging deity," Van Biema wrote, a "sinful and puny humanity, and the combination's logical consequence, predestination: the belief that before time's dawn, God decided whom he would save (or not), unaffected by any subsequent human action or decision." As evangelical writer Collin Hansen documented in his book on the movement, robust theological analysis has also been a core component of New Calvinist thinking. Emphasis on a sovereign God, clear-eyed preaching about grace and faith, and teaching saturated in scripture admonitions and imperatives—all hallmarks of American evangelicalism—have animated New Calvinist conversations. Similarly, a 2014 *Religion & Ethics NewsWeekly* profile highlighted the movement's devotion to an intellectual theology rooted in philosophical ideas, and also noted that a substantial number of Southern Baptists have adopted New Calvinism. In response to what they have perceived as a downturn in doctrinal rigor in favor of a simpler gospel message trimmed for the unchurched, seekers, and spiritual pilgrims, the New Calvinists have been unrelenting in their quest for theological certitude. Those whose theology does not measure up have quickly found themselves in the doctrinal crosshairs.[5]

One such critic is Southern Baptist stalwart and Calvinist partisan R. Albert Mohler. An author, editor, radio show host, and educator, he declared that Osteen's 2005 performance on *Larry King Live* "was not pretty." In a June 24, 2005, column on his website, Mohler argued that Osteen stumbled on the most important, basic doctrinal points and "even left the door open for atheists to go to heaven." Mohler emphasized that although he felt Osteen "obviously means well and loves to help people," his "message of smiling affirmation" ultimately failed to offer biblical encouragement since Osteen avoided talk of sin. The following day, Mohler reported on Joel Osteen's apology—the only critic to ever reference this letter—and praised him for what seemed to Mohler like genuine "humility and candor." He seemed pleased with Osteen's "clear and unambiguous affirmation of the exclusivity of the Gospel of

Jesus Christ" and found Osteen's apology "free from the evasions typical of the pseudo-apologies so often issued to the public. . . . The humility and honesty of the statement serve to fortify its authenticity." But Mohler's praise was conditional, as the apology did not settle all of his concerns. He has continued to target Osteen's work, including the smiling preacher's numerous television appearances. He has concluded that they offer "a display of confusion, evasion, and equivocation coming from one presented as a Christian pastor. What [we are] really seeing is the total theological bankruptcy of the word of faith movement and the gospel of positive thinking. Osteen cannot, or at least will not, speak even the simplest word of biblical conviction. He states his intention to stay in his 'lane' of glib affirmation."[6]

Mohler's role as a seminary president has provided him a platform from which to promote his opinion. His reaction to Osteen's comments on *Larry King Live* in 2005 and his sustained commentary since that time has represented one manifestation of New Calvinist opinion about America's most important minister. Mohler's belief that Osteen is soft on sin—Reformed Christianity regards sin as a vital doctrine—and part of a neopentecostal movement that he considers theologically bankrupt leads him to question Osteen's credentials as a pastor. Moreover, for Mohler, the theological thinness of Osteen's message and its alignment with the modern charismatic movement has undercut the legitimacy of his teaching. In his view, Osteen is not theological enough to be a preacher, and his lack of doctrinal depth is more suited to motivational speaking. Mohler's critique of Osteen has centered on theological disagreements, and therefore his problem with Osteen has essentially focused on interpretations of the Bible.

Subsequent attention to Osteen's ministry from evangelicals and nonevangelicals alike—mainline writers from *Christian Century* magazine and the online news source *Religion Dispatches*, for example, have critiqued Osteen since 2005—have generated a flurry of responses that ranged from utter dismissal to measured praise. This attention put many on notice that Osteen could be *the* next big thing in American evangelicalism. Although Osteen did not make *Time's* top-twenty-five list of noted evangelicals in late 2005, in 2006 David Van Biema and Jeff Chu's "Does God Want You to Be Rich?" referenced the smiling preacher. Their *Time* article profiled Lakewood member George Adams, who discovered both salvation and success through Osteen's teachings. Whether he was making the rounds on talk shows, sitting for interviews with local and national television affiliates, or giving his time to traditional print media journalists, after 2005 Osteen's name struck chords with both individuals and institutions.[7]

The appearance of Osteen's second book, *Become a Better You*, in late 2007 marked another watershed moment. He was very well known by that point, perhaps even a household name. The weeks leading up to publication witnessed a targeted marketing campaign to get the word out about his new book. Osteen's hometown newspaper, the *Houston Chronicle*, printed excerpts, and word about *Become a Better You* spread quickly both in Houston and throughout the nation.[8]

Such publicity efforts—especially Osteen's *60 Minutes* appearance in late 2007—afforded his critics another opportunity to respond. It was Westminster Theological Seminary professor and theologian Michael Horton who on the show provided the most pressing counterpoint to Osteen's theological claims. Horton said, "I think it's a cotton candy gospel. . . . [Osteen's] core message is God is nice, you're nice, be nice. . . . He uses the Bible like a fortune cookie."[9]

Horton's presence on *60 Minutes* was not insignificant. A prolific author, conference speaker, and ordained minister, he has long been a vocal critic of evangelicalism and a leading voice in the New Calvinist movement. For two decades, Horton has unfailingly called for what he has termed a "second Reformation." In pursuit of this objective, he first created an organization called Christians United for Reformation (CURE), a coalition of pastors and theologians concerned about the fate of American evangelicalism. Based in California, CURE gained a national following through a theological radio talk show Horton hosted called *White Horse Inn*. The organization also generated support through a monthly magazine called *Modern Reformation*. Increasing interest in questions about the doctrinal viability of evangelicalism in the mid-1990s led Horton to issue more formal statements about the need for a second Reformation. In a meeting on the campus of Harvard University—once the heart of Reformed Christianity in the United States—Horton and other delegates composed and signed the *Cambridge Declaration*, the founding statement of the new Alliance of Confessing Evangelicals (ACE). An interdenominational coalition of evangelical, Anglican, Lutheran, Presbyterian, and other conservative Protestants, ACE gave Horton's second Reformation message more visibility and a larger stage from which to issue critiques of American evangelicalism.[10]

Horton's call for a second Reformation coupled with his own reading of Protestant Christian history operates with what sociologist Christian Smith describes as a "sense of displaced heritage." As part of Protestant evangelicalism's "embattled and thriving" identity, Smith observes that notions of displaced heritage depend upon a reading of history and culture that ultimately pivots on a series of golden ages, followed by calamitous falls and heroic recoveries. For Horton, the sixteenth-century Protestant Reformation leaders Martin Luther and John Calvin, among others, helped to reassert the conviction that God is the prime mover of grace in the human experience. From his perspective, what the Reformation era recovered in terms of proper doctrine, nineteenth-century evangelicals squandered in a quest for relevance and cultural capital. Horton placed the blame for such doctrinal malaise on Charles Finney, a New York religious leader of the Second Great Awakening, and Protestant liberals of the early twentieth century. Horton's view of Protestant Christian history was not dissimilar to the perspective of those Worthen terms "God's idea men," leaders in the late-twentieth-century evangelical movement who highlighted intellectual deliberation in the promotion of a distinct Christian "worldview" against an encroaching secularism.[11]

Within Horton's narrative of Reformed Christianity and American Protestant history, some of his consistent targets have been modern televangelism, neopentecostalism, and the Word of Faith movement. For an edited volume, *The Agony of Deceit: What Some TV Preachers Are Really Preaching*, Horton recruited a host of essayists to denounce televangelism's impact on modern evangelicalism. Published in 1990 on the heels of a string of televangelist scandals, Horton aimed to reestablish what he considered sound doctrinal principles. Characteristically, he ended with a call for a second Reformation. He attempted to draw parallels between modern televangelists and Martin Luther's sixteenth-century nemesis John Tetzel, who popularized the sale of indulgences. Horton observed, "Today, unofficial, nonelected Protestant popes tyrannize the masses once more. Tetzels, purveyors of saving grace, pitch their hi-tech tents under the same sky." Horton fashioned the contribution of *The Agony of Deceit* as a new version of Protestant protest: "[W] e would like to think of this volume as the nailing of our theses to the door of the electronic church. Once again, let the cries of the people of God reach their Master's ears."[12]

Since *The Agony of Deceit*, Horton has continued to offer analyses of American evangelicalism. Thus, it is not surprising that he has spoken out vigorously to condemn Joel Osteen. For him, Osteen represents one of the latest examples of what is wrong with American evangelicalism. In the months following his appearance on *60 Minutes*, Horton continued to build a theological and historical case against Osteen. He devoted several *White Horse Inn* shows to Osteen's teachings and commented further on the smiling preacher in his 2008 book *Christless Christianity: The Alternative Gospel of the American Church.*[13]

Christless Christianity examined what Horton described as the theological scourge of "American Pelagianism." An early Christian writer who countered the teachings of fourth-century North African bishop Augustine, Pelagius contested the doctrine of inherent human fallibility and instead emphasized the possibility that humans could achieve salvation through their own will power. Horton also related Pelagianism to the doctrine of Arminianism, a theological posture popular during the Protestant Reformation. Arminianism prized human cooperation with divine intent in salvation. He contended that both Pelagianism and Arminianism found expression in the teachings of Charles Finney. In addition, according to Horton, Osteen's use of positive psychology has aligned with another heresy, Gnosticism. A teaching that emerged in the ancient world, Gnosticism held that secret knowledge of the spiritual realm released human ties to the physical world. Horton drew a straight line from ancient Gnosticism to Pelagius in the fourth century to Arminianism in the sixteenth century to the nineteenth-century ministrations of Charles Finney.[14]

For Horton, Joel Osteen has illustrated "self-salvation." He wrote, "To the extent that it reflects any theology at all [Osteen's] message represents a convergence of Pelagian self-help and Gnostic self-deification." According to Horton, Osteen has replaced the traditional gospel message of sin and salvation with short homilies on happy living and good advice. "Salvation is not a matter of divine rescue from the judgment that is coming on the world," Horton argued, "but rather a matter of self-improvement in order to have your best life now." While Horton has faulted Osteen for failing to understand human sin—a theological, biblical problem—his clarion call for a second Reformation has pivoted on anxieties of a displaced heritage that has emphasized a particular kind of historical recovery rooted in conservative, Reformed evangelicalism.[15]

Horton's neatly packaged, linear version of Christianity's doctrinal past has served to produce a narrative that relies on God's ultimate orchestration of human history. In this way, he has painted a way forward that involves a restoration of ideas and beliefs from a supposed golden age of Christian history. While not all individuals in the larger Reformed movement have appeared comfortable with his arguments and conclusions—for example, John Armstrong, a Chicago area minister and writer who is a friend of Horton's, has contested his dismissal of Osteen—Horton's influence is significant. He has taught that Reformed Christians must engage in perpetual doctrinal and intellectual combat to protect the Bible from its uncultured corrupters, many of whom are neo-pentecostal proponents of the prosperity gospel such as Joel Osteen.[16]

The way that Horton has aligned Osteen with a long history of doctrinal corruption comports with New Calvinism's emphasis on theology. In this formulation, the most intellectually robust and theologically literate are the true heirs of the Reformation. Furthermore, Osteen's inadequate focus on Jesus has led to a "Christless Christianity." Horton's excision of Osteen suggests that the main disagreement—much like Mohler's problem with Osteen—is about biblical interpretation and a particular Protestant, Reformed understanding of the scriptures. This illustrates how evangelicalism's crisis of authority has shaped the debate.

On the heels of Horton's critical comments, in 2008 prominent evangelical fundamentalist John MacArthur charged Osteen with serious doctrinal infractions. Trained at Talbot School of Theology, MacArthur, like Horton, has been a popular author, speaker, and writer. He has been pastor of Grace Community Church in California, president of Grace to You Ministries, which he founded in 1969, and host of a daily radio program of the same name. In the mid-1980s, he assumed the presidency of a Bible college and founded a seminary, Master's Theological Seminary. During that same decade, MacArthur began to publish a series of Bible commentaries, and by the mid-1990s, he combined years of preaching into a study Bible that includes reference notes to aid scripture study. In addition to his popularity among some evangelicals for his strategy of preaching the Bible verse by verse, MacArthur has long been a fierce critic of neopentecostalism. Although he has not emphasized Reformation theology precisely the same way as Horton, he has expressed sympathy with its history, its claims, and its teachings. And similar to Mohler and Horton, MacArthur's writings and teachings have surfaced in New Calvinist circles.[17]

In 1992, MacArthur published *Charismatic Chaos*, a revision of his 1978 book *The Charismatics: A Doctrinal Perspective*. He questioned the premium that neopentecostals had placed on religious experience. He argued that "[e]xperience . . . is not the test of biblical truth; rather, biblical truth stands in final judgment on experience." MacArthur devoted a final chapter to the Word of Faith movement and analyzed the writings and sermons of Kenneth Hagin, Charles Capps, Robert Tilton, Frederick K. C. Price, and Benny Hinn, among others. He criticized the movement's ideas about God, its presentations about Jesus, and its understanding of faith. He also expressed concerns that the interdenominational nature of neopentecostalism had promoted ecumenical tendencies potentially destructive to global Christianity.[18]

In late 2008, MacArthur issued his first public criticism of Joel Osteen in a sermon, "Your Best Life: Now or Later?," at Grace Community Church. MacArthur commented on Osteen's popularity and suggested that to focus on establishing "one's best life now" is to misunderstand Christianity and misapply the Bible "because in the world to come, you will only exist in a perpetual state of dying with no hope, no satisfaction, no meaning, no joy and no future and no relief from eternal suffering. That's the worst life possible. And this is your best life, if your next life is in hell."[19]

Two years later, MacArthur continued his critical analysis of Osteen at a Ligonier Ministries national convention. Ligonier Ministries has been the operation of Reformed theologian R. C. Sproul, a close colleague of Mohler, Horton, and MacArthur, and a respected teacher among the New Calvinists. In a presentation titled "Becoming a Better You," MacArthur likened the prosperity gospel to a "religious ponzi scheme" and unleashed a verbal assault: "Joel Osteen is . . . a mouthpiece for Satan; he's an agent for Satan. . . . [Osteen's teaching] is a false Christianity from hell." In another presentation, he stated, "You need to understand that [Joel Osteen] is pagan religionist, in every sense. He's a quasi-pantheist.

Jesus is a footnote that satisfies his critics and deceives his followers." MacArthur's presentations reprised his earlier sermon on Osteen, and he read numerous quotes from *Your Best Life Now*. He also called Osteen a "hyper-Pelagian," echoing Horton, and, in a closing prayer, a "danger to the cause of Christ." Whereas Horton set his criticism of Osteen most directly in relation to his reading of American evangelical history, MacArthur's exegetical attack on Osteen emanated most specifically from what he saw as Osteen's shallow reading of the Bible. In short, it was a crisis of authority over the scriptures.[20]

In late 2013, MacArthur again targeted neopentecostalism in a book called *Strange Fire: The Danger of Offending the Holy Spirit with Counterfeit Worship*. Unrelenting in his attacks on charismatic Christianity, MacArthur charged the movement with "gross doctrinal error" and stated that it "has warped genuine worship through unbridled emotionalism, polluted prayer with private gibberish, contaminated true spirituality with unbiblical mysticism, and corrupted faith by turning it into a creative force for speaking worldly desires into existence." No Pentecostal or neopentecostal teacher escaped MacArthur's rhetorical wrath, including Joel Osteen. He echoed his previous criticism, calling Osteen's prosperity gospel a "massive swindle," and expressed particular alarm with the smiling preacher's openness to Christians of numerous denominational backgrounds. "Osteen's doctrine is a shallow, saccharine variety of universalism," he exclaimed, an indicator that "a new wave of ecumenical inclusivism may be on the horizon." For MacArthur, Osteen and the wider charismatic movement were largely beyond the pale of orthodox Christianity.[21]

MacArthur's stature within the culture of conservative evangelicalism has given his words wide purchase. His historic relation to evangelical fundamentalism has led him to fixate on the notion of unfettered biblical authority. His conviction about the Bible's unchanging character has been foundational to his criticisms of the American evangelical movement generally and neopentecostalism most particularly. Any minute deterrence from these positions, exhibited especially by neopentecostals and charismatics, has grabbed MacArthur's attention.

A relatively recent development in New Calvinism, "Reformed rap" has signaled the movement's attempt to interface with hip-hop culture, spoken-word poets, and MCs. Reformed rappers set intellectual theology to beats using hooks, and formulate rhymes using Calvinist doctrines. Many of these artists have been active for many years, and have only recently received widespread attention. Texas native Lecrae, who has achieved some mainstream success, has headlined the movement, along with Dallas-based Tedashii and Los Angeles spoken-word artist Propaganda. While these artists have toured the United States and performed internationally, they have also taught in local congregations and attended theology conferences. Evangelical writers have praised the creative content of Reformed rap, and have pointed positively to its Calvinist message of transcendence and divine election, and its expressions of doctrinal certitude and theological conformity.[22]

Shai Linne has been one of Reformed rap's leading spokespersons. Originally from Philadelphia, he has affiliated with Capitol Hill Baptist Church in Washington, D. C., a New Calvinist congregation pastored by Mark Dever. Linne's records have explored systematic theology, Calvinist doctrines, eschatology, predestination, biblical authority, and the prosperity gospel. He received considerable attention in 2013 with the release of an album called *Lyrical Theology, Pt. 1: Theology*. Linne described the record as a "lyrical exposition" of the Bible, and made waves with a song called "Fal$e Teacher$." The dollar signs playfully indicated the critical tone of his message. He described the prosperity gospel as a "deception," "foul," "deceitful," "ungodly," "wicked," and riddled with "bogus statements" that have been "financially motivated." Like other New Calvinist critics of the prosperity gospel movement, Linne emphasized the Bible ("Use your discernment, let the Bible lead ya"), and cited numerous scripture passages. Similarly, he generalized all of the prosperity gospel proponents as money-obsessed and interested in nothing but financial gain, who "treat Jesus as a lottery ticket." He blasted the Trinity Broadcasting Network, on which prosperity messages have appeared, and likened the prosperity gospel to "a pyramid scheme" proffered by "heretics Christianizing the American Dream." While Linne's critique of the prosperity gospel aligned with New Calvinist dismissals, in "Fal$e Teacher$" he singled out specific pastors and teachers as proponents of the prosperity message. The song took particular aim at Joel Osteen. Linne rapped, "The gospel is He came to redeem us from sin/And that is the message forever I'll yell/If you're living your best life now/you're headed for hell." The song's chorus was even more direct:

Joel Osteen is a false teacher.

Creflo Dollar is a false teacher.

Benny Hinn is a false teacher.

I know they're popular but don't let them deceive ya.

T. D. Jakes is a false teacher.

Joyce Meyer is a false teacher.

Paula White is a false teacher.

Use your discernment, let the Bible lead ya.

Fred Price is a false teacher.

Kenneth Copeland is a false teacher.

Robert Tilton is a false teacher.

I know they're popular but don't let them deceive ya.

Eddie Long is a false teacher.

Juanita Bynum is a false teacher.

Paul Crouch is a false teacher.

Use your discernment, let the Bible lead ya.[23]

Linne reserved his harshest criticism for the smiling pastor, echoing MacArthur in his condemnation of Osteen to "hell." Exemplifying evangelicalism's crisis of authority, the Reformed rapper rebuked prosperity gospel teachers for using the Bible to guarantee financial success and earthy riches, and he deployed the New Calvinist rhetoric of cultural combat and doctrinal conflict. "And I know that some will label me a Pharisee/Because today the only heresy is saying that there's heresy/I'll dare to be specific and drop some clarity/On the popularity of the 'gospel' of prosperity."[24]

Street Preaching and Artistry

While many of the most vocal of Osteen's critics who have addressed doctrinal and biblical concerns have been New Calvinists, other detractors have taken equal exception to the smiling preacher's message even if they do not necessarily identify with Reformed Protestantism. Three examples—an Internet sleuth, a street preacher from Colorado, and an artist from the Answers in Genesis ministry—show the different ways in which Osteen's critics are connected to fundamentalist evangelicalism.

In April 2013, a website that appeared to be Joel Osteen's offered a stunning announcement from the smiling preacher: "I am leaving the Christian faith." The page offered a statement about Osteen's purported apostasy. It alluded to the criticism Osteen had received, and included a putative acknowledgment that he had adjusted the Christian message to "fit my own doctrine and dogma" and had been "preaching 'feel good Christianity.'" "Many of their criticisms are legitimate," Osteen supposedly admitted. But the clincher focused on the Bible: "I believe now that the Bible is a fallible, flawed, highly inconsistent history book that has been altered hundreds of times. There is zero evidence that the Bible is the holy word of God."[25]

With a mix of shock and surprise, as well as skepticism, the Internet was soon abuzz, and news outlets even reported on Osteen's alleged exit from the Christian faith. Shortly thereafter, Lakewood issued a clarification, stating that the website was fake and that the smiling preacher had been the target of a hoax. A few days later, Minnesotan Justin Tribble came forward as the hoax's purveyor, and said that he orchestrated it to bring attention to Osteen's clichéd sermons and "self-help platitudes." About Tribble's actions, Joel commented characteristically: "I feel too blessed, that life is too short to let things like this get you down."[26]

While Tribble's digital duplicity was shocking, the act of creating a fake website was not the most important aspect of the controversy. Key to the hoax was that he depicted Osteen as admitting to teaching a thin theology and decrying the Bible as "fallible" and full of "inconsistent history." Tribble's criticism, similar to many of Osteen's detractors, focused on biblical authority and thus spoke to evangelicalism's ongoing crisis about the scriptures.

Although some of Osteen's scoffers have excoriated him from a distance, a Colorado minister named Steve Bauer is one of the few who have countered the smiling preacher's message in person (another is independent evangelist and author Adam Key). A firefighter and paramedic, and a former atheist, Bauer has spent much of his free time street preaching, engaging people face to face with the Christian message. Bauer has located the inspiration for his approach in the expressive evangelistic techniques of Ray Comfort and Kirk Cameron, whose Way of the Master ministry has recommended open-air preaching and the dissemination of gospel tracts. The unrelenting street preacher has ministered to ordinary people passing on the sidewalk, as well as at Joyce Meyer meetings and outside sporting events such as the Super Bowl. As the founder of an organization called Watersource Ministries, Bauer has contended that "love for the lost" has motivated his street ministry and has coupled his practice of handing out gospel tracts with preaching. On this basis, he has claimed to pray regularly for Joel Osteen. Bauer has stated that churches have turned into sites of entertainment and in the process have failed to deliver a message of grace through faith. He has argued that advocates of the prosperity gospel most egregiously exhibit this kind of compromised Christianity.[27]

When Osteen's NOH traveled to the Pepsi Center in Denver in June 2012, Bauer mobilized around twenty-five volunteers from Watersource Ministries to preach against Osteen and hand out specially made anti–Joel Osteen gospel tracts. For several hours, while Osteen held his event inside the Pepsi Center, outside Bauer and his team preached tirelessly, engaged event attendees, and passed out nearly 5,000 tracts, according to their claims. On the top side of the tract, altered Federal Reserve and U.S. Treasury seals convey Bible verses along with a million-dollar denomination that flanks a slender, smiling Joel Osteen with oversized, sterling-white teeth. The "Treasury seal" Bible passage is 2 Corinthians 6: 9–10, verses in which the Apostle Paul describes survival despite difficulties and setbacks. The "Federal Reserve seal" includes biblical references, one from Ephesians, the other from Job. Lampooning the smiling preacher's Texas twang and questioning his legitimacy as a minister, a "Jole Olesteam" signature appears above the phrase "Department of Eternal Affairs." The backside of the tract prints a full gospel message of sin, faith, and salvation. Composed by evangelist Justin Peters for Watersource Ministries, the gospel message echoes MacArthur's emphasis on attaining one's best life in heaven as opposed to seeking it on earth.[28]

While Bauer's opinion of Osteen has been congruent with those of Osteen's New Calvinist doctrinal detractors, his methods of disagreement stand out, as does his contention that he has prayed for Osteen, instead of against him as MacArthur has done. In concert with MacArthur and Horton, the Joel Osteen million-dollar gospel tract bases its critique on argumentation from Bible passages. Thus, for Bauer, evangelicalism's crisis of authority has prompted him to hit the streets with the Bible in one hand, and Joel Osteen gospel tracts in the other.[29]

EPH1 4HECHOZUS

JOB FRT33N0N3

If you spend much time at all watching Christian television, you might think that it is God's will for everyone to be wealthy and to be physically healed. Many of the world's most popular preachers present the Gospel as little more other than a way to have "Your Best Life Now;" to be happy, wealthy, and physically whole. This may sound enticing, but it is not the true Gospel. The Bible is full of people who loved the Lord and served Him faithfully but were not wealthy and were sick. Job, the namesake of the oldest book in the Bible, says that "Man who is born of a woman is of few days and full of trouble" (Job 14:1). Our focus should not be on this life, but on the life to come. Where will you spend eternity? Are you like most people who think they will go to Heaven because they are good? Are you a good person? God's standard of goodness is the Ten Commandments. Have you kept the Ten Commandments? Have you ever told a lie? Have you ever stolen anything regardless of its value? Have you ever looked at another person with lust? Have you ever taken God's holy name in vain? If so, you, by your own admission, are a liar, a thief, an adulterer at heart, and a blasphemer. There are still six commandments left. Do you still consider yourself to be a good person? If God judges you by the Ten Commandments would you be found innocent or guilty? We would all be found guilty because "all have sinned" (Romans 3:23) and "the wages of sin is death" (Romans 6:23). We all deserve the wrath of God in Hell. But, the Good News is this: God loves you and has made a way to escape His wrath. Isn't that wonderful? God loves you! God sent His only begotten Son, Jesus Christ, to this earth. Jesus lived a sinless life and willingly laid down His life on the cross to pay the penalty of your sins and was then bodily raised from the dead. If you are willing to repent – to turn away – from sins and place your faith and trust in Jesus Christ, then you will be saved from the wrath of God and granted eternal life (Romans 5:9; Ephesians 2:8-9). No, God does not promise us our best life here on earth. If you are soundly saved, then your best life awaits you in Heaven for all of eternity. Read your Bible daily and thereby grow in the grace and knowledge of the Lord Jesus Christ.
For more information e-mail us at questions@watersourceministries.org

Figures 8.1 and 8.2. Joel Osteen million-dollar gospel tract. Artist: Esly Stampek. Text: Justin Peters. Source: Steve Bauer/Watersource Ministries. Used with permission.

If Bauer went public in a unique way with his Osteen criticism, artist Dan Lietha also creatively appraised the Houston preacher. Lietha has worked as an illustrator with the fundamentalist ministry Answers in Genesis. Most known for its vigorous support of creationism and active opposition to Darwinian science, Answers in Genesis, led by former high school science teacher Ken Ham, has also acted as a Christian apologetics organization. It has published books, magazines, a peer-reviewed science journal, and raised millions of dollars for museums and exhibits that promote a literal reading of Genesis and other parts of the Bible. Answers in Genesis has also directly employed researchers, writers, and artists to present its message in many forms. As a fundamentalist organization, Answers in Genesis has embraced theologically conservative beliefs, with a core conviction that the Bible is the only authority for

Figure 8.3. Dan Lietha, *After Eden* Joel Osteen cartoon, 2013. Source: Dan Lietha/
Answers in Genesis. Used with permission.

Christian life and practice. This posture has led the group and its ad-
herents to critique various other trends within evangelicalism, including the prosperity gospel. A 2013 cartoon of Joel Osteen that was part
of Lietha's *After Eden* line of illustrations depicted the smiling preacher
with a wide, toothy grin, firmly holding a Bible. But the Bible took the
form of a ventriloquist's prop, in which Joel's left hand moved the Bible's
mouth, thus controlling the message. The message Lietha communicated was that Osteen, rather than letting the Bible speak for itself—the

approach common in fundamentalist evangelicalism—instead finagled with scripture to fit it into the prosperity mold of his message. "You are worthy of God's love. God wants to make your life what you want it to be," Osteen's bubble quote read. "Your happiness is the most important thing." Lietha's cartoon protest of Osteen included a list of Bible verses, passages that referenced human sinfulness, the authority of the Bible, ethical thinking and living, and the responsibilities of pastors—all ideas Osteen's critics have addressed on some level.[30]

Osteen's New Calvinist detractors—and even those outside of New Calvinist circles—have issued denunciations in print, online, through lectures, sermons, rap music, and visual art. Collectively, the critics have argued that Osteen's message has not been spiritually demanding, requires very little sacrifice, and is detrimental to Christianity. Centering their criticism on disagreement over biblical interpretation, they have thus reflected a major aspect of evangelicalism's crisis of authority.

Joel Osteen's Piety of Resistance

By 2007 and in conjunction with the publication of *Become a Better You*, critics began more systematically to take account of Osteen's sermons, public statements, and publications. In response to increased scrutiny, Osteen developed a piety of resistance to answer the naysayers. It has offered finessed replies to direct, critical questions and has invoked anecdotes, stories, and statistics to document success and legitimacy while it has also deployed defenses of his prosperity message based on scripture passages and Bible stories. While Osteen's detractors reference the Bible to criticize his teachings, Osteen also uses the scriptures to counter the critics.

Osteen has emphasized that that he has faithfully embraced God's plan by offering messages of encouragement, positive thinking, and personal uplift. He has reminded critics that he is not a theologian; his job has not entailed translating Old Testament Hebrew or parsing New Testament Greek. On *Larry King Live* in 2006, for example, the host called on Osteen to reply to some particularly barbed criticism: "Ole Anthony, maybe you know him, president of the Trinity Foundation of Dallas, a critic of course, says of Joel, 'His popularity is a testimony of the spiritual infantilism of American culture. He's qualified to be an excellent

spiritual kindergarten teacher.' Funny. How do you react?" Osteen responded, "I hadn't heard that. I heard some other things he said. I don't
know, again, I'm doing what I feel like God has called me to do, and
judge it by the fruit. Come read my mails or listen to the phone calls or
come to the auditoriums where 20,000 people fill them." It is clear from
the exchange that Osteen has become well aware of what critics say. He
has appealed to his sense of pastoral vocation, and has invited the critics to dispute the results of his ministry, contest testimonies followers
offer, or challenge the numbers that he says show up to hear him preach.
In October 2007—the same month Osteen published *Become a Better
You*—on another *Larry King Live* show, King quoted a Michigan pastor, the Pentecostal-turned-Lutheran Robert Liichow, on Osteen's lack
of theological training. Osteen responded by saying that Jesus' disciples
did not receive advanced theological degrees. "[O]ne was a fisherman,
[another] a tax collector. They didn't have any formal training," he re-
torted. "The Bible says that God chooses people that, you know, are not
the most educated or the smartest, to confound other people." In response to the criticism that his message is "theology lite," Osteen told
King that weekly he and the Lakewood staff met people struggling with
diseases, addictions, and other life problems. "We deal with the real issues of life," Osteen continued. "I talk about forgiveness and how to have
faith when bad things happen and, you know, how to overcome and, you
know, love your enemies and things like that . . . we're helping people
where the rubber meets the road." That same month on *60 Minutes*, CBS
correspondent Byron Pitts also quoted Osteen's critics. Osteen pointed
to the testimonies that individuals had offered about how his message
had transformed their lives. He took pride in offering an uncomplicated
gospel, a "simple" message of hope and change that all people of any
background understood and embraced. In these ways, Osteen has strategically deflected his critics by insistence on his fulfillment of his God-
ordained role of encouragement and inspiration.[31]

Osteen's books, in which he has addressed the topic of adversity, have
also displayed his piety of resistance. He has suggested ways to address
self-doubt, but also strategies to tackle criticisms from enemies and naysayers. "No matter how successful we are," he wrote in *Your Best Life
Now*, "we all face challenges, struggles, and times when things don't go
our way."[32]

Many do not realize, Osteen wrote, "that God has a divine purpose for every challenge that comes into our lives. He doesn't send the problems, but sometimes He allows us to go through them." Osteen has not shied away from discussing trials, but he has categorically argued that God used difficulties to make life better in the long run. In his estimation, God has sent struggles to refine and perfect. "He will put people and circumstances in your path that grate on you like sandpaper," Osteen suggested, "but He will use them to rub off your rough edges." Rather than wilt in the face of difficulty, he has counseled positive thinking and a rugged individualism that participates with a larger divine plan. "Stand strong and fight the good fight of faith. God has called each of us to be champions; you are destined to win. If you will work with God and keep a good attitude, then no matter what comes against you, the Bible says that all things—not just the good things in life, but all things—will work together for your good."[33]

In *Become a Better You*, Osteen addressed negative thinking. In order to "be positive toward yourself," he recommended that one refrain from "listening to accusing voices." "Quit receiving all the accusations. Quit allowing the condemning voices to take root, crowding out the good things of God in your life," he wrote. Osteen then turned to the New Testament epistle of Ephesians to offer biblical advice. The Apostle Paul employs the imagery of an armored soldier to instruct followers to engage in spiritual battle; Osteen focused on the breastplate since "[i]t covers your heart, the center of your being, the way you think and feel about yourself deep inside." While the image of armor works indirectly for Osteen's defensive posture, it is striking that he discussed the imagery of a breastplate protecting the heart, the location of one's feelings. Despite his advice to "never take [criticism] personally," it appears that he has reflected on the voices of his critics quite intently.[34]

In a chapter titled "Handling Criticism," Osteen most directly replied to his critics. "Every one of us will have times when we are criticized," he admitted, "sometimes fairly, but more often unfairly, creating stress in our hearts and minds and tension in our relationships." According to Osteen, criticism did not come "in the spirit of blessing" but "with an intentional sting." He has taught that prominence inevitably draws out the critics. In Osteen's view, the criticism to which he has been subjected has often come from jealousy. "[I]f someone chooses to misinterpret my message or my motives, there's nothing I can do about it anyhow," he contended. "Now I don't let my critics upset me or steal my joy. I know most of the time it's not about me. The success God has given me stirs up the jealousy in them." Osteen wrote, "I realize that not everybody is going to understand me. I also recognize that it is not my job to spend all my time trying to convince [my critics] to change their minds. I'm called to plant a seed of hope in people's hearts. I'm not called to explain every minute facet of Scripture or to expound on deep theological doctrines or disputes that don't touch where real people live. My gifting is to encourage, to challenge, and to inspire."[35]

Osteen also developed his piety of resistance in *It's Your Time* (2009). He promoted strength in the midst of adversity and the promise of ultimate triumph. In a characteristic message of boundless optimism, he contended that "today's challenges are tomorrow's victories" because "[w]henever God is about to take you to a higher level, you will face stronger opposition." Utilizing the language of achievement, he wrote that, "stay[ing] focused on your dreams" often means "tun[ing] out negative voices coming from others and from within too." Osteen likened silencing accusers to plugging one's ears with cotton. "When I first started ministering," he admitted, "I overheard people saying, 'He can't preach. He's too young. He's not as good as his father.' So I found some cotton balls and put them in my ears. I've learned to always keep a fresh supply on hand."[36]

In *Every Day a Friday*, Osteen even more directly expressed a piety of resistance. By the time his fourth and fifth books appeared, he had had many years of experience in tuning out the critics. As he recalled his earliest days as Lakewood's new minister, Osteen admitted, "One of my problems was that I tried to keep everyone happy. I didn't want to lose anybody." Ultimately, he decided that he had to ignore the critics and embrace the reality that not everyone agreed with him. He realized that "you are anointed to be you." To listen to the critic's clamor was to "lose your identity and uniqueness. It lessens God's favor. So, I stepped into my own anointing." As a result of embracing his anointing, Osteen felt that he faced even more strident criticism. "So I became a professional ignorer," he stated resolutely. "The higher you go the more haters . . . the jealous, critical people and the small-minded people will come out of the woodwork. But don't be a people pleaser, be a God pleaser." Osteen cited Bible passages to claim God had ultimately avenged him. "Use your time and energy to move toward your God-given destiny," he suggested. "Avoid the trap of payback, and understand you cannot avenge yourself as God can avenge you. . . . He can take those who try and hurt you and use them to promote you." To prove his piety of resistance, Osteen told the story of a former critic who met him after a Sunday service. According to Osteen, the erstwhile scoffer said, "I was your biggest critic. I was always talking about you, blogging against you. And I came to one of your services to find something else to criticize. But I liked it so much I came back the next week. It's been six months. I haven't missed a service yet. Now I'm your biggest supporter." For Osteen, this legitimized his piety of resistance. "God wants to promote you in front of your opponents," he claimed. "Part of His justice is vindicating you so those who said you would fail see you succeeding and accomplishing your dreams."[37]

Osteen's piety of resistance has also included comparisons with the Old Testament prophet Isaiah, the Apostle Paul, and Jesus. Osteen invoked Isaiah to defend himself; he cited the verse "No weapon formed against us will prosper, but every tongue raised against us in judgment, You will show to be in the wrong." Osteen advised the criticized to "stay on the high road and keep doing your best" as "God will pour out His favor on you, in spite of your critics." While he drew a decidedly confrontational posture from the Bible, he also spiritualized the conflict with his critics. About the Apostle Paul, Osteen noted that other teachers became jealous of the "great crowds following him" and "ran him out of town." Paul responded to his critics, argued Osteen, by staying confident that he used God's call on his life to the best of his ability and "shak[ing] the dust off his feet." This, he said, symbolized ignoring the critics. From New Testament writings, Osteen recalled that Jesus counted as friends tax collectors and sinners, and as a result was often misunderstood and therefore "perpetually criticized for doing good." He wrote that "Jesus didn't change in a futile attempt to fit into everybody's mold. He didn't try to explain Himself and make everybody understand Him; He stayed focused and fulfilled His destiny." Osteen also described Jesus as "one of the most controversial and criticized people that ever lived." What he found most striking, however, was that Jesus "got more criticism from the religious crowd than He ever did from the secular crowd." Osteen stated that Jesus' detractors failed to pay attention to his message—"they were constantly trying to find fault and tell Him all that He was doing wrong"—as he traveled around and taught forgiveness and hope. In a rhetorically powerful move, Osteen aligned his convictions with the teachings and life of Jesus, which also gave a spiritual justification for his message in direct reply to his critics.[38]

Osteen has cited specific Bible passages to support his piety of resistance, while also connecting it to the broader frame of his message based on positive thinking and positive confession. He has used scripture passages from the prophet Isaiah and the Apostle Paul to illustrate that biblical characters encountered adversity, and survived critics because God ultimately blessed their boldness and sincerity. In Jesus, Osteen found not only a personal savior, but also a highly controversial teacher whose main enemies were religious leaders. By marshaling scripture passages in response to attacks from the scornful and the contemptuous, Osteen has spiritualized the controversies in which he has engaged and has contended with the critics by issuing a counteroffensive based on the Bible. Such power plays and volleys of scripture link the exchanges to part of evangelicalism's crisis of authority.

The rise of Joel Osteen to national prominence between 2004 and 2007 through the publication of bestselling books and television appearances led to extensive religious criticism. At the same time, leading preachers have come to Osteen's defense. In 2013, a California pastor and consultant named Phil Munsey who has chaired Osteen's Champions Network, a program of outreach to ministers, published a *Charisma* magazine article titled "The Joel Osteen Most People Don't Know." He reeled off an impressive number of statistics related to the resounding commercial success Osteen had become. Munsey also presented what he felt were relevant behind-the-scenes snapshots of Osteen as a father, a husband, and a person who, while not perfect, exhibited patience, tenderness, and an eagerness to love people regardless of their background. Munsey summed up what he felt was the Osteen most people do not know by writing that he had excelled at not being judgmental. "[W]hat some call weakness is really Joel's strength," Munsey argued. "Joel refuses with uncompromising conviction to use secular guest appearances to judge people. His kindness has kept the hearts and minds of millions receptive. Joel is a friend to sinners." Similarly, Hollywood pastor Philip

Wagner—leader of Oasis Church and a longtime friend of the Osteen family—defended the smiling preacher not through personal anecdotes but by a direct confrontation with Joel's critics. Wagner declared that he was embarrassed by the critics' "shameful" denunciations of Osteen, and demanded that they drop petty bickering and jealous criticisms. "I know Joel Osteen. I consider him a friend. I'm not a 'Joel Osteen fan'—I'm a friend," he affirmed. "I know him to be a genuine man, a humble man and know that he has a desire to lead people to become followers of Jesus Christ. He believes the same fundamental truths about the Bible and Christianity that mainstream Christianity teaches and preaches from the pulpits of America."[39]

These developments reinforce the historical parallels between Osteen and ministers such as Norman Vincent Peale and Oral Roberts. Many criticized Peale's teaching on positive thinking as slim banalities ill equipped to address alienation or disaffection. And few welcomed Oral Roberts's early forays into faith healing and televangelism. Critics warned against what they saw as Peale's and Roberts's doctrinal compromise in exchange for money and popularity. Both ministers at times felt the sting of critical commentary but attempted to stay true to their own philosophies. Peale harnessed positive thoughts to combat negativity and Roberts claimed that he had received God's anointing to explain his spiritual and material successes. Osteen in effect has combined the strategies Peale and Roberts used to deflect their critics, practices that speak to the smiling preacher's historical significance and cultural importance. Just as Peale and Roberts offered a soothing message for the stressful times of the mid-twentieth century, Osteen's teachings of the early 2000s offered an equally predictable presentation meaningful to many in the contemporary age of unrest.[40]

Osteen's popularity demonstrates that he has been, in fact, a leading evangelical personality, while many of the self-proclaimed guardians of evangelical doctrinal orthodoxy such as John MacArthur, R. Albert Mohler, and Michael Horton—and others, such as Reformed rapper Shai Linne—have questioned if his message is Christian at all. Street preachers and fundamentalist artists have also creatively interrogated Osteen's evangelical credentials. It seems that if Osteen were not an evangelical in his core convictions and teachings, then evangelical critics would have remained largely silent about him.

It is also important to observe that, in contradiction to Osteen's critics who have claimed that he has shuffled on human finitude and has refused to address sin, he has in fact deployed the word "sin" and has used it in relationship to pressing contemporary issues. Moreover, he has also defended the exclusive claims of the Christian message on numerous occasions. In a 2012 interview with Chris Wallace on Fox News, for example, Osteen emphatically observed, "I believe that Scripture says that being gay is a sin, but . . . I don't dislike anybody." Similarly, that same year, appearing as one of the first guests on Oprah Winfrey's *Next Chapter* talk show, the host asked him if there were multiple paths to heaven, and if gay people would reside in a realm of paradise. "I believe that Jesus is the way to the one God," Osteen stated, but clarified that his intent was to be as inclusive as possible. In this regard, in May 2008, Osteen met at Lakewood with Jay Bakker and other participants involved with American Family Outing (AFO) after a Sunday service. Bakker noted Osteen's cordiality, and the fact that Lakewood reserved seats for participants of AFO, but observed that Osteen "do[es] not share our convictions and that Lakewood Church is not yet ready for an open dialogue with LGBT families." About gay people, Osteen argued that he has understood the Bible to categorize homosexuality as sin. And in a 2013 *HuffPost Live* interview with Josh Zepps, he described living in a "fallen world" of evil and suffering. He also stated that he sided with the Bible, which he believes affirmed that the primary way to achieve eternal life centers on faith in Jesus. It is curious that after years of arguing that Osteen's supposedly meager theology illustrated his refusal to address some of Christianity's difficult teachings, Osteen's critics remained silent when he publicly did the sort of thing they had clamored for him to do—he declared homosexuality a "sin" and reiterated the exclusivist doctrines of the Christian gospel. Osteen's detractors, it seems, have refused to give him a second chance, the doctrine of which ironically sits at the very foundation of Christian biblical teaching to which both parties have devoted their lives.[41]

Significant as well is that most of Osteen's critics have been white males. Perhaps their energetic doctrinal gatekeeping has been a manifestation of anxieties about the shifting demographics of American Christianity, not to mention larger trends in American society that will soon leave Anglos in the statistical minority. Similarly, the growing Latino/a presence in U. S. society also likely means that neopentecostals and charismatics will comprise increasing shares of America's Christian congregations. The substantial number of evangelical detractors of Osteen who have sounded alarms of apocalyptic proportions—resonant with religious studies scholar Jason Bivins's description of evangelicalism's "religion of fear"—also likely speaks to inherent anxieties about the persistent neopentecostal presence in a highly fractured evangelical movement, yet more evidence of evangelicalism's crisis of authority.[42]

The pointed New Calvinist critiques put forward by the aging ministries of Mohler, Horton, and MacArthur—and the decreasing appeal of their stridently conservative theology—shows that spiritual sensibilities at the root of the prosperity gospel tradition that Osteen represents have long frustrated those whose commitments to propositional theology produce a clamorous resistance to change. This reveals striking historical ironies at play between Osteen and his critics. Osteen's New Calvinist skeptics, whose theology has prized God's absolute orchestration of human affairs, by the very nature of their anxious criticism have assigned Osteen a tremendous amount of material and historical agency. This seems to belie the New Calvinists' convictions about God's sovereignty. Using the same Bible, and engaging in similar acts of interpretation, Osteen has promised unfettered possibility while his critics have emphasized theological aspects of conformity, control, and order. Yet the utter predictability of Osteen's message of God's favor and goodness is in the end very similar to the predictability toward which his critics' propositional theology has aspired. Philosophically, therefore, Osteen and his critics have seemed more alike than different.[43]

The philosophical congruence between Osteen and his New Calvinist detractors further explains the cultural importance of his story and ties it to historical conflicts that reveal evangelicalism's rifts and scissions. Both parties have rooted their messages in particular interpretations of the Bible, and both have deployed defenses from Christian scripture in reply to one another. This shared basis of conflict has not just been an example of doctrinal infighting. It has been an illustration of deeply embedded intellectual conflict in the evangelical tradition out of which both Osteen and the New Calvinists have attempted to leverage the widest possible influence on American culture. The historical shape of evangelicalism's crisis of authority helped to frame the cultural conflicts between Osteen and the New Calvinists, and simultaneously produced fidelity to both propositional theology and a piety of resistance.

Conclusion

This book has argued that Joel Osteen is America's most notable twenty-first-century Christian minister. While Osteen and Lakewood do not represent the wide array of practices associated with evangelical Christianity in the U.S., let alone American Christianity as a whole, their histories illuminate key developments within American religious culture. With a television broadcast that beams into millions of homes, an Internet presence that engages at least as many fans and followers, and a radio program on SiriusXM heard by countless others, not to mention a steady stream of *New York Times* bestselling books and his role at pastor of the nation's largest megachurch, it is clear that Osteen's impact and influence has stretched far and wide.

How did this happen? And why does it matter?

First, this study has connected the historical and cultural factors that produced Osteen's privileged position, which included his historic and enduring connection to neopentecostalism, an influential movement that in part fueled the rise of megachurches and helped to birth the prosperity gospel. It has carefully excavated John Osteen's leading role in the neopentecostal movement, and both the personal factors and historical contingencies that led to his adoption of the prosperity gospel. In hindsight, these historical developments and cultural factors made Joel Osteen possible. The popularity of Joel in early-twenty-first-century Protestant Christianity, this study has documented, is inexplicable apart from understanding the larger significance of John's seven-decade ministry, its roots in Houston and the South, and its presence across the nation and throughout the world.

Second, this book has suggested that Osteen's pinnacle position in American Christianity resulted from the articulation of a positive, predictable, redundant, and consistent message delivered through television and across new media platforms. It has touched upon the central fact of Osteen's first career as a television producer—he is the only leading prosperity gospel proponent who brought two decades of media production experience into the pulpit—and the strategic partnerships he cultivated with ministry and media consultants. These factors translated into the innovative presentation and placement of his message on a wide variety of media modalities across a rapidly shifting media landscape at the dawn of the twenty-first century. Osteen's digitally dexterous ways also embraced more traditional methods of delivering his message, to which his Night of Hope events and Joel Osteen Radio program have attested.

Finally, this book has contended that Osteen emerged as America's leading evangelical minister around 2005 during a period of significant cultural clamor that saw Democrats and Republicans arguing over the role of religion and politics as the presidency of George W. Bush ended and the Obama era began. The important fact that Osteen, at the time, was neither specifically aligned with the Christian Right nor connected to the Religious Left, meant that his politics of positive thinking offered an appealing alternative across America's religious landscape. At the same time, Osteen's functionally conservative political positions on cultural questions evangelicals deemed important such as abortion or marriage equality aligned with Christian Right convictions. This book pointed out that Osteen's scrupulous avoidance of overtly politicizing his teachings contrasted with the combative rhetoric of the religious conservatives and the equally impassioned positions of religious progressives. Although Osteen's sermons and social opinions were not free from controversy, his approach rendered a popular message that connected to a wide diversity of individuals.

This book's overarching argument is that the story of Joel Osteen's rise to notoriety was neither a simple tale of divine providence, as he has maintained, nor solely the inevitable result of the smiling preacher's slick marketing or populist preaching. And the story of Joel Osteen has far exceeded the man himself; it has included the congregants of Lakewood along with the church's other teachers and preachers. Joel has never been the institution itself, but only one expression of the congregation's identity and one articulator of the church's aim and mission. Not everyone, however, most particularly the New Calvinists, believed in the possibilities that Osteen and Lakewood's message promised to deliver. Not long after Osteen stepped onto the national stage throughout 2004 and

2005, critics fiercely challenged the legitimacy of his ministry, contested the content of his message, and categorized him as just another glossy if highly successful televangelist seeking to cash in on his moment of fame. Fully aware of his detractors, Osteen skillfully answered the critics through a piety of resistance. The conflict was a contemporary version of evangelicalism's historic battles over biblical interpretation, its crisis of authority. Ultimately, the story of Osteen and Lakewood is one of human drama and historical contingency, a narrative deeply rooted in Houston's past and profoundly linked to neopentecostalism's place in American Christianity.

By 2014, Osteen found himself the pastor of a congregation of some 40,000 people—the country's largest—the author of immensely popular books, and a household name as twenty-first-century America's most notable evangelical preacher. In essence, fifteen short years after he became Lakewood Church's senior minister, Joel had become the embodiment and achieved the fulfillment of his own message—positive thinking, self-encouragement, and belief that God's consequential blessings inevitably bring progress and advancement—the story of salvation with a smile.

APPENDIX A: JOEL OSTEEN, "WHAT THE RESURRECTION MEANS TO US AS BELIEVERS" (1999)

Below is the text of Joel Osteen's first Easter sermon, preached in April 1999, six months before he assumed duties as Lakewood's senior pastor. As one of Osteen's earliest sermons, it is a remarkable historical artifact. The message captures an early attempt at public spoken ministry that strives to strike a balance between content and performance. At the time of this sermon's delivery, Osteen had been preaching full-time for roughly three months. While he would become head minister in October 1999, Osteen preached regularly from Lakewood's pulpit for much of that year. Contextually, Joel would publish his first *New York Times* bestseller five years later, and six years after this sermon, Lakewood would move into the Compaq Center.

Readers will note the unpolished discourse in this sermon, and the easy use of very colloquial and informal language. The topic is the Christian idea of the Resurrection, but references in the sermon meander between a variety of topics, most especially Joel's memories about his father. Absent in this sermon—but a style that became a staple of future messages—are clearly defined admonitions about positive thinking and positive confession. While the sermon is unscripted, in contrast to his later messages, there are distinct elements of an evangelical message including references to heaven, hell, and sin, the death of Christ, the Resurrection, faith, holy living, and service to God. Also strikingly clear are references to biblical passages and scripture stories. Exhibiting fluency with his father's messages, this sermon documents Joel's early usage of Lakewood's historic Bible confession and displays his routine use of humor to connect with audiences.

Before Lakewood Church moved to the Compaq Center in 2005 and thereafter rebuilt its website, the church made available online verbatim sermon manuscripts as well as sermon audio files at www.lakewood-church.org. Archived versions of Lakewood's previous web pages are available in the public domain via the Internet Archive Wayback Machine (www.archive.org), where I obtained this sermon and the one that follows in appendix B. In editing the sermon, I have removed the parenthetically identified congregational responses (e.g., "Applause," "Laughter") that appear in the transcript. I have edited the sermon into a more coherent, integrative paragraph format not necessarily in the original and silently spelled out Arabic numerals, capitalized proper nouns, and corrected grammatical inaccuracies. I have added footnotes for purposes of clarification. All other changes to the text, in the interest of readability, appear in brackets.

"What the Resurrection Means to Us as Believers," April 4, 1999

Well, as I say often, I'm always honored to have the opportunity to share with you.

Three or four months ago, I never dreamed I'd be up here on Easter Sunday. I've been in the background for so many years and I've got to tell you, that's a little bit less nerve-racking being back there. But I'm just glad to be here. I'm sure some of you visitors are wondering what this young kid's going to say to you today. And I want to tell you I'm wondering the same thing.

My mother has a real way of encouraging me. I've got to tell you this quick story. A couple of weeks ago on a Sunday night before service she asked me, she said, "Joel, are you going to be ready to preach Easter Sunday morning?" And it's a funny question because I had spoken several Sunday mornings before. And I said, "Well, unless you know something that I don't know, I'm going to be ready." And I said, "Why do you ask?" And she said, "Well, I just wanted to let you know there's going to be a lot of people there." Yea[h], this is really helping my nerves. She said, "There's going to be a lot of visitors and you're going to have to say something about Easter." I said, "No kidding, momma?" I'm thirty-six years old and she's as bad as my dad. But you know, I told my mother, I said, "Momma, this morning there were seven or eight thousand people there. The Lord lets you reach a level. You can only get so nervous, you know. It doesn't matter if there's seven thousand or seven hundred thousand. I've reached that point." And I told her, "The Lord only lets you get so nervous. My heart can only beat so fast, and I can only go to the bathroom so many times before I come out here."

But I've gotten a lot better. I'm not near as nervous. Forgive me, Lord, for lying. I am just as nervous. I saw Dr. [Reginald] Cherry,[1] and I thought I ought to ask Dr. Cherry, "My heart beats so fast, it's just like I'm doing aerobics up here. I shouldn't have to work out." I'm just thrilled to be up here. And I promised my mom I'd say something about Easter. So, before I forget, I want to tell you that the Easter Bunny [i]s going to be in the front lobby after church. I love to kid my mom. I don't know why but I get great enjoyment from doing it. I think it's the same thing my dad did. But I don't know. Anyway, it's kind of funny.

You know we miss my dad. And all of you, of course, know my dad's not here and some of you still write on television and say, "Where's Pastor Osteen?" Well, you know, January 23 he went on to be with the Lord. But thank God, for the life he lived. And I certainly honor his legacy and what he did for people and, you know, I can't talk about him without getting emotional. So I'm not going to talk about him. But it's the first Easter that he's not here and we honor the life that he lived. What a tremendous foundation that he built this church on. You can remain standing. We're going to hold up our Bibles. Remain standing. He built the church on such a tremendous foundation, you know. It's so wonderful. It's built on the foundation of the Word of God and the love of God for people. And that's just—one chapter's finished, the chapter of Daddy's life—but you know it's a new chapter. And I'm excited about the future. God's a progressive God.[2] He does new things. And you know He's got a bright future for all of you individually. And I believe He's got a bright future for this church. You know, you look up and you see it filled today and it's exciting to see what God's going to do. You know, all through the Bible when a great leader died, God raised up other leaders. And most of the time when the leaders died, the Church got stronger. The Church grew even more because the people were more committed and dedicated. And even when Jesus was crucified and died, they said, "You know Christianity is done away with." But you know what happened. It spread all over the world. So things are happening here and I'm excited about the future. And I'm so glad you're here with us this morning.

And let's hold up our Bibles, and we're going to make our confession. And let's make it like you mean it now. This is my Bible. I am what it says I am. I have what it says I have. I can do what it says I can do. Today I will be taught the Word of God. I boldly confess. My mind is alert. My heart is receptive. I will never be the same. I am about to receive the incorruptible, indestructible, ever-living seed of the Word of God. I will never be the same. Never, never, never. I'll never be the same. In Jesus' name. God bless you and you may be seated.

I'm not going to have you turn to any particular scripture right now because I'm going to quote a lot of scriptures today. As I've said already, I'm excited about the opportunity to share with you this Easter Sunday morning. Easter is a great time in Christianity—the day that we celebrate the Resurrected Savior. Isn't that great? We're not celebrating a dead god. We've got a risen Savior. Isn't that good news? Man, I'm excited about Easter. So many of the other religions, they celebrate the death of their leader. But thank God we can celebrate the resurrection and the life of our founder, the Lord Jesus Christ, our precious Savior.

And I want to talk to you a little while today about "What does the Resurrection mean to you and me as believers?" What does it mean? You know I believe the Bible is practical and is relevant for us today. What does an event that happened a couple thousand years ago; how does it affect my life? What significance does it play in my life? So, I want to talk to you a little bit about that. And in order to do that we need to go back a couple thousand years. Let me paint a picture for you. It's the day that Jesus was going to be crucified. Use your imagination. I can see Jesus. He's surrounded by a group of Roman soldiers. He's in the midst of those. His back is bloodied and bruised. He's just been beaten with a lead whip. And I can see one of the soldiers come up and he's so proud of this crown of thorns that he just made: thick, long, two- or three-inch thorns. And he goes over there and he places it on Jesus' head. And he thrust[s] it down. And you can feel the pain shoot through Jesus' body. And the sweat that's on His brow now becomes intermingled with the blood that's running down His face. And one of the Roman soldiers rips Jesus' clothes off Him. All He's got on is His loincloth. And they place on Him a purple robe, a robe signifying dignity. It's what the highest-ranking Roman officers wore. And they did this in order to make fun of Him. They wanted to insult Him, to mock Him, to make light of Him. And that's what they did. They placed Him in the circle. And they began to bow down in mockery. And they began to say, "Long live the King," and, you know, "Good health to the King." All mocking our Savior, our Lord and Jesus, a man who had done no wrong.

Sometimes to understand what the Resurrection means we need to see what Jesus went through and how He suffered the shame He bore for all of us. And at one point there, the mockery turned to violence. They took the purple robe off of Him and one translation talks about them blindfolding Him and punching Him with their fists and saying, "Prophesy to us now mister Messiah? Who hit you?" See, don't think for a minute He didn't feel the pain. Don't think [that] for a minute. He was human. He had emotions just like you and I do. But what a tremendous example He set for all of us. Don't you know, at one moment He could have called a legion of angels down there to wipe out all those around Him? But He didn't. He was so determined. He wanted to do His Father's will. He wanted to do what God had called Him to do. He willingly gave His life for us. He said at one point, "Father, this cup that I'm about to bear, it's so heavy; can You take it from me?" He said, "Nevertheless, not my will be done; but Thine [will] be done."

And you know what happened on that Friday before Resurrection Sunday? They took Him up to the cross. One account says around noon that day, and they nailed His hands into the cross. Have you ever thought about a spike going through your hand? Spikes going through your feet? I mean this is real pain, real suffering, real sorrow, and real heartache that the Lord suffered on our behalf. And it's amazing to me because Jesus was crucified between two sinners. And in Jesus' darkest hour, He was still reaching out, sharing His love and compassion. You know before it was over He had forgiven one of them their sins. In His darkest hour, He was still giving. And the Bible says the sun refused to shine that day when they nailed Him to the cross. A little while later, He cried out with a loud voice, He said, "My God, My God, why have you forsaken me?" He was forsaken so that you and I wouldn't have to be forsaken. He was paying the price for the sins of the world.

The Bible says, "All of us like sheep have gone astray." We've all done our own thing. But God laid on Him the iniquity or the sins of every one of us. He was bearing the sins of the world. You know a little later, I think one account says around three that afternoon, He lifted up His eyes toward heaven. And He said, "Father, into your hands do I commit my spirit." And the Son of God died. Laid down His head and died right there on the cross.

And so many interesting things happened when Jesus died. One, the Bible says there was a great earthquake. The very earth that Jesus spoke into existence revolted when it lost the one who created it. The very earth shook. And the Roman soldiers, this time they changed their story a little bit. They said, "Man, maybe He was the Son of God." But listen. Matthew 27:51 says that the very moment that Jesus died, the curtain in the temple that surrounded the presence of God was ripped in two from the top to the bottom. Now listen to this carefully because it's very significant. Back in those days, God didn't live in people like He does now. He lived in buildings. For a while, He lived in the Ark of the Covenant. But at this particular time, the people had built for Him a temple. And God lived in a sacred secluded area of the temple called the Holy of Holies. Now listen carefully. The Holy of Holies was surrounded by a curtain, a six-inch curtain. One translation calls it a veil. But it's interesting what happened there. That's where the presence of God was. Nobody could get close to that. None whatsoever. Once a year the priest would go in to ask forgiveness for the sins of the people. He'd do it once a year and God would atone their sins or cover their sins for the whole year. And it was a very critical ceremony that they went through. The priest would have to purify himself. He'd have to wear a special robe. And he'd even have a rope on him that when he walked in that if something happened when he went into the Holy of Holies—nobody would dare go in there, you could be killed in an instant—they'd have to pull him out if the sacrifice wasn't pleasing. So the priest would take this sacrifice into that Holy of Holies, the place where God actually lived.

And what's significant about when Jesus bowed his head and died, at that very moment the veil of the temple, that curtain that enclosed the presence of God, it was ripped in two, signifying that at that point God moved out of temples made by man and He moved into the hearts and lives of every one of His believers. Isn't that good news? See, that's the good news of the Resurrection. I mean that's one of the things, that God lives in us. We are the address of God. The Bible says, "What, know ye not that your bodies are temples of the Holy Ghost?" See, there's no more holy buildings. As much as this building is sacred in one sense, there's no more holy buildings. God lives in the hearts and lives of His people. But you've got to understand there still had to be a sacrifice. There still had to be a blood sacrifice.

So what was happening here? Well, in the book of John, John gives the account of Jesus when He just arose from the dead. And it's in John, chapter 20. You don't need to turn to it. Let me just tell you. Mary Magdalene was at the Garden tomb and she was sobbing. She's looking in there and she can't find the body of Jesus. And Jesus has appeared to her, behind her. Jesus says, "Woman, why are you weeping?" And she thought He was the gardener. She said, "Sir, if you've taken away His body, please tell me where and I'll go get Him?" And Jesus said, "Mary." No doubt she recognized Jesus' voice at that point. And she turned around and she said, "Rabbi, Teacher, Master." And no doubt, she was going to hug Him or to grab Him, maybe to embrace Him. In John 20:17, He said something that's very significant also. He said, "Mary, touch me not. I have not yet ascended unto my Father and to your Father; unto your God and to my God." See, there still had to be a blood sacrifice. And Jesus had shed His blood. And He had His holy blood on Him at that point. He had the precious blood of Jesus on Him. And it's interesting, because later when Jesus appeared to the disciples, He openly told them. He said, "Touch me, feel me, handle me." You know the story. He told doubting Thomas, "Feel the nail scars in my hand." Why did He tell Mary, "Don't touch me"? Well, the reason He did is He had just arisen from the dead. He had the blood, the precious blood, the sacrifice for the sins of the whole world on Him. And what He was saying, He said, "Mary, I'm about to go." And the Bible talks about in Hebrews how He went—He didn't go to the Holy of Holies this time because God moved out of that. He went into the very heavens themselves and He placed His blood as a sacrifice for our sins in the high court of heaven. And He offered it to God. And the good news about Easter is that God accepted the sacrifice of the blood of Jesus Christ.

See, no more do we have sin hanging on to us and pulling us down into the depths of hell. The price has already been paid. See, that's the beauty of the Resurrection. That's why I can stand up here with good news, smile at you, and preach with enthusiasm. Because you know our sins have already been forgiven. The Bible talks in Hebrews about how He went up there to obtain an eternal redemption for our sins. Think about that. We don't have to go and get them redeemed once a year anymore. Jesus paid the price forever. One translation says He gives us an eternal release from our sins. See, that's good news folks. Past, present, and future—the debt has already been paid. No wonder John the Baptist looked at Him at one point and said, "Behold the Lamb of God that takes away the sin of the world."

You see, back in the old covenant, the sins were only covered. Atonement means "to cover." And when you cover something, you know there's still a memory of it. You can still see something there. But folks, we live in a better covenant built on better promises when Jesus died and purchased our redemption. Our sins aren't covered, they're totally and completely washed away. Isn't that good news? One translation says that they're totally eradicated, totally erased. One of my favorite versions says that when Jesus died, He cleared our record. How many of you have had some things you've done in the past you're not real proud of? Well, listen, when you come to God, He clears your record. If the past is bothering you, if people are bringing up things in your past, or thoughts in your life, listen, you've got to remember that Jesus has cleared your record. You cast that down. That is not God bringing up the past, that's the enemy. And it's up to us to cast it down. Jesus paid all the price.

And some of you today don't want to come to God because you say, "Joel, you know, you're talking about some things I don't understand." Listen, this is what you need to understand. Your sins have already been forgiven if you will only accept the gift. The price has already been paid. Some of you say, "Well, Joel, I've done too much in the past and I don't live the right kind of life. You know when I clean myself up, I'll come to God." But that's not the way it works. You come to God just as you are. Give Him yourself just as you are. He says when you come to Him, He will make you a new creature. And what happens is none of us are where we want to be. You know God's working on all of us. You come to God just like you are and He'll start to mold you into that person that He wants you to be. Don't ever let that stop you from coming to God.

And Jesus at the Garden tomb, He told Mary there, "Mary, don't touch me," He said, "But go tell My disciples." And you know Jesus commands all of us. The Resurrection means to me that our sins are forgiven. And the Resurrection means to me that I should go out and tell this good news. It's too good to keep to ourselves. You know that? It's too good to keep to ourselves. Jesus commissions us to, you know, go out and make disciples. Tell the good news. Well, what's the good news? The good news is that the sins of the world have been forgiven. The debt has been paid in full. And that you can be washed in the precious blood of the Lamb.

Listen, folks, most of you here are born-again Christians. But what I want to say to you is this is when you share your faith, don't talk about the preacher, don't talk about the church, talk about the fact that their sins have already been forgiven. That's the good news. Listen, don't dangle people over the fires of hell. Lisa [Osteen Comes] and I always kid about you know we're going to dangle them over the fires of hell. Listen, that doesn't draw people to God. They know what kind of life they live. They know how bad they've lived. What you've got to do is talk about the goodness of God. Listen, it's the goodness of God that brings people to repentance. It's the goodness of God. One thing I always appreciated about my dad is that he instilled into us a good vision of who God was. We learned about a good God.

And then the other thing that the Resurrection means to me is it gives us the hope of heaven. Thank God, this world is not all. Do you all ever think about heaven? Heaven's hard for our finite minds to understand. It's hard for us to comprehend in one sense. But heaven is a real place. It's a place of indescribable beauty. And you know it's almost hard to describe it. Victoria and I were at the Galleria the other day, her home away from home. She lives part-time at our house and part-time at the mall. I'm sure the men can understand. We were up there late at night and the mall was all decorated for Easter. And there were a couple of areas of flowers. Maybe about as big as this platform. Yeah, probably about as big as this platform. And nobody was at the mall that night. It was late, and they'd just put these beautiful flowers out. And man, we walked through it and you could see the marvelous creation God made. And you started to—you could just sense the presence of God. When you looked at each flower so individually and meticulously made, you just thought this is magnificent. And the beautiful smell that was there, the aroma. That just made me think about heaven. And it reminded me of an account somebody gave about heaven. And they talked about the magnificent flowers in heaven. Think about heaven now, folks. They make streets out of gold. They talk about all the food up there. Somebody was kidding the other day: there's not going to be any low fat food in heaven. Thank God. I heard somebody kidding about. Let me think if

I can remember how it went. It was about this guy who went to heaven. Let me see if I can get it right. He went to heaven and he said, "Where's the low fat line?" And they said, "There's no low fat food in there." He got real angry. And they said, "Why are you so angry?" He said, "Well I'm angry because if my wife hadn't had me eating all that stuff, I'd been up here a long time ago." You know what he means, huh? We're going to this great place and we try to prolong our lives here. But you know he was talking about the flowers in heaven and how beautiful. And he talked about this sweet perfume-like aroma up there. And one thing that stuck · out in my mind, he said there were so many flowers that everywhere you walked you stepped on the flowers. He said, and you squashed them down; but he said it didn't matter. Because when you lifted up your leg, there was so much of the Resurrection power of Jesus there, the flowers just popped back up in place. Isn't that great? You know there's no death; there's no decay. Nothing can die up in heaven. There's no time. We're not going to get old. We're not going to age. You know there's no suffering, no heartache, and no pain. Daddy used to always say there's not going to be any more taxes in heaven. It's worth going because of that, isn't it? I heard somebody say the other day, you know, you've all heard this saying. There are only two things in life for certain: it's death and taxes. And they said, well at least death is still better than taxes because death doesn't get worse every time Congress meets.

But thank God we have the hope of heaven. We've got the hope of heaven. And, you know, take this in the right sense, but in this life there's question marks. We don't have all the answers. You know we have God's word. And I know we live in an evil world, but there are things we don't understand. And I don't understand it all. And I know Daddy didn't understand it all. We don't understand how—you know I don't understand when I watch the war how these little kids are involved, you know, at no fault of their own. I don't understand sometimes about a little baby being born addicted to crack cocaine at no fault of her own. You know, sometimes we look at life and we say, you know, it's not fair. It's not fair sometimes when a parent may be taken out of a life early and nobody to raise the little kids.

But, you know, the Resurrection of Jesus says to me that in the big picture of life Jesus stands there with His arms held open wide. And on the horizon of life, He says, "Look, don't worry about this life. I know you don't understand everything." He says this, He says, "Endure hardships, fight the good fight of faith, put your trust and confidence in me. But know that you're going to come to a place where there's not going to be any more tragedy, there's not going to be any more pain, there's not going to be any more suffering. You're not going to have any more questions when you come up there with me." Think of the hope that we have because of Easter Sunday morning. Isn't that good news?

You know I can't wait to get up to heaven to see my dad. You know, I can't wait to tell him that, "Hey, Daddy, I got up there and preached more than one time." You know, Daddy was always trying to get me up here. Through the years, he said, "Joel, they want to hear you." And I'd always say, "Daddy, as long as you're here, you're the preacher. They're coming to hear you." And you know I did the television production, like my mom said, for sixteen years. And I used to say, "Daddy, you preach and I'll make you look good. I promise you that." And Daddy loved that. He loved to look good. And we'd be out in public sometimes. And he'd introduce me. He'd say, "This is my son Joel. He does my television production." He'd smile real big and say, "He makes me look good."

I was thinking about the other day—I saw some of these kids this morning. They came in, in those big baggy pants that they wear. And sometimes we think, you know, what are they doing wearing this stuff? But you remember my dad? When he was only seventeen, he wore those pants up to here. It was the same thing. You know the styles come around and go around. But they were those big, big baggy pants. And they came down to bootleg, you know, I mean to a tight leg. And he was telling me a couple weeks before he died—he was just reminiscing. He was talking about he used to wear that hat and he had his coat on. It was called a zoot suit. I think I still have the chain. Or Momma has that chain. And he used to put his chain right there and he pulled that coat back. Man, he was a cool cat. And he'd wind up. He used to tell me how he'd do that. So don't you ever give up hope on these young people.

I'm going to tell you one more funny story about Daddy and then I'll quit. But Daddy, he loved to get—in his later years, he didn't have a whole lot of hair. And I can say this now that he's gone, otherwise, I'd be dead. He didn't have a whole lot of hair. Victoria, my wife, fixed his hair. And she used to fix it just right. Man, she could curve it right over. And then she'd get a couple cans of hair spray and spray it, you know. And he'd come out here and he'd be so proud of that hair. I'm talking about when we get to heaven we can reminisce. Don't you all tell him I told this. But I'll never forget one day he came up to the platform. He'd just had his hair done and we had a visiting minister. And they were going to pray over Daddy. And this guy was going to lay his hands on Daddy's head. And I'll never forget that hand came up and here comes Daddy's hand—like right there. Daddy was bold. He didn't mind doing anything. You should see the things he'd do in public sometimes. He would embarrass us. But I'll never forget that.

One time—I got to tell you this one last story. I told you one. But you all egg me on. You all are so easy to talk to. I'll tell you one more. We're supposed to be talking about Easter, but somehow this will tie in. One time we were down in the Amazon jungles, just me and him. And he'll kill me if he knows I told this. But we were there by the water and we were waiting for a boat to come pick us up. And I was probably about twenty. There was this other guy that was there and he spoke Spanish. He was about my age. And he had this little bitty—it was like a monkey, I guess it was a monkey. It looked just like a monkey. But it was only about that big. And this guy had it on his T-shirt. And he was just his pet. And he was running all over his shirt like, you know, just having fun. And we were so intrigued and we stopped and looked. Daddy, you know, he was bold. He said, "Can I see him?" And the guy said, "Sure." Well, he didn't speak English but he said yes. And he let that thing come on to Daddy's shirt and that thing just ran all over Daddy's shirt and we were having a lot of fun just watching it. But what Daddy didn't realize is Daddy had a shirt with buttons on the front. He didn't have a shirt like a T-shirt. And before you knew it, that monkey got inside his shirt. And it was the funniest thing because that started tickling him because he was running around. And Daddy was going like this—back and forth. I thought Daddy had a little bit of rhythm there for a minute. But, you got to hear the rest of it. It's funnier than that. So that guy comes over and he reaches in there and is trying to get it out of there. He got his hand in Daddy's shirt and man by this time I've walked way away. I didn't want to—I saw some people looking. But they couldn't get it out. And finally that little monkey came out the back of his neck. And when he hit Daddy's hair I think he thought it was some straw or some hay or something. He went wild in Daddy's hair. It took us forever to get [it] out. And you got to know my dad, how he didn't like to have his hair messed up. But when he got through, Daddy looked like a mad scientist or something. You know, Daddy's hair was real long because he wore it back. And man, he looked like Don King maybe.

All right, I got to quit. We're supposed to be talking about Easter, about the Resurrection. No, listen. I can't wait to get up there and reminisce. We've got the hope of going to see our loved ones. How many of you have loved ones there up in heaven? See, all of us do. And thank God for the good news about Easter. Let me wrap it up for just one second. The good news about Easter is this, is that God has already paid the price. He's already suffered. He's already borne the sins of the whole world. All we have to do is accept His forgiveness. Some people say, "You know Joel, you're giving people a license to sin when you say that." No, listen. When you really know God, you don't want to sin. You don't want to sin. You want to please God. And what the Resurrection of Jesus means to me is that my sins have already been forgiven, that I have good news to tell the world, that I want to live a holy, godly life. And that I have the hope of one day I'm going to heaven to spend eternity up there with all those who have gone before me. That's the good news of the Resurrection. That's the good news of the Resurrection.

Well, let's bow our heads in prayer. I want to say one thing to those of you who are viewing by television. Some of you maybe have never accepted Jesus. Maybe you've never asked Him to come into your heart. You know, it's a tragedy to die when God's already paid the price. When He's already borne your sins and sickness. You just have to accept this gift. And I want you to just pray a simple prayer with me. Maybe you don't know how to pray. But all you got to do is say this prayer and mean it with your heart. Say, Jesus, come into my heart. Save me. Be my Lord. Be my Savior. Jesus, I want to serve You all the days of my life. I'm not everything I want to be Jesus, but I know You'll make me into what You want me to be. Jesus, I'll serve You all the days. I'll give you 100 percent.

Well, I believe you prayed that prayer. And listen, what you ought to do is, if you can, come out here to Lakewood and be with us. We'd love to have you. If not, go to a good church in your neighborhood or in your area and support that pastor. Support that church in your attendance and your giving. Never regret giving your life to God. I hope you'll join us again next week.

APPENDIX B: JOEL OSTEEN, "VISION SUNDAY"
(1999)

The text below is Joel Osteen's inaugural sermon as Lakewood's senior pastor, delivered on October 3, 1999. In the message, Joel clearly demarcates his ministry from that of his father's, while he pays due respect to Lakewood's founder. Osteen links the church's outreach efforts to the evangelical imperative of missionary work based on extolling the gospel message of faith in Christ through service to others. Notably, he very clearly links these service rationales to biblical texts. Osteen unveils an ambitious list of plans for the Lakewood community, including job training classes, recovery groups, educational outreach, and an introductory class to the Christian life rooted in the quest for biblical literacy. The list of guest speakers who Osteen promises will visit Lakewood Church reads like an all-star lineup of neopentecostal celebrity pastors. It also reveals Joel's participation in neopentecostal preaching networks, a practice common in the movement's history. Finally, Joel invokes the first tagline he coined as Lakewood's pastor—"New Beginnings"—which not only distinguishes his ministry from that of his father's, but also reflects the idea of second chances that defines the substance of his message. Again, I have edited the sermon into a more coherent paragraph format, capitalized proper nouns, and corrected grammatical inaccuracies and stylistic inconsistencies in the interest of readability.

"Vision Sunday," October 3, 1999

I believe we're standing at a historic time in God's timetable. And what we do for God we must do now. Life is flying by. James 4:14 says, "What is your life? You are a mist that appears for a little while and then vanishes." In the scope of eternity, we are all here but for a split second.

I think it's so interesting that my daddy, Pastor John Osteen, died just eleven months before the new millennium. He could have gone to heaven a year from now or three years. But I believe God ordained it before the foundation of the world that you and I would be standing here at this very time about to launch this church into a new century. We are people of destiny.

We cannot remain stagnant; we must go further. If Daddy were here today, he would tell us the same thing—I knew him well—he would say, "Take it; run with the vision. The hour is late."

You didn't have to be around Daddy very long to catch a vision to reach the world. There are millions of people that have never even once heard the name of Jesus. It's up to you and me to remain faithful to give, and to go, and to pray for the lost and suffering of this world.

Over 90 percent of the unreached people groups live in the 10/40 Window framed on our auditorium world maps.[1] And over the years we have poured millions of dollars to better equip the native pastors and church leaders to spread the good news. It takes so little. Fifty dollars a month will support a native pastor and his family in India. Let's never lose our vision to reach out to help those who have never heard. And I stand here firmly committed to continuing our worldwide outreach. God help us if we ever forget about the people in other less fortunate countries that have never heard the Gospel once.

Let me challenge you to stir yourself up and be faithful to give to missions. Don't have a "me and my four, and no more" attitude. Believe God for more money, better jobs, and bonuses—not just for yourself, but to tell someone in a third-world country about the love and compassion of Jesus Christ.

And I have to warn you, I have big dreams. I dream of the day that we will not just give 5 million dollars a year to missions, but we'll give 50–60 million dollars each year. Listen, for that to happen, God's going to have to abundantly bless you. And He is able, if you are willing.

I don't know if any church in America has done more for world missions than Lakewood Church, and we are firmly committed to continuing and expanding our overseas outreaches.

But I have a burning desire to reach our own city as never before. The light that shines furthest shines brightest at home. Jesus told His disciples to reach their own city before they went to the other parts of the world. One man that Jesus healed wanted to follow Him. He said,

"No, no—first go home and tell your family and friends what God has done for you."

I think it's great to reach India and Africa and the other parts of the world, but God expects us also to do our part to reach out and love and care for and minister to those in need in our own city. Houston is a great city and it needs our help. And for years, you may have said, "We can't go to other nations; all we can do is give and pray." But friends, that's not true. Every one of you can go—go to your family, friends, neighbors, and co-workers and share God's love and compassion.

I am convinced that we are never going to get all the hurting, lonely people in a church building—it's up to us to go to them. We are never going to make the impact God wants us to until every one of us begins to reach out to those in need around us.

We all love the phrase, "Reach the unreached and tell the untold." And it is so true. But although we should never forget the unreached, it's equally as important to reach the reachable. Because whether somebody goes to hell from Africa or they go to hell from Sugar Land,[2] it's no different. And we each have the ability to positively affect change upon those around us.

God's not looking for people with great talent and great skill and great ability. He's simply looking for people that are willing, open, and obedient—people that are available for Him to use as a vessel to pour out His life into the lives of others. God has no arms to love except your arms. God has no voice to share the good news except your voice. God has no hands to care for the broken and wounded except your hands.

The true Gospel is a Gospel that reaches out and touches those in need. Helping hurting people is the closest thing to the heart of God. And when we really begin to reach out and touch the lives of those around us, this church won't be able to hold the people that will want to come and hear more about the goodness of God. The way we live, our lives are the best sermons you could ever preach. I am firmly committed to making a difference in this city.

We've talked about reaching the world and reaching our city—now I want to talk about how we want to help you. I am committed to doing everything we can to make Lakewood a better place to meet your needs and help you grow in your Christian walk. We want to develop strong families and strong leaders for the kingdom of God. I'm young—I have a lot of energy. This church leadership is young. My mom is young at heart; she can out work any of us!

God is leading us to do some new things. Beginning next Sunday night, my brother Paul is going to teach a class every Sunday night at 6:00 p.m. for people that have been born again in the past year. We're calling it "New Beginnings." It will be a four-week class to help people learn the basic truths of God's Word and how to live the Christian life. I want to help disciple and take care of the 100 to 200 people that come down to our altars each week.

Also beginning next Sunday, we're going to have a fellowship for any guests or visitors that you bring, immediately after the Sunday morning service. Your family and friends are important to us and we would love to have the honor of meeting them. This fellowship will also be open to anyone that wants to learn more about how to be involved in the church. Every week at least a couple dozen people ask me how to join Lakewood or how to be involved. That's going to happen every Sunday right after our morning service.

We're seriously praying about several other outreaches that we would like to start soon. We're in the final stages of development for a single-parent fellowship and network. This is so strong on our hearts—we are going to go to great efforts to strengthen and encourage and undergird our single parents.

We're developing a Homes at Risk ministry that is a mentoring program to help people that have troubled marriages. We know the enemy is attacking the family as never before and we believe we can take back what the enemy has stolen from us.

We are expanding our medical missions to not just overseas, but we are going to conduct health fairs right here on these grounds to provide medical screening and simple check-ups for the needy and elderly.

We have plans to begin a class to teach our Spanish-speaking friends English. We're going to have workshops to help people get better jobs, where we'll have trained staff to help you write your resume and we'll go through "mock" job interviews. After all, God expects us to do our part. There are a dozen more things we're praying about.

Listen, this is what the Gospel is all about. It's about caring and loving. Jesus said, "When I was hungry you fed Me; when I was thirsty you gave Me something to drink. When I was sick you comforted Me; when I was in prison you visited me. They said, When did we ever do that Jesus? He said, When you did it for the least of one of these you did it unto Me." We must make it a priority to take care of our own family here at Lakewood.

The children's church is running at record numbers and we're making some changes to help in the overcrowding. I received a fax from the nursery that said for the first time ever our newborn nursery was full to capacity.

God is enlarging our vision. The building is almost full every Sunday morning. We're praying seriously about sometime next year going to two Sunday morning services. We will make room for your family and friends. I am committed to developing strong families at Lakewood.

We have an exciting lineup of special speakers and events already scheduled for next year so that you can enjoy the five-fold ministry right here at Lakewood. They are: Jesse Duplantis, Rodney Howard-Browne, Joyce Meyer, R. W. Schambach, Kenneth Copeland, Jerry Savelle, [and] Nicky Cruz. Also, Marilyn Hickey and John Hagee may be coming.

You say, "Joel, what do you want from me?" Number one, I want you to reach out to your family and friends, minister to them, and then bring them to church. And the second thing is that we want you to be involved.

We have over thirty volunteer ministries and fellowships that you can help out in and be a part of everything from giving somebody a ride to church to comforting someone in their time of grief to shaking hands with people when they walk in the door. God's got something for you to do. Ephesians 5:16 says, "Be very careful how you live, not as unwise but wise, making the most of every opportunity."

And in the packet that we're about to pass out, there's a list of all the different ministries, and I want you to pray about what God wants you to do. And in the whole month of November, we're going to have booths set up so you can visit with the different ministries and sign up to help. Be involved—don't just sit back and let everybody else do the work. God wants to use you!

These are very exciting days. Daddy has passed the baton to me and to you. Now this is our day. God's counting on us.

Haggai prophesied, "The glory of the latter church will be greater than the glory of the former church."

I don't think we have even touched the surface of what God wants to do in our own lives and in the life of our church. I believe that we're entering into a whole new dimension today and that our greatest days are just ahead. This is a time of New Beginnings!

NOTES

INTRODUCTION

1 So as not to oversaturate the text with "Osteen" and to more easily identify to *which* Osteen I refer, I will often use first names only.

2 The work of philosopher Nimi Wariboko helps to explain my conceptualization of Lakewood's "Pentecost." He theorizes the "pentecostal principle" from the perspective of ethics and epistemology to create a "pneumatological methodology" in philosophy. "The pentecostal principle is the capacity to begin," Wariboko writes. "It encapsulates the notion that no finite or conditioned reality can claim to have reached its destiny. The movement of every existent to its destiny (full realization of potentialities) remains ever incompleteable because it is 'rooted' in the abyss of divine freedom . . . action corresponds with the human capacity to begin, a capacity that is decisively rooted in *natality*, birth and rebirth, the originality of each new human being entering into an ongoing social process." He continues, "Because of the demand of new beginning, more is expected from every moment and every life, and there is a radical openness to alternatives and surprises. The restlessness of all en-spirited life is recognized, understood, and grasped." Nimi Wariboko, *The Pentecostal Principle: Ethical Methodology in New Spirit* (Grand Rapids, MI: Eerdmans, 2012), 1–2, 197.

3 Multiple disciplines have produced scholarship on John Osteen, Joel Osteen, and Lakewood Church, grappling with their significance from the perspective of history, sociology, religious studies, rhetoric, psychology, and communications studies. This book offers the fullest historical account of Osteen and Lakewood to date.

   Historical studies of both John and Joel include David Edwin Harrell, *All Things Are Possible: The Healing and Charismatic Revivals in Modern America* (Bloomington: Indiana University Press, 1975), 180–187; David G. Roebuck, "Fundamentalism and Pentecostalism: The Changing Face of Evangelicalism in America," in *Faith in America: Changes, Challenges, New Directions, Volume 1: Organized Religion Today*, ed. Charles H. Lippy (Westport, CT: Praeger, 2006), 85–107; Shayne Lee and Phillip Luke Sinitiere, *Holy Mavericks: Evangelical Innovators and the Spiritual Marketplace* (New York: NYU Press, 2009), 25–51; Phillip Luke Sinitiere, "From the Oasis of Love to Your Best Life Now: A Brief History of Lakewood Church," *Houston History* 8/3 (Summer 2011): 2–9; Phillip Luke Sinitiere, "Preaching the Good News Glad: Joel Osteen's New Tel-e-vangelism," in *Global and Local Televangelism*, ed. Pradip Ninian Thomas and

Philip Lee (New York: Palgrave Macmillan, 2012), 87–107. John Osteen warranted an entry in Randall Balmer's useful *Encyclopedia of Evangelicalism* (Waco, TX: Baylor University Press, 2004), 516, although the entry overlooked Osteen's death in 1999. See also John D. Wilsey, "Joel Osteen," in *Baker Dictionary of Cults and Religions*, ed. H. Wayne House (Grand Rapids, MI: Baker, forthcoming).

Social scientific analyses and religious studies work that addresses the topic include William Martin, "Prime Minister," *Texas Monthly* (August 2005), reprinted in *Southern Crossroads: Perspectives on Religion and Culture*, ed. Walter H. Conser, Jr., and Rodger M. Payne (Lexington: University Press of Kentucky, 2008), 63–88; Mara Einstein, *Brands of Faith: Marketing Religion in a Commercial Age* (New York: Routledge, 2008), 120–146; Jeanne L. Tsai, Felicity F. Miao, and Emma Seppala, "Good Feelings in Christianity and Buddhism: Religious Differences in Ideal Affect," *Personality and Social Psychology Bulletin* 33/3 (March 2007): 409–421; Leanna K. Fuller, "Perfectionism and Shame: Exploring the Connections," *Journal of Pastoral Theology* 18/1 (Summer 2008): 44–60; Barbara Ehrenreich, *Bright-Sided: How the Relentless Promotion of Positive Thinking Has Undermined America* (New York: Metropolitan Books, 2009), 123–146; D. Michael Lindsey, *Faith in the Halls of Power: How Evangelicals Joined the American Elite* (New York: Oxford University Press, 2007), 130, 218–219; Luke Winslow, "Classy Morality: The Rhetoric of Joel Osteen," in *Uncovering Hidden Rhetorics: Social Issues in Disguise*, ed. Barry Brummett (Los Angeles: Sage, 2008), 123–139; Christine Miller and Nathan Carlin, "Joel Osteen as Cultural Selfobject: Meeting the Needs of the Group Self and Its Individual Members in and from the Largest Church in America," *Pastoral Psychology* 59 (2010): 27–51; Wayne R. Geiger, "Joel Osteen: A Critical Analysis of Sermonic Methodology" (M.A. Thesis, University of Central Missouri, 2009); Patricia Calderon, "The Media's Place in Religious Individualism: A Case Study of Lakewood Church" (M.A. Thesis, Texas A&M University, 2010); Helje Kringlebotn Sødal, "'Victor Not Victim': Joel Osteen's Rhetoric of Hope," *Journal of Contemporary Religion* 25/1 (January 2010): 37–50; Roger Finke and Chris Scheitle, *Places of Faith: A Road Trip across America's Religious Landscape* (New York: Oxford University Press, 2012), 37–62; Jillian Owens, "A Wide Net of Hope: Understanding the Success of Joel Osteen and Lakewood Church" (Senior Religious Studies Honors Thesis, University of Texas at Austin, 2012); Matthew Henderson, "'What Heaven's Gonna Look Like': Racial and Ethnic Diversity at Lakewood Church" (M.A. Thesis, University of Houston, 2012); Joseph W. Williams, *Spirit Cure: A History of Pentecostal Healing* (New York: Oxford University Press, 2013); Kate Bowler, *Blessed: A History of the American Prosperity Gospel* (New York: Oxford University Press, 2013); Todd M. Brenneman, *Homespun Gospel: The Triumph of Sentimentality in Contemporary American Evangelicalism* (New York: Oxford University Press, 2014); Katja Rakow, "Religious Branding and the Quest to

Meet Consumer Needs: Joel Osteen's 'Message of Hope,'" in *Religion and the Marketplace in the United States*, ed. Jan Stievermann, Philip Goff, and Detlef Junker (New York: Oxford University Press, 2015), 215–239.

4 Claire Bond Potter and Renee C. Romano, eds., *Doing Recent History: On Privacy, Copyright, Video Games, Institutional Review Boards, Activist Scholarship, and History That Talks Back* (Athens: University of Georgia Press, 2012). For *Salvation with a Smile*, I found the introduction (1–19) along with Renee C. Romano's "Not Dead Yet: My Identity Crisis as a Historian of the Recent Past" (23–44) and Julius H. Bailey's "'Cult' Knowledge: The Challenges of Studying New Religious Movements in America" (275–293) most helpful.

Among scholars of American religion, the following works and the various methodologies they employ informed the approaches I take in this study. See Randall Balmer, *Mine Eyes Have Seen the Glory: A Journey into the Evangelical Subculture in America*, 4th ed. (New York: Oxford University Press, 2006); Kathryn Lofton, *Oprah: The Gospel of an Icon* (Berkeley: University of California Press, 2011); Jonathan Walton, *Watch This!: The Ethics and Aesthetics of Black Televangelism* (New York: NYU Press, 2009); David Edwin Harrell, *All Things Are Possible*; David Edwin Harrell, *Oral Roberts: An American Life* (Bloomington: Indiana University Press, 1985); David Edwin Harrell, *Pat Robertson: A Life and Legacy* (Grand Rapids, MI: Eerdmans, 2010); Susan Friend Harding, *The Book of Jerry Falwell: Fundamentalist Language and Politics* (Princeton, NJ: Princeton University Press, 2000); Shayne Lee, *T. D. Jakes: America's New Preacher* (New York: NYU Press, 2005); Gerardo Marti, *Hollywood Faith: Holiness, Prosperity, and Ambition in a Los Angeles Church* (New Brunswick, NJ: Rutgers University Press, 2008); Mark J. Cartledge, *Testimony in the Spirit: Rescripting Ordinary Pentecostal Theology* (Burlington, VT: Ashgate, 2010); and Bowler, *Blessed*. For my own work, Bowler's excellent appendices most intelligently articulate the methodological questions, concerns, and opportunities of studying the prosperity gospel.

5 Harding, *The Book of Jerry Falwell*, xi; Manuel A. Vásquez, *More than Belief: A Materialist Theory of Religion* (New York: Oxford University Press, 2011), 1–17, 321–328.

6 Robert A. Orsi, *Between Heaven and Earth: The Religious Worlds People Make and the Scholars Who Study Them* (Princeton, NJ: Princeton University Press, 2004), 198.

7 Scholarship on evangelicalism and its many varieties is deep and wide. The studies most helpful in articulating my definition of evangelicalism include Randall Balmer, *The Making of Evangelicalism: From Revivalism to Politics and Beyond* (Waco, TX: Baylor University Press, 2010); Balmer, *Mine Eyes Have Seen the Glory*; David Bebbington, *Evangelicalism in Modern Britain* (London: Unwin Hyman, 1989), 2–3; Mark Noll, *American Evangelical Christianity: An Introduction* (Malden, MA: Blackwell, 2001), 7–108; Thomas S. Kidd, *The Great Awakening: The Roots of Evangelical Christianity in Colonial America* (New

Haven, CT: Yale University Press, 2007), xiv–xv; Douglas A. Sweeney, "Evangelicals in American History," in *The Columbia Guide to Religion in American History*, ed. Paul Harvey and Edward J. Blum (New York: Columbia University Press, 2012), 122–135; Molly Worthen, *Apostles of Reason: The Crisis of Authority in American Evangelicalism* (New York: Oxford University Press, 2014); Brenneman, *Homespun Gospel*, 16–17; and Steven P. Miller, *The Age of Evangelicalism: America's Born-Again Years* (New York: Oxford University Press, 2014). While Kidd's use of the Holy Spirit in his analysis of evangelicalism refers to revivals in North America during the 1700s, his definition can also apply to American evangelicalism more broadly.

8 Harrell, *All Things Are Possible*; Bowler, *Blessed*; Milmon Harrison, *Righteous Riches: The Word of Faith Movement in Contemporary African American Religion* (New York: Oxford University Press, 2005), 3–20; Candy Gunther Brown, "Introduction: Pentecostalism and the Globalization of Illness and Healing," in *Global Pentecostal and Charismatic Healing*, ed. Candy Gunther Brown (New York: Oxford University Press, 2011), 4–6.

9 Allan Anderson, *An Introduction to Pentecostalism* (New York: Cambridge University Press, 2004), 1–15, 144–165. See also Allan Anderson, "Varieties, Taxonomies, and Definitions," in *Studying Global Pentecostalism: Theories and Methods*, ed. Allan Anderson, Michael Bergunder, Andre Droogers, and Cornelius van der Laan (Berkeley: University of California Press, 2010), 13–29; Russell P. Spittler, "Pentecostal and Charismatic Spirituality," in *The New International Dictionary of Pentecostal and Charismatic Movements*, Revised and Expanded Edition, eds. Stanley M. Burgess and Eduard M. van der Maas (Grand Rapids: Zondervan, 2002), 1096–1102.

CHAPTER 1. JOHN OSTEEN'S PENTECOST

The epigraph comes from Joel Osteen, *Your Best Life Now* (New York: Warner Faith, 2004), 213.

1 John Osteen, *Rivers of Living Water: A Baptist Preacher's Experiences With the Power That Comes through the Holy Spirit* (Houston: Lakewood Church, 1975), 6–7; Sam Martin, *How I Led One and One Led a Million* (Houston: Lakewood Church, 2001), 2–5; John Osteen, "The Book of Revelation, Part 6" (1994), http://web.archive.org/web/19991022014946/http://www.lakewood-church.org/Sermons1994/511.html; Victoria Osteen, *Love Your Life: Living Happy, Healthy & Whole* (New York: Free Press, 2008), 25–26.

2 Joel Osteen, *The Christmas Spirit: Memories of Family, Friends, and Faith* (New York: Free Press, 2010), 5–8; 19–21; Joel Osteen, *Become a Better You: 7 Keys to Improving Your Everyday Life* (New York: Free Press, 2007), 61–62.

3 Osteen, *Rivers of Living Water*, 6–7; *John H. Osteen's Personal Testimony* Cassette (n.d.), Holy Spirit Research Center; Darren Dochuk, *From Bible Belt to Sunbelt: Plain-Folk Religion, Grassroots Politics, and the Rise of Evangelical Conservatism* (New York: W. W. Norton, 2010), xi–xxiv, 3–26.

4 Dochuk, *From Bible Belt to Sunbelt*, 57–60; Rick Ostrander, *Head, Heart, and Hand: John Brown University and Modern Evangelical Higher Education* (Fayetteville: University of Arkansas Press, 2003), 92–117. On John Brown University's early business connections, see Bethany Moreton, *To Serve God and Wal-Mart: The Making of Christian Free Enterprise* (Cambridge, MA: Harvard University Press, 2009), 161–163.

5 John Osteen, "The Unified Service" (M.R.E. Thesis, Northern Baptist Theological Seminary, 1944), 13, 49.

6 Ibid., 47, 49.

7 John Osteen, *This Awakening Generation* (Houston: John H. Osteen Evangelistic Association, 1967), 23–25; John H. Osteen File, Texas Baptist Historical Collection; *Central Baptist Church 75th Anniversary Book* (Baytown, TX: Central Baptist Church, 1996), 3.

8 Buck A. Young, "Baytown, TX," *Handbook of Texas Online*, https://www.tshaonline.org/handbook/online/articles/hdbo1; Julia Cauble Smith, "East Texas Oilfield," *Handbook of Texas Online*, https://www.tshaonline.org/handbook/online/articles/doe01; Darren Dochuk, "Blessed by Oil, Cursed with Crude: God and Black Gold in the American Southwest," *Journal of American History* 99 (June 2012): 51–61. While oil offered opportunity for many, as historian John D. Márquez documents, labor unrest, and racial discrimination marked the lives of others in Baytown. See John D. Márquez, *Black-Brown Solidarity: Racial Politics in the New Gulf South* (Austin: University of Texas Press, 2014), 65–113.

9 John H. Osteen File; *Central Baptist Church 75th Anniversary Book*, 3. *Youth on the March* aired on ABC nationally from 1949 to 1953 and on local affiliates from 1953 to 1958. See "'As This Is Our First Broadcast': Percy & Ruth Crawford and the Birth of Televangelism," Billy Graham Center Digital Archives, http://www2.wheaton.edu/bgc/archives/exhibits/Crawford/crawford02.htm; Bruce Shelly, "The Rise of Evangelical Youth Movements," *Fides et Historia* 18/1 (January 1986): 47–63.

In *Your Best Life Now*, Joel Osteen alludes to a divorce ending his father's ministry at Central Baptist Church, although he conceals the reasons why the marriage ended. "My dad married at a very early age—probably not one of the best decisions Daddy ever made—and, although he went into the relationship with the best of intentions, unfortunately, things didn't work out. The marriage failed. Daddy was heartbroken and devastated. He thought surely that his ministry was over, that God's blessings had lifted from his life. He didn't think he would ever preach again, much less have a family. Dealing with divorce was the darkest hour of my dad's life. . . . Daddy went through hell on earth. If you knew the circumstances surrounding the divorce he experienced, you would understand that he didn't take the easy road. . . . God not only restored my dad's ministry, He increased it" (176–178). See another version of the same story in Osteen, *Become a Better You*, 23–24.

10 David Russell interview, February 24, 2012.

11 John Osteen, *How God Baptized Me in the Holy Ghost and Fire* (Houston: John H.
    Osteen Evangelistic Association, 1961), 6–7; John Osteen, *How to Be Healed*
    (Houston: John H. Osteen Evangelistic Association, 1961), 9–10; John Osteen,
    Supernatural Manifestations in the Life of John H. Osteen (Houston: John H.
    Osteen Evangelistic Association, 1961), 3–4; John Osteen, *How to Demonstrate
    Satan's Defeat* (Houston: Lakewood Church, 1978), 47–50. On Dodie's baptism in
    the Holy Spirit, see John Osteen, "Meet Mrs. John Osteen and Our Children,"
    Praise 2/8 (October 1963): 4–5.
12 John H. Osteen File; John Osteen, "Baptized in the Holy Ghost and Fire," *Praise*
    2/7 (September 1964): 4–7; "Lakewood Baptist . . . Still Praising and Witnessing
    after Four Years!," *Praise* 2/1 (January/February 1963): 5–6; "They Shall Lay Hands
    on the Sick," *Praise* 2/7 (September 1964): 10–11; Jean Martin, "The Jean Martin
    Story: 'The Baptism of the Holy Spirit Revolution in My Life!,'" *Praise* 2/7
    (September 1963): 6–7. On neopentecostals who often described divine healing
    with reference to bones "popping," see Russell Spittler, "Pentecostal and
    Charismatic Spirituality," in *The New International Dictionary of Pentecostal and
    Charismatic Movements*, Revised and Expanded Edition, ed. Stanley M. Burgess
    and Eduard M. van der Maas (Grand Rapids, MI: Zondervan, 2002), 1101.
13 Robert S. Ellwood, *The Fifties Spiritual Marketplace: American Religion in a
    Decade of Conflict* (New Brunswick, NJ: Rutgers University Press, 1997), 1–26.
14 On Baptists and the post–World War II charismatic renewal, see Albert Frederick
    Schenkel, "New Wine and Baptist Wineskins: American and Southern Baptist
    Denominational Responses to the Charismatic Renewal, 1969–1980," and Helen
    Lee Turner, "Pentecostal Currents in the SBC: Divine Interpretation, Prophetic
    Preachers, and Charismatic Worship," in *Pentecostal Currents in American
    Protestantism*, ed. Edith L. Blumhoefer, Russell P. Spittler, and Grant Wacker
    (Urbana: University of Illinois Press, 1999), 152–167, 209–225; Vinson Synan,
    "Baptists Ride the Third Wave," *Charisma* (December 1986): 54–57; David Edwin
    Harrell, *All Things Are Possible: The Healing and Charismatic Revivals in Modern
    America* (Bloomington: Indiana University Press, 1975), 187; David Edwin Harrell,
    Oral Roberts: An American Life (Bloomington: Indiana University Press, 1985),
    423–424.
15 Harrell, *All Things Are Possible*, 135–137.
16 Harrell, *All Things Are Possible*, 146–149; Vinson Synan, *Under His Banner:
    History of Full Gospel Business Men's Fellowship International* (Costa Mesa, CA:
    Gift, 1992).
17 Synan, *Under His Banner*; John H. Osteen, "God Used the Full-Gospel
    Businessmen's Fellowship International to Deliver Me from between the Horns of
    a Dilemma," *Praise* 2/5 (June/July 1963): 4–5; E. M. Jones, "Raised Up of God to
    Stir Our Generation," *Voice* 7/6–7 (July–August 1959): 3–27; Jones, "Pentecost Is
    Not a Denomination: It Is an Experience," *Voice* 8/5 (June 1960): 4–9 (reprinted in
    Voice 9/3 [April 1961]: 25–29); Jones, "The Glory of God of Israel Has Returned!,"
    Voice 9/11 (December 1961): 1–6; Jones, "The Holy Ghost Falls at Seattle," *Voice*

10/9 (September 1962): 2–17; Don Scott, "I Found There is Reality in Knowing Jesus And Being . . . Filled with the Holy Spirit," in *The Methodists and the Baptism of the Holy Spirit*, ed. Jerry Jensen (Los Angeles: Full Gospel Businessmen's Fellowship International, 1963), 23; John Osteen, "This Southern Baptist Preacher Wept, Shook and Listened as . . . He Heard God Speak," in *The Baptists and the Baptism of the Holy Spirit*, ed. Jerry Jensen (Los Angeles: Full Gospel Businessmen's Fellowship International, 1963), 6–10, 30–31; John Osteen, *The Man You Could Have Been* Cassette (1963), Holy Spirit Research Center.

18   *John H. Osteen's Personal Testimony*; John Osteen, *This Awakening Generation*, 40; Aaron Mullen interview, June 16, 2011; Mel Montgomery, *The Genuine Flow: How the Faith Giants Flowed in the Spirit and How You Can Too* (Maitland, FL: Xulon, 2010), 34–36.

19   On Marvin Crow's involvement with Lakewood and FGBMFI, see convention advertisements, "See You in Albuquerque," *Voice* 11/3 (March 1963): 31, and "The Land of Enchantment," *Voice* 11/5 (May 1963): 17; Marvin Crow, "I Thought This Experience Had Ruined Our Service, Instead . . . Revival Fire Began to Burn," in *The Baptists and the Baptism of the Holy Spirit*, 19–21, 32; John Osteen, "This Baptist Preacher Saw It . . . and He Will Never Be the Same Again!," *Faith Digest* 6/7 (July 1961): 3–5; John Osteen, "Mexican Arena of Faith," *Faith Digest* 6/8 (August 1961): 3–9; John Osteen, "I Waited, I Wondered, I Witnessed," *Faith Digest* 7/4 (April 1962): 2–7; Harrell, *All Things Are Possible*, 187; Harrell, *Oral Roberts*, 423–424.

20   Burton W. Pierce, "Christianity at the Crossroads," *Pentecostal Evangel* (April 3, 1961): 4–5; Burton W. Pierce, "Spotlight on Evangelism," *Pentecostal Evangel* (July 16, 1961): 28; Burton W. Pierce, "Christian Church Minister Receives the Pentecostal Baptism," *Pentecostal Evangel* (September 3, 1961): 8–9, Flower Pentecostal Heritage Center Digital Collection.

21   John Osteen, *This Awakening Generation*, 46, 73; John Osteen, *You Can Change Your Destiny* (Houston: John H. Osteen Evangelistic Association, 1964), 7, 60–79; Robert S. Ellwood, *The Sixties Spiritual Awakening: American Religion Moving from Modern to Postmodern* (New Brunswick, NJ: Rutgers University Press, 1994).

22   John Osteen, *Telling the King's Household* (Houston: John H. Osteen Evangelistic Association, n.d.), Holy Spirit Research Center; John G. Turner, *Bill Bright and Campus Crusade for Christ: The Renewal of Evangelicalism in Postwar America* (Chapel Hill: University of North Carolina Press, 2008), 99–103.

23   "Our Readers Speak," *Praise* 2/1 (January/February 1963): 3–4; Dr. Hong Sit, "A Report to the People: The Amazing Story of Dr. Hong Sit," *Praise* 2/3 (April 1963): 12–14; Harry E. Martin, "This Catholic Man Says: I Must Testify," *Praise* 2/7 (August 1963): 10–11; John Osteen, *Rivers of Living Water*, 16–17.

24   John Osteen, "Lakewood Baptist . . . Still Praising and Witnessing after Four Years!," and "They Said It Wouldn't Last—But It Did . . . ," *Praise* 2/1 (January/February 1963): 5–6; C. O. Hobbs and Mrs. C. O. Hobbs, "Prominent Southern Baptist Family of Baytown, Texas Baptized in the Holy Ghost!," *Praise* 2/9

(November 1963): 12–13; Keith Hobbs, "The Gifts Are Operating in My Life," *Praise* 3/12 (February 1964): 7.

25 Quoted in Harrell, *All Things Are Possible*, 66–75, 138–144, 194–206; Kate Bowler, *Blessed: A History of the American Prosperity Gospel* (New York: Oxford University Press, 2013), 60–68.

26 Oral Roberts, "Open Letter to Magazine and Newspaper Editors: Oral Roberts Discusses Faith Healing," *Abundant Life* 11/2 (February 1957): 16–17, 28–29; R. F. DeWeese, "A Statement," *Abundant Life* 16/10 (October 1962): 22–23; Harrell, *Oral Roberts*, 170, 302–305.

27 Ibid.

28 C. Nelson, "Objections . . . to Divine Healing," *Christian Challenge* 12/11 (January 1964): 6–7, 10; unsigned editorial, "Divine Healing Is Not . . . ," *Christian Challenge* 13/5 (May 1964): 3, 6–7, Pentecostal Research Collection. On Juanita Coe, see Harrell, *All Things Are Possible*, 174–175.

29 John Osteen, "Do You Need Healing?," *Praise* 2/2 (March 1963): 13; John Osteen, "Prayer Cloths on Request," *Praise* 2/4 (May 1963): 4; John Osteen, "Do You Need Healing?," *Praise* 2/10 (December 1963): 8; John Osteen, "Do You Need Healing?," *Praise* 4/1 (March 1964): 5. On defense of the JOEA, see John Osteen, "Revival on Now, and It's Real News!," *Praise* 2/8 (September 1963): 14–15, and "Information for All Donors," *Praise* 4/1 (Winter 1965): 2. On prayer cloths and other "concrete mediators" of neopentecostalism's material culture, see Bowler, *Blessed*, 60, 144–145.

30 John Osteen, *You Can Change Your Destiny* (Houston: John H. Osteen Evangelistic Association, 1968), 59–69. See also A. A. Allen, "Heart Massaged to Life: Left Blood Clot on Brain," *Miracle Magazine* 9/9 (June 1964): 5; A. A. Allen, "'Aqua and White' Tent Dedication!," *Miracle Magazine* 10/1 (October 1964): 14–15, 20; A. A. Allen, "Documented Testimony," *Miracle Magazine* 11/12 (September 1966): 22; A. A. Allen, "Charlotte," *Miracle Magazine* 13/4 (January 1968): 20; A. A. Allen, "Actions Speak Louder than Words," *Miracle Magazine* (February 1968): 17; W. T. Jeffers, "Their Perfect Weekend," *Abundant Life* 11/7 (July 1957): 4; William P. Sterne, "A Great Revival in Denver," *Abundant Life* 17/2 (February 1963): 21. For neopentecostal attempts at legitimizing divine healing, see Harrell, *All Things Are Possible*, 84–93; Candy Gunther Brown, "Healing Words: Narratives of Spiritual Healing and Kathryn Kuhlman's Uses of Print Culture, 1947–1976," in *Religion and the Culture of Print in Modern America*, ed. Charles L. Cohen and Paul S. Boyer (Madison: University of Wisconsin Press, 2008), 271–297; Candy Gunther Brown, *Testing Prayer: Science and Healing* (Cambridge, MA: Harvard University Press, 2012), 99–154; Joseph W. Williams, *Spirit Cure: A History of Pentecostal Healing* (New York: Oxford University Press, 2013), 55–97.

31 Melody Harris interview, December 10 and December 20, 2010; Julia Duin interview, June 7, 2011. In *The Christmas Spirit*, Joel alludes to his father's frequent travels in the 1960s and the toll it took on the family (49–52). For Dodie's

comments on John's travel, see *Only the Beginning: John Osteen's 50 Years of Ministry* VHS (Houston: Lakewood Church, 1989).

CHAPTER 2. JOHN OSTEEN'S PROSPERITY GOSPEL

The epigraph comes from John Osteen, *The ABCs of Faith* (Houston: John Osteen Ministries, 1981), 46.

1   Melody Harris interview, December 10 and December 20, 2010. John Osteen first referred to Lakewood as the "Oasis of Love" in his book *How to Flow in the Super Supernatural* (Houston: Lakewood Church, 1972), 56. For more on the song "Oasis of Love," see David Ingles's web site, http://diministries.org/default2.asp. On the Jesus People movement, see John G. Turner, *Bill Bright and Campus Crusade for Christ: The Renewal of Evangelicalism in Postwar America* (Chapel Hill: University of North Carolina Press, 2008), 119–146; Preston Shires, *Hippies of the Religious Right: The Counterculture and American Evangelicalism in the 1960s and 1970s* (Waco, TX: Baylor University Press, 2007); Shawn David Young, "From Hippies to Jesus Freaks: Christian Radicalism in Chicago's Inner-City," *Journal of Religion and Popular Culture* 22/2 (Summer 2010), http://www.usask.ca/relst/jrpc/art22%282%29-jesusfreaks.html; Axel R. Schäfer, *Countercultural Conservatives: American Evangelicalism from the Postwar Revival to the New Christian Right* (Madison: University of Wisconsin Press, 2011); Larry Eskridge, *God's Forever Family: The Jesus People Movement in America* (New York: Oxford University Press, 2013).

2   David Edwin Harrell, *All Things Are Possible: The Healing and Charismatic Revivals in Modern America* (Bloomington: Indiana University Press, 1975), 225–239; Kate Bowler, *Blessed: A History of the American Prosperity Gospel* (New York: Oxford University Press, 2013), 60–76.

3   For FGBMFI information, see "November Tape Ministry," *Voice* 22/10 (November 1974): 13; "Photo Story: 1974 Dallas, Texas Regional Convention," *Voice* 22/11 (December 1974): 39; "Some 1975 FGBMFI Conventions, Rallies and Seminars in Retrospect," *Voice* 23/11 (December 1975): 38–39; "July–August Tape Ministry," *Voice* 24/7 (July/August 1976): 9; "Honolulu, Hawaii Regional Convention," *Voice* 25/4 (April 1977): 35; "Greatest Portland Convention Ever," *Voice* 25/8 (September 1977): 35; "Floridians Are First to Hold FGBMFI Convention," *Voice* 25/8 (September 1977): 36–37; "February Tape Ministry, Chicago World Convention," *Voice* 26/2 (February 1978): 25; "26th World Convention, New Orleans, July 2–7," *Voice* 27/8 (September 1979): 14–15.

4   John Osteen, "The Divine Flow of God's Love," *Voice* 21/8 (September 1973): 14–17. Osteen related the same story along with additional healing accounts in his 1978 book *The Divine Flow* (Houston: Lakewood Church, 1978), 10. On bones "popping" in neopentecostal healing, see Russell Spittler, "Pentecostal and Charismatic Spirituality," in *The New International Dictionary of Pentecostal and Charismatic Movements*, Revised and Expanded Edition, ed. Stanley M. Burgess and Eduard M. van der Maas (Grand Rapids: Zondervan, 2002), 1101.

5   John Osteen, "Hear Ye the Word of the Lord," *Voice* 27/10 (November 1979): 28–30.

6   Eva S. Moskowitz, *In Therapy We Trust: America's Obsession with Self-Fulfillment* (Baltimore: Johns Hopkins University Press, 2001), 218–244; Donald Meyer, *The Positive Thinkers: Religion as Pop Psychology from Mary Baker Eddy to Oral Roberts* (New York: Pantheon, 1980), 259–367; Bowler, *Blessed*, 64–67.

7   Osteen's comment about Hagin is from a 1983 interview with a California prosperity minister named Philip Wagner. See Philip Wagner, *Insights from Men of Faith* (Beverly Hills, CA: Oasis Publishing, 1987), 71–83.

    On Hagin and the Hagin–Osteen connection, see Harrell, *All Things Are Possible*, 185–186; Dale H. Simmons, *E. W. Kenyon and the Postbellum Pursuit of Peace, Power, and Plenty* (Lanham, MD: Scarecrow, 1997), 298–304; Milmon Harrison, *Righteous Riches: The Word of Faith Movement in Contemporary African American Religion* (New York: Oxford University Press, 2005), 3–19; Dale H. Simmons, "Positive Confession Theology," in *Encyclopedia of Pentecostal and Charismatic Christianity*, ed. Stanley M. Burgess (New York: Routledge, 2006), 377–380; Leonard Lovett, "Positive Confession Theology," in *The New International Dictionary of Pentecostal and Charismatic Movements*, 992–994; Scott Billingsly, "The Midas Touch: Kenneth E. Hagin and the Prosperity Gospel," in *Recovering the Margins of American Religious History: The Legacy of David Edwin Harrell Jr.*, ed. B. Dwain Waldrep and Scott Billingsley (Tuscaloosa: University of Alabama Press, 2012), 43–59; Bowler, *Blessed*, 44–46.

8   Billingsley, "Midas Touch"; Kenneth E. Hagin, *You Can Have What You Say!* (Tulsa: Kenneth Hagin Ministries, 1979), 3, 5, 7, 10; Sherry Andrews, "Keeping the Faith," *Charisma* (October 1981): 24–31; Vinson Synan, "The Faith of Kenneth Hagin," *Charisma* (June 1990): 62–70.

9   John Osteen, "How to Get Confession to Work for You," *A Revelation of the Name of Jesus and the Believer* Cassette Series (Houston: Lakewood Church, n.d.); Seth Dowland, "'Family Values' and the Formation of the Christian Right Agenda," *Church History* 78/3 (September 2009): 606–631; Daniel K. Williams, *God's Own Party: The Making of the Christian Right* (New York: Oxford University Press, 2010), 105–111, 143–153.

10 John Osteen, *There Is a Miracle in Your Mouth* (Houston: Lakewood Church, 1972), 29; John Osteen, *The Truth Shall Set You Free* (Houston: Lakewood Church, 1978), 21–22.

11 Osteen, *The Truth Shall Set You Free*, 7; John Osteen, *The Confessions of a Baptist Preacher* (Houston: John H. Osteen Publications, 1976), 7–8, 10, 13–14; Charles H. Kraft, "Spiritual Warfare: A Neocharismatic Perspective," in *The New International Dictionary of Pentecostal and Charismatic Movements*, 1091–1096.

12 Osteen, *How to Flow in the Super Supernatural*, 2; Osteen, *The Truth Shall Set You Free*, 7, 33, 43; W. Scott Poole, *Satan in America: The Devil We Know* (Lanham, MD: Rowman & Littlefield, 2009), 155–184.

13 On Church of the Redeemer, see Julia Duin, *Days of Fire and Glory: The Rise and Fall of a Charismatic Community* (Baltimore: Crossland Press, 2009). For an analysis of racial politics in Houston during this period, see Thomas R. Cole, *No Color is My Kind: The Life of Eldrewey Stearns and the Integration of Houston* (Austin: University of Texas Press, 1997), 13–99; David K. Chrisman, "Religious Moderates and Race: The Texas Christian Life Commission and the Call for Racial Reconciliation, 1954–68," and Brian H. Behnken, "Elusive Unity: African Americans, Mexican Americans, and Civil Rights in Houston," in *Seeking Inalienable Rights: Texans and Their Quests for Justice*, ed. Debra A. Reid (College Station: Texas A&M University Press, 2009), 97–122, 123–146. For images of William A. Lawson with Martin Luther King along with other ministers, see "William A. Lawson Eightieth Birthday Booklet," Reverend William A. Lawson Papers, Box 7, Folder 7.19, Woodson Research Center. On Houston's First Baptist, see "Negroes Picket Houston First Baptist Church," *Baptist News* (July 30, 1963), Southern Baptist Historical Library and Archives Digital Resources, http://media. sbhla.org.s3.amazonaws.com/1766,30-Jul-1963.pdf. I thank Derek Nease for bringing this document to my attention.

14 Melody Harris interview.

15 T. L. Osborn, *April 1984–December 1985*, Vol. 19 of *Faith Library in 23 Volumes* (Tulsa: OSPO International, 1997): 137. On Osborn's place in neopentecostal history, see Harrell, *All Things Are Possible*, 63–66, 169–172, and R. M. Riss, "Tommy Lee Osborn," in *The New International Dictionary of Pentecostal and Charismatic Movements*, 950–951. On Houston, see Joe R. Feagin, *Free Enterprise City: Houston in Political-Economic Perspective* (New Brunswick, NJ: Rutgers University Press, 1988).

16 On Osteen's national preaching events, see FGBMFI conference reports "By My Spirit," *Voice* 28/8 (September 1980): 18–19, "Signs and Wonders Now Detroit 83," *Voice* 31/4 (April 1983): 20–21, and "Detroit 83: The Tradition Continues," *Voice* 31/5 (May 1983): 20–21; Kenneth Copeland, "Report!," *Voice of Victory* 11/1 (January 1983): 7–8, Quentin J. Schulze Collection, Box 15, Folder 5, Heritage Hall; Lester Sumrall, "Campmeeting '85," *World Harvest* 24/4 (September/October 1985): 4; Vinson Synan interview, February 29, 2012. For Osteen's collaboration with Hagin, see "RHEMA Bible Training Center Presents John Osteen," Pentecostal Vertical File, Holy Spirit Research Center. John Osteen's articles in the charismatic press included "A Miracle in Your Mouth," *Charisma* (May 1979): 22–28; "Now the Spirit of the Lord Is Upon Me," *Testimony* 26/1 (1987): 1–7; "What You Say Is What You Get," *Charisma* (January 1989): 60–65; and "The Divine Flow," *Charisma* (May 1990): 72–78.

For feature articles in *Charisma* about Osteen, see Vinson Synan, "Baptists Ride the Third Wave," *Charisma* (December 1986): 54–57, and Steven Lawson, "John & Dodie Osteen: Their Oasis of Love Reaches a Troubled World," *Charisma* (September 1988): 44–50. Osteen featured updates about his television ministry in a monthly he published called *Manna*. See John Osteen,

"Our Television Ministry Is . . . Reaching Out Touching Lives," *Manna* (Spring 1986): 6–7, Pentecostal Vertical File, Holy Spirit Research Center; Dodie Osteen, "Be Part of John Osteen's Television Ministry," *Manna* (Spring 1987): 12–13, Flower Pentecostal Heritage Center.

For Osteen's national profile among leading televangelists of the 1980s, see Bobby C. Alexander, *Televangelism Reconsidered: Ritual in the Search for Human Community* (Atlanta: Scholars Press, 1994), 169. Although Alexander's study misspelled Osteen's last name in his May 27–June 3, 1990 survey, "John Oldstein" is a clear reference to Lakewood's minister. See also Charles Ward, "Praising the Lord: Charismatic Practices Mark Lakewood's Informal Service," *Houston Chronicle* (November 21, 1987).

17 John Osteen, "Now the Spirit of the Lord Is Upon Me"; Julia Duin, "Lakewood's New Building to Get Classy Send-off," *Houston Chronicle* (April 9, 1988); Julia Duin, "Charismatic Church a Big Success Story," *Houston Chronicle* (January 31, 1990); Cecil S. Holmes, "An Oasis of Energy," *Houston Chronicle* (February 22, 1997); Armando Villafranca and Cecil S. Holmes, "Worshippers Fondly Remember Lakewood Church Pastor's Integrity, Stand for Christ Gain Honor," *Houston Chronicle* (January 25, 1999); advertisement, "Announcing the Dedication of the New 8,2000 Seat Sanctuary at Lakewood Church," *Houston Post* (April 8, 1988); "Northeast's Lakewood Church to Build Largest Sanctuary in the City," *Northeast News* (February 24, 1987), Lakewood Church Vertical File, Houston Metropolitan Research Center; Bowler, *Blessed*, 77–111.

18 Judge Woodrow Seals to John H. Osteen, April 11, 1987, Box 40, Folder 15, Woodrow Seals Papers, Houston Metropolitan Research Center.

19 On the Systematic Bible Institute, see "Systematic Bible Institute Flyer," Reverend William A. Lawson Papers, Box 1, Folder 1.20, Woodson Research Center; and "Institute Started from Religious Conversation," *Forward Times* (February 6, 1960), 12, *Forward Times* Collection (microfilm), African American Library at the Gregory School. On Ernest L. Mays and Houston Bible Institute, see "Houston Bible Institute: The Past, Present and Future," [Houston Bible Institute] *News and Views* (Winter 1983): 3, and "Home Going Celebration for Dr. Ernest Lee Mays" (2000); *Houston Bible Institute Catalog* 1983–1985, College Archives, College of Biblical Studies; Jarvis Taylor, "The Houston Bible Institute and Ernest L. Mays' Strategy to Preserve the Character of the Black Church," paper delivered at the East Texas Historical Association Spring Meeting (February 2015), in possession of the author.

20 *Lakewood Bible Institute Student Handbook*, John H. Osteen Vertical File, Holy Spirit Research Center; "Let Lakewood Bible Institute Help You Become All God Wants You to Be!," *Manna* (Spring 1986): 11–14, Pentecostal Vertical File, Holy Spirit Research Center; *Lakewood Bible Institute 1985 Yearbook* (Houston: Lakewood Church, 1985), in possession of the author; Brady Mitchell interview, October 6, 2014.

21 Ibid.

22 Bowler, *Blessed*, 77–138; see also Kathleen Hladky, "I Double-Dog Dare You in Jesus' Name!: Claiming Christian Wealth and the American Prosperity Gospel," *Religion Compass* 6/1 (2012): 82–96; Joseph W. Williams, *Spirit Cure: A History of Pentecostal Healing* (New York: Oxford University Press, 2013).

23 Bowler, *Blessed*, 77–111, 178–186; John Osteen, *The Power of Words* VHS (Houston: Lakewood Church, 1988); John Osteen, *Confession That Brings Possession* Cassette Series (Houston: Lakewood Church, n.d.); John Osteen, *Four Principles in Receiving from God* (Houston: John Osteen Ministries, 1981), 5, 8, 12–14, 31–32.

24 Osteen, *There Is a Miracle in Your Mouth*, 6, 11–12, 20, 27.

25 Dodie Osteen, *Healed of Cancer* (Houston: Lakewood Church, 1986), 1, 15; James S. Olson, *Making Cancer History: Disease & Discovery at the University of Texas M.D. Anderson Cancer Center* (Baltimore: Johns Hopkins University Press, 2009), 163–213.

26 Saleim Kahleh interview, May 18, 2011; "This Is My Bible" confession, http://www.lakewood.cc/Downloads/PDF/ThisIsMyBible.pdf.

27 Simmons, "Positive Confession Theology"; Osteen, *There Is a Miracle in Your Mouth*, 6; Osteen, *ABCs of Faith*, 41; John Osteen, *Spiritual Food for Victorious Living* (Houston: John Osteen Ministries, 1985), 8; Osteen, "What You Say Is What You Get."

28 Lucy Rael, *Good Friday Service* VHS (Houston: Lakewood Church, 1986), Holy Spirit Research Center; Albert James Dager, "Stigmata: Is Lucy Rael for Real?" *Media Spotlight Special Report* (1989), http://www.mediaspotlight.org/pdfs/Stigmata-IsLucyRael-ForReal.pdf.

29 Dager, "Stigmata"; John Osteen, *Deception!: Recognizing True and False Ministries* (Houston: Lakewood Church, 1986), 3.

30 John Osteen, "Faith for our Families and Friends: A Harvest of Hope, Part 1" (1995), http://web.archive.org/web/19961109042300/http://www.lakewood-church.org/Sermons.html; Bowler, *Blessed*, 64–65.

31 Lakewood Church, "Seven Years of Harvest" (2000), http://web.archive.org/web/20040806161750/http:/www.lakewood.cc/mission_7years.htm.

32 David Edwin Harrell interview, September 16, 2011. As a visiting professor and Fulbright scholar in India in 1995, Harrell's path crossed Osteen's during one of John's India campaigns. Rekindling ties that stretched back to Harrell's research for *All Things Are Possible*, he interviewed Osteen during which time John identified Joel as he spoke about his succession plans for Lakewood.

33 Associated Press, "Man Once Questioned in Church Bombing Case Found Innocent," *Houston Chronicle* (June 22, 1990); Eric Hanson and Jerry Urban, "Bomb Hurts Pastor's Daughter: Lakewood Church Target of Explosive," *Houston Chronicle* (January 31, 1990); R. A. Dyer, "Church Bomb Probers Question Ex-Husband," *Houston Chroncle* (February 8, 1990); Richard Vara, "The Guiding Force of Lakewood Church," *Houston Post* (January 31, 1990); Steve Olafson and John Whitmire, "Daughter of Noted Pastor Hurt: Lakewood Explosion 'Like

Atomic Bomb,'" *Houston Post* (January 31, 1990); Norma Martin, "Bombing at Church Sparks Citywide Wave of Concern," *Houston Chronicle* (February 1, 1990).

34 Steve Brunsman, "One Year Ago, a Bomb Burst in Her Hands," *Houston Post* (January 30, 1991); Ken Lanterman, "Pastor Tells of Spiritual Bomb Alert," *Houston Post* (February 5, 1990); Stephen Strang, "After the Pipe Bomb," *Charisma* (April 1990): 8.

35 John Osteen, *Death & Beyond* VHS (Houston: Lakewood Television Productions, 1993). On neopentecostalism's simultaneous embrace of faith and medicine, see Williams, *Spirit Cure*, 81–97.

36 Randall J. Stephens and Karl W. Giberson, *The Anointed: Evangelical Truth in a Secular Age* (Cambridge, MA: Harvard University Press, 2011), 1–20, 182; Cecil Holmes, "Finding Hook to Bring in Flock," *Houston Chronicle* (August 22, 1992).

37 Ralph Reed, "An Active Faith: How Christians Are Changing the Soul of American Politics," in *The Columbia Documentary History of Religion in America since 1945*, ed. Paul Harvey and Philip Goff (New York: Columbia University Press, 2005), 404–409; John Osteen, *A Miracle for Your Marriage* (Houston: Lakewood Church, 1988), 5; John Osteen, *Love & Marriage* (Houston: John Osteen Ministries, 1980), 21, 31; John Osteen, "Building Secure Homes in an Insecure World, Part I" (n.d.), http://web.archive.org/web/20040824012955/http://www.lakewood.cc/sermon_john_classics.htm#.

38 John Osteen, *Unraveling the Mystery of the Blood Covenant* (Houston: Lakewood Church, 1987), 19–30, 37–40, 43, 45, 47, 66; Bowler, *Blessed*, 78–100.

39 John Osteen, *Seven Qualities of a Man of Faith* (Houston: Lakewood Church, 1990), 11, 30.

40 John Osteen, "Don't Limit God," *AZUSA 93 Conference* Cassette, Holy Spirit Research Center. On AZUSA 93 see Shayne Lee, *T. D. Jakes: America's New Preacher* (New York: NYU Press, 2005), 56–60; "Baccalaureate Commencement Oral Roberts University 1996" Program, University Archives, Oral Roberts University; Eric Hanson, "Brown to Be Sworn in as Houston Mayor Today," *Houston Chronicle* (January 2, 1998). On Lee Brown's inauguration, see "Mayor Lee P. Brown Inaugural Program," Dr. Lee P. Brown Papers, Box 152, Inaugural Address Folder, Woodson Research Center.

41 Villafranca and Holmes, "Worshippers Fondly Remember Lakewood Church Pastor's Integrity, Stand for Christ Gain Honor"; H.R. 57, "Honoring the Memory of Dr. John Osteen," http://www.legis.state.tx.us/billlookup/Text.aspx?LegSess=76R&Bill=HR57. California minister Ed Dufresne issued two collections of John Osteen's teachings: John Osteen, *How to Be Led by the Spirit of God* CD (Murrieta, CA: Ed Dufresne Ministries, 2009), and John Osteen, *Classics Collection, Volume 3* CD (Murrieta, CA: Ed Dufresne Ministries, 2010). See also Gary Simons, *Church by God's Design: Building a Modern Day Book of Acts Church* (Arlington, TX: Seven Pillars Publishing, 2010), 10; April Simons, *The Legacy Lives On* CD (Arlington, TX: High Point Church, 2010); John Osteen, *Keys to Daily Victory* CD (Houston: Joel Osteen Ministries, 2011); John Osteen,

Becoming a Man of Unwavering Faith, ed. Joel Osteen (New York: FaithWords, 2011); John Osteen, *Your Words Hold a Miracle: The Power of Speaking God's Word*, ed. Joel Osteen (New York: FaithWords, 2012); John Osteen, *Living in the Abundance of God*, ed. Joel Osteen (New York: FaithWords, 2013); John Osteen, *Power over the Enemy: Breaking Free from Spiritual Strongholds*, ed. Joel Osteen (New York: FaithWords, 2014).

CHAPTER 3. JOEL OSTEEN'S PROSPERITY GOSPEL, PART I
The epigraph comes from Joel Osteen's "Vision Sunday" sermon delivered in October 1999, and discussed below.

1   Joel Osteen, *Your Best Life Now: 7 Steps to Living at Your Full Potential* (New York: FaithWords, 2004), 214–217; Gary Simons, *Church by God's Design: Building a Modern Day Book of Acts Church* (Arlington, TX: Seven Pillars Publishing, 2010), 11–12.

2   See "John Osteen Tribute 1999," https://www.youtube.com/watch?v=Flwix4_IpTQ. An archived version of Lakewood's website includes an online letter that describes John's formal memorial service, http://web.archive.org/web/19990203144918/http:/www.lakewood-church.org/.

3   Joel Osteen, "Vision Sunday," (October 3, 1999), http://web.archive.org/web/19991012020750/http:/lakewood-church.org/. For the full text of this sermon, see appendix B.

4   Joel Osteen, *Historic Night of Hope in Jerusalem*, Trinity Broadcasting Network (February 3, 2011); Joel Osteen, Amazon.com interview for *Become a Better You*, http://www.amazon.com/Become-Better-You-Improving-Every/dp/0743296885; Joel Osteen, "Holding On to Your Dreams, Part 7: The Voice of Discouragement" (April 25, 1999), http://web.archive.org/web/20010303115912/http:/www.lakewood-church.org/Sermons1999/Sermons99.html.

5   Joel and Victoria Osteen, eds., *Hope for Today Bible* (New York: Free Press, 2009), x.

6   Joel Osteen, "HopeNote: Say It Out Loud," in ibid., 710.

7   Joseph W. Williams, *Spirit Cure: A History of Pentecostal Healing* (New York: Oxford University Press, 2013), 122–156.

8   For a helpful historical analysis of fundamentalism, see Matthew Avery Sutton, *American Apocalypse: A History of Modern Evangelicalism* (Cambridge, MA: Harvard University Press, 2014).

9   Joel Osteen, "HopeNote: God Turns It Around (Jonah 2:1)" and "Hope for Today: Another Chance," in *Hope for Today Bible*, 1002–1003.

10 Joel Osteen, "Hope for Today: God Will Rescue You (Daniel 3:17)," in ibid., 956.

11 Joel Osteen, "Hope for Today: Simple Trust (Luke 1:46–47)" and "HopeNote: Celebrate New Beginnings (Matthew 28:6)," in ibid., 1130, 1097.

12 Joyce Meyer, "The Last Days," Lakewood Church (February 2013).

13 Scott Billingsley, *It's a New Day: Race and Gender in the Charismatic Movement* (Tuscaloosa: University of Alabama Press, 2008), 80–84. See also Ken Walker,

"The Preacher Who Tells It Like It Is," *Charisma* (November 1998): 48–55; Vincent Newfield, "Teaching Beyond Words," *Charisma* (April 2012): 20–26; "Joyce Meyer" in *Encyclopedia of Evangelicalism*, Revised and Expanded Edition, ed. Randall Balmer (Waco, TX: Baylor University Press, 2004), 454. On T. D. Jakes, Joyce Meyer and the 1993 AZUSA meeting, see Shayne Lee, *T. D. Jakes: America's New Preacher* (New York: NYU Press, 2005), 61–83; Shayne Lee and Phillip Luke Sinitiere, *Holy Mavericks: Evangelical Innovators and the Spiritual Marketplace* (New York: NYU Press, 2009), 63–65.

14 Joyce Meyer, *Battlefield of the Mind: Winning the Battle in Your Mind* (New York: Warner Faith, 1995), 11, 42, 45, 53, 67, 69, 81, 89, 108, 169; Joyce Meyer, *Power Thoughts: 12 Strategies to Win the Battle of the Mind* (New York: FaithWords, 2010), 77, 89.

15 Meyer, *Battlefield of the Mind*, 145, 178; Meyer, *Power Thoughts*, 27, 193–195, 241.

16 Kate Bowler, *Blessed: A History of the American Prosperity Gospel* (New York: Oxford University Press, 2013), 178–225.

17 Joyce Meyer, "Love Life Ministry Conference: 30th Anniversary," *Charisma* (April 2012): 15, 26.

18 Joel Osteen, *Every Day a Friday: How to Be Happier 7 Days a Week* (New York: FaithWords, 2011), 220–221. An announcement about Maxwell's INJOY leadership conference appears on an archived page of Lakewood's website, http://web. archive.org/web/200011100135/http://www.lakewood-church.org/.

19 John Maxwell, "How a Biblical Miracle Works," Lakewood Church (April 2012).

20 Anthony Baldacchi interview, June 19, 2012; Robert H. Schuller, "Foreword," in John C. Maxwell, *The Success Journey: The Process of Living Your Dreams* (Nashville: Thomas Nelson, 1997), ix–x. On Schuller's "possibility thinking," see Dennis Voskuil, *Mountains into Goldmines: Robert Schuller and the Gospel of Success* (Grand Rapids, MI: Eerdmans, 1983), 71–131. On Schuller's "thinking big," see Dr. Robert H. Schuller, *The Miracle of Thinking Big* (Garden Grove, CA: Garden Grove Community Church, 1975), William Martin Collection, Box 112, Robert Schuller Folder, Woodson Research Center.

21 Maxwell, *Success Journey*, 26, 30–31; John C. Maxwell, *Be All You Can Be!: A Challenge to Stretch Your God-Given Potential* (Wheaton, IL: Victor Books, 1987), 52, 62.

22 Maxwell, *Success Journey*, 39, 83, 103; Maxwell, *Be All You Can Be!*, 96; John C. Maxwell, *Failing Forward: Turning Mistakes into Stepping Stones for Success* (Nashville: Thomas Nelson, 2000), 126.

23 Joel Osteen, *Become a Better You: 7 Keys to Improving Your Everyday Life* (New York: Free Press, 2007), 65.

24 Joel Osteen, "Holding On to Your Dreams" (February 21, 1999); Joel Osteen, "Holding On to Your Dreams, Part 2: Persistence & Determination" (March 7, 1999); Joel Osteen, "Holding On to Your Dreams, Part 3: II Kings 6" (March 21, 1999); Joel Osteen, "Holding On to Your Dreams, Part 4: What to Learn in the Dark Hours" (March 28, 1999); Joel Osteen, "Holding On to Your Dreams, Part 5: 3 Things to Do in the Midst of Trouble" (April 11, 1999); Joel Osteen, "Holding On to

Your Dreams, Part 6: Don't Limit God" (April 18, 1999); Joel Osteen, "Holding On to Your Dreams, Part 7: The Voice of Discouragement" (April 25, 1999); Joel Osteen, "Holding On to Your Dreams, Part 8: Do All You Can Do to Make Your Dreams Come True" (May 2, 1999); all http://web.archive.org/web/20010303115912/http:/www.lakewood-church.org/Sermons1999/Sermons99.html.

25 Joel Osteen, "Winning the Battle of the Mind, Part 1" (May 9, 1999); Joel Osteen, "Winning the Battle of the Mind, Part 2" (May 23, 1999); Joel Osteen, "Winning the Battle of the Mind, Part 4" (June 6, 1999); Joel Osteen, "Winning the Battle of the Mind, Part 6: No Condemnation" (June 20, 1999); all http://web.archive.org/web/20010303115912/http:/www.lakewood-church.org/Sermons1999/Sermons99.html.

26 Joel Osteen, "Winning the Battle of the Mind, Part 7: 3 Things to Do Not to Faint" (June 27, 1999); Joel Osteen "Winning the Battle of the Mind, Part 11: Your Imagination" (August 1, 1999); Joel Osteen, "Winning the Battle of the Mind, Part 12: Hearing the Voice of God" (August 8, 1999); Joel Osteen "Winning the Battle of the Mind: Part 13" (August 15, 1999), all http://web.archive.org/web/20010303115912/http:/www.lakewood-church.org/Sermons1999/Sermons99.html.

CHAPTER 4. JOEL OSTEEN'S PROSPERITY GOSPEL, PART II

The epigraph comes from Emily DePrang, "Gimme Shelter," *Texas Observer* (July 8, 2014), http://www.texasobserver.org/gimme-shelter/.

1 Joel Osteen, *You Can, You Will: 8 Undeniable Qualities of a Winner* (New York: FaithWords, 2014), 23–24.

2 Donald Meyer, *The Positive Thinkers: Popular Religious Psychology from Mary Baker Eddy to Norman Vincent Peale and Ronald Reagan* (Middletown, CT: Wesleyan University Press, 1988), xv.

3 Joel Osteen, "Be Positive," *Six Steps to Enjoying Life* Cassette Series (Houston: Joel Osteen Ministries, 2001); Joel Osteen, "Developing a Warrior Mentality," *Letting Go of the Past* Cassette Series (Houston: Joel Osteen Ministries, 2002).

4 Joel Osteen, *Thinking The Right Thoughts* CD (Houston: Joel Osteen Ministries, 2003); Joel Osteen, *30 Thoughts for Victorious Living* (Houston: Joel Osteen Ministries, 2003), 1, 12, 18; Joel Osteen, "Get Up On the Inside," on *Be Determined!* DVD (Houston: Joel Osteen Ministries, 2003); Joel Osteen, *Living in a Positive Frame of Mind* DVD (Houston: Joel Osteen Ministries, 2005); Joel Osteen, "Freedom from Wrong Mindsets," on *Living a Resurrected Life* CD (Houston: Joel Osteen Ministries, 2008).

5 Joel Osteen, *Your Best Life Now: 7 Steps to Living At Your Full Potential* (New York: FaithWords, 2004), 104, 107–108; Joel Osteen, *Become a Better You: 7 Keys to Improving Your Everyday Life* (New York: Free Press, 2007), 130.

6 Joel Osteen, *Every Day a Friday: How to Be Happier 7 Days a Week* (New York: FaithWords, 2011), 261–263, 266–269.

7   Kathryn Lofton, "The Preacher Paradigm: Promotional Biographies and the Modern-Made Evangelist," *Religion and American Culture* 16/1 (Winter 2006): 95–123.

8   Joel Osteen, "Life-Giving Words," on *The Power of Words* CD (Houston: Joel Osteen Ministries, 2001).

9   Joel Osteen, "Speaking Faith-Filled Words," "Be an Encourager," and "Speaking a Blessing," on *Life-Changing Words* DVD (Houston: Joel Osteen Ministries, 2004).

10   Osteen, *Become a Better You*, 109, 111–112; Joel Osteen, *It's Your Time: Activate Your Faith, Achieve Your Dreams, and Increase in God's Favor* (New York: Free Press, 2009), 112, 118–119.

11   John Osteen, *Your Words Hold a Miracle: The Power of Speaking God's Word*, ed. Joel Osteen (New York: FaithWords, 2012), 13, 67, 165; Joel Osteen, *I Declare: 31 Promises to Speak Over Your Life* (New York: FaithWords, 2012), v–xii.

12   I first began thinking of a "providence of positive outcomes" after reading Chicago pastor John Armstrong describe Osteen's "personal divine providence." See John Armstrong, "Joel Osteen on Divine Providence: Amazing," (February 22, 2011), http://www.johnharmstrong.com. On the idea of "victory" in the prosperity gospel movement, see Kate Bowler, *Blessed: A History of the American Prosperity Gospel* (New York: Oxford University Press, 2013), 178–225.

13   Osteen, *Your Best Life Now*, 195–204.

14   Osteen, *Become a Better You*, 329–339, 351–362.

15   Osteen, *It's Your Time*, 107, 114, 177, 187, 195, 199, 205.

16   Ibid., 233–244.

17   Peter J. Thuesen, *Predestination: The American Career of a Contentious Doctrine* (New York: Oxford University Press, 2009), 1–13, 200–218.

18   "Good God, He's RIPPED!!!," *TMZ* (February 2, 2012), http://www.tmz.com/2012/02/02/joel-osteen-topless-ripped-photo-stomach/; Nicola Menzie, "Megachurch Pastor Joel Osteen's 'Healthy' Physique Stuns Public," *Christian Post* (February 2, 2012), http://global.christianpost.com/news/megachurch-pastor-joel-osteens-healthy-physique-stuns-public-photo-68586/. TMZ eventually removed Osteen's shirtless photo from its website, but the image is available elsewhere online.

19   Jessica Martinez, "Top 10 Fittest Christian Leaders List Includes Joel Osteen, Rick Warren," *Christian Post* (March 18, 2014), http://www.christianpost.com/news/top-10-fittest-christian-leaders-list-includes-joel-osteen-rick-warren-116338/.

20   R. Marie Griffith, *Born Again Bodies: Flesh and Spirit in American Christianity* (Berkeley: University of California Press, 2004), 160–250; Lynne Gerber, *Seeking the Straight and Narrow: Weight Loss and Sexual Reorientation in Evangelical America* (Chicago: University of Chicago Press, 2011).

21   Michelle A. Vu, "Interview: Joel Osteen on the Prosperity Gospel, Crystal Cathedral, and Jesus," *Christian Post* (April 29, 2012), http://www.christianpost.com/news/interview-joel-osteen-on-prosperity-gospel-crystal-cathedral-and-jesus-74040/.

22 Along with the essays in Katherine Attanasi and Amos Yong, eds., *Pentecostalism and Prosperity: The Socio-Economics of the Global Charismatic Movement*, (New York: Palgrave Macmillan, 2012), the following works have alerted me to various material dimensions of the prosperity gospel's message: James K. A. Smith, "What's Right with the Prosperity Gospel?" *Calvin Forum* 16/3 (Fall 2009): 8–9; James K. A. Smith, *Thinking in Tongues: Pentecostal Contributions to Christian Philosophy* (Grand Rapids, MI: Eerdmans, 2010), 41–43; Amos Yong, *In the Days of Caesar: Pentecostalism and Political Theology* (Grand Rapid, MI: Eerdmans, 2010), 23–26, 257–268; Jason Hackworth, *Faith Based: Religious Neolibralism and the Politics of Welfare in the United States* (Athens: University of Georgia Press, 2012), 30–47; Donald Miller and Tetsunao Yamamori, *Global Pentecostalism: The New Face of Christian Social Engagement* (Berkeley: University of California Press, 2007), 39–67; Calvin L. Smith, "The Politics and Economics of Pentecostalism," in *The Cambridge Companion to Pentecostalism*, ed. Cecil M. Robeck, Jr., and Amos Yong (New York: Cambridge University Press, 2014), 175–194.

23 In Joel's books, he recounts family testimonials of divine healing. See, for example, *Your Best Life Now*, 25–26, 63, 85–86, 126–127, 162, 225; and *Become a Better You*, 15, 62–65.

24 On the relationship between the gradual eclipse of charismatic spiritual expressions such as divine healing and speaking in tongues due to bourgeois wealth and material attainment, see for example, Bowler's *Blessed*, Attanasi and Yong's *Pentecostalism and Prosperity*, and the work of James K. A. Smith cited above. Also important is Matthew Avery Sutton, *Aimee Semple McPherson and the Resurrection of Christian America* (Cambridge, MA: Harvard University Press, 2007), and Paul Alexander, *Signs and Wonders: Why Pentecostalism Is the World's Fastest Growing Religion* (San Francisco: Josey-Bass, 2009), 61–78.

25 "HopeNote: Healthy in Body and Spirit," in *Hope for Today Bible*, ed. Joel and Victoria Osteen (New York: Free Press, 2009), 1448.

26 *The Dr. Oz Show*, "Medical Miracles" (November 17, 2011), http://www.doctoroz.com/videos/joel-osteen-medical-miracles-pt-1.

27 Osteen, *It's Your Time*, 131, 146, 157.

28 Joel Osteen, "Staying Healthy Physically," on *Healthy Living* CD (Houston: Lakewood Church, 2006).

29 Osteen, "Eating Healthier," ibid.

30 Osteen, "Living at Your Ideal Weight," ibid. In *Your Best Life Now*, Osteen told a story about "Carly," who, despite her large body size, eventually became CEO of her company (55); in *Become a Better You*, he offered a story about "Stacey," an overweight woman whose eventual shedding of her excess pounds he attributed to her positive mindset (360). See also Alan Wolfe, *The Transformation of American Religion: How We Actually Live Our Faith* (Chicago: University of Chicago Press, 2003), 158–161.

31 Carol V. R. George, *God's Salesman: Norman Vincent Peale and the Power of Positive Thinking* (New York: Oxford University Press, 1993), 103–162.

32   Barbara Ehrenreich, *Bright-Sided: How Positive Thinking Is Undermining America* (New York: Picador, 2009), 123–146.

33   Joel Kotkin, "The Next Great World City," *American* 2/2 (March/April 2008): 32–39; Kerry Hannon, "30 Cities to Restart Your Career," *Daily Beast* (October 6, 2010), http://www.thedailybeast.com/articles/2010/10/07/best-places-to-restart-your-career.html?cid=hp:beastoriginalsC2; Bill White, "Inaugural Speech" (January 2, 2008), http://newswirehouston.com/2008/01/02/mayor-bill-whites-inauguration-speech-january-2–2008/?doing_wp_cron=1348183879.382215023040 7714843750; Annise Parker, "2012 Inaugural Address" (January 3, 2012), http://www.houstontx.gov/mayor/inauguration2012.html. I thank Ty Cashion for directing me to Joel Kotkin's article.

34   Rice University's Kinder Institute has made available much of the data from the Houston Area Survey. For measures of religiosity, see http://kinder.rice.edu/content.aspx?id=2147486188.

35   Richard Vara, "From the Rodeo Arena to the Pulpit," *Houston Chronicle* (May 17, 2008): F1, F4; Angela K. Brown, "Hats and Boots Are Fine Here, Y'all," *Houston Chronicle* (January 10, 2009): F4; Lori Rodriguez, "Patrons Keep the Faith in Folk Healers," *Houston Chronicle* (August 13, 2006): B1, B8; R. Andrew Chesnut, *Devoted to Death: Santa Muerte, the Skeleton Saint* (New York: Oxford University Press, 2012); Timothy Wyatt, "Iglesia De La Luz Del Mundo," *Houston History* 8/3 (Summer 2011): 26–29; Barbara Karkabi, "Looking Inward," *Houston Chronicle* (February 23, 2008): F1, F4; Barbara Karkabi, "A Stretch Toward God," *Houston Chronicle* (June 3, 2006): F1, F4; David Barron, "KSBJ Makes a Splash Across FM Dial," *Houston Chronicle* (June 15, 2012), http://blog.chron.com/sportsmedia/2012/06/ksbj-makes-a-splash-across-fm-dial/; Richard Vara, "Radio María: Church at Home," *Houston Chronicle* (February 23, 2008): F1, F4; Andrew Guy, Jr., "Running with the Praise Man," *Houston Chronicle* (December 26, 2006): E1, E12; Salatheia Bryant, "Broadcasting a Message," *Houston Chronicle* (February 16, 2008): F1, F4; Jennifer Gramman, "Lone Star Christianity," *That! Texas Magazine* 8/2 (April–May 2008): 22–24; Lindsay Wise, "New Faith, Changed Man," *Houston Chronicle* (June 14, 2008): F1, F4; Fenggang Yang and Helen Rose Ebaugh, "Transformations in New Immigrant Religions and Their Global Implications," *American Sociological Review* 66 (April 2001): 269–288; Elias Bongmba, "Portable Faith: The Global Dimensions of African Initiated Churches (AIC)," in *African Immigrant Religions in America*, ed. Jacob Olupona and Regina Gemignani (New York: NYU Press, 2007), 102–129; Kafah Bachari Manna, "Breaking Bread: The Pink Iftar Movement," *Houston History* 8/3 (Summer 2011): 23–25; Barbara Karkabi, "Dinner Dialogues Will Involve a Lot of 'Respectful Listening,'" *Houston Chronicle* (October 13, 2007): F1, F4; Richard Vara, "Racing to Spread God's Word," *Houston Chronicle* (May 24, 2008): F1, F3; Richard Vara, "A Church They Can Relate To," *Houston Chronicle* (June 21, 2008): F1, F4; Tara Dooley, "The Making of a Cardinal," *Houston Chronicle* (December 1, 2007): F1; Eileen McClelland, "A Doubleheader at the Ballpark," *Houston Chronicle* (August 4,

2007): F1, F4; Tania Ganguli, "God Felt in Many Guises on Gridiron," *Houston Chronicle* (December 23, 2012): A1, A21; Ken Chitwood, "Church Offers Sanctuary for Freethinkers," *Houston Belief* (October 25, 2012), http://www.chron.com/life/houston-belief/article/Church-offers-sanctuary-for-freethinkers-3982205.php; Nancy Cook War, "Catholic Megacenter Serves Houston's Charismatics," *Charisma* (October 1997): 38–41; Bret Mavrich, "God's Defense Attorney," *Christianity Today* (December 17, 2014), http://www.christianitytoday.com/ct/2014/december/gods-defense-attorney.html?utm_source=ctdirect-html&utm_medium=Newsletter&utm_term=12613996&utm_content=322175872&utm_campaign=2013. On Fr. Cedric Pisegna, see "Profile: Live with Passion!" (September 2014), *Liguorian.org*, https://frcedric.org/html/Liguorian_Live_With_Passion.pdf, and "Fr. Cedric Pisegna, C. P., Passionist Religion," Box 7, Folder 58, Barbara Karkabi Papers, Special Collections, University of Houston.

36 The Hartford Institute for Religion Research maintains an updated website of megachurch data. As of 2012 statistics show that nationally, 40 percent of megachurches are nondenominational, while 16% are Southern Baptist. Megachurches associated with the United Methodist Church account for only 2 percent of megachurches nationally. See "Profile of Total North American Megachurches," Hartford Institute of Religion Research, http://hirr.hartsem.edu/megachurch/megastoday_profile.html.

37 Figures discussed in this paragraph come from data presented in Bowler, *Blessed*, appendices A and B. See also Scott Thumma and Dave Travis, *Beyond Megachurch Myths* (San Francisco: Wiley, 2007). On the self-reported membership totals from megachurches, see the online Database of Megachurches in the U.S. above.

38 Bill Shepson, "He's Doing His Father's Business," *Charisma* (August 2000): 76–78; Ernest Herndon, "How a Big Church Grew Bigger," *Charisma* (June 2004): 42–50; Mark A. Shibley, *Resurgent Evangelicalism in the United States: Mapping Cultural Change Since 1970* (Columbia: University of South Carolina Press, 1996); Darren Dochuk, "Evangelicalism Becomes Southern, Politics Becomes Evangelical: From FDR to Ronald Reagan," in *Religion and American Politics: From the Colonial Period to the Present*, Second Edition, ed. Mark A. Noll and Luke E. Harlow (New York: Oxford University Press, 2007), 297–325.

39 Daniel K. Williams, *God's Own Party: The Making of the Christian Right* (New York: Oxford University Press, 2010), 245–276; Nancy Gibbs and Michael Duffy, "How the Democrats Got Religion," *Time* (July 12, 2007), http://www.time.com/time/magazine/article/0,9171,1642890,00.html; Jim Wallis, *God's Politics: Why the Right Gets It Wrong and the Left Doesn't Get It* (San Francisco: HarperCollins, 2005); Jim Wallis, *Great Awakening: Reviving Faith and Politics in a Post-Religious Right America* (San Francisco: HarperCollins, 2008); David P. Gushee, *The Future of Faith in American Politics: The Public Witness at the Evangelical Center* (Waco, TX: Baylor University Press, 2008); E. J. Dionne, *Souled Out: Reclaiming Faith and Politics after the Religious Right* (Princeton, NJ: Princeton University Press, 2009); Peter G. Heltzel, *Jesus and Justice: Evangelicals, Race, and American Politics* (New

Haven, CT: Yale University Press, 2009); Amy Sullivan, *The Party Faithful: How and Why the Democrats Are Closing the God Gap* (New York: Scribner's, 2008); David R. Swartz, *Moral Minority: The Evangelical Left in an Age of Conservatism* (Philadelphia: University of Pennsylvania Press, 2012), 255–266; Brantley Gasaway, *Progressive Evangelicals and the Pursuit of Social Justice* (Chapel Hill: University of North Carolina Press, 2014), 270–278. For the Jim Wallis quote, see "Jim Wallis Interview, July 22, 2004," *One Nation under God?* Film Project Materials, Box 1, Folder 1.115, Woodson Research Center. See also Robert Wuthnow, *Rough Country: How Texas Became America's Most Powerful Bible-Belt State* (Princeton, NJ: Princeton University Press, 2014).

40   Hackworth, *Faith Based*, 30–47; Kathryn Lofton, "The Sigh of the Oppressed? Marxism and Religion in America Today," *New Labor Forum* 21/3 (Fall 2012): 58–65; Sean McCloud, *Divine Hierarchies: Class in American Religion and Religious Studies* (Chapel Hill: University of North Carolina Press, 2007), 7, 9–30, 90–101, 135–166, 168–169. While McCloud does not directly address the prosperity gospel, his analysis does include Pentecostal congregations. For additional class analysis of the prosperity gospel, see Catherine A. Brekus, "The Perils of Prosperity: Some Historical Reflections on Christianity, Capitalism, and Consumerism in America," in *American Christianities: A History of Dominance & Diversity*, ed. Catherine A. Brekus and W. Clark Gilpin (Chapel Hill: University of North Carolina Press, 2011), 279–306; and Gerardo Marti, "'I Determine My Harvest': Risky Careers and Spirit-Guided Prosperity in Los Angeles," in *Pentecostalism and Prosperity*, 131–150.

41   *Larry King Live*, "Interview with Joel Osteen" (June 20, 2005), http://transcripts. cnn.com/TRANSCRIPTS/0506/20/lkl.01.html; Daniel Calder, "Joel Osteen: The New Face of Christianity," *Guardian* (March 6, 2010), http://www.theguardian. com/world/2010/mar/07/joel-osteen-america-pastor; Jason C. Bivins, *Religion of Fear: The Politics of Horror in Conservative Evangelicalism* (New York: Oxford University Press, 2008).

CHAPTER 5. JOEL OSTEEN'S TEL-E-VANGELISM

The epigraph comes from Joel Osteen, *Your Best Life Now: 7 Steps to Living at Your Full Potential* (New York: Warner Faith, 2004), 93.

1   Osteen, *Your Best Life Now*, 111.

2   Joel Osteen, *Become a Better You: 7 Keys to Improving Your Everyday Life* (New York: Free Press, 2007), 250–251, 260–261; Joel Osteen, *Every Day a Friday: How to Be Happier 7 Days a Week* (New York: FaithWords, 2011), 37–38.

3   Pradip N. Thomas and Philip Lee, "Global and Local Televangelism: An Introduction," in *Global and Local Televangelism*, ed. Pradip Ninian Thomas and Philip Lee (New York: Routledge, 2012), 1–2.

4   Jeffrey K. Hadden and Charles E. Swann, *Prime Time Preachers: The Rising Power of Televangelism* (Reading, MA: Addison-Wesley, 1981); Jeffrey K. Hadden, "The Rise and Fall of Televangelism," *ANNALS of the American Academy of Political*

and Social Science 527 (May 1993): 113–130; J. Gordon Melton, Phillip Charles Lucas, and Jon R. Stone, *Prime-Time Religion: An Encyclopedia of Religious Broadcasting* (Phoenix, AZ: Oryx, 1997); Michele Rosenthal, *American Protestants and TV in the 1950s: Responses to a New Medium* (New York: Palgrave Macmillan, 2007); Jonathan Walton, *Watch This!: The Ethics and Aesthetics of Black Televangelism* (New York: NYU Press, 2009), 19–45; Christopher Owen Lynch, *Selling Catholicism: Bishop Sheen and the Power of Television* (Lexington: University Press of Kentucky, 1998); Heather Hendershot, *What's Fair on the Air?: Cold War Right-Wing Broadcasting and the Public Interest* (Chicago: University of Chicago Press, 2011), 102–136; Michael Stamm, "Broadcasting Mainline Protestantism: The Chicago Sunday Evening Club and the Evolution of Audience Expectations from Radio to Television," *Religion and American Culture* 22/2 (Summer 2012): 233–264; Lerone A. Martin, *Preaching on Wax: The Phonograph and the Making of Modern African American Religion* (New York: NYU Press, 2014).

5   Hadden, "The Rise and Fall of Televangelism"; David Edwin Harrell, *Oral Roberts: An American Life* (Bloomington: Indiana University Press, 1985); Kathleen Hladky, "I Double-Dog Dare You in Jesus' Name!: Claiming Christian Wealth and the American Prosperity Gospel," *Religion Compass* 6/1 (2012): 82–96; Darren E. Grem, "Selling a 'Disneyland for the Devout': Religious Marketing at Jim Bakker's Heritage USA," in *Shopping for Jesus: Faith in Marketing in the USA*, ed. Dominic Janes (Washington, DC: New Academia Press, 2008), 137–160; Steve Bruce, *Pray T. V.: Televangelism in America* (New York: Routledge, 1990); Janice Peck, *The Gods of Televangelism: The Crisis of Meaning and the Appeal of Religious Television* (Cresskill, NJ: Hampton Press, 1993); Walton, *Watch This!*, 145–165; Dennis J. Bekkering, "From 'Televangelist' to 'Interevangelist': The Emergence of the Streaming Video Preacher," *Journal of Religion and Popular Culture* 23/2 (July 2011): 101–117. I thank Peter Schuurman for bringing the Bekkering article to my attention.

6   On People for the American Way, see "The Media Fairness Project: Responding to the One-Sided 'Truths' of Moral Majoritarian TV Evangelists Pamphlet," William Martin Papers, Box 87, Religious Right Media Folder, Woodson Research Center. For Norman Lear, see "Norman Lear Interview, May 6, 2008," *One Nation under God?* Film Project Materials, Box 3, Folder 44, Woodson Research Center.

7   Phillip Luke Sinitiere, "Ted Haggard and Saint James Church," *Religion in American History* blog (June 2, 2010), http://usreligion.blogspot.com/2010/06/ted-haggard-and-saint-james-church.html; Joe Maxwell, "Praise and Dismay for Senate Scrutiny of Ministries' Finances," *Christianity Today* (November 6, 2007), http://www.christianitytoday.com/ct/2007/novemberweb-only/145–25.0.html; Lillian Kwan, "Grassley Asks Televangelists Again for Cooperation," *Christian Post* (January 18, 2008), http://www.christianpost.com/news/grassley-asks-televangelists-again-for-cooperation-30903/; Jacqueline L. Salmon, "Probe Biased, Televangelists Say," *Washington Post* (May 24, 2008), http://www.washingtonpost.

com/wp-dyn/content/article/2008/05/23/AR2008052302679.html; Sarah Pulliam
Bailey, "A Voice For Sanity," *Christianity Today* 53/11 (November 2009): 42–45; and
Sarah Posner, "Grassley Staff Memo on Televangelists Makes Clear Religious
Right Opposition to Government Oversight," *Religion Dispatches* (January 7, 2011),
http://www.religiondispatches.org/dispatches/sarahposner/3999/grassley_staff_
memo_on_televangelists_makes_clear_religious_right_opposition_to_govern-
ment_oversight/. The Senate Finance Committee's initial queries to televangelists
along with its final report are available in "Grassley Seeks Information from Six
Media-based Ministries" (November 6, 2007), http://finance.senate.gov/
newsroom/ranking/release/?id=baa4251a-ee70–48af-a324–79801cd07f18, and
"Grassley Releases Review of Tax Issues Raised by Media-based Ministries"
(January 6, 2011), http://finance.senate.gov/newsroom/ranking/
release/?id=5fa343ed-87eb-49b0–82b9–28a9502910f7.

8   Susan Friend Harding, *The Book of Jerry Falwell: Fundamentalist Language and
Politics* (Princeton, NJ: Princeton University Press, 2000), 247–269.

9   Pew Research Center's Religion & Public Life Project, "Religion and Electronic
Media" (November 6, 2014), http://www.pewforum.org/2014/11/06/religion-and-
electronic-media/2/. This study accounted not only for generational differences in
media consumption, but examined race and ethnicity as well as electronic
evangelistic practices compared to face-to-face interactions.

10   Joel Osteen, "Holding onto Your Dreams, Part 7: The Voice of Discouragement,"
(April 25, 1999), http://web.archive.org/web/20010303115912/http:/www.lakewood-
church.org/Sermons1999/Sermons99.html.

11   Osteen, *Become a Better You*, 72–73, 250–251.

12   Ibid., 260–261.

13   Quoted in Jim Asker, "Lakewood Pastor Has Camera-Ready Message: 'Oasis of
Love' Congregation Aims at TV Audience," *Houston Post* (April 2, 1983); Osteen,
Every Day a Friday, 111.

14   Tara Dooley, "Spreading Its Word"; Osteen, *Every Day a Friday*, 37–38.

15   John Osteen, *The Power of Words* VHS (Houston: Lakewood Church, 1988); John
Osteen, *How to Follow God's Peace* VHS (Houston: Lakewood Church, 1989).

16   Bobby C. Alexander, *Televangelism Reconsidered: Ritual in the Search for Human
Community* (Atlanta: Scholars Press, 1994), 163–183. The survey listed "John
Oldstein" as a show viewers watched; "Oldstein" is a clear reference to Osteen (169).

17   *Welcome to Lakewood* VHS (Houston: Lakewood Church, 1993).

18   The "New Beginnings" tagline appears at the beginning of the three-cassette tape
series found in Joel Osteen, *Six Steps to Enjoying Life: You Can Experience Real
Joy, Happiness and Purpose . . . Everyday!* (Houston: Joel Osteen Ministries, 2001).

19   The "champion" tagline and video is from Joel Osteen, *Having a Relaxed and Easy
Going Attitude* VHS (Houston: Lakewood Church, 2003), and Joel Osteen, *Living
a Lifestyle of Giving: Showing God's Kindness and Mercy* DVD (Houston: Joel
Osteen Ministries, 2002).

20 Ibid.

21 Joel Osteen, *You Can, You Will: 8 Undeniable Qualities of a Winner* (New York: FaithWords, 2014), 96–97.

22 James A. Beverly, *Holy Laughter and the Toronto Blessing* (Grand Rapids, MI: Zondervan, 1995); *Larry King Live*, "Interview with Joel Osteen," (June 20, 2005), http://transcripts.cnn.com/TRANSCRIPTS/0506/20/lkl.01.html; *Larry King Live*, "Interview with Joel and Victoria Osteen" (October 16, 2007), http://transcripts.cnn.com/TRANSCRIPTS/0710/16/lkl.01.html. On the declining influence of religious leaders more generally, see Mark Chaves, *American Religion: Contemporary Trends* (Princeton, NJ: Princeton University Press, 2011), 69–72.

23 Phil Cooke, *Branding Faith: Why Some Churches and Nonprofits Impact Culture and Others Don't* (Ventura, CA: Regal, 2008), 33; Alex Murashko, "Christian TV Program Producer Discusses Joel Osteen, Today's Televangelism," *Christian Post* (May 9, 2013), http://www.christianpost.com/news/christian-tv-program-producer-discusses-joel-osteen-todays-televangelism-95558/.

24 Phil Cooke, *The Last TV Evangelist: Why the Next Generation Couldn't Care Less about Religious Media and Why It Matters* (Huntington Beach, CA: Conversant Media Group, 2009), 17–18, 70. Emphasis in original. Murashko, "Christian TV Program Producer Discusses Joel Osteen, Today's Televangelism."

25 Mara Einstein, *Brands of Faith: Marketing Religion in a Commercial Age* (New York: Routledge, 2008), 120–146; Jennifer Dawson, "Church Sells The Tube to Network," *Houston Business Journal* (November 26, 2006), http://www.bizjournals.com/houston/stories/2006/11/27/story1.html?page=all.

26 Duncan Dodds, "Marketing and Creating a Brand" Handout, Lakewood Church Leaders in Ministry Conference (October 13–15, 2006), 1–2.

27 Ibid.

28 Ibid. For more on Dodds, see Lee and Sinitiere, *Holy Mavericks*, 33; Phillip Luke Sinitiere, "Preaching the Good News Glad: Joel Osteen's Tel-e-vangelism," in *Global and Local Televangelism*, 87–107; Richard Young, *The Rise of Lakewood Church and Joel Osteen* (New Kensington, PA: Whitaker House, 2007), 128–130.

29 Stephanie Samuel, "Joel Osteen Says New SiriusXM Channel Will Offer a More Personal Look Into Their Lives," *Christian Post* (October 3, 2014), http://www.christianpost.com/news/joel-osteen-says-new-siriusxm-channel-will-offer-a-more-personal-look-into-their-lives-127438/; Allan Turner, "Lakewood Church Launches New Satellite Ministry," *Houston Chronicle* (October 31, 2014), http://www.houstonchronicle.com/news/houston-texas/houston/article/Lakewood-Church-launches-satellite-radio-ministry-5862249.php#/0. On postwar trends and the cultural politics of contemporary religious radio, see Tona J. Hangen, *Redeeming the Dial: Radio, Religion and Popular Culture in America* (Chapel Hill: University of North Carolina Press, 2002), 142–158. I thank Jerry Park and Matt Henderson for alerting me to the *Houston Chronicle* article.

30 Osteen, *Your Best Life Now*, 295.

31 ControlBoot.tv, "Jon Swearingen Interview: A Chat with Joel Osteen's TV Director" (August 28, 2013), http://www.controlbooth.tv/?p=3645.

32 "Jon Swearingen Interview"; "Broadcast TV and Technologies for Live Worship" Handout, Lakewood Church Leaders in Ministry Conference (October 13–15, 2006).

33 Charity R. Carney, "Lakewood Church and the Roots of the Megachurch Movement in the South," *Southern Quarterly* 50/1 (Fall 2012): 60–78, and Jeanne Halgren Kilde, "Reading Megachurches: Investigating the Religious and Cultural Work of Church Architecture," in *American Sanctuary: Understanding Sacred Spaces*, ed. Louis P. Nelson (Bloomington: Indiana University Press, 2006), 225–249. Also key is Kate Bowler's "aesthetics of triumph" in *Blessed: A History of the American Prosperity Gospel* (New York: Oxford University Press, 2013), 197–199.

34 Lee and Sinitiere, *Holy Mavericks*, 35–37; *Lakewood Church Grand Opening* DVD (Houston: Lakewood Church, 2005); Jennifer Mathieu, "Power House," *Houston Press* (April 4, 2002), http://www.houstonpress.com/2002-04-04/news/power-house/; Seth Olivier interview, August 6, 2014.

35 Da'dra Greathouse, "Overcoming Lies with the Truth," *Hope for Today* 5/2 (Summer 2012): 26–27; Paul Osteen, "A Father's Heart," *Hope for Today* 5/1 (Spring 2012): 14–15; Paul Osteen, "Sunshine at the End of the Room," *Hope for Today* 5/2 (Summer 2012): 19–22; Paul Osteen, "To the Least of These: 2 Weeks in Cameroon," *Hope for Today* 3/2 (Fall 2010): 10–12.

36 On Oral Roberts, see Walton, *Watch This!*, 61.

37 Joel Osteen, *An Evening with Joel Osteen Live* DVD (Houston: Joel Osteen Ministries, 2004).

38 Grant Wacker, *America's Pastor: Billy Graham and the Shaping of a Nation* (Cambridge, MA: Harvard University Press, 2014), 158–159.

39 For more on the Central Texas event, see Lee and Sinitiere, *Holy Mavericks*, 48.

40 Ibid.

41 Fieldnotes, Night of Hope (February 25, 2011), Corpus Christi, Texas. I thank Kimberly Hill for local Corpus Christi media materials that reported on the Osteen event.

42 I viewed each of the Historic Night of Hope events on Trinity Broadcasting Network, which aired on the Houston affiliate KETH.

43 Ibid.

44 Ibid.

45 Jill Stevenson, *Sensational Devotion: Evangelical Performance in Twenty-First-Century America* (Ann Arbor: University of Michigan Press, 2013), 162–227. While Stevenson's book connects sensational devotion to experiences within megachurches, I borrow her innovative explanation of religious appeal for NOH and HNH events because these stadium events have employed elements similar to those of an ordinary Lakewood service (e.g., praise music, sermon, Jumbotron) and always host well over 2,000 attendees.

CHAPTER 6. LAKEWOOD'S CHARISMATIC CORE

The epigraph comes from the DVD of Lakewood's fiftieth-anniversary service, referenced below.

1 *Lakewood Church 50th Anniversary* DVD (Houston: Lakewood Church, 2009); Marybeth Carlyle interview, May 20, 2012.

2 *Lakewood Church 50th Anniversary* DVD.

3 Joel Osteen, *The Christmas Spirit: Memories of Family, Friends, and Faith* (New York: Free Press, 2010), 22–48.

4 Dodie Osteen, *The Healing of a Lady Named Dodie* Cassette (June 6, 1986), Holy Spirit Research Center; Dodie Osteen, *Healed of Cancer* (Houston: Lakewood Church, 1986).

5 Osteen, *Healed of Cancer*, 8, 16, 30.

6 Osteen, *Healed of Cancer*, 61–73; Candy Gunther Brown, *Testing Prayer: Science and Healing* (Cambridge, MA: Harvard University Press, 2012), 99–154; Candy Gunther Brown, "Pentecostal Healing Prayer in an Age of Evidence-Based Medicine," *Transformation: An International Journal of Holistic Mission Studies* (2014): 1–16.

7 Osteen, *The Healing of a Lady Named Dodie*; Saleim Kahleh interview, May 18, 2011; Dodie Osteen, *Choosing Life One Day at a Time: A Daily Devotional for Men and Women* (New York: Free Press, 2001), 17; Deborah Wrigley, "Lakewood Starts Drive-Through Healing Service," *ABC News 13/KTRK* (February 8, 2010), http://abc13.com/archive/7266019/.

8 Lisa Osteen Comes, *You Are Made for More!* (New York: FaithWords, 2012), 41–60. In a commendable decision that I gather was in the interest of respecting her ex-husband's privacy—and her current family and spouse, Kevin Comes—Osteen Comes used the pseudonym of "Tom" in her book to refer to George Allan Jackson. I discovered the name George Allan Jackson in a *Houston Chronicle* article about Lisa's survival of a pipe bomb blast in 1990. See references below.

9 Ibid., xi–xii, 54–56.

10 Ibid., 56, 82–102, 123–143; Lisa [Osteen] Comes, *6 Lies the Devil Uses to Destroy Marriages* (Houston: Lakewood Church, 1988), 43; Seth Dowland, "'Family Values' and the Formation of the Christian Right Agenda," *Church History* 78/3 (September 2009): 606–631.

11 Associated Press, "Man Once Questioned in Church Bombing Case Found Innocent," *Houston Chronicle* (June 22, 1990); Eric Hanson and Jerry Urban, "Bomb Hurts Pastor's Daughter: Lakewood Church Target of Explosive," *Houston Chronicle* (January 31, 1990); R. A. Dyer, "Church Bomb Probers Question Ex-Husband," *Houston Chronicle* (February 8, 1990); Richard Vara, "The Guiding Force of Lakewood Church," *Houston Post* (January 31, 1990); Steve Olafson and John Whitmire, "Daughter of Noted Pastor Hurt: Lakewood Explosion 'Like Atomic Bomb,'" *Houston Post* (January 31, 1990); Norma Martin, "Bombing at

Church Sparks Citywide Wave of Concern," *Houston Chronicle* (February 1, 1990); Osteen Comes, *You Are Made for More!*, 1–17.

12 Osteen Comes, *You Are Made for More!*, 11–17; Lisa Osteen [Comes], *Overcoming Opposition: How to Succeed in Doing the Will of God* (Houston: Lakewood Church, 1990), 6–7.

13 See the following sermon handouts: Lisa Osteen Comes, "Designed for Destiny" (January 7, 2009); Lisa Osteen Comes, "Ten Distractions from Destiny" (February 4, 2009); Lisa Osteen Comes, "The Joy of Speaking in Tongues" (May 23, 2012).

14 Marcos Witt, *Señor, ¿en Qué Puedo Servirte?* (Nashville, TN: Nelson, 1997); *How to Overcome Fear and Live Your Life to the Fullest* (New York: Atria, 2007), 184–193. Joel Osteen wrote the foreword to Witt's book, and praised his co-pastor for showing "how to confront fear directly; you will find keys to help you determine what your fear is and why you are afraid. Most important of all, Marcos will help you to focus your attention on God and His love, power, and promises to help you" (xiii).

15 Shayne Lee and Phillip Luke Sinitiere, *Holy Mavericks: Evangelical Innovators and the Spiritual Marketplace* (New York: NYU Press, 2009), 38–39; Phillip Luke Sinitiere, "From the Oasis of Love to Your Best Life Now: A Brief History of Lakewood Church" *Houston History* 8/3 (Summer 2011): 2–9; "Marcos Witt Says Goodbye to Lakewood Church" (September 12, 2012), Canzion Group Press Release, http://www.canzion.com/marcoswitt/index_eng.html; "Marcos Witt—Se Despide De Joel Osteen & Lakewood Church 09/16/12," https://www.youtube.com/watch?v=XfVxscOkMhw; "Marcos Witt—Lakewood Church: Tristeza e interrogantes surgen tras su renuncia," *NoticiaCristiana.com* (September 17, 2012), http://www.noticiacristiana.com/iglesia/pastor/2012/09/marcos-witt-lakewood-church-tristeza-e-interrogantes-surgen-tras-su-renuncia.html; Nínro Ruíz Peña, "Danilo Montero designado por Marcos Witt como pastor principal de Iglesia Lakewood," *NoticiaCristiana.com* (June 26, 2012), http://www.noticiacristiana.com/iglesia/mega-iglesias/2012/06/danilo-montero-designado-por-marcos-witt-como-pastor-principal-de-iglesia-lakewood.html. I thank Kristen Bullock for her assistance in translating the YouTube video of Marcos and Miriam Witt's final Lakewood service as well as the *NoticiaCristiana* article that announced his departure.

16 Gastón Espinosa, *Latino Pentecostals in America: Faith and Politics in Action* (Cambridge, MA: Harvard University Press, 2014), 391. See also Arlene Sánchez-Walsh, "Santidad, Salvación, Sanidad, Liberación: The Word of Faith Movement among Twenty-First-Century Latina/o Pentecostals," in *Global Pentecostal and Charismatic Healing*, ed. Candy Gunther Brown (New York: Oxford University Press, 2011), 151–168.

17 *Lakewood Church 50th Anniversary* DVD; Osteen, *The Christmas Spirit*, 129–133.

18 Osteen, *The Christmas Spirit*, 134; George Luke, "Marcos Witt: The Worship Leader Speaks about His Ministry," *Cross Rhythms* (July 21, 2005), http://www.crossrhythms.co.uk/articles/music/Marcos_Witt_The_worship_leader_speaks_about_his_ministry/14257/p1/. For background to the connections between

Houston and Latin America, see Rubén Hernández-León, *Metropolitan Migrants: The Migration of Urban Mexicans to the United States* (Berkeley: University of California Press, 2008), and Zulema Valdez, *The New Entrepreneurs: How Race, Class, and Gender Shape American Enterprise* (Stanford, CA: Stanford University Press, 2011).

19 R. Andrew Chesnut, *Competitive Spirits: Latin America's New Religious Economy* (New York: Oxford University Press, 2003).

20 "Alberto Mottesi su Espada Masonica, Profetiza a Marcos Witt," (July 16, 2013), https://www.youtube.com/watch?v=fjDhNo6nEco; "Marcos Witt—Lakewood Church." I thank Arlene Sánchez-Walsh for bringing the Mottesi–Witt relationship to my attention, and Kristen Bullock for translation assistance.

21 See the Pew Research Center's Religion & Public Life studies "Changing Faiths: Latinos and the Transformation of American Religion" (April 25, 2007), http://www.pewhispanic.org/2007/04/25/changing-faiths-latinos-and-the-transformation-of-american-religion/, and "The Shifting Religious Identity of Latinos in the United States" (May 5, 2014), http://www.pewforum.org/2014/05/07/the-shifting-religious-identity-of-latinos-in-the-united-states/.

22 *Great Day Houston*, "Victoria Osteen," (September 2013); Melanie Saxton, "A Chat with TV Host Deborah Duncan," *Houston Lifestyles & Homes* (May 1, 2013), http://houstonlifestyles.com/deborah-duncan/.

23 R. Marie Griffith, *God's Daughters: Evangelical Women and the Power of Submission* (Berkeley: University of California Press, 1997).

24 Osteen, *The Christmas Spirit*, 97–122; Victoria Osteen, *Love Your Life: Living Happy, Healthy & Whole* (New York: Free Press, 2008), 46–47, 119; Melanie Saxton, "Marriage, Motherhood, and Her Passion for Childhood Literacy," *Houston Lifestyles & Homes* (September 1, 2011), http://houstonlifestyles.com/victoria-osteen/.

25 Joel Osteen, "Holding On to Your Dreams" (February 21, 1999), http://web.archive.org/web/20010303115912/http://www.lakewood-church.org/Sermons1999/Sermons99.html; Osteen, *Love Your Life*, 105–106.

26 Osteen, *Love Your Life*, 3, 28, 41–53, 76, 79.

27 Ibid., 151, 187–207.

28 Griffith, *God's Daughters*.

29 Osteen, *Love Your Life*, 169–170, 172.

30 Margaret Lamberts Bendroth, *Fundamentalism and Gender: 1875 to the Present* (New Haven, CT: Yale University Press, 1993), 97–127; Marabel Morgan, "The Total Woman," in *Jerry Falwell and the Rise of the Religious Right: A Brief History with Documents*, ed. Matthew Avery Sutton (New York: Bedford/St. Martin's, 2013), 110–114. On Marabel Morgan and the conservative politics of evangelicalism, sexuality, and gender, see Steven P. Miller, *The Age of Evangelicalism: America's Born Again Years* (New York: Oxford University Press, 2014), 24–27, and Amy DeRogatis, *Saving Sex: Sexuality and Salvation in American Evangelicalism* (New York: Oxford University Press, 2014), 62–65.

31 Victoria Osteen, *Hooray for Today!* (New York: Little Simon Inspirations, 2009); Victoria Osteen, *Hooray for Wonderful Me!* (New York: Little Simon Inspirations, 2009); Victoria Osteen, *Hooray for My Family!* (New York: Little Simon Inspirations, 2009); Victoria Osteen, *Unexpected Treasures* (New York: Little Simon Inspirations, 2009); Victoria Osteen, *Gifts from the Heart* (New York: Little Simon Inspirations, 2010).

32 Todd M. Brenneman, *Homespun Gospel: The Triumph of Sentimentality in Contemporary American Evangelicalism* (New York: Oxford University Press, 2014), 100–112. I thank Todd Brenneman for helpful discussions about the role of evangelical children's literature and sentimentality in relation to my cultural reading of Victoria Osteen's books.

33 Kate Bowler, *Blessed: A History of the American Prosperity Gospel* (New York: Oxford University Press, 2013), 178–225; Paul Alexander, *Signs and Wonders: Why Pentecostalism Is the World's Fastest Growing Faith* (San Francisco: Josey-Bass, 2009), 131–150.

34 Harvey Rice, "Airline Incident Delays Osteens' Vail Vacation," *Houston Chronicle* (December 21, 2005), http://www.chron.com/news/houston-texas/article/Airline-incident-delays-Osteens-Vail-vacation-1936199.php; Juan A. Lozano, "Victoria Osteen, Joel Osteen's Wife, Accused of Assaulting a Flight Attendant," *HuffPost Good News* (September 6, 2008), http://www.huffingtonpost.com/2008/08/06/joel-osteens-wife-accused_n_117311.html; James C. McKinley, Jr., "Jury Finds Pastor Did Not Assault a Flight Attendant," *New York Times* (August 14, 2008), http://www.nytimes.com/2008/08/15/us/15houston.html?_r=0; Brian Rogers, "Jurors: Attendant 'Exaggerated' Osteen Conflict," *Houston Chronicle* (August 14, 2008), http://www.chron.com/life/houston-belief/article/Jurors-Attendant-exaggerated-Osteen-conflict-1777790.php.

35 Gina Sunseri, "Osteen's Wife on Trial for Temper Tantrum," *ABC News* (August 6, 2008), http://abcnews.go.com/TheLaw/story?id=5524479; Barbara Ehrenreich, *This Land Is Their Land: Reports from a Divided Nation* (New York: Picador, 2009), 225–228; *Larry King Live*, "Interview with Joel and Victoria Osteen," (December 22, 2006), http://transcripts.cnn.com/TRANSCRIPTS/0612/22/lkl.01. html. A copy of Victoria Osteen's statement appears on http://www.forgottenword. org/victorialetter.html.

36 "Victoria Osteen, 'Do Good for Your Own Self' Not for God" (August 28, 2014), https://www.youtube.com/watch?v=koIBkYlocHk. See also R. Albert Mohler, Jr., "The Osteen Predicament—Mere Happiness Cannot Bear the Weight of the Gospel," *AlbertMohler.com* (September 3, 2014), http://www.albertmohler.com/2014/09/03/the-osteen-predicament-mere-happiness-cannot-bear-the-weight-of-the-gospel/; Michael Brown, "An Open Letter and Appeal to Joel and Victoria Osteen: Rebuke in Love, Exhort and Encourage," *Christian Post* (September 10, 2014), http://www.christianpost.com/news/an-open-letter-and-appeal-to-joel-and-victoria-osteen-rebuke-in-love-exhort-and-encourage-126176/; Matt K. Lewis, "In Defense of the Prosperity Gospel: Let's Cut Victoria Some

Slack," *This Week* (September 3, 2014), http://theweek.com/article/index/267390/in-defense-of-the-prosperity-gospel.

37 Billy Hallowell, "Pastor Joel Osteen's Wife Hits Back at 'Critics and Cynics' and Addresses Furor Over Her Viral Sermon about Worshipping God," *The Blaze* (September 5, 2014), http://www.theblaze.com/stories/2014/09/05/exclusive-victoria-osteen-responds-to-evangelical-furor-over-viral-youre-not-doing-it-for-god-clip/; Heather Alexander, "Critics Assail Recent Sermon by Lakewood Co-Pastor Victoria Osteen," *Houston Chronicle* (September 6, 2014), http://www.houstonchronicle.com/news/houston-texas/houston/article/Critics-assail-recent-sermon-by-Lakewood-5738922.php.

38 See the sermon handouts, Paul Osteen, "Living a Balanced Life, Part 1" (June 3, 2004), and Paul Osteen, "The Good Samaritan: Who Is My Neighbor and How Should I Love Him/Her?" (October 6, 2004).

39 Robert Wuthnow, *Boundless Faith: The Global Outreach of American Churches* (Berkeley: University of California Press, 2009), 140–187. See also Brian M. Howell, *Short-Term Mission: An Ethnography of Christian Travel Narrative and Experience* (Downers Grove, IL: InterVarsity Press Academic, 2012); Robert J. Priest, Douglas Wilson, and Adelle Johnson, "U.S. Megachurches and New Patterns of Global Mission," *International Bulletin of Missionary Research* 34/2 (April 2010): 97–104; Mark A. Noll, *The New Shape of World Christianity: How American Experience Shapes Global Faith* (Downers Grove, IL: InterVarsity Press Academic, 2009); Donald Miller and Tetsunao Yamamori, *Global Pentecostalism: The New Face of Christian Social Engagement* (Berkeley: University of California Press, 2007), 50–55.

40 Paul Osteen, "A Father's Heart," *Hope for Today* 5/1 (Spring 2012): 14–15; Paul Osteen, "Sunshine at the End of the Room," *Hope for Today* 5/2 (Summer 2012): 19–22.

41 Paul Osteen, "To the Least of These: 2 Weeks in Cameroon," *Hope for Today* 3/2 (Fall 2010): 10–12.

42 Paul Osteen, "Africa Sermon" (October 2012) and "Thoughts as I Leave Chitokoloki" (July 2011), *PaulOsteen.com* (accessed December 2014, offline as of April 2015).

43 Paul Osteen, "Giving Thanks and Looking Forward" (January 2014), *PaulOsteen.com* (accessed December 2014, offline as of April 2015); Wuthnow, *Boundless Faith*; Priest, Wilson, and Johnson, "U.S. Megachurches and New Patterns of Global Mission."

CHAPTER 7. THE REDEMPTIVE SELF

The epigraph comes from Connie Selvaggi, *What's inside Lakewood Church?: One Woman's Account of Spiritual Conflict and Renewal* (Bogotá, Columbia: Procreditor, 2010), 5–6.

1 Alexis Grant, "I Fell in Love with a Megachurch," *Salon* (January 29, 2012), http://www.salon.com/2012/01/29/i_fell_in_love_with_a_megachurch/.

2   Dan P. McAdams, *The Redemptive Self: Stories Americans Live By*, Revised and
    Expanded Edition (New York: Oxford University Press, 2013), xi–xx, 125–147. It is
    important to note that religion (in this case Christianity), is not *the* organizing
    theme of McAdams's narrative psychology, only one dimension of generativity's
    presence across American culture.

3   Matthew Henderson, "'What Heaven's Gonna Look Like': Racial and Ethnic
    Diversity at Lakewood Church" (M.A. Thesis, University of Houston, 2012). On
    Lakewood's racial diversity, see also Robert D. Putnam and David E. Campbell,
    American Grace: How Religious Divides and Unites Us (New York: Simon &
    Schuster, 2010), 308. On nondenominational congregations, see Mark Chaves,
    American Religion: Contemporary Trends (Princeton, NJ: Princeton University
    Press, 2011), 55–59, and Alan Wolfe, *The Transformation of American Religion: How
    We Actually Live Our Faith* (Chicago: University of Chicago Press, 2003), 38–49. On
    Houston's diversity, see the Rice University report by Michael O. Emerson, Jenifer
    Bratter, Junia Howell, P. Wilner Jeanty, and Mike Cline, "Houston Region Grows
    More Racially/Ethnically Diverse, with Small Declines in Segregation" (Houston:
    Kinder Institute for Urban Research and Hobby Center for the Study of Texas,
    2013), 5.

4   This paragraph reproduces reflections from my work as a member of the
    Congregations and Social Change seminar at Calvin College in 2011. Led by
    Davidson College sociologist Gerardo Marti, seminar participants read selections of
    sociological, historical, and ethnographic literature on congregations. I have found
    the following sources helpful in processing and reflecting on the congregational
    history and character of Lakewood Church: Nancy Ammerman, *Congregation and
    Community* (New Brunswick, NJ: Rutgers University Press, 1997); Donald E. Miller,
    Reinventing American Protestantism: Christianity in the New Millennium (Berkeley:
    University of California Press, 1997); Penny Edgell Becker, *Congregations in Conflict:
    Cultural Models of Local Religious Life* (New York: Cambridge University Press,
    1999); Kimon Howland Sargeant, *Seeker Churches: Promoting Traditional Religion in
    a Non-Traditional Way* (New Brunswick, NJ: Rutgers University Press, 2000);
    Nancy L. Eiesland, *A Particular Place: Urban Restructuring and Religious Ecology in
    a Southern Exurb* (New Brunswick, NJ: Rutgers University Press, 2000); Paul
    Lichterman, *Elusive Togetherness: Church Groups Trying to Bridge America's
    Divisions* (Princeton, NJ: Princeton University Press, 2005); Jonathan Walton,
    Watch This!: The Ethics and Aesthetics of Black Televangelism (New York: NYU
    Press, 2009); Jonathan Walton, "From Where Two or Three (Thousand) Are
    Gathered in My Name!: A Cultural History and Ethical Analysis of African
    American Megachurches," *Journal of African American Studies* 15/2 (2011): 133–154;
    Kendra Hadiya Barber, "'What Happened to All the Protests?': Black Megachurches'
    Responses to Racism in a Colorblind Era," *Journal of African American Studies* 15/2
    (2011): 218–235; Quentin Schultze, *Televangelism and American Culture: The Business
    of Popular Religion* (Grand Rapids, MI: Baker Academic, 1991).

5   Robert Wuthnow, *After Heaven: Spirituality in America since the 1950s* (Berkeley: University of California Press, 1998), 168–198.

6   Philip Wagner, *Insights from Men of Faith* (Beverly Hills, CA: Oasis Publishing, 1987), 71–83.

7   On Oasis, see Gerardo Marti, *Hollywood Faith: Holiness, Prosperity, and Ambition in a Los Angeles Church* (New Brunswick, NJ: Rutgers University Press, 2008).

8   Brady Mitchell interview, October 6, 2014. On black Houston during this period, see Robert D. Bullard, *Invisible Houston: The Black Experience in Boom and Bust* (College Station: Texas A&M University Press, 1987), 3–31. On Houston's racial politics and economic democracy during this period, see Wesley G. Phelps, *A People's War on Poverty: Urban Politics and Grassroots Activists in Houston* (Athens: University of Georgia Press, 2014). See also Robert Wuthnow, *Rough Country: How Texas Became America's Most Powerful Bible-Belt State* (Princeton, NJ: Princeton University Press, 2014), 247–255.

9   Preston Wilson interview, November 5, 2010, and November 12, 2010; Jarvis Middleton interview, January 4, 2011, and August 25, 2011.

10 Scott Thumma and Dave Travis, *Beyond Megachurch Myths: What We Can Learn from America's Largest Churches* (San Francisco: Josey-Bass, 2007), 44–54; Charity R. Carney, "Lakewood Church and the Roots of the Megachurch Movement in the South," *Southern Quarterly* 50/1 (Fall 2012): 60–78.

11 Ken Chitwood, "Church Life for Children with Autism," *Houston Chronicle* (April 11, 2013), http://www.houstonchronicle.com/life/houston-belief/article/Church-life-for-children-with-autism-4427423.php#/0. Craig Johnson Ministries also hosts a website detailing Connor's story through autobiographical statements and YouTube videos, http://connormoments.com/.

12 Jillian Owens, "A Wide Net of Hope: Understanding the Success of Joel Osteen and Lakewood Church" (Senior Religious Studies Honors Thesis, University of Texas at Austin, 2012). See also "Receiving, Giving, Connection," *Lakewood Church Blogs* (June 29, 2012), https://www.lakewoodchurch.com/Pages/Ministry.aspx?mid=1085&month=06%202012, and Tuan Hoang, "LifeGroups—It's All about the Atmosphere," *Lakewood Church Blogs* (June 20, 2012), https://www.lakewoodchurch.com/pages/BlogDetail.aspx?bid=5060.

13 *Fox 26 News*, "Houston Human Trafficking Walk-a-Thon Raises Awareness" (January 28, 2013), https://www.youtube.com/watch?v=S-Bq6oU1NSE; Barclay Torrance interview, April 13, 2013; Omri Elisha, *Moral Ambition and Social Outreach in Evangelical Megachurches* (Berkeley: University of California Press, 2011), 1–35. See also Thumma and Travis, *Beyond Megachurch Myths*, 78–90; Calvin L. Smith, "The Politics and Economics of Pentecostalism," in *The Cambridge Companion to Pentecostalism*, ed. Cecil M. Robeck, Jr., and Amos Yong (New York: Cambridge University Press, 2014), 175–194; Wuthnow, *Rough Country*, 392–393, 404–405.

14 Joel and Victoria Osteen, *God's Promises for a New Beginning* (Houston: Joel Osteen Ministries, 2008); Steve Austin, *Foundations: Building Your Life with Christ* (Houston: Lakewood Church, 2012).

15 Marcos Witt and Lisa Comes, *Growing Strong: Six Keys to Grow in Christ* DVD (Houston: Lakewood Church, 2010).

16 Field notes (October 2005); "Developing Faith for the Mercies of God and His Comfort" (October 2005), Compass class handout.

17 "Developing Faith for the Mercies of God and His Comfort"; James S. Bielo, *Words upon the Word: An Ethnography of Evangelical Group Bible Study* (New York: NYU Press, 2009), 58–63; James S. Bielo, "Textual Ideology, Textual Practice: Evangelical Bible Reading in Group Study," in *The Social Life of Scriptures: Cross-Cultural Perspectives on Biblicism*, ed. James S. Bielo (New Brunswick, NJ: Rutgers University Press, 2009), 157–175.

18 T. M. Luhrmann, *When God Talks Back: Understanding the American Evangelical Relationship to God* (New York: Knopf, 2012), 3–38, 101–131.

19 Selvaggi, *What's Inside Lakewood Church?*, 13–59, 121.

20 Stanley Morrison interview, November 20 and November 30, 2011.

21 Ibid.

22 See the Lakewood men's ministry class handouts, "Spiritual Warfare 101: What is the Invisible War?," "Spiritual Warfare 201: How to Prepare Yourself for Spiritual Battle," "Spiritual Warfare 301: How to Do Battle with the Enemy and Win," "Spiritual Warfare 401: How to Gain Deliverance from Demonic Influence," and "Your Manhood Plan!!!," and Robert Lewis, *The Quest for Authentic Manhood* (Nashville: Lifeway Press, 2009). On ideas about conservative Christian manhood in contemporary American evangelicalism, see Seth Dowland, "A New Kind of Patriarchy: Inerrancy and Masculinity in the Southern Baptist Convention, 1979–2000," in *Southern Masculinity: Perspectives on Manhood and the South Since Reconstruction*, ed. Craig Thompson Friend (Athens: University of Georgia Press, 2009), 246–268, and Ryan Harper, "New Frontiers: *Wild at Heart* and Post-Promise Keeper Evangelical Manhood," *Journal of Religion and Popular Culture* 24/1 (Spring 2012): 97–112. On the practice of prayer and white Christian masculinity, see Charles H. Lippy, *Do Real Men Pray?: Images of the Christian Man and Male Spirituality in White Protestant America* (Knoxville: University of Tennessee Press, 2005), 143–205.

23 Richard Merchant interview, September 8, 2011, and February 2, 2012.

24 Ibid.

25 Ibid.

26 Raymond and Angela Gordon interview, November 6, 2014.

27 Ibid.

28 Ibid.

29 Ibid.

30 Ibid.

31 Teri Burrell interview, August 21, 2012.

32 Ibid.

33 The CBS affiliate in Houston, KHOU, produced a story on Unconditional Love Ministries, "What's Right: Former Stripper Using Ministry to Help Others in the Business," *KHOU.com* (February 28, 2013), http://www.khou.com/story/news/local/outreach/2014/07/22/11977966/.

34 Teri Burrell interview.

CHAPTER 8. JOEL OSTEEN'S PIETY OF RESISTANCE

The epigraph comes from Hank Hanegraaff, *The Osteenification of American Christianity* (Charlotte, NC: Christian Research Institute, 2014), 11–13. See also Hank Hanegraaff, "Osteenification and What It Portends," *Philosophical Fragments* (March 19, 2014), http://www.patheos.com/blogs/philosophicalfragments/2014/03/19/osteenification-and-what-it-portends/; Hank Hanegraaff, *Christianity in Crisis: 21st Century* (Nashville, TN: Thomas Nelson, 2009), xvi–xvii.

1 John Leland, "A Church That Packs Them In, 16,000 at a Time," *New York Times* (July 18, 2005), http://travel.nytimes.com/2005/07/18/national/18lakewood.html?pagewanted=all&_r=0; Jennifer Harper, "Flock Replaces Rockers, Rockets at Megachurch," *Washington Times* (June 20, 2005), http://www.washingtontimes.com/news/2005/jun/20/20050620–011432–1952r/?page=all; Lakewood Church, *Grand Opening: A Remarkable Journey, 1959–2005* DVD (Houston: Lakewood Church, 2005).

2 *Larry King Live*, "Interview with Joel Osteen" (June 20, 2005), http://transcripts.cnn.com/TRANSCRIPTS/0506/20/lkl.01.html.

3 *Larry King Live*, "Interview with Joel and Victoria Osteen" (December 22, 2006), http://transcripts.cnn.com/TRANSCRIPTS/0612/22/lkl.01.html. Osteen's original apology letter is no longer available at his website; however, it appears in its entirety at http://www.joelosteenblog.com/2005/07/13/joel-osteens-letter-about-the-interview/.

4 Molly Worthen, *Apostles of Reason: The Crisis of Authority in American Evangelicalism* (New York: Oxford University Press, 2014), 264.

5 David Van Biema, "The New Calvinism," *Time* (March 12, 2009), http://www.time.com/time/specials/packages/article/0,28804,1884779_1884782_1884760,00.html; Collin Hansen, *Young, Restless, Reformed: A Journalist's Journey Among the New Calvinists* (Wheaton, IL: Crossway, 2008); Drew Angerer, "Evangelicals Find Themselves in the Midst of a Calvinist Revival," *New York Times* (January 3, 2014), http://www.nytimes.com/2014/01/04/us/a-calvinist-revival-for-evangelicals.html; "The New Calvinism," *Religion & Ethics NewsWeekly* (April 4, 2014), http://www.pbs.org/wnet/religionandethics/2014/04/03/april-4–2014-new-calvinism/22607/. Reformed Blacks of America maintains a web presence (reformedblacksofamerica.org), as does Reformed African American Network (http://www.raanetwork.org/). The publications of Anthony J. Carter, among many others, have provided something of a history of this growing movement. See Anthony J. Carter, *On Being Black and Reformed: A New Perspective on the*

African-American Experience (Phillipsburg, NJ: Presbyterian and Reformed, 2003); Anthony J. Carter, *Experiencing the Truth: Bringing the Reformation to the African-American Church* (Wheaton, IL: Crossway, 2008); Anthony J. Carter, *Glory Road: The Journeys of 10 African-Americans into Reformed Christianity* (Wheaton, IL: Crossway, 2009).

6   For his biography, see "Richard Albert Mohler," in *Encyclopedia of Evangelicalism*, Revised and Expanded Edition, ed. Randall Balmer (Waco, TX: Baylor University Press, 2004), 463. Albert Mohler, "The Limits of Encouragement" (June 24, 2005), http://www.albertmohler.com/2005/06/24/the-limits-of-encouragement/; "Joel Osteen Issues Apology" (June 25, 2005), http://www.albertmohler.com/2005/06/25/joel-osteen-issues-apology/. For additional Mohler pieces, see "Prosperity Theology with a Smile" (March 30, 2006), http://www.albertmohler.com/2006/03/30/prosperity-theology-with-a-smile/, and "'Staying in His Lane'—Joel Osteen's Gospel of Affirmation without Salvation" (September 21, 2012), http://www.albertmohler.com/2012/09/21/joel-osteen-explains-stance-on-homosexuality/.

7   David Van Biema, "The 25 Most Influential Evangelicals in America," *Time* (February 27, 2005): 34–45; David Van Biema and Jeff Chu, "Does God Want You to Be Rich?," *Time* (September 18, 2006): 48–56. Representative *Christian Century* features include Jason Byassee, "Be Happy," *Christian Century* (July 12, 2005), 20–23, and John M. Buchanan, "Positive Influence," *Christian Century* (July 26, 2005), 3. Candace Chellew-Hodge has given sustained attention to Osteen at *Religion Dispatches*. Representative posts include "Is Joel Osteen, *Success* Mag Cover Boy, Really 'God's Best'?" *Religion Dispatches* (November 19, 2009), http://www.religiondispatches.org/dispatches/candacechellew-hodge/2045/is_joel_osteen__success_mag_cover_boy__really__god_s_best_; "'Living in Favor, Abundance, and Joy' (Unless You're Gay)," *Religion Dispatches* (January 25, 2011), http://www.religiondispatches.org/dispatches/candacechellew-hodge/4099/_living_in_favor__abundance__and_joy___unless_you_re_gay_; "C'mon, Joel, Swerve a Little Bit," *Religion Dispatches* (September 23, 2012), http://www.religiondispatches.org/dispatches/candacechellew-hodge/6419/c_mon__joel__swerve_a_little_bit_.

8   Tara Dooley, "At Home in the World," *Houston Chronicle* (October 14, 2007): G1, G6; Joel Osteen, "Learning to Live in Peace with Ourselves," *Houston Chronicle* (October 15, 2007): E2; Joel Osteen, "Identify What's Holding You Back and Do Something About It," *Houston Chronicle* (October 16, 2007): E12; Joel Osteen, "Learn to Embrace the Place Where You Are," *Houston Chronicle* (October 17, 2007): E2; Joel Osteen, "Stay Passionate about Your Life," *Houston Chronicle* (October 18, 2007): E5. See also Osteen's Borders Books promotional spot on "Borders Presents" with Rich Fahle, https://www.youtube.com/watch?v=VR7tCUK4mLo.

9   *60 Minutes*, "Joel Osteen Answers His Critics" (October 14, 2007), http://www.cbsnews.com/stories/2007/10/11/60minutes/main3358652.shtml?tag=contentMain;contentBody.

10   "Michael Scott Horton," in *Encyclopedia of Evangelicalism*, 342.

11   Michael S. Horton, *Putting Amazing Back into Grace: Who Does What in
     Salvation?* (Grand Rapids, MI: Baker, 1994), 11–20; Michael S. Horton, "The Crisis
     of Evangelical Christianity: Reformation Essentials," *Modern Reformation* 3/2
     (March/April 1994): 12–19; Christian Smith, *American Evangelicalism: Embattled
     and Thriving* (Chicago: University of Chicago Press, 1998), 120–153; Worthen,
     Apostles of Reason, 220–240. On Horton and the New Calvinists, see Hansen,
     Young, Restless, Reformed, 109–112.

12   Michael S. Horton, ed. *The Agony of Deceit* (Grand Rapids, MI: Zondervan, 1990),
     243–251.

13   For a survey of Horton's view of American religious history and American
     religious culture, see his books *Made in America: The Shaping of Modern
     American Evangelicalism* (Grand Rapids, MI: Baker, 1991), *Beyond Culture Wars:
     Is America a Mission Field or Battlefield?* (Chicago: Moody, 1994), *Where in the
     World Is the Church?: A Christian View of Culture and Your Role in It* (Chicago:
     Moody, 1995), and *In the Face of God: The Dangers and Delights of Spiritual
     Intimacy* (Nashville, TN: Thomas Nelson, 1997).

14   Michael S. Horton, *Christless Christianity: The Alternative Gospel of the American
     Church* (Grand Rapids, MI: Baker, 2008), 29–69.

15   Ibid., 65–100.

16   John Armstrong founded a ministry called ACT 3 and has blogged about Osteen
     since 2005. He found Horton's "hermeneutical system" lamentably unwilling to
     consider God's activity operating outside of a "Lutheran-Reformed paradigm." As
     such, unlike the majority of Osteen's evangelical critics, Armstrong argued that
     Osteen's teaching might have something meaningful to say. Armstrong described
     himself as "not a big 'fan' of Joel Osteen," but stated, "I believe he has some helpful
     things to teach me. . . . I personally know folks who attended Osteen's meetings in
     Chicago precisely because they deeply appreciate his ministry and believe they are
     helped by it." See John Armstrong, "The Popularity of Joel Osteen," (May 9, 2005);
     John Armstrong, "Further Reflections on Joel Osteen," (May 13, 2005); John
     Armstrong "How Joel Osteen Has Impacted My Life," (May 17, 2005); all http://
     johnharmstrong.com/.

17   Iain H. Murray, *John MacArthur: Servant of the Word and Flock* (Carlisle, PA:
     Banner of Truth Trust, 2011). On MacArthur and the New Calvinists, see Hansen,
     Young, Restless, Reformed, 103–108.

18   John MacArthur, *Charismatic Chaos* (Grand Rapids, MI: Zondervan, 1992), 16, 19,
     266–267, 291–296.

19   John MacArthur, "Your Best Life: Now or Later?," *Grace to You*, http://www.gty.
     org/Resources/Sermons/80–334.

20   John MacArthur, "Becoming a Better You" (March 23, 2008), 2010 Christless
     Christianity West Coast Conference (Ligonier Ministries), http://www.ligonier.
     org/learn/conferences/christless-christianity-2010-west-coast/becoming-a-better-
     you/; John MacArthur, "A True Knowledge of the True God, Part 1" (May 23,

2010), http://www.gty.org/resources/Sermons/90–397. On Sproul and the New Calvinists, see Hansen, *Young, Restless, Reformed*, 107–108, and Jeff Kunerth, "Sanford Evangelist R. C. Sproul Influences a Younger Generation of Conservatives," *Orlando Sentinel* (July 24, 2010), http://www.orlandosentinel.com/news/local/seminole/os-sproul-profile-20100724,0,2955003.story.

21 John MacArthur, *Strange Fire: The Danger of Offending the Holy Spirit with Counterfeit Worship* (Nashville, TN: Thomas Nelson, 2013), xiv–xvi, 10–11, 15, 50–53.

22 See "Reformed Rap and Hip Hop," *Christianity Today* (May 2, 2011), http://www.christianitytoday.com/ct/2011/may/spot-reformedrap.html; Russell Moore, "W. W. Jay-Z?," *Christianity Today* (May 10, 2013), http://www.christianitytoday.com/ct/2013/may/ww-jay-z.html. The cover of the May 2013 issue of *Christianity Today* featured a photo of Lecrae with the headline "Why the Gospel Needs Hip Hop."

23 Shai Linne, *Lyrical Theology, Pt. 1: Theology* (Philadelphia: Lamp Mode Records, 2013). See also Melissa Steffen, "Reformed Rapper Calls Out 12 Popular Pastors as 'False Teachers,'" *Christianity Today* (April 11, 2013), http://www.christianitytoday.com/gleanings/2013/april/reformed-rapper-calls-out-12-popular-pastors-as-false.html?paging=off; Anugrah Kumar, "Rapper Shai Linne Explains Why He Named Names in Fal$e Teacher$," *Christian Post* (April 28, 2013), http://www.christianpost.com/news/rapper-shai-linne-explains-why-he-named-names-in-fale-teacher-94851/.

24 Ibid.

25 Jennifer Leong, "Joel Osteen 'Too Shallow' for Man behind Internet Hoax," *ABC News* (April 10, 2013), http://abcnews.go.com/blogs/headlines/2013/04/joel-osteen-too-shallow-for-man-behind-internet-hoax/; Robert Stanton, "Man behind Hoax Explains Why He Targeted Houston Pastor," *Houston Chronicle* (April 10, 2013), http://www.chron.com/news/houston-texas/houston/article/Osteen-hoaxer-says-he-s-a-big-fan-of-pastor-4424495.php; Sami K. Martin, "Joel Osteen 'Resigns' a Hoax; Pastor Attacked with False Statement," *Christian Post* (April 8, 2013), http://www.christianpost.com/news/joel-osteen-resigns-a-hoax-pastor-attacked-with-false-statement-93453/.

26 Ibid.

27 Steve Bauer interview, July 9, 2012. Pastor Adam Key, a member of Psalm 24 Ministries, in 2007 self-published *Your Best Lie Now: The Gospel According to Joel Osteen*. The cover of Key's book features a mockup of a smiling Joel, echoing the cover of *Your Best Life Now*. In bold, red strokes, Key's cover depicts Osteen with devil horns protruding from his forehead, and a sinister-looking goatee that evokes Anton LaVey, founder of the Church of Satan. Like Bauer, Key has sought to address Osteen in person. He preached outside of Lakewood Church in Houston in 2007. A five-minute YouTube video of Key's street preaching shows the cover of his book displayed prominently next to a large sign that reads, "Joel is LYING to you." See "Preaching outside Joel Osteen's Lakewood Church in Houston" (August 4, 2007), http://www.youtube.com/watch?v=Nu9k6o-GgVk.

28 Ibid.

29   Ibid.

30   I thank Kate Bowler for drawing my attention to Lietha's *After Eden* Osteen
      illustration. On Answers in Genesis, see Randall J. Stephens and Karl W.
      Giberson, *The Anointed: Evangelical Truth in a Secular Age* (Cambridge, MA:
      Harvard University Press, 2011), 21–60.

31   *Larry King Live*, "Interview with Joel and Victoria Osteen" (December 22, 2006),
      http://transcripts.cnn.com/TRANSCRIPTS/0612/22/lkl.01.html; *Larry King Live*,
      "Interview with Joel and Victoria Osteen" (October 16, 2007), http://transcripts.cnn.
      com/TRANSCRIPTS/0710/16/lkl.01.html; *60 Minutes*, "Joel Osteen Answers His
      Critics" (October 14, 2007), http://www.cbsnews.com/stories/2007/10/11/60minutes/
      main3358652.shtml?tag=contentMain;contentBody. Robert Liichow was one of
      Osteen earliest online critics, starting in 2005. See, for example, Robert S. Liichow,
      "The Leaven of Lakewood," at http://www.rapidnet.com/~jbeard/bdm/exposes/
      osteen/Leaven.htm. See also "A Smile, a Chair and a Prayer for You at Lakewood," at
      http://www.newdiscernment.org/NewJoelOsteenNov07.htm.

32   Joel Osteen, *Your Best Life Now: 7 Steps to Living at Your Full Potential* (New York:
      Warner Faith, 2004), 205–212.

33   Ibid.

34   Joel Osteen, *Become a Better You: 7 Keys to Improving Your Life Every Day* (New
      York: Free Press, 2007), 88, 91. At the end of this chapter, Osteen writes of
      watching an online parody of himself smiling with sparkling teeth, "sort of like a
      toothpaste commercial" (240). It is telling that Osteen placed this anecdote in a
      chapter on how to handle criticism. He wrote that he "laughed" at the parody. "I
      thought to myself, *That doesn't bother me one bit. I smile a lot. If somebody doesn't
      like it, I'll smile some more. Who knows? Maybe Crest or Colgate will want to
      sponsor our television program!*" (240).

35   Ibid., 229–230, 236–238.

36   Joel Osteen, *It's Your Time: Activate Your Faith, Achieve Your Dreams, and Increase
      God's Favor* (New York: Free Press, 2009), 222, 228–229.

37   Joel Osteen, *Every Day a Friday: How to Be Happier 7 Days a Week* (New York:
      FaithWords, 2011), 76–77, 102–103, 105–106; Joel Osteen, *You Can, You Will: 8
      Undeniable Qualities of a Winner* (New York: FaithWords, 2014), 21–41.

38   Osteen, *Become a Better You*, 236–237; Joel Osteen, "HopeNote: Rise above the
      Critics," in *Hope for Today Bible*, ed. Joel and Victoria Osteen (New York: Free
      Press, 2009), 1062.

39   Phil Munsey, "The Joel Osteen Most People Don't Know," *Charisma* (July 25,
      2013), http://www.charismanews.com/us/40377-the-joel-osteen-most-people-
      don-t-know; Philip Wagner, "What's the Problem with Joel Osteen?"
      Philipwagner.com (June 29, 2014), http://www.philipwagner.com/blog/
      whats-the-problem-with-joel-osteen.

40   Peale's critics printed their objections in both secular magazines and the
      Christian press. See Carol V. R. George, *God's Salesman: Norman Vincent Peale
      and the Power of Positive Thinking* (New York: Oxford University Press, 1993),

128–150. On Roberts and his critics, see W. E. Mann, "Supersalesman of Faith Healing," *Christian Century* (September 5, 1956): 1018–1019; Hayes Jacobs, "Oral Roberts: High Priest of Faith Healing," *Harper's* (February 1962): 37–43, Quentin J. Schultze Papers, Box 38, Folders 6 and 7, Heritage Hall; and David Edwin Harrell, *Oral Roberts: An American Life* (Bloomington: Indiana University Press, 1985), 151–182.

41 "Joel Osteen on Claims He Preaches 'Prosperity Gospel,' Why Scripture Says 'Being Gay Is a Sin,'" *Fox News Insider* (April 29, 2012), http://insider.foxnews.com/2012/04/29/joel-and-victoria-osteen-respond-to-critics-on-fox-news-sunday; Brittney R. Villalva, "Joel Osteen on Oprah: 'Homosexuality Is a Sin, But Repentance Leads to Heaven,'" *Christian Post* (January 9, 2012), http://www.christianpost.com/news/joel-osteen-on-oprah-homosexuality-is-a-sin-but-repentance-leads-to-heaven-66723/; "Lakewood Church's Joel Osteen Meets with Jay Bakker following 'American Family Outing,'" *OutSmart* (June 2008): 26, Lakewood Church Vertical File, Houston Metropolitan Research Center.

42 Jason C. Bivins, *Religion of Fear: The Politics of Horror in Conservative Evangelicalism* (New York: Oxford University Press, 2008).

43 I thank Anthony Smith, Charity Carney, and Arlene Sánchez-Walsh for helpful conversations about the points I raise in this paragraph. Books on the complexities and tensions of evangelicalism's propositional theology of the Bible include Christian Smith, *The Bible Made Impossible: Why Biblicism Is Not a Truly Evangelical Reading of Scripture* (Grand Rapids, MI: Brazos, 2011); Peter Enns, *Inspiration and Incarnation: Evangelicals and the Problem of the Old Testament* (Grand Rapids, MI: Baker Academic, 2005); Brian Malley, *How the Bible Works: An Anthropological Study of Evangelical Biblicism* (Walnut Creek, CA: Alta Mira, 2004); and Mark A. Noll, *Jesus Christ and the Life of the Mind* (Grand Rapids, MI: Eerdmans, 2011), 75–98, 125–145. On the declining popularity of conservative theology, see Mark Chaves, *American Religion: Contemporary Trends* (Princeton, NJ: Princeton University Press, 2011), 33–37.

APPENDIX A

1 Reginald Cherry, a Houston-based, degreed physician of Christian conviction, is a long-time friend and associate of the Osteen family. He served as one of Dodie Osteen's doctors during her battle with cancer. See Dodie Osteen, *Healed of Cancer* (Houston: Lakewood Church, 1986), 61–66.

2 Starting in 1999, and in sermons and publications since, Osteen has described God as a "progressive God." Osteen does not use "progressive" for its center-left political connotations. Rather, for Osteen "progressive" evokes the "Pentecost" theme of second chances or starting over. With "progressive," Osteen has expressed the idea that with faith God always improves life circumstances and always does so in more broadly beneficial ways.

APPENDIX B

1 According to cultural geographer Hannes Gerhardt, "The 10/40 window is a rectangular swath of land between 10 and 40 degrees north of the equator where the least evangelized populations of the world live. This geographical imaginary, and the subsequent maps produced to present it, serve as a tool to depict undeveloped, impoverished, and frequently also demonic spaces that are seen as desperately in need of intervention" (167–168). As a "geographical imaginary," the construct of the 10/40 Window is commonplace in evangelical missionary discourse and sermons. The 10/40 Window is also a highly politicized rhetorical register of Christian humanitarianism, particularly in today's globalized age. "Rather than forceful persuasion and outright conversion," writes cultural geographer Ju Hui Judy Han, "current rhetoric stresses reaching out and creating connections, emphasizing humanitarian aid and cultural exchange as the preferred mode of missionary encounter" (184). Han explains the broad geopolitical factors involved: "As demonstrated by the 10/40 Window, evangelicals are armed with a master narrative about the inexorable forces of Christianity and capitalist modernity and they continue to embark on a territorialized strategy for world evangelization. . . . [T]hese strategies do not simply regurgitate imperial hostilities of the past or unquestioningly endorse American unilateralism. Instead, we see missionary subjectivities forged in the context of Third World liberation, global capitalism and hegemonic humanitarianism" (200). See Hannes Gerhardt, "The Problematic Synergy between Evangelicals and the U.S. State in Sub-Saharan Africa," and Ju Hui Judy Han, "Reaching the Unreached in the 10/40 Window: The Missionary Geoscience of Race, Difference and Distance," in *Mapping the End Times: American Evangelical Geopolitics and Apocalyptic Visions*, ed. Jason Dittmer and Tristan Sturm (Burlington, VT: Ashgate, 2010), 157–182 and 183–207.

2 Sugar Land is a suburb of Houston located on the city's southwest side. See Bettye J. Anhaiser, "Sugar Land, TX," *Handbook of Texas Online*, http://www.tshaonline.org/handbook/online/articles/hfs10.

BIBLIOGRAPHY

MANUSCRIPT AND ARCHIVAL COLLECTIONS

African American Library at the Gregory School (Houston, Texas)
    Forward Times Collection (microfilm)
Calvin College, Heritage Hall (Grand Rapids, Michigan)
    Quentin J. Schultze Collection
Central Baptist Church (Baytown, Texas)
    Church Anniversary File
College of Biblical Studies (Houston, Texas)
    Charismatic Vertical File
    Holy Spirit Vertical File
    College Archives
Flower Pentecostal Heritage Center (Springfield, Missouri)
    Digital Collections
    John H. Osteen Books
General Baptist Convention of Texas (Dallas, Texas)
    Texas Baptist Historical Collection
    John H. Osteen File
Houston Metropolitan Research Center (Houston, Texas)
    Woodrow Seals Papers
    Churches Vertical File
    Lakewood Church Vertical File
Northern Baptist Theological Seminary
    Seminary Archives
Oral Roberts University, Holy Spirit Research Center (Tulsa, Oklahoma)
    University Archives
    Pentecostal Vertical File
    VHS Collection
    Cassette Collection
Regent University (Virginia Beach, Virginia)
    Pentecostal Research Collection
Rice University, Woodson Research Center (Houston, Texas)
    William Martin Papers
    One Nation under God? Film Project Materials
    Reverend William A. Lawson Papers
    Dr. Lee P. Brown Papers

San Jacinto Baptist Association (Baytown, Texas)
    John H. Osteen File
Southern Baptist Historical Library and Archives (Nashville, Tennessee)
    Digital Resources
University of California, Santa Barbara (Santa Barbara, California)
    American Religions Collection
University of Houston (Houston, Texas)
    Barbara Karkabi Papers
University of North Carolina at Chapel Hill (Chapel Hill, North Carolina)
    The Southern Folklife Collection
    Full Gospel Businessmen's Fellowship International Collection
Wheaton College, Billy Graham Center (Wheaton, Illinois)
    Digital Archives

INTERVIEWS

Preston Wilson, November 5 and November 12, 2010, by telephone.
Melody Harris, December 10 and December 20, 2010, by telephone.
Jarvis Middleton, January 4 and August 25, 2011, Houston, Texas.
Saleim Kahleh, May 18, 2011, Houston, Texas.
Julia Duin, June 7, 2011, by telephone.
Aaron Mullen, June 16, 2011, Houston, Texas.
Richard Merchant, September 8, 2011, and February 2, 2012, Houston, Texas.
David Edwin Harrell, September 16, 2011, by telephone.
Stanley Morrison, November 20 and November 30, 2011, Houston, Texas.
Ray Buford, November 20, 2011, Houston, Texas.
David Russell, February 24, 2012, Humble, Texas.
Vinson Synan, February 29, 2012, Virginia Beach, Virginia.
Ralph Lee, March 25, 2012, Houston, Texas.
Marybeth Carlyle, May 20, 2012, Humble, Texas.
Anthony Baldacci, June 19, 2012, Houston, Texas.
Steve Bauer, July 9, 2012, by telephone.
Teri Burrell, August 21, 2012, Houston, Texas.
Barclay Torrance, April 13, 2013, by telephone.
Seth Olivier, August 6, 2014, Trenton, New Jersey.
Brady Mitchell, October 6, 2014, Houston, Texas.
Raymond and Angela Gordon, November 6, 2014, Houston, Texas.

AUDIO AND VIDEO SOURCES

"Alberto Mottesi su Espada Masonica, Profetiza a Marcos Witt." July 16, 2013. https://www.youtube.com/watch?v=fjDhNo6nEco.
"Houston Human Trafficking Walk-a-Thon Raises Awareness." *Fox 26 News*. January 28, 2013. https://www.youtube.com/watch?v=S-Bq6oU1NSE.

Lakewood Church. *Only the Beginning: John Osteen's 50 Years of Ministry*. VHS. Houston: Lakewood Church, 1989.

———. *Welcome to Lakewood*. VHS. Houston: Lakewood Church, 1993.

———. *Grand Opening: A Remarkable Journey, 1959–2005*. DVD. Houston: Lakewood Church, 2005.

———. *Lakewood Church 50th Anniversary*. DVD. Houston: Lakewood Church, 2009.

Linne, Shai. *Lyrical Theology, Pt. 1: Theology*. Philadelphia: Lamp Mode Records, 2013.

MacArthur, John. "Becoming a Better You." Ligionier Ministries 2010 Christless Christianity West Coast Conference. http://www.ligonier.org/learn/conferences/christless-christianity-2010-west-coast/becoming-a-better-you/.

"Marcos Witt—Se Despide De Joel Osteen & Lakewood Church 09/16/12." https://www.youtube.com/watch?v=XfVxscOkMhw.

Osteen, Dodie. *The Healing of a Lady Named Dodie*. Cassette. June 6, 1986.

Osteen, Joel. *The Power of Words*. CD. Houston: Joel Osteen Ministries, 2001.

———. *Six Steps to Enjoying Life*. Cassette Series. Houston: Joel Osteen Ministries, 2001.

———. *Letting Go of the Past*. Cassette Series. Houston: Joel Osteen Ministries, 2002.

———. *Living a Lifestyle of Giving: Showing God's Kindness and Mercy*. DVD. Houston: Joel Osteen Ministries, 2002.

———. *Be Determined!* DVD. Houston: Joel Osteen Ministries, 2003.

———. *Having a Relaxed and Easy Going Attitude*. VHS. Houston: Lakewood Church, 2003.

———. *Thinking the Right Thoughts*. CD. Houston: Joel Osteen Ministries, 2003.

———. *An Evening with Joel Osteen Live*. DVD. Houston: Joel Osteen Ministries, 2004.

———. *Life-Changing Words*. DVD. Houston: Joel Osteen Ministries, 2004.

———. *Living in a Positive Frame of Mind*. DVD. Houston: Joel Osteen Ministries, 2005.

———. *Healthy Living*. CD. Houston: Lakewood Church, 2006.

———. *Living a Resurrected Life*. CD. Houston: Joel Osteen Ministries, 2008.

———. *Historic Night of Hope: Jerusalem*. Trinity Broadcasting Network. February 3, 2011.

Osteen, John. *The Man You Could Have Been*. Cassette. 1963.

———. *The Power of Words*. VHS. Houston: Lakewood Church, 1988.

———. *How to Follow God's Peace*. VHS. Houston: Lakewood Church, 1989.

———. *Death & Beyond*. VHS. Houston: Lakewood Television Productions, 1993.

———. "Don't Limit God." *AZUSA 93 Conference*. Cassette. 1993.

———. *How to Be Led by the Spirit of God*. CD. Murrieta, CA: Ed Dufresne Ministries, 2009.

———. *Classics Collection, Volume 3*. CD. Murrieta, CA: Ed Dufresne Ministries, 2010.

———. *Keys to Daily Victory*. CD. Houston: Joel Osteen Ministries, 2011.

———. *A Revelation of the Name of Jesus and the Believer*. Cassette Series. Houston: Lakewood Church, n.d.

———. *Confession That Brings Possession*. Cassette Series. Houston: Lakewood Church, n.d.

———. *John H. Osteen's Personal Testimony*. Cassette. n. d.

"Preaching outside Joel Osteen's Lakewood Church in Houston." August 4, 2007. http://www.youtube.com/watch?v=Nu9k6o-GgVk.

Rael, Lucy. *Good Friday Service*. VHS. Houston: Lakewood Church, 1986.

Simons, April. *The Legacy Lives On*. CD. Arlington, TX: High Point Church, 2010.

"What's Right: Former Stripper Using Ministry to Help Others in the Business." *KHOU.com*. February 28, 2013. http://www.khou.com/story/news/local/outreach/2014/07/22/11977966/.

Witt, Marcos, and Lisa (Osteen) Comes. *Growing Strong: Six Keys to Grow in Christ*. DVD. Houston: Lakewood Church, 2010.

Wrigley, Deborah. "Lakewood Starts Drive-Through Healing Service." *ABC News 13/ KTRK*. February 8, 2010. http://abc13.com/archive/7266019/.

MAGAZINES, NEWSPAPERS, AND OTHER PERIODICALS, (PRINT AND ONLINE)

Abundant Life

The American

Baptist News

The Blaze

Charisma

Christian Century

Christian Challenge

Christian Post

Christianity Today

Cross Rhythms

Daily Beast

Forward Times

Guardian

Harper's Magazine

Hope for Today

Houston Belief

Houston Business Journal

Houston Chronicle

Houston Lifestyles & Homes

Houston Post

Houston Press

Huffington Post

Manna

Media Spotlight Special Report

Miracle Magazine

Modern Reformation

New York Times

Northeast News

NoticiaCristiana.com

Orlando Sentinel

OutSmart

Pentecostal Evangel
Praise
Religion Dispatches
Religion & Ethics NewsWeekly
Salon
Texas Monthly
Texas Observer
That! Texas Magazine
This Week
Time
TMZ
Voice
Voice of Victory
World Harvest
Washington Post
Washington Times

BOOKS, ARTICLES, ESSAYS, SERMONS, AND OTHER SOURCES (PRINT AND DIGITAL)

Alexander, Bobby C. *Televangelism Reconsidered: Ritual in the Search for Human Community.* Atlanta: Scholars Press, 1994.

Alexander, Paul. *Signs and Wonders: Why Pentecostalism Is the World's Fastest Growing Religion.* San Francisco: Josey-Bass, 2009.

Ammerman, Nancy. *Congregation and Community.* New Brunswick, NJ: Rutgers University Press, 1997.

Anderson, Allan. *An Introduction to Pentecostalism.* New York: Cambridge University Press, 2004.

———. "Varieties, Taxonomies, and Definitions." In *Studying Global Pentecostalism: Theories and Methods,* 13–29. Edited by Allan Anderson, Michael Bergunder, Andre Droogers, and Cornelius van der Laan. Berkeley: University of California Press, 2010.

Anhaiser, Bettye J. "Sugar Land, TX." *Handbook of Texas Online.* http://www.tshaonline.org/handbook/online/articles/hfs10.

Armstrong, John. "Joel Osteen on Divine Providence: Amazing." February 22, 2011. http://www.johnharmstrong.com.

Attanasi, Katherine, and Amos Yong, Editors. *Pentecostalism and Prosperity: The Socio-Economics of the Global Charismatic Movement.* New York: Palgrave Macmillan, 2012.

Austin, Steve. *Foundations: Building Your Life with Christ.* Houston: Lakewood Church, 2012.

Bailey, Julius H. "'Cult' Knowledge: The Challenges of Studying New Religious Movements in America." In *Doing Recent History: On Privacy, Copyright, Video Games, Institutional Review Boards, Activist Scholarship, and History That Talks Back,* 275–293. Edited by Claire Bond Potter and Renee C. Romano. Athens: University of Georgia Press, 2012.

Balmer, Randall, Editor. *Encyclopedia of Evangelicalism*, Revised and Expanded Edition. Waco, TX: Baylor University Press, 2004.

———. *Mine Eyes Have Seen the Glory*. Fourth Edition. New York: Oxford University Press, 2006.

———. *The Making of Evangelicalism: From Revivalism to Politics and Beyond*. Waco, TX: Baylor University Press, 2010.

Barber, Kendra Hadiya. "'What Happened to All the Protests?': Black Megachurches' Responses to Racism in a Colorblind Era." *Journal of African American Studies* 15/2 (2011): 218–235.

Bebbington, David. *Evangelicalism in Modern Britain*. London: Unwin Hyman, 1989.

Becker, Penny Edgell. *Congregations in Conflict: Cultural Models of Local Religious Life*. New York: Cambridge University Press, 1999.

Behnken, Brian H. "Elusive Unity: African Americans, Mexican Americans, and Civil Rights in Houston." In *Seeking Inalienable Rights: Texans and Their Quests for Justice*, 123–146. Edited by Debra A. Reid. College Station: Texas A&M University Press, 2009.

Bekkering, Dennis J. "From 'Televangelist' to 'Interevangelist': The Emergence of the Streaming Video Preacher." *Journal of Religion and Popular Culture* 23/2 (July 2011): 101–117.

Bendroth, Margaret Lamberts. *Fundamentalism and Gender: 1875 to the Present*. New Haven, CT: Yale University Press, 1993.

Beverly, James A. *Holy Laughter and the Toronto Blessing*. Grand Rapids, MI: Zondervan, 1995.

Bielo, James S. *Words upon the Word: An Ethnography of Evangelical Group Bible Study*. New York: NYU Press, 2009.

———. "Textual Ideology, Textual Practice: Evangelical Bible Reading in Group Study." In *The Social Life of Scriptures: Cross-Cultural Perspectives on Biblicism*, 157–175. Edited by James S. Bielo. New Brunswick, NJ: Rutgers University Press, 2009.

Billingsly, Scott. *It's a New Day: Race and Gender in the Charismatic Movement*. Tuscaloosa: University of Alabama Press, 2008.

———. "The Midas Touch: Kenneth E. Hagin and the Prosperity Gospel." In *Recovering the Margins of American Religious History: The Legacy of David Edwin Harrell Jr.*, 43–59. Edited by B. Dwain Waldrep and Scott Billingsley. Tuscaloosa: University of Alabama Press, 2012.

Bivins, Jason C. *Religion of Fear: The Politics of Horror in Conservative Evangelicalism*. New York: Oxford University Press, 2008.

Bongmba, Elias. "Portable Faith: The Global Dimensions of African Initiated Churches (AIC)." In *African Immigrant Religions in America*, 102–129. Edited by Jacob Olupona and Regina Gemignani. New York: NYU Press, 2007.

Bowler, Kate. *Blessed: A History of the American Prosperity Gospel*. New York: Oxford University Press, 2013.

Brekus, Catherine A. "The Perils of Prosperity: Some Historical Reflections on Christianity, Capitalism, and Consumerism in America." In *American Christianities: A*

History of Dominance & Diversity, 279–306. Edited by Catherine A. Brekus and W. Clark Gilpin. Chapel Hill: University of North Carolina Press, 2011.

Brenneman, Todd M. *Homespun Gospel: The Triumph of Sentimentality in Contemporary American Evangelicalism*. New York: Oxford University Press, 2013.

Brown, Candy Gunther. "Healing Words: Narratives of Spiritual Healing and Kathryn Kuhlman's Uses of Print Culture, 1947–1976." In *Religion and the Culture of Print in Modern America*, 271–297. Edited by Charles L. Cohen and Paul S. Boyer. Madison: University of Wisconsin Press, 2008.

———. "Introduction: Pentecostalism and the Globalization of Illness and Healing." In *Global Pentecostal and Charismatic Healing*, 3–28. Edited by Candy Gunther Brown. New York: Oxford University Press, 2011.

———. *Testing Prayer: Science and Healing*. Cambridge, MA: Harvard University Press, 2012.

———. "Pentecostal Healing Prayer in an Age of Evidence-Based Medicine." *Transformation: An International Journal of Holistic Mission Studies* (August 2014): 1–16.

Bruce, Steve. *Pray T.V.: Televangelism in America*. New York: Routledge, 1990.

Bullard, Robert D. *Invisible Houston: The Black Experience in Boom and Bust*. College Station: Texas A&M University Press, 1987.

Calderon, Patricia. "The Media's Place in Religious Individualism: A Case Study of Lakewood Church." M.A. Thesis, Texas A&M University, 2010.

Canzion Group Press Release. "Marcos Witt Says Goodbye to Lakewood Church." September 12, 2012. http://www.canzion.com/marcoswitt/index_eng.html.

Carney, Charity R. "Lakewood Church and the Roots of the Megachurch Movement in the South." *Southern Quarterly* 50/1 (Fall 2012): 60–78.

Carter, Anthony J. *On Being Black and Reformed: A New Perspective on the African-American Experience*. Phillipsburg, NJ: Presbyterian and Reformed, 2003.

———. *Experiencing the Truth: Bringing the Reformation to the African-American Church*. Wheaton, IL: Crossway, 2008.

———. *Glory Road: The Journeys of 10 African-Americans into Reformed Christianity*. Wheaton, IL: Crossway, 2009.

Cartledge, Mark J. *Testimony in the Spirit: Rescripting Ordinary Pentecostal Theology*. Burlington, VT: Ashgate, 2010.

Chaves, Mark. *American Religion: Contemporary Trends*. Princeton, NJ: Princeton University Press, 2011.

Chesnut, R. Andrew. *Competitive Spirits: Latin America's New Religious Economy*. New York: Oxford University Press, 2003.

———. *Devoted to Death: Santa Muerte, the Skeleton Saint*. New York: Oxford University Press, 2012.

Chrisman, David K. "Religious Moderates and Race: The Texas Christian Life Commission and the Call for Racial Reconciliation, 1954–68." In *Seeking Inalienable Rights: Texans and Their Quests for Justice*, 97–122. Edited by Debra A. Reid. College Station: Texas A&M University Press, 2009.

Cole, Thomas R. *No Color Is My Kind: The Life of Eldrewey Stearns and the Integration of Houston*. Austin: University of Texas Press, 1997.

Comes, Lisa (Osteen). *6 Lies the Devil Uses to Destroy Marriages*. Houston: Lakewood Church, 1988.

———. "Designed for Destiny." Sermon Handout. January 7, 2009.

———. "Ten Distractions from Destiny." Sermon Handout. February 4, 2009.

———. "The Joy of Speaking in Tongues." Sermon Handout. May 23, 2012.

———. *You Are Made for More!* New York: FaithWords, 2012.

Cooke, Phil. *Branding Faith: Why Some Churches and Nonprofits Impact Culture and Others Don't*. Ventura, CA: Regal, 2008.

———. *The Last TV Evangelist: Why the Next Generation Couldn't Care Less about Religious Media and Why It Matters*. Huntington Beach, CA: Conversant Media Group, 2009.

Crow, Marvin. "I Thought This Experience Had Ruined Our Service, Instead . . . Revival Fire Began to Burn." In *Baptists and the Baptism of the Holy Spirit*, 19–21, 32. Edited by Jerry Jensen. Los Angeles: Full Gospel Businessmen's Fellowship International, 1963.

DeRogatis, Amy. *Saving Sex: Sexuality and Salvation in American Evangelicalism*. New York: Oxford University Press, 2014.

"Developing Faith for the Mercies of God and His Comfort." Lakewood Compass Class Handout. October 2005.

Dionne, E. J. *Souled Out: Reclaiming Faith and Politics after the Religious Right*. Princeton, NJ: Princeton University Press, 2009.

Dochuk, Darren. "Evangelicalism Becomes Southern, Politics Becomes Evangelical: From FDR to Ronald Reagan." In *Religion and American Politics: From the Colonial Period to the Present*, Second Edition, 297–325. Edited by Mark A. Noll and Luke E. Harlow. New York: Oxford University Press, 2007.

———. *From Bible Belt to Sunbelt: Plain-Folk Religion, Grassroots Politics, and the Rise of Evangelical Conservatism*. New York: W.W. Norton, 2010.

———. "Blessed by Oil, Cursed with Crude: God and Black Gold in the American Southwest." *Journal of American History* 99 (June 2012): 51–61.

Dowland, Seth. "'Family Values' and the Formation of the Christian Right Agenda." *Church History* 78/3 (September 2009): 606–631.

———. "A New Kind of Patriarchy: Inerrancy and Masculinity in the Southern Baptist Convention, 1979–2000." In *Southern Masculinity: Perspectives on Manhood and the South since Reconstruction*, 246–268. Edited by Craig Thompson Friend. Athens: University of Georgia Press, 2009.

Duin, Julia. *Days of Fire and Glory: The Rise and Fall of a Charismatic Community*. Baltimore: Crossland Press, 2009.

Ehrenreich, Barbara. *Bright-Sided: How Positive Thinking Is Undermining America*. New York: Picador, 2009.

———. *This Land Is Their Land: Reports from a Divided Nation*. New York: Picador, 2009.

Eiesland, Nancy L. *A Particular Place: Urban Restructuring and Religious Ecology in a Southern Exurb*. New Brunswick, NJ: Rutgers University Press, 2000.

Einstein, Mara. *Brands of Faith: Marketing Religion in a Commercial Age*. New York: Routledge, 2008.

Elisha, Omri. *Moral Ambition and Social Outreach in Evangelical Megachurches*. Berkeley: University of California Press, 2011.

Ellingson, Stephen. *The Megachurch and the Mainline: Remaking Religious Tradition in the Twenty-first Century*. Chicago: University of Chicago Press, 2007.

Ellwood, Robert S. *The Sixties Spiritual Awakening: American Religion Moving from Modern to Postmodern*. New Brunswick, NJ: Rutgers University Press, 1994.

———. *The Fifties Spiritual Marketplace: American Religion in a Decade of Conflict*. New Brunswick, NJ: Rutgers University Press, 1997.

Emerson, Michael O., Jenifer Bratter, Junia Howell, P. Wilner Jeanty, and Mike Cline. "Houston Region Grows More Racially/Ethnically Diverse, with Small Declines in Segregation." Houston: Kinder Institute for Urban Research and Hobby Center for the Study of Texas, 2013.

Enns, Peter. *Inspiration and Incarnation: Evangelicals and the Problem of the Old Testament*. Grand Rapids, MI: Baker Academic, 2005.

Eskridge, Larry. *God's Forever Family: The Jesus People Movement in America*. New York: Oxford University Press, 2013.

Espinosa, Gastón. *Latino Pentecostals in America: Faith and Politics in Action*. Cambridge, MA: Harvard University Press, 2014.

Feagin, Joe R. *Free Enterprise City: Houston in Political-Economic Perspective*. New Brunswick, NJ: Rutgers University Press, 1988.

Finke, Roger, and Chris Scheitle. *Places of Faith: A Road Trip across America's Religious Landscape*. New York: Oxford University Press, 2012.

Fuller, Leanna K. "Perfectionism and Shame: Exploring the Connections." *Journal of Pastoral Theology* 18/1 (Summer 2008): 44–60.

Gasaway, Brantley. *Progressive Evangelicals and the Pursuit of Social Justice*. Chapel Hill: University of North Carolina Press, 2014.

Geiger, Wayne R. "Joel Osteen: A Critical Analysis of Sermonic Methodology." M.A. Thesis, University of Central Missouri, 2009.

George, Carol V. R. *God's Salesman: Norman Vincent Peale and the Power of Positive Thinking*. New York: Oxford University Press, 1993.

Gerber, Lynne. *Seeking the Straight and Narrow: Weight Loss and Sexual Reorientation in Evangelical America*. Chicago: University of Chicago Press, 2011.

Gerhardt, Hannes. "The Problematic Synergy between Evangelicals and the U.S. State in Sub-Sharan Africa." In *Mapping the End Times: American Evangelical Geopolitics and Apocalyptic Visions*, 157–182. Edited by Jason Dittmer and Tristan Sturm. Burlington, VT: Ashgate, 2010.

Grem, Darren E. "Selling a 'Disneyland for the Devout': Religious Marketing at Jim Bakker's Heritage USA." In *Shopping for Jesus: Faith in Marketing in the USA*, 137–160. Edited by Dominic Janes. Washington, DC: New Academia Press, 2008.

Griffith, R. Marie. *God's Daughters: Evangelical Women and the Power of Submission.* Berkeley: University of California Press, 1997.

———. *Born Again Bodies: Flesh and Spirit in American Christianity.* Berkeley: University of California Press, 2004.

Gushee, David P. *The Future of Faith in American Politics: The Public Witness at the Evangelical Center.* Waco, TX: Baylor University Press, 2008.

Hackworth, Jason. *Faith Based: Religious Neoliberalism and the Politics of Welfare in the United States.* Athens: University of Georgia Press, 2012.

Hadden, Jeffrey K. "The Rise and Fall of Televangelism." *Annals of the American Academy of Political and Social Science* 527 (May 1993): 113–130.

Hadden, Jeffrey K., and Charles E. Swann. *Prime Time Preachers: The Rising Power of Televangelism.* Reading, MA: Addison-Wesley, 1981.

Hagin, Kenneth E. *You Can Have What You Say!* Tulsa, OK: Kenneth Hagin Ministries, 1979.

Han, Ju Hui Judy. "Reaching the Unreached in the 10/40 Window: The Missionary Geoscience of Race, Difference and Distance." In *Mapping the End Times: American Evangelical Geopolitics and Apocalyptic Visions,* 183–207. Edited by Jason Dittmer and Tristan Sturm. Burlington, VT: Ashgate, 2010.

Hangen, Tona J. *Redeeming the Dial: Radio, Religion, and Popular Culture in America.* Chapel Hill: University of North Carolina Press, 2002.

Hankins, Barry G. *American Evangelicals: A Contemporary History of a Mainstream Religious Movement.* Lanham, MD: Rowman & Littlefield, 2008.

Hansen, Collin. *Young, Restless, Reformed: A Journalist's Journey among the New Calvinists.* Wheaton, IL: Crossway, 2008.

Hanegraaff, Hank. *Christianity in Crisis: 21st Century.* Nashville, TN: Thomas Nelson, 2009.

———. "Osteenification and What It Portends." *Philosophical Fragments.* March 19, 2014. http://www.patheos.com/blogs/philosophicalfragments/2014/03/19/osteenification-and-what-it-portends/.

———. *The Osteenification of American Christianity.* Charlotte, NC: Christian Research Institute, 2014.

Harding, Susan Friend. *The Book of Jerry Falwell: Fundamentalist Language and Politics.* Princeton, NJ: Princeton University Press, 2000.

Harper, Ryan. "New Frontiers: *Wild at Heart* and Post-Promise Keeper Evangelical Manhood." *Journal of Religion and Popular Culture* 24/1 (Spring 2012): 97–112.

Harrell, David Edwin. *All Things Are Possible: The Healing and Charismatic Revivals in Modern America.* Bloomington: Indiana University Press, 1975.

———. *Oral Roberts: An American Life.* Bloomington: Indiana University Press, 1985.

———. *Pat Robertson: A Life and Legacy.* Grand Rapids, MI: Eerdmans, 2010.

Harrison, Milmon. *Righteous Riches: The Word of Faith Movement in Contemporary African American Religion.* New York: Oxford University Press, 2005.

Harvey, Paul, and Philip Goff, Editors. *The Columbia Documentary History of Religion in America since 1945.* New York: Columbia University Press, 2005.

Heltzel, Peter G. *Jesus and Justice: Evangelicals, Race, and American Politics*. New Haven, CT: Yale University Press, 2009.

Hendershot, Heather. *What's Fair on the Air?: Cold War Right-Wing Broadcasting and the Public Interest*. Chicago: University of Chicago Press, 2011.

Henderson, Matthew. "'What Heaven's Gonna Look Like': Racial and Ethnic Diversity at Lakewood Church." M.A. Thesis, University of Houston, 2012.

Hernández-León, Rubén. *Metropolitan Migrants: The Migration of Urban Mexicans to the United States*. Berkeley: University of California Press, 2008.

Hill, Samuel S., Editor. *New Encyclopedia of Southern Culture, Volume 1: Religion*. Chapel Hill: University of North Carolina Press, 2006.

Hladky, Kathleen. "I Double-Dog Dare You in Jesus' Name!: Claiming Christian Wealth and the American Prosperity Gospel." *Religion Compass* 6/1 (2012): 82–96.

"Horton, Michael Scott." In *Encyclopedia of Evangelicalism*, Revised and Expanded Edition, 342. Edited by Randall Balmer. Waco, TX: Baylor University Press, 2004.

Horton, Michael S., Editor. *The Agony of Deceit*. Grand Rapids, MI: Zondervan, 1990.

———. *Made in America: The Shaping of Modern American Evangelicalism*. Grand Rapids, MI: Baker, 1991.

———. *Beyond Culture Wars: Is America a Mission Field or Battlefield?* Chicago: Moody, 1994.

———. *Putting Amazing Back into Grace: Who Does* What *in Salvation?* Grand Rapids, MI: Baker, 1994.

———. "The Crisis of Evangelical Christianity: Reformation Essentials." *Modern Reformation* 3/2 (March/April 1994): 12–19.

———. *Where in the World Is the Church?: A Christian View of Culture and Your Role in It*. Chicago: Moody, 1995.

———. *In the Face of God: The Dangers and Delights of Spiritual Intimacy*. Nashville, TN: Thomas Nelson, 1997.

———. *Christless Christianity: The Alternative Gospel of the American Church*. Grand Rapids, MI: Baker, 2008.

Howell, Brian M. *Short-Term Mission: An Ethnography of Christian Travel Narrative and Experience*. Downers Grove, IL: InterVarsity Press Academic, 2012.

H.R. 57. "Honoring the Memory of Dr. John Osteen." http://www.legis.state.tx.us/billlookup/Text.aspx?LegSess=76R&Bill=HR57.

"Joel Osteen on Claims He Preaches 'Prosperity Gospel,' Why Scripture Says 'Being Gay Is a Sin.'" *Fox News Insider*. April 29, 2012. http://insider.foxnews.com/2012/04/29/joel-and-victoria-osteen-respond-to-critics-on-fox-news-Sunday.

Key, Adam. *Your Best Lie Now: The Gospel According to Joel Osteen*. Raleigh, NC: Lulu, 2007.

Kidd, Thomas S. *The Great Awakening: The Roots of Evangelical Christianity in Colonial America*. New Haven, CT: Yale University Press, 2007.

Kilde, Jeanne Halgren. "Reading Megachurches: Investigating the Religious and Cultural Work of Church Architecture." In *American Sanctuary: Understanding Sacred*

Spaces, 225–249. Edited by Louis P. Nelson. Bloomington: Indiana University Press, 2006.

Kraft, Charles H. "Spiritual Warfare: A Neocharismatic Perspective." In *The New International Dictionary of Pentecostal and Charismatic Movements*, Revised and Expanded Edition, 1091–1096. Edited by Stanley M. Burgess and Eduard M. van der Maas. Grand Rapids, MI: Zondervan, 2002.

Lee, Shayne. *T. D. Jakes: America's New Preacher*. New York: NYU Press, 2005.

Lee, Shayne, and Phillip Luke Sinitiere. *Holy Mavericks: Evangelical Innovators and the Spiritual Marketplace*. New York: NYU Press, 2009.

Lewis, Robert. *The Quest for Authentic Manhood*. Nashville, TN: Lifeway Press, 2009.

Lichterman, Paul. *Elusive Togetherness: Church Groups Trying to Bridge America's Divisions*. Princeton, NJ: Princeton University Press, 2005.

Liichow, Robert. "The Leaven of Lakewood." http://www.rapidnet.com/~jbeard/bdm/exposes/osteen/Leaven.htm.

———. "A Smile, A Chair and A Prayer for You at Lakewood." http://www.newdiscernment.org/NewJoelOsteenNov07.htm.

Lindsey, D. Michael. *Faith in the Halls of Power: How Evangelicals Joined the American Elite*. New York: Oxford University Press, 2007.

Lippy, Charles H. *Do Real Men Pray?: Images of the Christian Man and Male Spirituality in White Protestant America*. Knoxville: University of Tennessee Press, 2005.

Lofton, Kathryn. "The Preacher Paradigm: Promotional Biographies and the Modern-Made Evangelist." *Religion and American Culture* 16/1 (Winter 2006): 95–123.

———. *Oprah: The Gospel of an Icon*. Berkeley: University of California Press, 2011.

———. "The Sigh of the Oppressed? Marxism and Religion in America Today." *New Labor Forum* 21/3 (Fall 2012): 58–65.

Lovett, Leonard. "Positive Confession Theology." In *The New International Dictionary of Pentecostal and Charismatic Movements*, Revised and Expanded Edition, 992–994. Edited by Stanley M. Burgess and Eduard M. van der Maas. Grand Rapids, MI: Zondervan, 2002.

Luhrmann, T. M. *When God Talks Back: Understanding the American Evangelical Relationship to God*. New York: Knopf, 2012.

Lynch, Christopher Owen. *Selling Catholicism: Bishop Sheen and the Power of Television*. Lexington: University Press of Kentucky, 1998.

Malley, Brian. *How the Bible Works: An Anthropological Study of Evangelical Biblicism*. Walnut Creek, CA: Alta Mira, 2004.

MacArthur, John. *Charismatic Chaos*. Grand Rapids, MI: Zondervan, 1992.

———. "Your Best Life: Now or Later?" March 23, 2008. http://www.gty.org/Resources/Sermons/80-334.

———. *Strange Fire: The Danger of Offending the Holy Spirit with Counterfeit Worship*. Nashville, TN: Thomas Nelson, 2013.

Manna, Kafah Bachari. "Breaking Bread: The Pink Iftar Movement." *Houston History* 8/3 (Summer 2011): 23–25.

Márquez, John D. *Black-Brown Solidarity: Racial Politics in the New Gulf South*. Austin: University of Texas Press, 2014.

Marti, Gerardo. *Hollywood Faith: Holiness, Prosperity, and Ambition in a Los Angeles Church*. New Brunswick, NJ: Rutgers University Press, 2008.

———. "'I Determine My Harvest': Risky Careers and Spirit-Guided Prosperity in Los Angeles." In *Pentecostalism and Prosperity: The Socio-Economics of the Global Charismatic Movement*, 131–150. Edited by Katherine Attanasi and Amos Yong. New York: Palgrave Macmillan, 2012.

Martin, Lerone A. *Preaching on Wax: The Phonograph and the Making of Modern African American Religion*. New York: NYU Press, 2014.

Martin, Sam. *How I Led One and One Led a Million*. Houston: Lakewood Church, 2001.

Martin, William. "Prime Minister." In *Southern Crossroads: Perspectives on Religion and Culture*, 63–88. Edited by Walter H. Conser and Rodger M. Payne. Lexington: University Press of Kentucky, 2008.

Maxwell, John C. *Be All You Can Be!: A Challenge to Stretch Your God-Given Potential*. Wheaton, IL: Victor Books, 1987.

———. *The Success Journey: The Process of Living Your Dreams*. Nashville, TN: Thomas Nelson, 1997.

———. *Failing Forward: Turning Mistakes into Stepping Stones for Success*. Nashville, TN: Thomas Nelson, 2000.

———. "How a Biblical Miracle Works." Lakewood Church. April 2012.

McAdams, Dan P. *The Redemptive Self: Stories Americans Live By*. Revised and Expanded Edition. New York: Oxford University Press, 2013.

McCloud, Sean. *Divine Hierarchies: Class in American Religion and Religious Studies*. Chapel Hill: University of North Carolina Press, 2007.

Melton, J. Gordon, Phillip Charles Lucas, and Jon R. Stone. *Prime-Time Religion: An Encyclopedia of Religious Broadcasting*. Phoenix, AZ: Oryx, 1997.

Meyer, Donald. *The Positive Thinkers: Religion as Pop Psychology from Mary Baker Eddy to Oral Roberts*. New York: Pantheon, 1980.

———. *The Positive Thinkers: Popular Religious Psychology from Mary Baker Eddy to Norman Vincent Peale and Ronald Reagan*. Middletown, CT: Wesleyan University Press, 1988.

"Meyer, Joyce." In *Encyclopedia of Evangelicalism*, Revised and Expanded Edition, 454. Edited by Randall Balmer. Waco, TX: Baylor University Press, 2004.

Meyer, Joyce. *Battlefield of the Mind: Winning the Battle in Your Mind*. New York: Warner Faith, 1995.

———. *Power Thoughts: 12 Strategies to Win the Battle of the Mind*. New York: FaithWords, 2010.

———. "The Last Days." Lakewood Church. February 2013.

Miller, Christine, and Nathan Carlin. "Joel Osteen as Cultural Selfobject: Meeting the Needs of the Group Self and Its Individual Members in and from the Largest Church in America." *Pastoral Psychology* 59 (2010): 27–51.

Miller, Donald E. *Reinventing American Protestantism: Christianity in the New Millennium*. Berkeley: University of California Press, 1997.

Miller, Donald E., and Tetsunao Yamamori. *Global Pentecostalism: The New Face of Christian Social Engagement*. Berkeley: University of California Press, 2007.

Miller, Steven P. *The Age of Evangelicalism: America's Born-Again Years*. New York: Oxford University Press, 2014.

"Mohler, Richard Albert." In *Encyclopedia of Evangelicalism*, Revised and Expanded Edition, 463. Edited by Randall Balmer. Waco, TX: Baylor University Press, 2004.

Montgomery, Mel. *The Genuine Flow: How the Faith Giants Flowed in the Spirit and How You Can Too*. Maitland, FL: Xulon, 2010.

Moreton, Bethany. *To Serve God and Wal-Mart: The Making of Christian Free Enterprise*. Cambridge, MA: Harvard University Press, 2009.

Morgan, Marabel. "The Total Woman." In *Jerry Falwell and the Rise of the Religious Right: A Brief History with Documents*, 110–114. Edited by Matthew Avery Sutton. New York: Bedford/St. Martin's, 2013.

Moskowitz, Eva S. *In Therapy We Trust: America's Obsession with Self-Fulfillment*. Baltimore: Johns Hopkins University Press, 2001.

Murray, Iain H. *John MacArthur: Servant of the Word and Flock*. Carlisle, PA: Banner of Truth Trust, 2011.

Noll, Mark A. *American Evangelical Christianity: An Introduction*. Malden, MA: Blackwell, 2001.

——. *The New Shape of World Christianity: How American Experience Shapes Global Faith*. Downers Grove, IL: InterVarsity Press Academic, 2009.

——. *Jesus Christ and the Life of the Mind*. Grand Rapids, MI: Eerdmans, 2011.

Olson, James S. *Making Cancer History: Disease & Discovery at the University of Texas M.D. Anderson Cancer Center*. Baltimore: Johns Hopkins University Press, 2009.

Orsi, Robert A. *Between Heaven and Earth: The Religious Worlds People Make and the Scholars Who Study Them*. Princeton, NJ: Princeton University Press, 2004.

Osborn, T. L. *Faith Library in 23 Volumes*. Vol. 19, *April 1984–December 1985*. Tulsa, OK: OSPO International, 1997.

Osteen, Dodie. *Healed of Cancer*. Houston: Lakewood Church, 1986.

——. *Choosing Life One Day at a Time: A Daily Devotional for Men and Women*. New York: Free Press, 2001.

Osteen, Joel. "Holding On to Your Dreams." Lakewood Church. February 21, 1999. http://web.archive.org/web/20010303115912/http:/www.lakewood- church.org/Sermons1999/Sermons99.html.

——. "Holding On to Your Dreams, Part 2: Persistence & Determination." March 7, 1999. http://web.archive.org/web/20010303115912/http:/www.lakewood- church.org/Sermons1999/Sermons99.html.

——. "Holding On to Your Dreams, Part 3: II Kings 6." March 21, 1999. http://web.archive.org/web/20010303115912/http:/www.lakewood- church.org/Sermons1999/Sermons99.html.

———. "Holding On to Your Dreams, Part 4: What to Learn in the Dark Hours." March 28, 1999. http://web.archive.org/web/20010303115912/http:/www.lakewood- church. org/Sermons1999/Sermons99.html.

———. "Holding On to Your Dreams, Part 5: 3 Things to Do in the Midst of Trouble." April 11, 1999. http://web.archive.org/web/20010303115912/http:/www.lakewood-church.org/Sermons1999/Sermons99.html.

———. "Holding On to Your Dreams, Part 6: Don't Limit God." April 18, 1999. http:// web.archive.org/web/20010303115912/http:/www.lakewood- church.org/Sermons1999/Sermons99.html.

———. "Holding On to Your Dreams, Part 7: The Voice of Discouragement." April 25, 1999. http://web.archive.org/web/20010303115912/http:/www.lakewood- church.org/ Sermons1999/Sermons99.html.

———. "Holding On to Your Dreams, Part 8: Do All You Can Do to Make Your Dreams Come True." May 2, 1999. http://web.archive.org/web/20010303115912/http:/www. lakewood- church.org/Sermons1999/Sermons99.html.

———. "Winning the Battle of the Mind, Part 1." May 9, 1999. http://web.archive.org/ web/20010303115912/http:/www.lakewood- church.org/Sermons1999/Sermons99. html.

———. "Winning the Battle of the Mind, Part 2." May 23, 1999. http://web.archive.org/ web/20010303115912/http:/www.lakewood- church.org/Sermons1999/Sermons99. html.

———. "Winning the Battle of the Mind, Part 4." June 6, 1999. http://web.archive.org/ web/20010303115912/http:/www.lakewood- church.org/Sermons1999/Sermons99. html.

———. "Winning the Battle of the Mind, Part 6: No Condemnation." June 20, 1999, http://web.archive.org/web/20010303115912/http:/www.lakewood- church.org/Sermons1999/Sermons99.html.

———. "Winning the Battle of the Mind, Part 7: 3 Things to Do Not to Faint." June 27, 1999. http://web.archive.org/web/20010303115912/http:/www.lakewood- church.org/ Sermons1999/Sermons99.html.

———. "Winning the Battle of the Mind, Part 11: Your Imagination." August 1, 1999. http://web.archive.org/web/20010303115912/http:/www.lakewood- church.org/Sermons1999/Sermons99.html.

———. "Winning the Battle of the Mind, Part 12: Hearing the Voice of God." August 8, 1999. http://web.archive.org/web/20010303115912/http:/www.lakewood- church.org/ Sermons1999/Sermons99.html.

———. "Winning the Battle of the Mind: Part 13." August 15, 1999. http://web.archive. org/web/20010303115912/http:/www.lakewood- church.org/Sermons1999/Sermons99.html.

———. *30 Thoughts for Victorious Living.* Houston: Joel Osteen Ministries, 2003.

———. *Your Best Life Now: 7 Steps to Living at Your Full Potential.* New York: Faith-Words, 2004.

———. *Become a Better You: 7 Keys to Improving Your Everyday Life*. New York: Free Press, 2007.

———. *It's Your Time: Activate Your Faith, Achieve Your Dreams, and Increase in God's Favor*. New York: Free Press, 2009.

———. *The Christmas Spirit: Memories of Family, Friends, and Faith*. New York: Free Press, 2010.

———. *Every Day a Friday: How to Be Happier 7 Days a Week*. New York: FaithWords, 2011.

———. *I Declare: 31 Promises to Speak over Your Life*. New York: FaithWords, 2012.

———. *You Can, You Will: 8 Undeniable Qualities of a Winner*. New York: FaithWords, 2014.

Osteen, Joel, and Victoria Osteen. *God's Promises for a New Beginning*. Houston: Joel Osteen Ministries, 2008.

———, Editors. *Hope for Today Bible*. New York: Free Press, 2009.

Osteen, John. "The Unified Service." M.R.E. Thesis, Northern Baptist Theological Seminary, 1944.

———. *How God Baptized Me in the Holy Ghost and Fire*. Houston: John H. Osteen Evangelistic Association, 1961.

———. *How to Be Healed*. Houston: John H. Osteen Evangelistic Association, 1961.

———. *How You May Receive the Baptism of the Holy Ghost*. Houston: John H. Osteen Evangelistic Association, 1961.

———. *The Supernatural Gifts of the Spirit*. Houston: John H. Osteen Evangelistic Association, 1961.

———. *Supernatural Manifestations in the Life of John H. Osteen*. Houston: John H. Osteen Evangelistic Association, 1961.

———. "This Southern Baptist Preacher Wept, Shook and Listened As . . . He Heard God Speak." In *The Baptists and the Baptism of the Holy Spirit*, 6–10, 30–31. Edited by Jerry Jensen. Los Angeles: Full Gospel Businessmen's Fellowship International, 1963.

———. *This Awakening Generation*. Houston: John H. Osteen Evangelistic Association, 1964.

———. *The Bible Way to Spiritual Power*. Houston: John Osteen, 1968.

———. *How to Release the Power of God*. Houston: John H. Osteen, 1968.

———. *You Can Change Your Destiny*. Houston: John H. Osteen Evangelistic Association, 1968.

———. *How to Flow in the Super Supernatural*. Houston: Lakewood Church, 1972.

———. *Pulling Down Strongholds*. Houston: Lakewood Church, 1972.

———. *There Is a Miracle in Your Mouth*. Houston: Lakewood Church, 1972.

———. *Rivers of Living Water: A Baptist Preacher's Experiences with the Power That Comes through the Holy Spirit*. Houston: Lakewood Church, 1975.

———. *The Confessions of a Baptist Preacher*. Houston: John H. Osteen, 1976.

———. *The Divine Flow*. Houston: John Osteen Ministries, 1978.

———. *How to Claim the Benefits of the Will*. Houston: Lakewood Church, 1978.

———. *How to Demonstrate Satan's Defeat*. Houston: Lakewood Church, 1978.

———. *The Truth Shall Set You Free*. Houston: Lakewood Church, 1978.

———. *The Believer's #1 Need*. Houston: Lakewood Church, 1980.

———. *Keep What God Gives*. Houston: Lakewood Church, 1980.

———. *Love & Marriage*. Houston: John Osteen Ministries, 1980.

———. *Receive the Holy Spirit*. Houston: Lakewood Church, 1980.

———. *Saturday's . . . Coming!* Houston: Lakewood Church, 1980.

———. *The Sixth Sense . . . Faith*. Houston: Lakewood Church, 1980.

———. *The ABCs of Faith*. Houston: John Osteen Ministries, 1981.

———. *Four Principles in Receiving from God*. Houston: John Osteen Ministries, 1981.

———. *How to Minister Healing to the Sick*. Houston: Lakewood Church, 1981.

———. *Seven Facts about Prevailing Prayer*. Houston: Lakewood Church, 1981.

———. *What to Do When Nothing Seems to Work*. Houston: Lakewood Church, 1981.

———. *What to Do When the Tempter Comes*. Houston: Lakewood Church, 1981.

———. *A Place Called There*. Houston: Lakewood Church, 1982.

———. *How to Receive Life Eternal*. Houston: Lakewood Church, 1985.

———. *Spiritual Food for Victorious Living*. Houston: John Osteen Ministries, 1985.

———. *Deception!: Recognizing True and False Ministries*. Houston: Lakewood Church, 1986.

———. *Overcoming Hindrances to Receiving the Baptism of the Holy Spirit*. Houston: John Osteen Ministries, 1987.

———. *Unraveling the Mystery of the Blood Covenant*. Houston: Lakewood Church, 1987.

———. *Believing God for Your Loved Ones*. Houston: Lakewood Church, 1988.

———. *A Miracle for Your Marriage*. Houston: Lakewood Church, 1988.

———. *Seven Qualities of a Man of Faith*. Houston: Lakewood Church, 1990.

———. *Becoming a Man of Unwavering Faith*. Edited by Joel Osteen. New York: FaithWords, 2011.

———. *Your Words Hold a Miracle: The Power of Speaking God's Word*. Edited by Joel Osteen. New York: FaithWords, 2012.

———. *Living in the Abundance of God*. Edited by Joel Osteen. New York: FaithWords, 2013.

———. *Power over the Enemy: Breaking Free from Spiritual Strongholds*. Edited by Joel Osteen. New York: FaithWords, 2014.

———. *Telling the King's Household*. Houston: John H. Osteen Evangelistic Association, n.d.

"Osteen, John H." In *Encyclopedia of Evangelicalism*, Revised and Expanded Edition, 516. Edited by Randall Balmer. Waco, TX: Baylor University Press, 2004.

Osteen, Justin. *A Letter to My Friend*. Houston: John Osteen, 1983.

Osteen, Lisa. *Overcoming Opposition: How to Succeed in Doing the Will of God*. Houston: Lakewood Church, 1990.

Osteen, Paul. "Living a Balanced Life, Part 1." Sermon Handout. June 3, 2004.

———. "The Good Samaritan: Who Is My Neighbor and How Should I Love Him/Her?" Sermon Handout. October 6, 2004.

Osteen, Victoria. *Love Your Life: Living Happy, Healthy & Whole*. New York: Free Press, 2008.

———. *Hooray for My Family!* New York: Little Simon Inspirations, 2009.

———. *Hooray for Today!* New York: Little Simon Inspirations, 2009.

———. *Hooray for Wonderful Me!* New York: Little Simon Inspirations, 2009.

———. *Unexpected Treasures*. New York: Little Simon Inspirations, 2009.

———. *Gifts from the Heart*. New York: Little Simon Inspirations, 2010.

Ostrander, Rick. *Head, Heart, and Hand: John Brown University and Modern Evangelical Higher Education*. Fayetteville: University of Arkansas Press, 2003.

Owens, Jillian. "A Wide Net of Hope: Understanding the Success of Joel Osteen and Lakewood Church." Senior Religious Studies Honors Thesis, University of Texas at Austin, 2012.

Parker, Annise. "2012 Inaugural Address." January 3, 2012. http://www.houstontx.gov/mayor/inauguration2012.html.

Peck, Janice. *The Gods of Televangelism: The Crisis of Meaning and the Appeal of Religious Television*. Cresskill, NJ: Hampton Press, 1993.

Pew Research Center's Religion & Public Life Project. "Changing Faiths: Latinos and the Transformation of American Religion." April 25, 2007. http://www.pewhispanic.org/2007/04/25/changing-faiths-latinos-and-the-transformation- of-american-religion/

———. "The Shifting Religious Identity of Latinos in the United States." May 5, 2014. http://www.pewforum.org/2014/05/07/the-shifting-religious-identity-of-latinos-in-the- united-states/.

———. "Religion and Electronic Media." November 6, 2014. http://www.pewforum.org/2014/11/06/religion-and-electronic-media/2/.

Phelps, Wesley G. *A People's War on Poverty: Urban Politics and Grassroots Activists in Houston*. Athens: University of Georgia Press, 2014.

Poole, W. Scott. *Satan in America: The Devil We Know*. Lanham, MD: Rowman & Littlefield, 2009.

Potter, Claire Bond, and Renee C. Romano. "Introduction." In *Doing Recent History: On Privacy, Copyright, Video Games, Institutional Review Boards, Activist Scholarship, and History That Talks Back*, 1–19. Edited by Claire Bond Potter and Renee C. Romano. Athens: University of Georgia Press, 2012.

Priest, Robert J., Douglas Wilson, and Adelle Johnson. "U. S. Megachurches and New Patterns of Global Mission." *International Bulletin of Missionary Research* 34/2 (April 2010): 97–104.

"Profile: Live with Passion!" September 2014. *Ligourian.org*. https://frcedric.org/html/Liguorian_Live_With_Passion.pdf.

Putnam, Robert D., and David E. Campbell. *American Grace: How Religion Divides and Unites Us*. New York: Simon & Schuster, 2010.

Rakow, Katja. "Religious Branding and the Quest to Meet Consumer Needs: Joel Osteen's 'Message of Hope.'" In *Religion and the Marketplace in the United States*,

215–239. Edited by Jan Stievermann, Philip Goff, and Detlef Junker. New York: Oxford University Press, 2015.

Riss, R. M. "Tommy Lee Osborn." In *The New International Dictionary of Pentecostal and Charismatic Movements*, Revised and Expanded Edition, 950–951. Edited by Stanley M. Burgess and Eduard M. van der Maas. Grand Rapids, MI: Zondervan, 2002.

Roebuck, David G. "Fundamentalism and Pentecostalism: The Changing Face of Evangelicalism in America." In *Faith in America: Changes, Challenges, New Directions, Volume 1: Organized Religion Today*, 85–107. Edited by Charles H. Lippy. Westport, CT: Praeger, 2006.

Romano, Renee C. "Not Dead Yet: My Identity Crisis as a Historian of the Recent Past." In *Doing Recent History: On Privacy, Copyright, Video Games, Institutional Review Boards, Activist Scholarship, and History That Talks Back*, 23–44. Edited by Claire Bond Potter and Renee C. Romano. Athens: University of Georgia Press, 2012.

Rosenthal, Michele. *American Protestants and TV in the 1950s: Responses to a New Medium*. New York: Palgrave Macmillan, 2007.

Sánchez-Walsh, Arlene. "Santidad, Salvación, Sanidad, Liberación: The Word of Faith Movement among Twenty-First-Century Latina/o Pentecostals." In *Global Pentecostal and Charismatic Healing*, 151–168. Edited by Candy Gunther Brown. New York: Oxford University Press, 2011.

Sargeant, Kimon Howland. *Seeker Churches: Promoting Traditional Religion in a Non-Traditional Way*. New Brunswick, NJ: Rutgers University Press, 2000.

Schäfer, Axel R. *Countercultural Conservatives: American Evangelicalism from the Postwar Revival to the New Christian Right*. Madison: University of Wisconsin Press, 2011.

Schenkel, Albert Frederick. "New Wine and Baptist Wineskins: American and Southern Baptist Denominational Responses to the Charismatic Renewal, 1969–1980." In *Pentecostal Currents in American Protestantism*, 152–167. Edited by Edith L. Blumhofer, Russell P. Spittler, and Grant Wacker. Urbana: University of Illinois Press, 1999.

Schuller, Robert H. *The Miracle of Thinking Big*. Garden Grove, CA: Garden Grove Community Church, 1975.

Schultze, Quentin. *Televangelism and American Culture: The Business of Popular Religion*. Grand Rapids, MI: Baker Academic, 1991.

Scott, Don. "I Found There Is Reality in Knowing Jesus and Being . . . Filled with the Holy Spirit." In *The Methodists and the Baptism of the Holy Spirit*, 23. Edited by Jerry Jensen. Los Angeles: Full Gospel Businessmen's Fellowship International, 1963.

Selvaggi, Connie. *What's inside Lakewood Church? One Woman's Account of Spiritual Conflict and Renewal*. Bogotá, Columbia: Proceditor, 2010.

Senate Finance Committee. "Grassley Seeks Information from Six Media-based Ministries." November 6, 2007. http://finance.senate.gov/newsroom/ranking/release/?id=baa4251a-ee70-48af-a324-79801cd07f18.

———. "Grassley Releases Review of Tax Issues Raised by Media-based Ministries." January 6, 2011. http://finance.senate.gov/newsroom/ranking/release/?id=5fa343ed-87eb-49b0- 82b9-28a9502910f7.

Shelly, Bruce. "The Rise of Evangelical Youth Movements." *Fides et Historia* 18/1 (January 1986): 47–63.

Shibley, Mark A. *Resurgent Evangelicalism in the United States: Mapping Cultural Change since 1970.* Columbia: University of South Carolina Press, 1996.

Shires, Preston. *Hippies of the Religious Right: The Counterculture and American Evangelicalism in the 1960s and 1970s.* Waco, TX: Baylor University Press, 2007.

Simons, Gary. *Church by God's Design: Building a Modern Day Book of Acts Church.* Arlington, TX: Seven Pillars Publishing, 2010.

Simmons, Dale H. *E. W. Kenyon and the Postbellum Pursuit of Peace, Power, and Plenty.* Lanham, MD: Scarecrow, 1997.

———. "Positive Confession Theology." In *Encyclopedia of Pentecostal and Charismatic Christianity*, 377–380. Edited by Stanley M. Burgess. New York: Routledge, 2006.

Sinitiere, Phillip Luke. "Ted Haggard and Saint James Church." *Religion in American History Blog.* June 2, 2010. http://usreligion.blogspot.com/2010/06/ted-haggard-and-saint-james- church.html.

———. "From the Oasis of Love to Your Best Life Now: A Brief History of Lakewood Church." *Houston History* 8/3 (Summer 2011): 2–9.

———. "Preaching the Good News Glad: Joel Osteen's Tel-e-vangelism." In *Global and Local Televangelism*, 87–107. Edited by Pradip Ninian Thomas and Philip Lee. New York: Palgrave Macmillan, 2012.

Smith, Calvin L. "The Politics and Economics of Pentecostalism." In *The Cambridge Companion to Pentecostalism*, 175–194. Edited by Cecil M. Robeck, Jr., and Amos Yong. New York: Cambridge University Press, 2014.

Smith, Christian. *American Evangelicalism: Embattled and Thriving.* Chicago: University of Chicago Press, 1998.

———. *The Bible Made Impossible: Why Biblicism Is Not a Truly Evangelical Reading of Scripture.* Grand Rapids, MI: Brazos, 2011.

Smith, James K. A. "What's Right with the Prosperity Gospel?" *Calvin Forum* 16/3 (Fall 2009): 8–9.

———. *Thinking in Tongues: Pentecostal Contributions to Christian Philosophy.* Grand Rapids, MI: Eerdmans, 2010.

Smith, Julia Cauble. "East Texas Oilfield." *Handbook of Texas Online.* https://www.tshaonline.org/handbook/online/articles/doe01.

Sødal, Helje Kringlebotn. "'Victor Not Victim': Joel Osteen's Rhetoric of Hope." *Journal of Contemporary Religion* 25/1 (January 2010): 37–50.

"Spiritual Warfare 101: What Is the Invisible War?" Lakewood Men's Ministry Class Handout. November 2011.

"Spiritual Warfare 201: How to Prepare Yourself for Spiritual Battle." Lakewood Men's Ministry Class Handout. November 2011.

"Spiritual Warfare 301: How to Do Battle with the Enemy and Win." Lakewood Men's Ministry Class Handout. November 2011.

"Spiritual Warfare 401: How to Gain Deliverance from Demonic Influence." Lakewood Men's Ministry Class Handout. November 2011.

Spittler, Russell. "Pentecostal and Charismatic Spirituality." In *The New International Dictionary of Pentecostal and Charismatic Movements*, Revised and Expanded Edition, 1101. Edited by Stanley M. Burgess and Eduard M. van der Maas. Grand Rapids, MI: Zondervan, 2002.

Stamm, Michael. "Broadcasting Mainline Protestantism: The Chicago Sunday Evening Club and the Evolution of Audience Expectations from Radio to Television." *Religion and American Culture* 22/2 (Summer 2012): 233–264.

Stephens, Randall J., and Karl W. Giberson. *The Anointed: Evangelical Truth in a Secular Age*. Cambridge, MA: Harvard University Press, 2011.

Stevenson, Jill. *Sensational Devotion: Evangelical Performance in Twenty-First-Century America*. Ann Arbor: University of Michigan Press, 2013.

Sullivan, Amy. *The Party Faithful: How and Why the Democrats Are Closing the God Gap*. New York: Scribner's, 2008.

Sutton, Matthew Avery. *Aimee Semple McPherson and the Resurrection of Christian America*. Cambridge, MA: Harvard University Press, 2007.

———. *American Apocalypse: A History of Modern Evangelicalism*. Cambridge, MA: Harvard University Press, 2014.

Swartz, David R. *Moral Minority: The Evangelical Left in an Age of Conservatism*. Philadelphia: University of Pennsylvania Press, 2012.

Sweeney, Douglas A. "Evangelicals in American History." In *The Columbia Guide to Religion in American History*, 122–135. Edited by Paul Harvey and Edward J. Blum. New York: Columbia University Press, 2012.

Synan, Vinson. *Under His Banner: History of Full Gospel Business Men's Fellowship International*. Costa Mesa, CA: Gift, 1992.

Thomas, Pradip N., and Philip Lee. "Global and Local Televangelism: An Introduction." In *Global and Local Televangelism*, 1–20. Edited by Pradip Ninian Thomas and Philip Lee. New York: Palgrave Macmillan, 2012.

Thuesen, Peter J. *Predestination: The American Career of a Contentious Doctrine*. New York: Oxford University Press, 2009.

Thumma, Scott, and Dave Travis. *Beyond Megachurch Myths: What We Can Learn from America's Largest Churches*. San Francisco: Josey-Bass, 2007.

Tsai, Jeanne L., Felicity F. Miao, and Emma Seppala. "Good Feelings in Christianity and Buddhism: Religious Differences in Ideal Affect." *Personality and Social Psychology Bulletin* 33/3 (March 2007): 409–421.

Tuner, Helen Lee. "Pentecostal Currents in the SBC: Divine Interpretation, Prophetic Preachers, and Charismatic Worship." In *Pentecostal Currents in American Protestantism*, 209–225. Edited by Edith L. Blumhoefer, Russell P. Spittler, and Grant Wacker. Urbana: University of Illinois Press, 1999.

Turner, John G. *Bill Bright and Campus Crusade for Christ: The Renewal of Evangelicalism in Postwar America*. Chapel Hill: University of North Carolina Press, 2008.

Valdez, Zulema. *The New Entrepreneurs: How Race, Class, and Gender Shape American Enterprise*. Stanford, CA: Stanford University Press, 2011.

Vásquez, Manuel A. *More than Belief: A Materialist Theory of Religion*. New York: Oxford University Press, 2011.

Voskuil, Dennis. *Mountains into Goldmines: Robert Schuller and the Gospel of Success*. Grand Rapids, MI: Eerdmans, 1983.

Wacker, Grant. *America's Pastor: Billy Graham and the Shaping of a Nation*. Cambridge, MA: Harvard University Press, 2014.

Wagner, Philip. *Insights from Men of Faith*. Beverly Hills, CA: Oasis Publishing, 1987.

———. "What's the Problem with Joel Osteen?" June 29, 2014. http://www.philipwagner.com/blog/whats-the-problem-with-joel-osteen.

Wallis, Jim. *God's Politics: Why the Right Gets It Wrong and the Left Doesn't Get It*. San Francisco: HarperCollins, 2005.

———. *Great Awakening: Reviving Faith and Politics in a Post-Religious Right America*. San Francisco: HarperCollins, 2008.

Walton, Jonathan. *Watch This!: The Ethics and Aesthetics of Black Televangelism*. New York: NYU Press, 2009.

———. "From Where Two or Three (Thousand) Are Gathered in My Name!: A Cultural History and Ethical Analysis of African American Megachurches." *Journal of African American Studies* 15/2 (2011): 133–154.

Wariboko, Nimi. *The Pentecostal Principle: Ethical Methodology in New Spirit*. Grand Rapids, MI: Eerdmans, 2012.

White, Bill. "Inaugural Speech." January 2, 2008. http://newswirehouston.com/2008/01/02/mayor-bill-whites-inauguration-speech-january- 2–2008/?doing_wp_cron=1 348183879.3822150230407714843750.

Wolfe, Alan. *The Transformation of American Religion: How We Actually Live Our Faith*. Chicago: University of Chicago Press, 2003.

Wyatt, Timothy. "Iglesia De La Luz Del Mundo." *Houston History* 8/3 (Summer 2011): 26–29.

Williams, Daniel K. *God's Own Party: The Making of the Christian Right*. New York: Oxford University Press, 2010.

Williams, Joseph W. *Spirit Cure: A History of Pentecostal Healing*. New York: Oxford University Press, 2013.

Wilsey, John D. "Joel Osteen." In *Baker Dictionary of Cults and Religions*. Edited by H. Wayne House. Grand Rapids, MI: Baker, forthcoming.

Winslow, Luke. "Classy Morality: The Rhetoric of Joel Osteen." In *Uncovering Hidden Rhetorics: Social Issues in Disguise*, 123–139. Edited by Barry Brummett. Los Angeles: Sage, 2008.

Witt, Marcos. *Señor, ¿en Qué Puedo Servirte?* Nashville, TN: Nelson, 1997.

———. *How to Overcome Fear and Live Your Life to the Fullest*. New York: Atria, 2007.

Worthen, Molly. *Apostles of Reason: The Crisis of Authority in American Evangelicalism*. New York: Oxford University Press, 2014.

Wuthnow, Robert. *The Restructuring of American Religion*. Princeton, NJ: Princeton University Press, 1988.

———. *After Heaven: Spirituality in America since the 1950s*. Berkeley: University of California Press, 1998.

———. *Boundless Faith: The Global Outreach of American Churches*. Berkeley: University of California Press, 2009.

———. *Rough Country: How Texas Became America's Most Powerful Bible-Belt State*. Princeton, NJ: Princeton University Press, 2014.

Yang, Fenggang, and Helen Rose Ebaugh. "Transformations in New Immigrant Religions and Their Global Implications." *American Sociological Review* 66 (April 2001): 269–288.

Yong, Amos. *In the Days of Caesar: Pentecostalism and Political Theology*. Grand Rapids, MI: Eerdmans, 2010.

Young, Buck A. "Baytown, TX." *Handbook of Texas Online*. https://www.tshaonline.org/handbook/online/articles/hdb01.

Young, Richard. *The Rise of Lakewood Church and Joel Osteen*. New Kensington, PA: Whitaker House, 2007.

Young, Shawn David. "From Hippies to Jesus Freaks: Christian Radicalism in Chicago's Inner- City." *Journal of Religion and Popular Culture* 22/2 (Summer 2010). http://www.usask.ca/relst/jrpc/art22%282%29-jesusfreaks.html.

"Your Manhood Plan!!!" Lakewood Men's Ministry Class Handout. November 2011.

INDEX

ABOUT THE AUTHOR

Phillip Luke Sinitiere is Visiting Assistant Professor of History at Sam Houston State University. He is author or editor of several books, including *Holy Mavericks: Evangelical Innovators and the Spiritual Marketplace* (NYU Press).